THE BOOK OF A DEVOUT POP PICKER

Hot Tub Publishing 2017

The Book of a Devout Pop Picker
ISBN 978-0-9576753-5-3
First published 2017 in Great Britain

Hot Tub Publishing Limited
Tiverton, Devon, UK
info@hottubpublishingltd.co.uk

For Bump, Bean
and their wonderful mum

Introduction

When elder members of the family died, one of the things I noticed was that pieces of their writing were often more precious that photographs. Excited gasps would greet the discovery of yellowing sheets covered with sincere expression; typed or handwritten, it didn't matter; stories of wartime evacuations, reflections on tragedy and torment; grumbles, euphoric thoughts, jokes, poems, wishes. As they were passed round, you heard things like "Ooh, ain't that just like her?" or "Cor, you can really *hear* him saying that, can't you?" Because you could.

I began wanting to leave my voice behind in the same way, for my children. A memoir would do the trick; they would probably like that. But I didn't want to burden them with anything heavy or best-left-lying, let alone plague them with details of early girlfriends. They'd never forgive me. If I was going to leave behind a voice, it would have to be a relaxed one; it would have to be on the subject of something I was knowledgeable and naturally enthusiastic about, something which had always been with me. That decision was easy to make.

They have grown up in a house where my vinyl records and CDs, boxes and boxes of them, lovingly tended and brooded over, are a constant storage issue. We have often explored them together. Occasionally, they have done so independently. A couple of Christmases ago, my son recommended that I check out the B-side of Boney M's 'Mary's Boy Child/Oh My Lord', about which I knew nothing because I'd never played it. I felt both chastened and proud (I can now recommend it to you; it's called 'Dancing in the Streets'). So they interact with them. They're a part of their lives. I have sometimes wondered: what will they do with them when I die? Will they sell them? *Could* they sell them? Might they instead become enthusiastic new owners?

Whatever they did, I thought, they would have to understand their value first. My left-behind voice would be their guide. That's how I took the decision to explain things from scratch, assuming the reader to be a complete novice in the subject; to tell it all as I had seen it, with its various links and connections – *my* links and connections. Not only that, but to illustrate the way in which records now basking in the status of "classic" were received when they first appeared, because it's often a far cry from how posterity has come to view them. And, in addition, to show what it was like buying and owning vinyl in the era when it was the core format. And if any other things occur to me, I'll do those too. I'm going to tell them what I know, what I remember noticing and what I remember thinking. In my voice. The one that they rely on. The one that makes them laugh.

Instinct told me to write anonymously. I had vague ideas about this giving it some character, but I didn't think it through – it just felt right. Later, however, as I began wishing a wider audience for it, I was pleased with the the decision. Nobody out there cares who I am, with my treasured collection and big opinions. But if I became an unspecified *someone* with a treasured collection and big opinions, I might just remind the reader of themselves a bit. The anonymity had gone from being a vague gimmick to being a device. I was away. Now all I had to do was make it entertaining.

And truthful. Because our memories are fallible. Records make their own impressions, under their own steam, not always informed by context or background facts. You like it, you don't like it, or you shrug about it and say it's alright. It does what it does. A work of art making its own impression. This book is a history of impressions and I set out to write it purely from memory in order to convey this idea. It was an idea that felt good, but I'm afraid I had to abandon it.

When I was at secondary school, there was a jazzy soul record called 'Mellow Mellow Right On' by Lowrell. I remember talking about it to a kid I knew. He was surprised and impressed that I, a white boy with my apparent musical tastes, had even heard of it. Of course I had heard of it. It was a hit. Only a minor one, but a hit nevertheless. It was played on the mainstream radio station that I listened to endlessly. It had caught my attention because its feel was slightly outside my experience. It shouldn't have been a surprise to him.

But perhaps he had come to it via a different route; maybe a wise older brother, or a visit to one of those record shops that cool people hung out in. Perhaps he had no idea that it had crept into the pop charts. It doesn't matter, because it's the conversation I remember, a shared experience of a record between two people who didn't often share experiences of records.

What does matter, however, was the fact that, in remembering it, I was incorrect about its date. I thought it had been in 1977, but it wasn't – it was 1979, which is a big deal if you're me. I haven't used the anecdote in the book, but had I done so purely from memory, I might have got the facts wrong. So: which memories can we be so sure about that we don't have to check? It's a good question. I learned to check. I don't intend to get any facts wrong. We ought to be accurate.

I took ages settling on a title. I thought about *Memoirs of* and *The Story of*, as well as having a few stabs at the short and charismatic. But in the end I decided. There is an important medieval text called *The Book of Margery Kempe*, significant because (a) it was written in English rather than Latin, (b) it was about a woman and (c) it was the biography of a commoner rather than one of the lives of the saints. She was an ordinary soul, a follower rather than one of the followed, so it matched my subject quite well. She also believed herself to have special gifts as a worshipper, and that seemed to fit too. I was comfortable with the clunkiness of *The Book of*. I had found my idea.

I hope the *Devout* bit is obvious. I am a true believer. The intensity of my experience with records and my understanding of their role in my life is genuinely and profoundly spiritual. I tend to be a bit frivolous when I talk about it, but that's just excitement.

If this book has one core proposition, it's this: a good record is a good record regardless of who or what is behind it. I can't stand fashion.

I can't stand peer pressure. Sometimes we are told that a record is important when we don't even know how it goes. Sometimes a record is more important to us than others seem to think it should be.

There has been a recent shift in music writing towards finding merit in "guilty pleasures" - records that we like but feel we should keep quiet about. It's slowly becoming okay to say that releases composed and tailored by corporation staff, promoted to mass audiences and put out under the name of artists who had not written the songs, perhaps not even played on the records, and whose image had been manipulated and controlled by marketing people, should nevertheless be afforded some credibility if they are good. This is to be applauded. It is something many of us have understood all our lives.

One

I was born at my South London home in the autumn of 1963, in the eye of a cultural hurricane. Days earlier, a lively and tuneful guitar band called the Beatles had appeared before royalty as part of a variety bill at the London Palladium and the whole country had seen it on TV. Before this, they had merely been the most famous and successful group in the land. Now they were the national agenda. Everyone, not just teenagers, knew their names, where they came from and how long their hair was. For years, midwives had been in the habit of twisting the hair of a newborn around their finger into a shape they called a kiss-curl, but the one that attended my mother brushed mine straight down my forehead. "There," she said. "You can be a Beatle baby."

Membership of the Beatles Fan Club was among the gifts on my first birthday. The only detail of this I remember is being sent a flexi-disc at Christmas containing a seasonal message from them to us. I think we got two of these before my membership lapsed. The messages were warm and funny, full of the wit, silliness and easy charm that had endeared the group to so many so quickly. Fan Club members loved and treasured them. Our hyper-active dog chewed ours up. Mum and Dad were cross, but I was only fascinated, both by the dents his teeth had made in the soft, bendy plastic and by the effect they had on play.

In any case, there were plenty of un-chewed alternatives in the house. It was the smaller ones that I was drawn to. I could reach them. I could hold them. I liked their size and shape. I liked the range of designs on the labels, the different colours and logos. I liked the patterns made by the writing.

Their main credits were centred, usually at the foot of the label: the song title, the writers' names and the name of the act; three or more lines in different type, one above the other. Each set formed a blob of words whose unique shape helped me to identify them. Mum said I was working the record player before I turned three, safely before I could read, so the shapes were helpful.

Sometimes they seemed linked to the theme. Dad had a Peter Sellers EP (Extended Play seven-inch), the cover of which showed Sellers in a bowler hat polishing the statuette at the front of his Rolls-Royce. To me, the word-blob on the label looked like an upside-down bowler hat. The shapes also helped to form an impression of a record before I listened to it; a visual representation of its stature. There were deep, grand ones; thin, slick ones; willowy, elegant ones.

But the music created the real effect. As I listened, I recognised that I wasn't just hearing sounds – I was getting feelings. It was doing things to me, all sorts of things. A record might amuse or delight me; it might make me bounce; it might frighten or warn me; it might send apprehensive tingles through my insides, offering glimpses of a grown-up world for which I was not yet ready. This was clearly serious stuff.

Right from the start, my soundtrack had variety. That Peter Sellers EP included a drunk singing behind the wheel of a screeching car, ending with his screams as he crashed it, as well as a version of the big-band standard 'All the Things You Are' - the character sitting in his bath, fantasising about performing before hundreds, until the orchestra fades to leave the slow, echoing drip of the tap and his wife banging impatiently on the door. There was a yodelling record on the peach-coloured Polydor label that my parents had picked up on holiday in Austria – rather exotic for a pair of Nonconformist cockneys – which I found no more than curious. There were classical and military EPs. There was a single by Bob Dylan which first introduced me to the sight of the blood-orange CBS label, as well as the sound of a voice I couldn't stand. There was a blue one on Philips by Joan Baez, which I also found myself avoiding.

But I certainly did not avoid an EP called *Excerpts from At the Drop of a Hat* by Michael Flanders and Donald Swann; a double act using two voices and a piano to produce live recordings of spellbinding expression and wit; four songs so clever and funny that I would bounce excitedly as I listened to them. I could say all the words, even the ones I didn't understand. 'The Song of Reproduction' made fun of Hi-Fi geeks and included the wonderful phrase "flutter on your bottom". 'A Transport of Delight' was about London buses; it used a chorus that became longer with each verse and included a bus conductor yelling "Ged' ahht of it!" in a manner familiar to me from relatives. Then there was 'The Hippopotamus', which took brilliant liberties with rhyming and had a truly great chorus beginning "Mud, mud, glorious mud".

But my favourite was 'The Gnu Song', about an animal fed up at being poorly appreciated in comparison to its cousins the bison, the okapi, the moose and even, for heaven's sake, the hartebeest. The gnu's complaints consisted of a series of rants wherein each word beginning with 'n' had a 'g' fixed to its front bumper, hence for example "the g-nicest work of g-nature in the zoo".

I would listen to these over and over again, my enthusiasm encouraged by parents who took time to explain what the lyrics meant, leading me to a deeper appreciation of songs that might otherwise have only been fun. Thus did I learn that lyrics matter greatly, that they make a contribution to the overall effect of a record and should therefore be good.

As for the Beatles, we had the *Twist and Shout* EP, the title track of which is still one of the most thrilling experiences available to humankind. It seemed important, grown-up and mystifying, like eavesdropping on an emotionally-charged conversation with no chance of understanding anything apart from the mood. Yet I became familiar with it, and with the other three tracks, enjoying the contrast between them; from the screaming hysteria of 'Twist and Shout' to the wistful sound of 'There's a Place' and my first experience of a pop song in "waltz time", 'A Taste of Honey'. I liked 'Do You Want to Know a Secret' best. I knew about secrets. It was here that I first encountered the idea of being "in love". The song made it sound cosy and sweet.

Having begun to understand this, I found I could interpret the meaning of the other tracks. 'There's a Place' was about having a special place to go to. Easy. 'A Taste of Honey' was about food, and 'Twist and Shout' was about thrashing around in a panic. You could tell this by the singer's voice, and I wasn't surprised that he was unhappy; you only had to look at the sleeve.

The cover shot showed the four of them jumping in the air above a pile of bomb-site bricks, and part of the image had been blurred by the action, making it seem that one of John Lennon's feet was horribly mangled. I had seen people with missing body parts and various deformities - my grandparents' generation had after all lived through World War II - so I simply registered this, and sympathised. His situation had given rise to all this anger, which had led to twisting, shouting and shaking a baby. I had no concept of how it was being shaken or whether it was in any danger, just that shaking was taking place and that it was a baby on the receiving end.

However, beside it in our living room was something to help me clarify this baby thing: 'Where Did Our Love Go' by the Supremes. The baby in this song was definitely not a newborn, but an older object of sad longing, and through its lyric I developed some early, small ideas about burning, yearning feelings and being hurt so bad – a different hurt to the one experienced when clattering into a metal napkin bucket or suffering a wasp sting.

The intro reminded me of the sound of shoes echoing their clip-clapping progress up the stone stairwells of flats where my grandparents, aunts and cousins lived, a prelude to a door being thrown open to greetings, hugs and biscuits. I remember being captivated by the B-side, 'He Means the World to Me', which was eventful and a little rough around the edges, even to the extent of being out of tune. I can still summon the image that its metallic sounds conjured in my imagination, of a cavernous, abandoned factory; water dripping onto decaying machinery from its leaking roof. No idea why. Must have seen it somewhere.

I'm not sure if I sang along to these songs, but I would soon become an enthusiastic sing-alonger and it may be that the turning point was 'We Shall Not Be Moved' by Australian group the Seekers. A traditional gospel song, it was on the B-side of their hugely successful single 'The Carnival Is Over'. I sang along to 'We Shall Not Be Moved' with gusto, clear and pleasant images of brothers together and trees standing by the water-side playing in my mind thanks to the lyrics, which I understood as a collection of disjointed phrases, strange but learnable; eventually, at least – what I initially sang, and repeatedly requested, was 'Me a Dolly Moon'. I imagine that it set me off bouncing around the room as well, since it was probably the first record I got to know that builds steadily from a sober intro to an exciting, wild thrash of a final chorus. I guess you would say that's gospel for you, but I was only little.

In time, baby sisters started appearing and adult attention was divided. It meant I was left to explore this expanding world of records for longer periods without direct supervision. An important aspect of this was getting to know the functionality of the record player. Ours was a Dansette, perhaps a Dansette Bermuda, although I can't be certain of this, even after research. So if you can identify the precise model from the following description, your team gets the points.

To play a record in the proper way, you fixed it on a little steel pole standing in the middle of the turntable, called a spindle, which fit snugly through the hole in the centre of the disc. There it was held up by a triangular catch, while an angled plastic lever was swung over and down to fully stabilise it. On a dial to the bottom-right of the turntable was a lever the size of a fingernail, operating a dial which clicked round in a semicircle to set the thing in motion; heavy work for little fingers. The turntable began to move, reaching its requisite speed as the triangular catch retracted, letting the record fall onto its rubber mat. The playing arm then sailed across and landed, the needle finding the run-in groove at the start of the record. Seconds later the music began.

You could reliably stack several discs on the spindle; it was unusual for the machine to make a mistake and release two at once. If you left it to run, they would play one after the other, the breaks between them containing the sounds of the run-out grooves, a few clicks, bumps and pauses, then the needle landing on the next run-in as your anticipation built, sometimes ridiculously. It would all come to rest once the arm had lifted itself from the run-out of the final disc and returned to its stand. Such delights would remain commercially available until the mid-1970s.

The playing arm's bulbous head held the stylus containing the playing needle - essentially the same kit that superstar DJs were using decades later and which is becoming popular again as I write. Our head contained a cartridge that you could rotate, allowing you to switch between two needles: the one suitable for singles playing at 45 revolutions per minute as well as for LPs (long players) playing at 33, and the more heavy-duty one for playing now-defunct 78s. A different fingernail dial to the left of the turntable controlled the speed by clicking up and down from 78, to 45, to 33; and then to 16, for heaven's sake. I don't think I ever handled a record that was supposed to play at 16, although I experimented with the setting, of course.

Playing records at the wrong speed made for good investigation, but never for very long, and often just to make records I didn't like sound more interesting, perhaps the yodelling one or something by Bob Dylan. Placing the needle on the record and pushing the turntable round the wrong way also produced interesting results. I discovered the tone dial too, enabling me to thin and fatten the sound at will, and before long I had tweaked and morphed all my regulars in as many ways as my ingenuity could allow. More experiments would follow.

In the meanwhile, I was beginning to develop a picture of records having a life of their own in the big wide world. They were on the radio. They were in other people's houses. They were in shops. Sometimes they were on the radio and in other people's houses, and then in shops too. Some records were in house after house and shop after shop, then leaping out of the radio every few hours, day after day for weeks and weeks. I say radio, but I think everybody probably still called it the wireless then. I know for sure my dad did. I can hear his voice: "*I heard it on the wireless.*" Anyway, because of this, I became familiar with the sound of records we didn't have at home, records of consequence, records that sounded huge and important and grown-up.

Mum often sat me on the kitchen surface as she busied herself; my sisters in cots or playpens somewhere safe behind us. I have a clear image of perching on the Formica, with a sea of flour next to me as she got busy with the pastry. I can see the wiggly wire of the resting tray and I can hear the gentlemanly voices of the presenters. I can also hear 'River Deep, Mountain High' by Ike and Tina Turner, its frantic pace, spooky orchestration and hysterical vocals disturbing my innards. Years later, when I would see it written about for the first time, it would be described as a "monster hit". It was indeed monstrous. It scared me.

In the same ballpark, but not quite as scary, was 'I Got You Babe' by Sonny and Cher; the same big sound, but a steadier tempo; enormous, swinging chord changes and that woodwind part in the chorus that made me think of swans gliding up and down on a pond. There seemed to be so much going on in these records, so much detail, I felt I couldn't possibly tame them. I didn't get the chance, because we didn't have our own copies and I hadn't started demanding them yet.

Two others I remember from that time were 'My Boy Lollipop' by Millie, and 'The Loco-Motion' by Little Eva. These would have been oldies even then. I imagined Eva to have been anything but little, such was the scale and power of the record's sound. In my mind I saw a stocky woman belting it out from a large, muscular mouth adorned with ruby red lipstick, a picture in keeping with the furious blare going on around her. 'My Boy Lollipop' was as big, but lighter, more fun; straightforward expressions of the first rush of love set to a jaunty rhythm, a record able to engage the affection of just about everybody. When it came on, people smiled, did silly little dances, sang along with the words they could make out, plus a few others they had on standby. Adults I knew filled in the gaps with phrases like "me diddle I-dee".

My investigations continued beyond home turf. When visiting other people's homes, I would peer around trying to decide where their records might be kept. Books may have been visible but records weren't. They were hidden in cupboards and cabinets, some made for the purpose. I don't ever remember seeing them kept messily, but then they were valuable things. By 1970 their price would have fallen dramatically in real terms but in the late 50s they had been at a premium.

Mum's cousin told me she hadn't been able to afford more than one a week on her wages before I was born. Her copies of the important hits were handled with reverence and tucked well away. She wouldn't even show them to me until I was older.

Finally and under duress, she made great ceremony of playing me her 78 of the Everly Brothers' cute ballad of hapless longing 'All I Have to Do Is Dream', twice only, before returning it to its secure storage facility. I wondered how tense her walks home from the shop must have been.

Nan and Grandad had their stash under the lid of their piano stool. I was always rumbled when I peeped at them because I could never close the heavy lid without a giveaway clunk. Therein lay singles by crooner Perry Como, a tamer, post-army Elvis Presley, and plink-a-plonk keyboard instrumentals by Russ Conway and Winifred Atwell, some of which I have come to revere. In the improved conditions of the late 50s they had been able to buy a new record player, so they then had to get things to play on it, hence the 45s. This was a fairly typical scenario although some, like my grandparents on my dad's side, had owned a gramophone for some time and had built up a stack of 78s from the 1940s and 50s that included music-hall ditties and religious songs, as well as records by jazz smoothies Nat 'King' Cole and Bing Crosby.

In some houses and flats we visited, the children had not yet left home; in others they had left recently. Either way, there would be a deposit of records, mostly from the rock 'n' roll era which, by the time I was three, was very much over. I was occasionally allowed to hold them under close supervision; I certainly wasn't allowed to play them. Mum was convinced that I would get this record thing out of my system, letting me loose at home on that assumption. But at other people's houses, very different rules applied. Nobody in their right mind was going to let a three-year-old boy handle their expensive consumer goods when they were prone to being chipped and scratched anyway, never mind what he might do with the record player and its fascinating needle.

Yet they must have played them to me, because two in particular loomed large. First, 'Right Said Fred' by comedy actor Bernard

Cribbins. This is the tale of three removal men getting an unnamed object into a house, their unsubtle ideas for making it fit causing substantial damage to both the object and the house, all of which they cheerfully take in their stride while pausing for regular tea breaks. It's full of character, peppered with sound effects and slickly produced.

Second, 'Rocking Goose' by Johnny and the Hurricanes. This was an instrumental featuring a call-and-response of sorts, the call being a four-note phrase on a distorted organ, the response being a goose honking on the beat, its sound made seemingly by abusing some poor brass instrument in an echo chamber. This makes it sound comical, and there is indeed an explicit sense of fun about it, but the record stands out mainly for its energy and head-splitting volume. They did tend to mix them loud in those days, but even so, 'Rocking Goose' is a remarkable racket – furiously paced and big on the effects. One final, elongated honk brings two-and-a-bit minutes of madness to a close, leaving the listener in a condition which, whatever else it may consist of, is certain to include elements of sheer disbelief. The B-side is good, too, 'Revival' being a mid-paced rocker using the melody of 'When the Saints Go Marching In'. I would, no doubt, have been confused when subsequently bumping into the original.

Uncovering these and others to satisfy the curiosity of a small boy led to discussions about which one belonged to whom and how it had come to be in the house when the initials scrawled on the label related to someone who lived streets away. I heard stories about how so-and-so lent them a record and never asked for it back, or asked if they could store a pile of them at their house for safekeeping; or conversely, bitter tales of records borrowed and never returned, stolen at parties, or kidnapped by older siblings when they moved out. Sad, sometimes tragic tales of betrayal and loss. Happily for me, the outcome of these outpourings was often that I was given time to listen to one or two more while they scratched their heads trying to remember who 'PF' was.

It was at Nan and Grandad's that I was most often left when Mum had to be elsewhere, and I assume that in time they became happier for me to use the record player because I got to spend a lot of time with a few firm favourites. I was particularly keen on Neil Sedaka's rumbustious 'Happy Birthday Sweet Sixteen', my first experience of sixteen being touted as the age at which girls are finally liberated from the miserable business of not having a boyfriend.

There was also a Bobby Vee B-side called 'Remember Me, Huh?' This is a real gem, the thoughts of a guy trying hard to be dignified about his girl leaving him, but letting the facade slip. I was immediately absorbed and moved by the drama. Its melody and chord structure support the subject excellently. The A-side, 'A Forever Kind of Love', pales by comparison.

Apart from knowing for sure that I had meaningful relationships with these records, my memories of that time are patchy and I can't be sure which ones relate directly to one another. As I write this, I am approximating, making assumptions as safely as possible, so that what I say is either true or highly likely. Crisp, clear recollections like the abandoned factory image conjured up by that Supremes B-side, or being frightened by 'River Deep, Mountain High' are precious. But the most precious memory of all concerns a shop.

I was taken to the West End of London to look for toys. I remember it being warm outside. In a crowded, bustling, narrow street was a shop called Galt's. It sold wooden toys including musical ones, among them xylophones with colourful keys. As bodies pushed endlessly past we played with the samples, and in the background there was music; loud, compelling, on-the-beat music with the sound of what seemed to be wooden blocks. I directly linked the toys with the music, and whenever I saw wooden toys subsequently I remembered this scene.

I now know the record to have been another Supremes song, 'Love Is Like an Itching in My Heart', with its stomping beat and prominent glockenspiel, and that the Galt's in question was in Carnaby Street, Swinging London's most iconic fashion alley. Thus do I have a clear memory of listening to the new sound by the Supremes, in Carnaby Street, in 1966, as I shopped for musical instruments. Far too cool to even think about.

Speaking of cool, it's about time the Beatles were mentioned again. Not every Fab Four single made its way into our house, but there was one double A-side that truly had something for all the family. One side was 'Eleanor Rigby', a bleak social comment whose maturity consigned their "yeah yeah yeah" period firmly to the past. My parents and others spent time telling me what it was about. I understood what lonely people were and what dying was, but adults seemed particularly affected by it. *We have to remember that some people are lonely, that they're not as fortunate as we are, and it's very sad.*

This was a genuine thing. Mum in particular often spoke to me about issues that cropped up in lyrics. There were important aspects of the emerging counter-culture that she felt an affinity with, but the real root of her responses was straightforward Christian compassion. 'Eleanor Rigby' meant time to pause and think. Me? I was a small boy and preferred the other side, 'Yellow Submarine', a brash piece of silliness designed to engage children and be approved of by grandparents, with a chorus they could sing along to in unison. Unfortunately, some, for example me, sang along to all of it, including the middle part with its indecipherable maritime commands and odd sound effects. People must have thought I needed treatment.

My indulgences were nevertheless allowed to continue. Mum still assumed it was a phase that I would grow out of, one that would soon be eclipsed by traditional young boy pursuits. So she let it run. I did like other things. I had tea sets and doctors' sets. I had bears. I had a Tap-Tap set, where you secured colourful wooden shapes on a cork board with a hammer and brass tacks. I had Fuzzy Felt, with zoo animals and a family of four to position in friezes. The wooden xylophone I've already mentioned. I possibly had my first bits of Lego by then. Dad had built a three-sided shop front with a counter to place my toy till on and serve customers from. Oh, and I also had a drum kit. A kid's drum kit, featuring a bass skin decorated with upturned red crotchets, a snare, two toms and a cymbal. Fantastic. Grandad had played drums in the army and may have tried to coach me. I have no memory of how he got on.

These things were a big deal. I loved my toys. Many were played with for years, on and off. It was just that records were never off. Not ever. Every adult in my world knew this. So I was bought them as gifts to cheer me up when I was ill, I was bought more as birthday presents and even more as Christmas gifts. If I had heard something I liked on the radio or the TV, people knew about it. Sometimes, even when it wasn't a special occasion, some grown up or other would turn up with a copy. I had begun to have an influence on the music that was brought into the house.

So what came? Well the Beatles, obviously. They were taking a real shine to those odd sound effects and by the autumn of 1967 I had encountered more of them. 'Baby You're a Rich Man', the B-side of 'All You Need Is Love', featured an eerie warbling which could have been some exotic eastern instrument but then again might have been the panicking fly trapped in a bottle that I was envisaging. That was merely curious, but the final part of 'Strawberry Fields Forever' was downright disturbing. As the song faded, what I imagined to be some demented underground train came creeping from its tunnel to loom over me, clanging and rattling deafeningly for long moments before returning to the darkness, no less unnerving for its disappearance.

I wasn't that keen on the song. I found it dull, but I would dare myself to sit through it until the Spooky Express had come and gone. It was the aural equivalent of monsters behind the bedroom curtains. I would peer towards the record, a chill running through me, knowing those sounds were on there somewhere.

This was an early experience of being affected by a record so heavily that I needed another to make things alright again. I needed an antidote. In 1967, the prime option would have been the Monkees' 'I'm a Believer'. This was a smashing record; its sound a rich, dense sweetness, its beat seemingly woven from sunshine, its theme the experience of being suddenly rescued from the feeling that you are never going to get anyone special to love you, that everything you try will always go wrong and you should forget it because the disappointments are too crushing and too frequent. Then one day it goes right - fantastically, breathlessly right in Widescreen Technicolor, your faith is restored and you are a Believer.

This was universally relevant songwriting from the very top drawer, a masterclass in how to connect with an audience. Plus the singer's voice sounded brilliant. Plus it had a keyboard riff on the chorus that went *a-barmbarm barmbarm bom*! Bloody great. Anybody who didn't feel better for listening to it was as odd as a Beatles sound effect.

The alternative antidote to 'Strawberry Fields Forever' was at an even shorter reach, since, if you simply turned the 45 over, you had 'Penny Lane' with its intricate, unfolding melody, busy arrangement and uplifting feel – despite the setting, the very strange setting, in pouring rain while customers were shaved, with firemen rushing in and everything. It was as if someone had flicked a whole pack of cards in the air so that they tumbled down all around as you listened, each one printed with a short evocative phrase which somehow landed perfectly on the precise part of the tune for which it was destined. It was wonderful, there was so much of it to get to know and its sound effects were much easier on the ear.

I am also happy to report that the dog's destruction of Christmas flexi-discs from the Beatles Fan Club had not meant the end of flexies in the house. There were others, and one in particular that I had on heavy rotation for months. It came from the Smiths Crisps company. Someone in the family must have sent off for it.

'When It Comes to the Crunch (It's Smiths It Is)' was a song advertising its range of snacks, designed to get the kids on board by approximating the fab 'n' groovy pop sounds of the day. This it seems to have knowingly achieved, yet I can't think of another record from the era that sounded quite like it. The insistent, driving go-go beat, twangy lead guitar and cry of "*Come on everybody, do the Crunch!*" makes it almost a parody of mid-60s pop cool. Indeed it would have sat comfortably on the soundtrack of a turn-of-millennium Austin Powers movie. Except that it was about crisps.

If this makes it sound risible I certainly wasn't mocking it at the time. 'Crunch' was great to bounce on the sofa to and as loud as heck. The B-side, 'Rhythm and Crunch', was an instrumental version of the same song, my first experience of this. Now, thrillingly, I could sing along without competition from the actual vocalist.

In May 1968, a third sister was born. This left Mum at home with four of us for the summer. Little surprise then, that my memories of this time are almost all of being in the house. The radio must have been on pretty constantly, which would have been good thinking on Mum's part. It would have distracted both of us, as well as giving us a shared topic of conversation as she swept from one chore to another. This is not pure conjecture; a large number of the songs I know best are from that year. Some – the ones we had copies of – I got to know in intricate detail; every beat, every twist and turn of the arrangement, every nook and cranny of the vocal parts. I had my special favourites, Mum had hers, some we liked equally.

My growing experience of language meant that I could increasingly 'get' adult turns-of-phrase in lyrics. My experience was set to develop in other ways, too: I would start infant school that autumn. But here's a big one. In the early weeks of that year, I was taken to a record shop in Camberwell, which I think was called Page 39 and, holding money up to the counter, I shyly asked for 'The Ballad of Bonnie and Clyde' by Georgie Fame. My first time.

For many reasons this was a new phase, but particularly so in terms of my musical intake. Never before had my diet contained so much current music. And what current music it was: a blizzard of captivating melodies, soaring ballads, hippy mythologies, huge stompers and poetic melodrama; warning, accusing, longing and lamenting, dripping in atmosphere. Perhaps it seemed that way to me because I was a titch and it was new. Perhaps though, it had something to do with the recent launch of a certain BBC radio station.

In the mid-60s there were two different experiences of listening to popular music on the radio. The first was the BBC Light Programme, which was not actually a programme but an entire station, one of two serving the entertainment and information needs of Brits. The Light Programme sometimes played new pop records, in intensive but carefully edited bursts on shows such as *Saturday Club*, on which the Beatles were regular guests. The other was a number of commercial stations which for legal reasons could not operate on British soil, and therefore broadcast in defiance either from the continent or from ships moored in the seas around the coast.

These were dubbed 'pirate stations'. They played a pure diet of hip new sounds and were rougher around the edges because of their fluctuating signal strength, their blaring, charismatic jingles and the outsider personalities of their disc jockeys. Guess which of the two was more popular with rebellious youngsters. Finally a law was passed that shut the pirates down, and being good capitalist pirates many of them accepted offers of work from a new station catering legitimately for the youthful pop audience, part of a comprehensive reorganisation of BBC radio. Hence Tony Blackburn, John Peel, Emperor Rosko, Kenny Everett and others were soon plying their trade on Radio 1, which went on air in September 1967.

I was oblivious to these momentous events despite being a regular radio listener. We usually had Jimmy Young's show on before lunch, its cartoony cry of *What's the recipe today, Jim?* heralding more kitchen tips for housewives. The only other show that I can be sure I listened to was *Junior Choice*, first hosted by Leslie Crowther, whose relatively un-studied style of presentation made him easy to like. Its predecessor on the Light Programme had been *Children's Hour*, and *Junior Choice* picked up its baton after the reorganisation, playing pretty much the same stuff but with a growing quota of current pop hits. It went out on Radio 1 and Radio 2 simultaneously for an hour and a half on Saturday morning and an hour on Sunday.

The playlist consisted of nursery rhymes, gospel songs, movie soundtracks, TV themes and musical stories like 'Tubby the Tuba', the tale of an under-valued brass instrument who wanted his own tune to play so he could be like other members of the orchestra. We had a copy of the version by Danny Kaye, Britain's favourite Yank. Its flip offered the tale of 'The Little Fiddle' which is barking mad: Kaye narrates in the persona of a German music professor who makes farm animal noises as he approximates classical pieces, and although the objective may have been to introduce youngsters to a range of orchestral themes, its effect may simply have been to give them nightmares about being chased around fields by brass instruments. Feel free to investigate.

Another *Junior Choice* favourite was the sprightly theme from Prokofiev's *Peter and the Wolf,* which served to familiarise young listeners with classical sounds in a more straightforward way. But I already had my favourite. We owned an EP of *The Sorcerer's Apprentice* by Dukas and I was nuts about it. The piece is featured in the Disney movie *Fantasia*, with Mickey Mouse as the apprentice. Mum kept telling me about this, repeatedly mentioning this wonderful movie that I had no chance of seeing. However it did mean that I knew the story. The sorcerer goes out, leaving orders for the apprentice to clean, sweep and fetch water. The apprentice thinks he can use magic to complete his tasks, but loses control of what he unleashes and the place is a flooded wreck by the time the boss returns, whereupon, seeing the mess, he gives the apprentice a good ass whoopin'. What a tune it is, or rather, what a series of rich, tense, overlapping tunes it is. Perhaps it, too, got played on *Junior Choice*, blowing more tiny minds than just mine.

Remembering the programme makes me think of weekend breakfast dishes, of mixing egg yolk and tomato ketchup together in swirls on my plate, studying half-eaten slices of toast and deciding what their shape reminded me of, occupying an island of concentration in a sea of expanding family hubbub as I listened to 'Puff the Magic Dragon' by Peter, Paul and Mary, 'Three Wheels on My Wagon' by the New Christy Minstrels, 'Alexander Beetle' by Melanie Safka (although I'm probably being chronologically inaccurate here and veering deep into the post-Leslie Crowther era of Ed "Stewpot" Stewart) or something by Pinky & Perky.

Now then: Pinky & Perky. A pair of marionette upright pigs in dungarees and berets, with their own TV show on which they performed songs including Beatles ones. I know this because it was their version of 'All My Loving' that I heard first. This is one of the Beatles' very best and the memory is difficult to deal with. Pinky & Perky had a backing band. They were marionette birds with moptop hairdos. They were called the Beakles. In the midst of Beatlemania this must have seemed the most reasonable thing in the world.

The riveting sounds and novelties delivered by *Junior Choice* would be the staple diet of British children for many years to come. But by the end of 1968, I had something that could compete with it. Thanks to that third sister and all those weeks indoors with Mum, I had daytime radio and a full induction into the darker world of grown-up pop. In time, the balance of power would shift towards this newer influence until, like the neglected Puff, *Junior Choice* would have to slip back into its cave. But that was a long way off. 'Tubby the Tuba' still had equal status with 'Strawberry Fields Forever', but the pull of this new world was powerful: the sounds, the seriousness, the sheer importance.

Here I encountered harrowing tragedies, records whose arrangements and orchestration matched their dramatic themes. In these moral epics, men had sinned, lost battles with conscience, betrayed the ones they loved and now dealt with the consequences; weeping, regretting, pleading, but resigned to their fate. Similar songs had been around for years, but this batch was an update and a British update to boot. It may be that the disappearance of the pirates and launch of Radio 1 had upped the stakes, making the need to grab mainstream attention more urgent and requiring record-making expertise of greater cunning to rise to the challenge. It may simply have been the evolution of songwriting at work. In any case it was all very new to me, and one record in particular seemed to provide a bridge between this world and that of the *Junior Choice* playlist: 'Stop Stop Stop' by the Hollies.

This was the first I knew of the Hollies and I assumed that the band's name was an onomatopoeic reference to the main riff which begins the record, played on what sounds like, and for all I know is, an electrified banjo. *Hoddly hol hol, hoddly hoddly hol hol.* Better the Hollies than the Hoddlies, I suppose.

It belongs in the *Children's Hour/Junior Choice* camp because it came out a couple of years before my third sister did, but it belongs in the new world too because of its seedy theme. A man goes to a club to see an exotic dancer. He watches her, finding excitement in her every movement, getting increasingly hot under the collar as she snakes between the tables. He knows that one is not supposed to touch, but this feast of the senses is overwhelming and he launches himself at her, out of control, sending tables and drinks flying until finally being grabbed by bouncers and thrown out.

The listener's moral compass ensures that this incident is recognised as totally unacceptable and if such dreadful places didn't exist there would be no occasion for it anyway. Fine. Job done. Except that it isn't, for although you might think that our hero would creep away in shame and rather die than show his face there again, it becomes clear that this has happened on several previous occasions and is almost certain to be repeated.

It's the kind of episode that might have been edited out of a *Carry On* film, yet no adult declared it inappropriate and I listened to it until every little bit was familiar. *Hoddly hol hol, hoddly hoddly hol hol.* It had a strong B-side which I played almost as much. 'It's You' is a break-up song with a good tune and a harmonica as its lead instrument. It's one of the few occasions on which the harmonica has done anything other than annoy me.

Thus does 'Stop Stop Stop' provide the bridge to the concentration of fabnificence that was 1968, which I unveil by means of a record that I had no awareness of at the time but which Mum loved; 'I've Gotta Get a Message to You' by the Bee Gees. I do so because of the subject, a guy trying to communicate for one last time with his lover before he is executed for murder. The harrowing theme is wrapped in swirling strands of orchestral silk, with a dominant part of the arrangement being the chiming of a lead guitar so distorted it sounds like a child's toy piano, harmonising with the sorrowful melody and backing vocal. Sweet, tearful tragedy. How is the listener to feel about a killer receiving his comeuppance? Well in this case sad, clearly; the record sees to that.

How different from 'The Ballad of Bonnie and Clyde' by Georgie Fame. This coincided with a *Bonnie and Clyde* movie starring Warren Beatty and Faye Dunaway whose level of violence was controversial. Georgie Fame came out of the mod scene, mixing blues and jazz to make records with a cool, dinner-clubby feel. This one was stodgily blues, but with the embellishments of piano and brass evoking the 1930s. The sassy narrative tells of a violent life of violent robbery which comes to a violent end. Crime and punishment of a different hue: live by the sword, die by the sword. It taught me some great American phrases: *waitin' for heat to die down, reachin' for the sky, hollerin', high tailin' it out of town, carbines openin' up, lyin' in a pool of blood.*

Best of all, though, were the guns. Lots and lots of guns. There are two bullet-riddled passages on the record, the first being the middle eight, where machine-gun and rifle fire mix with the sirens as the subjects flee the authorities and the band swings through the tune of the verse. The second is at the end, when the Feds catch them by surprise. The music stops and there is just the guns, long, long moments of them before, at funeral pace now, the band reappears so that Georgie can confirm the baddies are dead, and play out a final, mocking, good-riddance kind of motif to end the record.

Just as powerful an experience was 'Last Night in Soho' by Dave Dee, Dozy, Beaky, Mick and Tich. Tell me about that name. More outlaw tales, more tragic endings, another woman left weeping. It was set in the underworld where a man who thought he had left the bad life behind is sucked back in, talked into doing one more job for the mob, but this time going down for it. Resigned to his fate and hating himself for the life he has thrown away, he is led off to where love cannot help.

The arrangement and orchestration support the despairing lyric thoroughly and in impressive detail. There is a sound on the intro, a clanging downward slide on an instrument that I've never been confident about naming, which is typical of the way the atmosphere is established. No sunlight here, no hope of redemption. The melody in the verse is every bit as good as the one in the chorus is unusual. *Last night in Soho, I let my love go.* A lamenting refrain, the last note of which slides up a third, but seems as though it has risen much further. I've heard nothing like it anywhere else.

As a kid I found it gripping, as an adult I have barrels of respect for it. It was a serious record that I understood and Soho was a place I had been to: in those days you could still park a car there and go shopping on Regent Street. Most of all though, I loved the tune. I belted it out at full tilt as its drama unfolded all over again on yet another repeat play.

Imprisonment and death were constant companions in 1968, yet doom-laden melodrama also translated well into songs of simple heartbreak, reflecting the self-absorbed, obsessively analytical state of love's victims. In the blue corner: 'Fox on the Run' by Manfred Mann.

This terrific lyric is about a woman of status swanning into a poor boy's life, taking what he has to give, then abandoning him; leaving him to suffer just as a wounded fox is left to die. He is haunted by the spectre of the hurt chasing him down; he knows it will get him in the end. The record fades out to a slowed tempo; you hear the panting of an exhausted runner and the sound of distant howling. It's coming to get him.

This single should be put in front of music students as an example of how to use metaphor and simile in a pop lyric. It should be put in front of them again to demonstrate how effectively a verse and chorus can complement each other, especially when the verse and chorus in question are so well-crafted. Liverpool songwriter Tony Hazzard was responsible for this little belter. He also wrote something for the Hoddlies – sorry, Hollies – called 'Listen to Me', which has a similar and equally endearing feel.

'Fox on the Run' is the only record from that time that I have retained the original copy of. My initials are clearly visible in the white arc of the Fontana label in Mum's handwriting and the thing's still perfectly playable. Sadly, the same cannot be said of many other 45s I had access to. I had not yet learned to care for them and I'm afraid some were treated like laboratory rats in my enthusiasm to experiment. 'Stop Stop Stop' sounded amazing at 78rpm and Pinky & Perky were fascinating at 16. I played records without the rubber disc covering the turntable, even once being caught trying to lift the whole turntable away. I drew on records in crayon and tried to play them. I had mixed results trying to peel the labels off, but some you could tease up at the spindle hole.

Additionally, of course, I pushed the centres out. Most 45s had removable centres, presumably so they could be adapted for use in jukeboxes where they were dropped onto fat centre fixtures rather than having to negotiate a spindle. In the manufacturing, narrow arcs were cut to make a circle around the spindle hole, leaving four little spikes to hold the centre in place. With a bit of prodding these would start to weaken until one would pop, leaving an increasingly wobbly and off-centre centre to do a less effective job of keeping the record straight as it spun.

This corrosive process was riveting. Once the centre was completely removed, the young scientist was then faced with the challenge of putting it back. This, obviously, was done with sticky tape. Just as obviously, it looked horrible and never worked. Not all records came with removable centres: the same release could come with solid centres, as well as black plastic ones with three spokes that you could take out if you were careful, and which I have heard referred to curiously as spiders.

That yodelling single had one of these and removing it was my gateway to the delights of playing records deliberately off centre, so that the tone rose and fell giddily and the playing arm swung in and out as the turntable spun. It was the kind of thing that caused adults to drop whatever they were doing and fly into the room with alarm in their voices. Some time in the 70s, the neat little three-legged spider was replaced by a futuristic update with a wavy pattern. This was a pain in the arse. Not only was it ugly, but the spindle hole was too big and you had to fiddle about to centre it manually. Yodellers were okay warped, but I wasn't having it with anything I liked.

As with the pre-1968 period, I was aware of records that were out there doing big things in the world even if they weren't favourites in our house. They were on the radio and in shops, lurking in the background for months on end, which in the case of unnerving things like 'Fire' by the Crazy World of Arthur Brown, was where I was happy for them to stay. They were also at wedding receptions. Mum had hundreds of cousins and they all seemed to get married within the space of a few years, with the result that we were going to church halls and community buildings a lot.

Here we ran between tables when there was grown up stuff like speeches going on, ate chicken drumsticks and crisps, or hid from cousins who were older than us and didn't smile back. We also danced to loud music, with adults joining in several glasses to the good, beaming and singing their heads off, ignorance of the words being no obstacle, many a *dee digh doe* and a *digh doe day*. 'Mony Mony' by Tommy James and the Shondells, 'Baby Come Back' by the Equals, 'Hi Ho Silver Lining' by Jeff Beck: huge, stompy, hand-clappy tunes in whose company I felt very grown up, and yet will always make me think of kids being lifted into the air and swung around, or getting themselves into ring-a-roses circles, or skidding across the polished floor on their knees, or diving through the legs of an indulgent uncle. These occasions would have given me my first experience of teenagers yelling "Oh I love this one!" and scraping chairs back as they sprang to their feet, grabbing others to join them in homage. They never grabbed me. Aunts, uncles and grandparents were my dance floor community and that suited me just fine. To me, dancing meant bouncing and I bounced until I was dragged away.

Many in the family have a particular memory of me at one of these receptions. I was with a slightly older cousin; we were on tiptoe, holding on to the edge of the stage and staring up at the curtain, oblivious to the world around us because we were singing along at the tops of our voices to 'Hey Jude'. This was the new Beatles single, the first on their recently-launched Apple label. The single itself looked beautiful; a rich, dappled-green apple image covering the label on the A-side, a white cross-section of it on the reverse, showing its core and pips. No record label had looked like this before, certainly not in our house with its collection of Columbia, Parlophone and Fontana designs, which seemed suddenly frumpy by comparison. It was lovely. But then there was the record itself.

It is one of a handful that I have rediscovered at intervals, spending years not being at all bothered about it, but then, suddenly, having it once again flood my waking hours, seeming like the most magnificent thing in creation. I have tried and failed to find a throwaway chord change, a shard of perfunctory instrumentation or that'll-do delivery. Every nook and cranny of it has meaning and purpose.

Now I'm certain that at the time, I spent the first half of it twiddling my thumbs waiting for that epic, tantric coda to begin – I would have been told off for dumping the needle at the point where *better, better, better* climbs to its screamed summit – but I definitely knew all the words and sang them in sincere tribute to the passion in the grooves, in recognition of all the swoons and tingles it was sending through me. Not so sure how my accompaniment actually sounded, but I wouldn't have given a stuff, even in the hysterical parts. I was lost in it. So was my cousin, gripping the edge of the stage on tiptoe at a wedding reception.

'Hey Jude' was to be the last Beatles song I would spend proper time with until 'Yesterday' was released as a single in a 1976 reissues flurry. I imagine their break-up two years later was a big deal but I had no idea it was happening. Yet I knew all about the end of the Seekers. One day I was told there was going to be a TV special that evening with the Seekers on, and at the end of it they were going to "split up".

I was horrified. I knew about splitting: pieces of wood split down the middle, conker cases split open, I would split my head open on a kerb if I didn't look where I was going. I had visions of the stage rising during the final song and squashing them against the ceiling. What had they done to deserve this? I watched the show peeping between my fingers. As the end credits rolled they were still performing, very much alive. Thankfully the cameras were switched off before they did the dirty deed. I can't remember if I voiced this misconception or not, but I remember the distress. And they'd done all those nice songs, too.

How did I know about all those nice songs? Well they had a thumping great *Best Of* album out and it was selling by the truckload. We had one, with its cover shot of the group in painfully formal attire, singer Judith Durham seemingly wearing a wedding cake designed by a six year-old. I didn't question any of it at the time of course; its look and sound were fine, and both would have a lasting effect. Those vocal harmonies and muscular tunes would do the job of a head massage as I grew older; warming and reassuring; somewhere I could always go for a hug.

Judith Durham's voice is clean and strong, one of the very best from the 60s. A teenage girlfriend that I was particularly keen on was a dead ringer for her on that cover, minus the dress. It was years after the relationship ended that I realised this: it seemed to explain a lot. Thus are our love maps often forged, in the security and wonders of childhood.

Through this *Best Of*, I found out about more than 'The Carnival is Over' and 'Me a Dolly Moon'. There was their first, excellent chart-topper 'I'll Never Find Another You', which Mum had sung to me when I was small, as well as the cracking 'Georgy Girl' and 'Morningtown Ride', the latter a well-fashioned lullaby whose appeal is deservedly enduring and which I already knew from *Junior Choice*.

So it wasn't all 45s, there were albums too. I assume I was dissuaded from touching them, at least to begin with. They seemed like a lot of bother anyway. Two covers – *two* covers, an outer cardboard one and fiddly paper inner sleeve – to grapple with, plus having to negotiate that fingernail lever to change the turntable speed to 33. We usually listened to albums together.

There were nevertheless a couple that had been bought especially for me. Before I turned five, I was taken to the cinema for the first time, to see Disney's *The Jungle Book*. I remember it being an uncomfortable experience, queuing for ages at the Elephant & Castle with nothing to look at but the back of people's legs, then getting inside a rowdy dark area and seeing very little of the film, although I do remember seeing the bit at the end with the vultures. Despite this, I did get to know the songs, which as the whole world knows are completely brilliant: 'The Bare Necessities', 'I Wanna Be Like You', 'That's What Friends Are For'. We longed to own them, but original soundtrack recordings were then flatly unavailable and so we had to make do with *Songs From The Jungle Book*, a set of cover versions on the budget MFP (Music For Pleasure) label licensed by EMI.

The other was *Ken Dodd and the Diddymen*, from the TV series of the same name, also on MFP. Ken Dodd was a comedian and singer, with little rosy-cheeked marionette friends who conformed to social and national stereotypes for the entertainment of millions. Among their ranks was an Irish one called Mick the Marmeliser, marmelising being what he would do to you if you pissed him off. There was

Harry Cart, the yokel; Little Evan and Wee Hamish (no prizes) and an upper-class one called Sir Nigel Ponsonby-Smallpiece. They marched along the streets of Knotty Ash – an actual district of Liverpool – singing in helium voices and looking ridiculous. However, on record it worked a certain charm.

The main theme, 'Song of the Diddymen', catchy and familiar from the telly, for some reason begins side two. Side one opens with a narrative-plus-dialogue on how they all got together to make the record, its star being Sir Nigel due to his fabulous guffawing. They then spoil it a bit by singing a couple of jolly songs in a medley, but this is all but forgiven when the second track begins. 'Where's Me Shirt?' deserves recognition. Surreal and chaotic, it laments the plight of those throughout history who have found themselves *sans chemise*, doing so to a driving Tijuana-like rhythm. It's the only track on the album not to feature the Diddymen; it's Ken Dodd going berserk all by himself. Everybody ought to listen to it at least once, just to say they've done it.

I imagine my parents wished they could have kept it down to once; but then they had albums of their own to console them. Both liked *Live at PJ's* by Trini Lopez, containing 'If I Had a Hammer' and a good version of 'La Bamba'. 'If I Had a Hammer' was a real favourite in the house. It was written by the protester's protester Woody Guthrie and was ubiquitous on the folkie/Civil Rights circuit. We had Bob Dylan and Joan Baez, so we had that too.

Another *Best Of* was that of earnest folkies Peter, Paul and Mary, originators of 'Puff the Magic Dragon' and habitual Dylan tributeers; their version of his flagship song 'Blowin' in the Wind' had been their first hit. The compilation featured this, plus its own version of 'If I Had a Hammer', plus the wistful, captivating '500 Miles'. This song of loss provided me with the novel experience of having to explain what the matter was, when in fact I had just gone quiet and still, not wanting anyone to see me, hoping they would leave me alone, probably blushing a bit. Records can do that sometimes. '500 Miles' has been covered often, every version a living joke next to that one. The trio pose as mobsters on the cover, the guys carrying instrument cases, presumably to conceal their weapons. Guns everywhere when I was a kid.

No guns, however, on *Honky Tonk Classics* by Andy "Plymouth" Rocke, although it may well have had a few aimed at it. This was a curiosity: a collection of classical compositions by Brahms, Tchaikovsky and others, performed in saloon-bar style on an upright piano with the occasional saxophone or clarinet chipping in to help. It was given to Mum by a friend who thought that because she liked classical music she would find it amusing. She didn't. She hated it. Unwisely however, she didn't get rid of the thing and in time it was discovered by a small child who thought it was hilarious.

I did silly dances to it, demanding that adults watched. The poor sods. It was on the Gala label, which I never encountered in any other context. The vinyl was more brittle than I was used to. There was a crack in our copy which made it all but impossible to play the first tune on either side. In my experimental moods this was irresistible. I found that if I lifted one side of the crack it would click askew, making a little ramp for the needle to jump off as the disc revolved. I watched to see how many different places it would settle in. Eventually the crack spread beyond the first track and the thing was doomed.

Doomed like a character from a 1968 pop record. But I should set the record straight, or at least straighter than those characters were. If I've been allowing the impression to persist that 1968 was all condemned felons and relentless, unfathomable misery, I need to mention 'Jesamine' by the Casuals. Mum went silly over this sweeping, silken love song and I have clear memories of her singing it at the top of her voice as she moved through the house.

A record of similar charm and prettiness - and an even bigger hit - was Amen Corner's '(If Paradise Is) Half As Nice'. This came on the candy pink Immediate label, looking as sweet as it sounded. It ends with a long fade-out where the verse and chorus are sung in harmony, and I remember sitting on the bath trying to sing both at once, switching from one to the other according to which I thought was carrying the feel better. It ought to have been deeply annoying, yet I'm tempted to think that Mum simply enjoyed my enjoyment. For the first half an hour or so anyway.

I should also point out that, for the purposes of this narrative, 1969 is an honorary part of 1968. The Amen Corner record topped the charts in '69, and 'Fox on the Run' by Manfred Mann took until January of that year to climb to the Top 10. Later there was 'Dizzy' by Tommy Roe, which I played obsessively, loving the lyrics about whirlpools and spinning, since spinning until I got dizzy had been one of my favourite pastimes long before I heard it. I understood how this translated into a falling-in-love situation too; I was no longer needing much help getting literal meaning from lyrics and 'Dizzy', bless it, was never going to present much of a challenge in that regard.

It was on the Stateside label, with the letter 'S' on its logo turned into a dollar sign, the first to come into our house since 'Where Did Our Love Go' by the Supremes. There was also 'My Sentimental Friend' by Herman's Hermits, a decent song rendered soppy by its title but elevated by a spectacular chorus. Strum through it on a guitar and you'll realise how good it is.

We now have an almost complete picture of this young life in thrall to music, but there remain two important pillars left to cover. The first is the drums. I would fall madly in love with the sound of drums and in time would play them to a reasonable standard. The record that fully sealed this for me would come a little later, but those with prominent drum parts were already making their mark. I give you the Tremeloes' 'Helule Helule' (*pron. Hel-oo-lay*); a record that races along, wind in its hair, by way of an intense, frantic bongo pattern and carefree mood.

It forms part of that British entertainment tradition in which life in the Caribbean is presented as a continuous interplay between love, rum and di coconut tree. White people on stages everywhere brightened their grins, practised their jungle cries and adjusted their accents in tribute to this lightness of being. Nice escapism; better than a rainy day in Manchester I grant you, but not what you might call representative.

Yet such things were merely "a bit of fun": that is largely how they were presented and largely how they were received. In the decades to come this phrase would form the case for the defence against various musical crimes, but "a bit of fun" is certainly how I took 'Helule Helule' in 1968. I loved it. Why? Because of that sound of drums; that fantastic, rich texture of clattering drums.

Its busy lyric is a warning to men about the windy weather of marriage, hinting that getting hitched might not be a price worth paying for yer sport, whether beneath di coconut tree or anywhere else. Additionally, the record provided the British football terrace with one of its most enduring tunes, as in *Fergie, Fergie, what's the score? Fergie, what's the score?* You know the one. 'Helule Helule' is where that comes from. The windy weather lyric has further resonance, since the record reminds me of a relentlessly stormy and wet caravan holiday in Norfolk, spending hours around a tiny table with lined washing brushing our faces. If someone had offered us the Caribbean they would have lost fingers.

Drums of a different kind featured on 'Hurdy Gurdy Man' by Donovan. These ones didn't arrive in a neat, busily-woven tapestry of tuneful percussion; they sounded like empty canisters tumbling down stone steps. Drummers habitually mark the passage of one section to another with a "fill": a flurry of beats on the snare or around the kit, lasting up to a bar, which builds anticipation of the next bit and also provides the drummer with a chance to demonstrate skill and artistry. If it adds something to the overall character of the record, so much the better. This is certainly the case with 'Hurdy Gurdy Man'. This is fill nirvana. No drummer should be allowed this much fun. The record is delicious; a fat chunk of psychedelic pop blare whose heavy atmosphere I was very happy to wander around in.

Donovan delivered hits of character and quality. We had four of them gathered on an EP called *Mini Monster*, with a grainy image of a tyrannosaurus rex on the label to further engage four-year-olds. In addition to the above number, there was the gently catchy 'Mellow Yellow', the delightfully sweet and partially-in-French 'Jennifer Juniper' and a silly song called 'There Is a Mountain'. I call it silly because its lyric pushed at the doors of perception in a way typical of prevalent trends but not in a way that I could respect it for. I'll expand later.

Psychedelia was raging all around but Donovan was as far as my parents wanted to go. We had no Jimi Hendrix, no Cream, we didn't even have a copy of *Sgt. Pepper's Lonely Hearts Club Band*, but we did have Donovan. Hearing him sing about an electrical banana in 'Mellow Yellow' was my first experience of surrealism in a lyric and to me it was just a fun piece of wordplay. I knew about bananas and I knew they were not electrical. There was similar silliness at the end of 'Hurdy Gurdy Man'. In the final chorus, the eponymous hero is suddenly joined by the roly-poly man, who is sung about in the same reverential way, so that we now had this mythical hippy figure cavorting in the mist with a jam pudding. Brilliant.

Now the previous winter, I may have heard the Beatles' single 'Hello Goodbye' and dismissed it as pointless drivel. I can imagine this with a degree of confidence because that's how I feel about it now. However, had we acquired a copy, I would have become familiar with its B-side, 'I Am the Walrus'. I wonder what I would have made of that: someone claiming to be a walrus in a land of egg men, where people sit on giant cornflakes and substances drip from the eyes of dead dogs. That and all the disorientating background noise too – the return of the Spooky Express.

But we didn't have that. We had Donovan and his mains-operated fruit, a reasonable compromise by a nice family in the Christian tradition. To add to which, their four-year-old felt able to pick fault with it, which brings us back to 'There Is a Mountain'. Despite the title, Donovan is plainly unsure about whether indeed there is a mountain or not. The chorus goes round in circles on the matter: there is a mountain, then there isn't a mountain, then there is one. I didn't get it. I would have understood had it been a garden bird dipping in and out of a hedge, but how does such confusion arise with a mountain, for goodness' sake?

The second of these two important pillars was that I started school. This would increasingly bring me into contact with the opinions and tastes of other children and adults but, equally importantly, it meant pocket money. Mum decided that I should get 3/- 6d (three and a half shillings) so that I could spend sixpence a day on sweets. I didn't spend any of it on sweets. I saved it up and bought records. My purchasing decisions were now open to influence by my new peer group, but I was also witnessing more situations in which tunes could demonstrate their popularity.

The Move were a band from Birmingham who had recently been top of the charts with the majestic 'Blackberry Way', a record whose chorus refrain "I can see you, I don't need you" compelled you to sing along. When the hearing test came to our school, I was sitting in the office listening to bleeps on headphones and moving buttons from one box to another when the door burst open and an older boy bounded in. The nurse sternly asked him for a name and, when given it, quickly checked the list on the table. "No," she said, "I don't need you." This clearly reminded him of 'Blackberry Way' because, as he swung the door closed behind him, he was singing its chorus rather loudly which made me laugh, to the clear annoyance of the nurse. I was playing it half to death at home and the idea that I was sharing it with this much bigger, brash and confident boy was an electrifying one.

Football had not yet caught my imagination, and so whenever I encountered older children it was records that I wanted to ask about. Being older children, they often ignored me completely, but more usually, sneered at my preferences because in addition to 'Blackberry Way' there were also things like 'My Sentimental Friend'.

Perhaps, though, I was most disappointed when they spoke enthusiastically about records I had never heard of. I would feel myself shrink when this happened: I knew so much and yet, clearly, I knew so little. In many cases these kids would have been influenced by the tastes of older siblings, and there was a widening gulf in the music business between artists recording hit singles for teenyboppers and more mature, credible ones constructing hit albums. The latter were unlikely to be featured on *Junior Choice* and I was not yet watching *Top of the Pops* regularly.

In early 1970, I was seriously unnerved by the sight of Jethro Tull – an albums band who did bother having hit singles – performing 'Witch's Promise' on said show. Their front man spent the song pulling the kind of face you worry about appearing at your bedroom window. When I listened to records at home, the images that ran through my mind were rich, colourful and right on the edge of my experience, but I wasn't quite ready for stuff like that.

So my points of reference remained relatively limited. Yet I had made a start and, after all, when 'Witch's Promise' was out I was still getting used to being six. I had spent my first years spreading roots: I had established a reverence for strong lyrics and meaning, I had developed a taste for powerful and detailed arrangements setting an atmosphere and I had enjoyed the rewards of being comfortable with a wide range of genres. I had even, as we have seen, begun building a stock of images that would eventually inform my interest in girls.

But 1970 was a funny time. Life had been awash with current music for the previous two-and-a-bit years but I remember very little from 1970. There were two probable reasons for this. Firstly, at the end of 1969, we moved house, somewhere bigger for a family of six, so there would have been new routines, new distractions, new places for things to be tucked away - records and record players for instance. I assume that I just got out of the habit, or that to go to the other room to play records would have taken me away from everybody else and, for now at least, that was not the point.

The other reason was that my parents' marriage was failing. By the spring of 1971, Dad would have moved out. Mum took great care to ensure that our lives continued smoothly, and they did, but whether there was an atmosphere in the house that made certain types of recreation seem inappropriate I'm not sure. Still, in any kind of memoir, this is the type of thing you have to mention.

Two

On the morning of Christmas Day 1970, I went into my back garden and played in the snow. I have a clear memory of this: the deep, crisp fall covering our new, much longer garden, the view down the side path to the back window and, within, the flickering light coming from the TV. It was the last time I would play in the snow on Christmas Day for forty years, when I would be sliding down toboggan runs on baby-changing mats with my own children. So it was unusual.

What was also unusual, given previous habits, was that it marked the end of a twelve-month break from record buying in our house. We didn't have a single 45 from that whole year. Some of the possible reasons for this I have already speculated on, but coincidently, we were beginning to do things on weekend mornings: swimming, church, a drama club and, curiously, a children's music group, about which I remember little apart from posh surroundings and posh kids.

The sum total of all this was missing *Junior Choice*. The programme was now under the auspices of Ed "Stewpot" Stewart, whose chipper, grubby-kneed enthusiasm would remain synonymous with weekend breakfasts for an era. Yet it seems he hadn't had the chance to enthuse me with anything from his playlist for a while.

Perhaps, though, the very fact of the festive season was making a difference. Christmas shopping would have meant visiting more stores than usual, many with piped music, or just as likely, it would have meant sitting in a locked car listening to the radio, enabling

Mum to "pop in here for a minute". Something must have happened, because new records began trickling back. Over the next few years, this trickle would become a bubbling stream before, finally, swelling to a shimmering, stomping, blaring torrent that provided a backdrop to everything and made the world wonderful.

Junior school and cub scouts would mean gangs of friends with whom to huddle and share. We would share football and we would share television, but pop had something for everybody and a part to play in any occasion. It was for exalting and it was for vilifying. It was for singing along to, regardless of your grasp of the lyric, and for moving to, regardless of your familiarity with grace. When it was enchanting and exciting, it was on your side; when it was baffling and alarming, it helped you take your next steps. It was for imitating in solemn reverence and it often begged to have the piss taken out of it. It bent your mind and made your insides go funny. It made you want to march up and down, yelling at the top of your voice; it made you go quiet and imagine. I would know about all of this before I left primary school.

Dancing and miming aside, performing other tasks while listening to a record was not really doing it properly. You gave it your full attention. You listened with the lid up too, so you could watch it spin on the turntable.

The experience was becoming more interesting because this was an era when the design of mainstream UK record labels was changing. The big labels in the 60s had come in a range of colours: the magenta, then the sky blue, of Pye; the navy blue of Decca and Fontana; the blood orange of CBS. But many, including Parlophone (the Beatles, the Hollies), Columbia (the Seekers) and RCA-Victor (the Monkees) were monochrome. The credits on these labels were centred and their logos positioned neatly at the top, making symmetry standard, although the EMI-owned ones, which included Parlophone and Columbia, were a tad jazzier for positioning a giant '45' on the right-hand side.

By 1974, all of these had revolutionised their look or disappeared, making way for new players. RCA had been the first to re-design, changing to an expanse of orange with a bubble-writing logo down the side in white, and the Victor bit shrunk to a secondary presence. The soon-to-be-dominant Bell label, sometimes silver on black but usually the inverse, had arcs forming a rainbow shape right across the top. The pot of gold at the end? A bell with a record resting against it. There were the rich greens of Harvest, with funny blobby shapes denoting the planting of a seed. Its parent company, EMI, would launch its own home label, a futuristic hug of red and caramel. The RAK design was perhaps the most striking of all. It was entirely given over to the image of a yacht on the open sea. This was the label owned by Mickie Most and it may have been the picture of a vessel he bought with the proceeds of his production successes in the 60s. The idea has just occurred to me as I type.

These labels were ubiquitous in my junior school years because it was their releases that we spent our pocket money on or had bought for us at birthdays; they were part of the view and we carried them around in our heads as reference points. In time, singles would begin to have their credits stamped into a plastic ring rather than printed on paper and so, from an aesthetic perspective, this was a special time. Watching a plastic ring going round would never really compare.

In my world, RCA's orange was the most visible. This was mainly due to the label being home to a band called the Sweet (we will get to them soon) and also because its roster included Perry Como, Al Martino, Jim Reeves and the girthy, balladeering version of Elvis Presley - artists who had been followed by senior members of the family since the 50s. RCA singles popped up everywhere when I visited grandparents, aunts, uncles and also my dad, once he had his new flat.

The music lover that never bought 45s was a rare creature. Cassette tapes were not yet widespread and I have never had any kind of brush with the world of 8-track cartridges, plastic bricks that plugged in somewhere and played somehow, although they had their devotees.

There was, however, reel-to-reel tape, played on a contraption the size of a small stove. Music was often shared in my family through records being recorded live onto these machines. You put the record on, pointed a microphone at it, clicked down the play-and-record keys, then sat quietly until it had finished and you could press the stop key. If you sneezed, or if someone slammed a door in the next room, the recording would pick it up. Even in those far-behind-us days of putting in a bit of effort to get your entertainment, this was a tormenting faff. So format options were limited and vinyl it tended to be.

It was still proportionately expensive - an album was a serious outlay - but singles were something you could afford to buy spontaneously and people of every age did so. When I looked on Dad's sideboard I would find RCA's orange on an Elvis Presley hand-wringer, indicative, I imagined, of his personal situation. When I lifted the lid of Nan and Grandad's piano stool now, I was stared up at by RCA's orange on a Perry Como single; a big hit for the reason that so many other nans and grandads were buying it, too.

On television, the main outlet for pop was the BBC's *Top of the Pops* and it would remain so for a long time. For now, it was coming on just as I was going to bed. I watched it occasionally and I don't think I was particularly impressed. But there were other places for a kid to access music. *Blue Peter*, which has out-lasted *Top of the Pops*, has always been a kind of on-screen scout meeting. Its magazine format sometimes allowed room for chart acts to do their stuff among the display stands, sofas and dog mats, while the programme's mature presenters smiled and nodded to the beat with professional aplomb.

Then there were the Monkees. They had their own show, which was how they had been launched in the first place, as an American version of the Beatles. It was a sitcom about a band who every now and then took a break from their zany, irreverent doings to perform songs, some of which were rather good. The zany, irreverent humour of the Beatles was natural and off-the-cuff, whereas the Monkees' was scripted. Nonetheless the show worked and gave them a ratings hit as well as a string of chart successes in 1967-8 including, of course, 'I'm a Believer'. It was being repeated well into the 70s.

Taking a similar idea in a different direction was *The Banana Splits* show. This starred a giant dog with a lisp, a laid-back lion, a monkey with a huge fixed grin and a hairy elephant with a bicycle horn for a voice. They were a club and had a den like a psychedelic dolls' house. The chaotic, slapstick-ridden format was subject to musical interludes, where footage of the gang riding theme park attractions or cavorting through crowds to the delight of children was accompanied by original songs performed by them because they were also a band.

These songs came in various styles but all had a sunny, smiley, hand-clappy feel made from similar ingredients to those of the Monkees. The show's unforgettable main theme, 'The Tra La La Song', is an example of it in concentrate with knobs on. Chase sequences in the *Scooby Doo, Where Are You!* series featured songs made of the same stuff. Other examples included a *Dr Doolittle* animation in which the doctor would flip open the top of his treatment case to reveal a band of crickets ready to launch into a song to the finger-popping delight of all present. No, I didn't make that up. This clean-cut, saccharine sound was rife and it was epitomised by two records in particular: 'I'm a Believer', and 'Sugar, Sugar' by the Archies.

Coming from the same management team as the Monkees, 'Sugar, Sugar' was a shameless piece of corporate pop manufacture, recorded by session performers but presented to the world by a band of cartoon kids. Deeply cynical, yes, but that only matters if the record is rubbish. This isn't. The song is an uncomplicated tribute to when love is going right, when it is all sugar, honey and candy. The lyric pumps out confectionery references like a marshmallow machine-gun and if this takes things beyond saturation level it matters little, because, when love is going that well, perspective is an irrelevance - life is a brilliant and beautiful high.

That's exactly what 'Sugar, Sugar' is. Its sound is immaculate. Its beat is infectious. It's got an excellent riff. Listening to it is like being hugged by someone who smells nice; it quickens the pulse and relieves the mind of its duties. It swept all before it in the autumn of 1969 and those who doggedly make perspective their business have been moaning about it ever since. It was the last word in a genre labelled "bubblegum" (more bloody sweets) and it would resonate well into the 70s, not least in the TV shows we were watching.

The other giant style of the time was country, which in the UK meant the American strand but also British folk. Among the records echoing in the background as I played in the snow that Christmas was 'When I'm Dead and Gone' by the duo McGuinness Flint, one of whom had been in Manfred Mann. This acoustic crowd-pleaser owed its character to a strummed mandolin that added depth to the sound and a feeling of celebration to the subject of a man insisting that his woman lives on happily after his demise. You rocked from side to side as you sang along.

You did the same to a tune not far behind it in the Christmas Day chart, 'Ride a White Swan' by T. Rex. It too had a strong melody, stimulating and comforting at the same time, but its twanging, three note riff and the trembling strangeness of the singer's voice gave it an additional edge. Its lyric was a lot of pseudo-hippy nonsense about tall hats and gowns and travelling around on wildlife, and yet it worked a powerful charm; Mum would remember it as one of her favourite songs of the era. Both of these charismatic records had a contemporary folky feel and were hugely popular, but we didn't own a copy of either. We were, however, soon to buy a very different record climbing the chart that holiday: Clive Dunn's 'Grandad'.

Clive Dunn was an actor who had risen to fame in the cast of *Dad's Army*, a monster hit of a sitcom about the home guard troupe in a coastal town during World War II. In it, he played a manic corporal much older than himself and did so convincingly, with the result that when he performed 'Grandad' he could simply be a cuddlier, more sedate version of the same character.

There he sat, in a rocking chair, going on about photographs, lollipops, motor cars and other things that were extraordinary in his childhood, as if muttering and chuckling to himself in the corner, pausing only to listen to a children's choir and their mawkish refrain about how lovely Grandad is. It had a gentle accompaniment of brass and ukulele and was released at that point in the calendar when there is a three-line whip on goodwill, sentimentality and being with the family. It was the sound of the record-buying public having its arm twisted.

Demand for it duly grew throughout the holiday. It was requested by legions of *Junior Choice* listeners and by mid-January it was the nation's best selling single. I'm not sure how often I played our copy. My grandads were both worldly cockneys who would have smiled politely at a dedication before turning back to the paper to pick another horse.

I certainly didn't play it as much as I played 'The Pushbike Song' by the Mixtures, which appeared soon afterwards. I loved this one, with its cheery banjo lead and loudly whispered backing vocal of *ch, ch-ch – oh, ch – ah*! The verses tell the story of an urban cycle ride with a pretty girl and the chorus describes what happens to wheels and pedals as a bike moves. What's not to like? Cleanly produced, full of percussive hooks and as catchy as a candy cactus. A worthy distraction for all the family.

These records, with their soothing sounds and homely, innocent themes, were a real contrast with what I had been imbibing two or three years earlier; partly due to current trends and partly due to our domestic situation. Mum had begun buying records for all of us kids to join in with. My sisters took to 'Sweet Caroline' by Neil Diamond, belting out the chorus with serious frowns. Neil Diamond was the man who had written 'I'm a Believer' and was now a big-time performer in his own right, his voice a uniquely rich blend of smooth and rugged.

We also had 'Rose Garden' by Lynn Anderson, an exceptional country record with a muscular lyric about maturity in relationships. Its orchestration is great and its melody relentless, delivering a rush to each section – there really isn't a dull moment. It taught me the word "melancholy" and the chorus began with the phrase "I beg your pardon" which provided a pleasing link to burping and farting. Or 'blowing off', as we said in those days. These records were fine things but they didn't throw my switches like 'The Pushbike Song', or indeed as the next one I would spend pocket money on: 'Bridget the Midget (the Queen of the Blues)' by Ray Stevens.

'Bridget the Midget' is a novelty classic. You kind of have to hear it to believe it. Essentially, it's a recording of a long-awaited concert by the eponymous star, wherein Stevens is part narrator, part compere. A big band fires up before settling into a boogie-woogie rhythm as he begins his announcements. Bridget finally takes the stage and launches into a routine of call-and-response, woo-yeah-yeahs and rousing choruses, indulged, roared on and applauded by the supposedly vast audience. She sounds like an American cousin of the Diddymen.

Stevens reappears to introduce her backing group – Strawberry and the Shortcakes, fact hounds – but also to yell at an obsessed fan who has invaded the stage, deliriously proclaiming that he digs it, really digs it. For years I thought he was saying "I *did* it", wondering what it was he had done - had he touched Bridget? She didn't sound distressed. He fails to interrupt the show, although he does return to have another grapple with Stevens' increasingly frantic character as the record fades. It's a bit of silly fun; but elaborate silly fun, carried off with style and polish. It was the kind of intense experience I hadn't had for a while. I wanted to climb in through the speaker and be there.

In fashion terms, the early part of the decade represented the maturing and settling down of what the late sixties were famous for. It takes a little while for the attire of trend-setters to filter down to the high street. Long hair, miniskirts and tie-dyes may have been centre stage in San Francisco, Monterrey and Woodstock before 1970, but not in the middle bit of South London that I grew up in.

When you watch footage of *Top of the Pops* from 1971, you see girls dancing in mini-or maxi-length skirts or dresses, with straight hair and big-eye make up. They have long, silky sleeves that billow at the cuff, they wear purely decorative belts made from links of suede and they may or may not be wearing tights. My teacher in the first year of junior school looked exactly like this, so did the teacher in the next room. The male teacher I was to have the following year wore tie-dye shirts to work and had a beard level with his chest.

Hippy styles were now mainstream, and to the untrained eye, fashion shots of 1971 look indistinguishable from those of the following four years. The trained eye might even struggle. On a camping holiday that summer we befriended a young chap in the tent next to us, who had a thin beard and a languid manner as well as a well-thumbed copy of *The Hobbit*. Mum admired him because his mates had pulled out of the holiday at the last minute but he had decided to go anyway and see what transpired. The freedom of the open road, the purity of doing your own thing.

Peace 'n' Love may have been in tatters as an administrative option, but its romantic ideas had put down deep roots, engendering tribal loyalties that would endure. They connected Mum and the young chap. They connected all sorts of people with a yearning for that thing called freedom (one of the most abused words in our language). They didn't connect me, though. I was too busy listening to 'Bridget the Midget'.

Actually I was listening to lots of stuff on that summer holiday and not just on the car radio, because this was the summer that I discovered jukeboxes and how to feed them with these 10-new-pence pieces that were then just a few months old. In truth, I absorbed most of it through other people's choices; there was only one record I spent my own money on. I had fallen head over heels in love with it at the start of the holiday. I was insufferable until taken to buy it. Once it was home, I sat transfixed before the record player for repeat play after repeat play. It dwarfed everything else in my life. It was called 'Co-Co' and it was by the Sweet.

Set firmly beside di coconut tree, it tells of a bewitching boy dancing along the shore beneath the stars at midnight, his laughter echoed by the sound of the island's drums. Jungle drums and an island boy with a name that references chocolate: if your dodgy-ometer is bleeping it's because it's working properly. But remember this was 1971. The verse starts in a low murmur, gradually building, until bursting into a chorus of bright fireworks, the lyrics to which seem to be from the south Pacific rather than the Caribbean - *Ho chi kaka ho, Co-Co*. Check it out. Still, my seven-year-old ears had no problem with any of it and I sang along without a care.

The main hook, however, was the percussion. The record opens with a herald of high tom-toms, then there's a nifty little pattern played on what to me sounded like saucepans and empty milk bottles, until steel pans join in to signal the beginning of the first verse. The whole lot reappears in the chorus to form an interwoven mesh of accentuated rhythms that put me in something close to a shamanistic trance. It was like 'Helule Helule', but groovier, more expressive. There was no longer any doubt that I would one day be a drummer. By the end of 1972 the Sweet would become my first favourite band, a group whose next release I would be longing for and whose chart fortunes I would follow with chewed fingernails. But, like every other record I had known so far, I saw 'Co-Co' as a thing in its own right.

Our holiday was warm and sunny and we spent much of our time wandering up and down the campsite, often by ourselves while Mum got things ready or had a doze on the grass. We learned how to deal with wasps, as well as with other children who found friendliness too much bother. Moving between the tents, we would pick up the sound of transistor radios, which rarely played anything other than Radio 1. We had ours on at breakfast time. When I hear some 1971 records now, I think only of tents and grass and trapping wasps in jam jars.

There were two fields. We were in the one nearest the road. If you walked to the other one you went past an old railway coach convert-ed into a healthily smelly chicken coop, and a pen housing a donkey called Pedro that was led round twice a day for rides if you had 15p to spare. He didn't mind being stroked and patted and there was usually a line of children there. The other field was bordered by high, dense trees which cast long shadows across the grass. In a near corner was a cabin with tables and benches that sold ice cream, drinks and snacks. This was where the jukebox was.

Mum sometimes took us in here for a late afternoon treat, and with her there I was less self-conscious about having a good look. The im-age of a classic Wurlitzer jukebox is a familiar one, with its illumi-nated arched shapes in bright colours, but it was other models that the likes of us came into contact with. In transport cafés we found ones that had a coin slot and selection buttons on each table, with listings displayed in rigid plastic booklets which were fixed to the wall and sticky to the touch. The campsite one was more like those we saw in pub family rooms; a black trapezium, its speaker concealed by a silver, red and black mesh, with its tickets in a single block at the back, hand-written. After long, challenging moments dealing with a stranger's handwriting, I found one that said 'Co-Co'. Wicked. Or, as we said in those days, 'neat'.

To my disappointment, the girl who served us our fizzy drinks did not sit bolt upright with a wide-eyed look of joy as it came on. I imagine that my sisters wanted a choice of their own, but I can't remember. What I do remember is months and years watching the way that different types of jukeboxes worked, from the ones that lowered the centre-less disc to a horizontal position, to ones that spun the disc vertically, bringing the stylus up to play it. When I came across one that wouldn't let you see its inner workings at all, I felt ripped off.

I have never seriously wanted to own one, but they are fascinating things. To have the choice of a mere hundred tunes, you had to have a contraption the size of a washing machine strapped to a tumble drier. There are still jukeboxes in the MP3 era, albeit digital equivalents. Their innards are suitably compact, but some of them are free-standing, full-size replicas of the Wurlitzer.

I will mention two other records that I know for sure got selected in that cabin. The first was playing as the girl serving was chatting with a group her own age. 'I'm Gonna Run Away from You' by Tami Lynn was an infectious stomper of a soul tune which had been overlooked when it first came out in the mid-sixties. It was not alone in having that experience. Britain was gradually finding its funky feet. There were increasing amounts of assertive, socially aware black music becoming available to a population for whom the Civil Rights movement was a very recent memory; but a key part of that process was the general pop audience learning to fully appreciate the output of the Motown Corporation.

Motown had been set up in 1959 by black Detroit entrepreneur Berry Gordy Jr. His ambition was to make rhythm 'n' blues pop that would appeal to kids of all backgrounds. This was a contentious ambition, but using jazz musicians, talented local songwriters and young vocalists raised on doo-wop and gospel, he managed it in spectacular fashion. These recordings had been issued in the UK via agreements with various labels including Stateside, but in 1965 EMI launched the Tamla-Motown label to do it properly, its first release being by the Supremes, Gordy's star act.

Motown records were consistently at the top of the US charts but, with a few exceptions, they were nowhere near as successful here. By 1969 the British public was apologising for this by packing the Top 20 with as many Motown releases past and present as it could lay its hands on, from such names as the Four Tops, Smokey Robinson & the Miracles, Stevie Wonder, Martha & the Vandellas, Marvin Gaye and, soon, the sparkling, brand-new Jackson 5.

At the same time, the flourishing northern soul scene was celebrating rare sixties records made by little-remembered artists on regional US labels, tunes of a similarly tuneful, danceable style. Some of them were so popular that they were re-issued and sold by the sackful, hence 'I'm Gonna Run Away from You' being cool for a group of youngsters on our camp site. The record was an instant party. Northern soul fans eschewed Motown chart hits, but as far as the general public was concerned, it was all part of the same landscape.

You may have noticed that, so far, I have avoided using the term "number one" to denote a record outselling all others in a given week. That's because it had made no impact on me. I wouldn't get the significance of it until I became a regular listener of the Sunday teatime chart countdown on Radio 1 in the spring of 1973. Before then, I had simply been aware of some records as being bigger and more important than others, whether or not I liked them. Sometimes this was because of their sound, which is not as illogical as it may initially seem: all-conquering pop records do have a great sound. At other times, however, it was because I had noticed how people everywhere were affected by them; dancing and singing to them at parties, making reference to them in conversation, humming them absent-mindedly, or having a copy and playing it, playing it, playing it.

That camping holiday is particularly potent in my memory and there are records in addition to those I have mentioned that give it its flavour. But in truth, the summer of 1971 was carved up between three almighty number ones. The second, 'Get It On' by T. Rex, I have no memory of whatsoever. But the first and third I definitely do, and the first was the other record I remember going on in that cabin.

Imagine that you are a parent. Imagine that you are packing your bags and the baby's things in preparation for leaving your eldest child without warning, while singing a song in imitation of a small bird, which you repeat several times in an atmosphere of glee. Your eldest child overhears this as they drift off to sleep, comforted. But when they wake up the next morning they discover that they have been deserted; and all they are left with is that song going round and round in their head. Child abandonment and emotional abuse – nice.

This is the storyline on the record. You might think someone in power would step in. But they didn't. Nobody stepped in, because it sounded like just a bit of jolly, light-hearted fun, some old forgotten nursery rhyme revived by a cheery pop group. It created a mood: smile, dance and sing along to the nonsense chorus. This is the tune that might have been played by the Pied Piper of Hamelin: *Come with me, kids of all ages, come with me.* The record sold 10 million copies worldwide and was the UK's number one for five weeks. It was 'Chirpy Chirpy Cheep Cheep' by Middle of the Road and you underestimate it at your peril.

The lead singer's voice really is unlike any other - shrill, nasal, vibrato, commanding – as it delivers the song's dark meaning in simple refrains which, in the verse, is echoed by the male backing. And when I say echoed, I mean echoed. There is a megaton of reverb on it, in complete contrast to the lead, which gives the sound a cavernous depth. The only other things filling this depth are the prominent bass that plods through the verse and then bounces all over the place in the chorus, crisp drums and hi-hat, together with the merest twinkle of rhythm guitar.

It's an extraordinary record; loud, giddy and unhinged. But all people heard was the skip and the hand-clap. This was a record you could have a carefree sing and dance to, with your grandchildren in a sunlit garden, in a rosy-cheeked circle at the Village Hall, or in a taverna on a Spanish holiday.

Alternatively, it was that lowbrow pile of crap that annoyed the hell out of anyone with standards. On those rare occasions when it gets played on the radio nowadays, this is the reaction of DJs: they are apologetic, gently distancing themselves from the decision to playlist it. They will allow themselves a self-conscious chuckle and a sharp intake of breath, before moving on to something nice by Bruce Springsteen.

They will pay for their insolence. It's a badass. A few customers at the campsite cabin clearly appreciated it. So did the family living in the flat above my dad's. They had a perpetual air of heightened enthusiasm and wanted to talk endlessly when we were introduced, faces big and bursting with smile. 'Chirpy Chirpy Cheep Cheep' was one of their favourite subjects; when it was mentioned, their smiles grew even bigger and one or other of them would hurry away and put it on to deliver their fix. The Pied Piper had them right where he wanted them.

The third of those big number ones came at the end of the summer when we were back in London, but before we leave the holiday, there is one more link with my earlier childhood. Keith Potger had been a member of the Seekers and, following their split, he formed a group intended for a similar audience called, imaginatively, the New Seekers. He soon decided it would be best to concentrate on management, leaving band membership to them young 'uns and, once the line-up had settled down, they began a run of successes big enough to rival that of the "old" Seekers. Their first major hit was 'Never Ending Song of Love' and if you wanted to hear it at any point that August, all you had to do was turn on the radio.

It was a thigh-slapping, camp fire singalong about somebody loving somebody else and knowing that they would from the moment they met. It had a yodelling bit in it, which wasn't yodelling at all but falsetto harmony with lots of reverb; yet if you mentioned "the yodelling bit" in 'Never Ending Song of Love' everybody knew what you were talking about. It was everywhere. Except number one. It spent five weeks at number two, first under 'Get It On' by T.Rex, then behind one of the most stunning records of the period.

Diana Ross was the lead singer of the Supremes but left in 1970 to go it alone and be groomed for movie stardom. Her early solo singles were lavish productions, with big orchestration, dramatic arrangements and choral backing vocals. Her first Top 10 hit, 'Ain't No Mountain High Enough', was ostentatious twaddle, but the next, 'Remember Me', was much better. The third was called 'I'm Still Waiting'.

At seven I knew nothing about the singer, I just sensed that this record I was suddenly hearing a lot was a serious, important one; a class apart. Most love songs give us unreality, because they depict the thoughts and feelings of intense moments when we are not our normal, level-headed selves. The unreality in 'I'm Still Waiting' is different. It provokes our romantic imagination like some Gothic horror of the heart. Its arrangement, its succession of melodies, its whole atmosphere - I get goose bumps just thinking about it.

It tells the story of a shy five-year-old girl, besotted with an older boy who, fully aware of her feelings for him, teases her to tears. Some time later, his family announce that they are moving away and her world collapses. As he leaves, he tells her to forget about him and to look out for love which will one day come from somewhere. But she grows to a young adult and it hasn't happened. His parting words echo celestially in the chorus, full of reassurance and promise; love will come from somewhere. But then it plummets to her reality: *but I'm still waiting.* He is the only one.

Why doesn't she go and look for him? Because this isn't the movies. He's probably living perfectly happily, having forgotten all about her. We know she fears this, because there is a second part to the chorus in which she states *I'm just a fool, I'm just a fool to keep waiting.* And this is the idea we're left with. At the end she admits her longing and cries out for him to come back, but the backing vocal is unaffected, relentlessly repeating *I'm just a fool, I'm just a fool to keep waiting,* as the record fades.

This is spine-tingling stuff. From one angle, the girl is a romantic heroine, uncompromisingly holding out for true love. But from all others, she is just a fool; left to stew in it, heartbroken and powerless.

We are walking through the back streets of Brixton on a warm day. Mum is guiding the double pushchair with two of my sisters in, the third walking alongside. I am a few paces behind, listening to music coming from open bay windows in these big houses. It's 'I'm Still

Waiting' that I can hear. I can hear it from several windows and, in some cases, it's on very loud indeed. I was struck by the evidence, both here and elsewhere, of this record wielding so much power over so many. It spent four weeks on top of the charts.

Perhaps the most remarkable thing about it is that it was never intended to be a single at all. Ross' 1970 album *Everything Is Everything* had a few glossy cover versions and a couple of cute originals but was largely inconsequential. Except for side one track five. That's where 'I'm Still Waiting' was located.

Now, the thing about this position was that it was the penultimate track on the side one, and the penultimate track on side one is not where singles were positioned in those days. There did seem to be unspoken rules about the positioning of singles on albums and the penultimate track on side one would have been a flagrant contravention. By all means have a single as the opening track of either side, or the last. Side one track three was an acceptable spot, so was track two as long as there was also a single on track one. Come on, keep up. But not the penultimate track on side one. If you put a single there, you would probably get hauled before some album ordering committee and asked to explain yourself.

So there sat 'I'm Still Waiting', a buried album filler, until Radio 1 breakfast-time DJ and Motown nut Tony Blackburn began campaigning for it to be released as a single because it was too good not to be. His substantial clout was brought to bear. Out it came and Britain went silly. Good work, Tone.

For me back then, 'Co-Co' was the main event of the summer. It would remain my top play until eclipsed by some other favourite single. But a year on, I would be playing LPs more; mainly due to one specific commercial innovation.

Compilation albums had been around for years; the *Best Of* and the *Greatest Hits* were an established part of the landscape. There had also been LPs featuring multiple artists, released by labels as showcases for their roster and the musical niche they occupied.

But 1972 brought something fresh. Albums began to appear featuring hits from different acts as well as across different genres - pop, country, rock and soul mixed in together. Companies such as K-Tel and Ronco, who had hitherto made their money selling kitchen gadgets and devices for removing various types of unwanted hair, acquired the right to release original recordings by artists on a sweep of labels including RCA, Polydor and Bell. They crammed twenty of them onto two sides, gave their collections flash titles and advertised them on TV.

These adverts were thrilling. Loud, breathless announcements and electrifying blasts of music, edited to ensure that it was the most charismatic bits of each song that you heard, one after the other, bang, bang, bang. You were left with a dry mouth, a thumping heart and a burning need to spend £1.99. Compilations of hit songs had been available previously but not by the original artists. The *Top of the Pops* series – nothing to do with the show – featured tame re-recordings by session musicians and were popular because they sold for under a quid. The ad campaigns of K-Tel, Ronco and Dutch label Arcade shrank the appeal of these albums to mere price.

First off the blocks was K-Tel's *20 Dynamic Hits*, then came Arcade's *20 Fantastic Hits*, which my aunt and uncle had. Both of these flew to the top of the album chart. The formula was proving lucrative. It was *20 Fantastic Hits volume 2* that I pestered for, mainly because it had a song on it by the Sweet.

They had caught my attention again that spring with 'Poppa Joe', a single which was effectively 'Co-Co' in a new suit. It had steel pans, percussion that sounded like saucepans and empty milk bottles, and a lyric about a man selling coconut rum in the marketplace to customers who, according to the first verse, beat on the drums whenever he appears. He should put his prices up. The chorus goes "Poppa rumbo rumbo hey Poppa Joe coconut", over a rhythm so pleasing that you kind of forgive it.

Its most remarkable feature however is the repeated modulation. Let me explain. A piece of music modulates when it changes key, in other words when it all shifts up a tone. It happens a lot in pop, giving the impression of everything being "raised", usually at the final chorus so that things go out on a high. It's an effective device. Usually it happens once. In 'Poppa Joe' it happens four times. *Four times.* A few other records do it even more, but not with these results. The falsetto backing vocal is, to begin with, a benign component of the whole sound, laid-back and happy; you hardly notice it. Three key changes later however, it has become a conspicuous squawk, desperately gasping for breath with bulging eyes, close to snapping under the strain behind the usually assured, manly lead. It's hilarious.

Yet to me, back then, it was merely a feature of a record that thrilled me from head to toe, just like 'Co-Co' before it. It didn't do as well, but as far as I was concerned, it was massive. The Sweet were beginning to establish themselves in my mind as a generally good bet and so, when their name cropped up on the *20 Fantastic Hits volume 2* advert, I made my enthusiasm apparent.

My pocket money had been increasing by sixpence, then by two-and-a-half new pence, each September, and now stood at 25p. I did not have £1.99 and saving up would take ages, so Mum decided to make a special exception and buy it on behalf of the whole family, because with all those other songs on it there was going to be something for everyone. But I would have to look after it and put it back in its cover properly. A very good deal, eagerly accepted.

The cover was colourful, mainly blue and yellow, but with interspersed photos of the artists in black and white. A little cloud shape bore the legend "As advertised on TV". You don't say. Among the other tracks on it were a couple we already had on 45, gifts from the previous Christmas; a likeable Middle of the Road song called 'Soley, Soley' and the record that enabled the New Seekers to put their frustration over being stuck at number two firmly behind them: 'I'd Like to Teach the World to Sing (in Perfect Harmony)'. This is a let's-put-all-those-nasty-guns-down-and-be-nice-to-each-other kind of song but the record has a good sound and one absolute killer chord change. It went to number one in January and stayed there for a month. The tune had originally been conceived to soundtrack an ad campaign for a cola drink in a red tin.

The Sweet song was called 'Little Willy'. It had come out after 'Poppa Joe' and hadn't registered with me at all. Now I had this new album I found I didn't like it. No steel bands, no coconuts, nothing. I felt cheated.

'Little Willy' is actually a straightforwardly catchy piece of pop-rock about a local tearaway, happy to play on the possibility that its title might make some people think of a small penis. To me, though, it was just silly and boring and I was still smarting from this disappointment when adverts started appearing for *Ronco's 20 Star Tracks*. This one had 'Poppa Joe' on it, representing the good old days when the Sweet made proper records.

I made a fuss about getting it even though I had the single. I was prepared to do anything. There may have been talk of additional chores to earn the money, but in the end the deal was this: I would pay for half of it by foregoing four weeks' pocket money and Mum would pay for the other half. It was made clear there would be no more deals of this type and if I wanted more albums I would have to wait for Christmas or birthdays. So we got *20 Star Tracks*, with black and white pictures of the artists in little stars among purple and orange swirls on the cover.

I explored both compilations studiously, quickly establishing my preferences, finding it really hard to return them to the inner sleeves, but generally keeping my side of the bargain. I got to know Jethro Tull's 'Life Is a Long Song' and Joan Baez's 'The Night They Drove Old Dixie Down'; both revelations, as my previous encounters with these acts had been negative. I marvelled at the sore-throat voices of Joe Cocker on 'Delta Lady', and Derek – for I assumed it was Derek – on he and his Dominoes' 'Layla'. I loved 'Run to Me' by the Bee Gees, mainly because the verse is gorgeous, but partly out of defiance, as my friend's Mum had dubbed it "soppy rubbish" that summer in response to my outburst of enthusiasm when it came on the radio.

In attending to these albums I also began developing the skills necessary for lifting and replacing the needle to move quickly between tracks, via the odd blunder that shamefully left marks and clicks on the vinyl. Mum wanted me to play the whole side and wait for the one I wanted, but that would have been torture. Illicit lifting and replacing seemed the only reasonable option. A good job I could be absorbed by all this; I couldn't buy any new singles with my pocket money tied up in repayments. Four weeks is a long time when you're not quite nine.

I may have amused myself for some of this period by exploring new stacks of vinyl in other people's houses. On these visits, adults would converse in that assertive friendliness that they use when building useful relationships, their children sitting quietly with squash and biscuits in the golden moments before restlessness begins; but one of them would be gently shuffling across the fluffy carpet towards a glass cabinet housing the records. He would be noticed and reminded about not touching, then made small by his parent's humorous assumption that the host didn't have 'Poppa Joe' by the Sweet, an assumption that the host would happily confirm.

I nevertheless recognised that hosts tended to have *Bridge over Troubled Water* by Simon and Garfunkel, with its oh-so-familiar grainy cover images in greens and blues, and often something by Cat Stevens, a name I recognised from the inclusion on *20 Star Tracks* of 'Morning Has Broken', which we often sang in assembly. My closest friends all had the *Bridge over Troubled Water* album somewhere in their lounge. It was practically obligatory.

In addition, they almost definitely had a copy of the *Oliver!* soundtrack. This musical had been in the cinema for a few years but continued to exert a powerful hold. It's a great movie, and the central stars were a pair of boys not much older than us. The success of the stage play meant that its songs were already well known but the movie took them to a new level. Singing 'Consider Yourself' became a favourite way of lampooning cockneys, especially if you were prepared to impersonate the extras and skip up and down with your thumbs under imaginary jacket lapels. 'As Long as He Needs Me' is a character's defiant declaration of love for the man who is abusing her and who would ultimately batter her to death. Lovely. Big-stage belter Shirley Bassey, my dad's favourite pin-up girl, had enjoyed a hit with this before I was born. Women I knew years later, perfectly sane individuals, would suddenly throw their heads back in that way that you would only ever do in a musical, and cry "As long as hay nayds mayyyy" just because something inside had made them.

By contrast with this extrovert, communal demographic listening to their movie soundtracks on up-to-date stereo record players, I had a friend in the next street whose mum prepared tea by cutting the corners off tea bags and pouring their contents into the tea pot and whose dad had a massive collection of 78s. I was being given a whirlwind tour of the house when we burst through the door of his room. He stood, startled, shellac disc balanced on one hand, beside a pre-war gramophone complete with giant trumpet speaker, saying nothing; not hostile, but not wanting us to stay either. The room was about seven yards square and every part of each wall was filled with packed record shelves, the coarse edges of the 78 sleeves interrupted only by occasional cardboard markers. Alphabetical? Chronological? By genre? I was only in there for a few seconds but this image of reverential record ownership is still sharp.

Reverence is an important component of music enjoyment. But the opposite is every bit as valid and often just as satisfying. The three pillars holding up the Temple of Mockery are: mishearing lyrics, corrupting them on purpose and lampooning records thorough performance.

Mishearing lyrics is an integral part of being a pop listener and one of the richest sources of humour in our culture. I was chirping all sorts of nonsense to 'Co-Co' and 'Poppa Joe'. I won't share these with you but I'm happy to tell tales on others.

The 1982 hit 'Golden Brown' by the Stranglers, reputedly about heroin, uses lyrics such as "With my mind she runs / Throughout the night" to personify its subject. The mother of my children remembers listening to the first part of this and hearing "with my Manchirons", assuming it to be a race that the crew of the Starship Enterprise might have encountered. In the same year, Adam Ant's 'Goody Two Shoes' dealt with responses to the singer's sober lifestyle. The chorus went "Don't drink, don't smoke – what *do* you do?" This was a particular favourite of one of my sisters, except that she sang "Don't drink, don't smoke – what doodle-oodle."

Both were teenagers when these records appeared, proving that our need to sing along often overrides our desire for the security of correctness, something we must conclude to be healthy.

I'm not sure how old I was when I first heard someone parody a song by purposefully altering the lyric. This is something that we are all born with the instinct to attempt. People seem to do it automatically, changing a lovingly-crafted phrase to something rude, or at least silly. In many cases, with some sentimental or pretentious tosh, it is well-deserved, but justice rarely comes into it.

There was a Diana Ross song called 'Reach Out and Touch (Somebody's Hand)'. One night at cub scouts I heard an older boy loudly singing "Reach out and touch somebody's crutch". Now I realised there was a flaw in this; that the joke lay in the reference to grabbing somebody's crotch, rather than their hobbling stick, but that crotch didn't rhyme. Yet the meaning was clear, and once I'd got over the shock of his intimidating rudeness, I realised it was quite funny.

Performing a mocking rendition was another, well-established means of lampooning a record and it was rife among my peers. The year after those compilation LPs arrived in our house, there was a single called 'Heart of Stone' by Kenny, a mid-tempo stomp designed for the school disco and with that nursery rhyme feel often used by songwriters to subconsciously hook the listener. It also had a deadened, pounding drum sound which characterised in particular those records released on the Bell and RAK labels. But it was the screeching lead vocal that made it such an extraordinary din and a legitimate target for parody.

A boy in my class was quite disturbed by its effect and this drove him to made up a dance routine, which I doubt was inspired by any *Top of the Pops* performance. It involved shuffling from side to side, shoulders hunched and elbows out, calling "Come on everybody, let's do the Hust-Hustoe!" This warrants an explanation. Hust-Hustoe was how he had heard the song's title before discovering it was actually 'Heart of Stone' but, having thought about it, he had decided that Hust-Hustoe sounded better and would make a great name for a new dance craze, one to demonstrate how silly new dance crazes generally were. For the next two weeks, whenever he was summoned across the playground by friends or asked to put the rulers away by a teacher, he would refuse, leaping back into character and replying "No! I must do the Hust-Hustoe!" And off he would go again, shoulders up, elbows out, fully encouraged by the giggling of onlookers.

Mishearing lyrics is an everyday issue when you are about nine. Singing the wrong words to a new favourite can be a humbling experience when someone laughingly corrects you in front of a playground crowd: "It's not *constably* changing, it's *constantly* changing" ('How Can I Be Sure', David Cassidy). However, if the new favourite in question is an instrumental, none of this applies. In the weeks leading up to my ninth birthday such a thing appeared. It came from nowhere, sounded like nothing else and almost everybody I knew had a reason to like it. It was by Lieutenant Pigeon and it was called 'Mouldy Old Dough'.

On *Top of the Pops*, you saw a grinning, bearded drummer, a lad-about-town bass player in flared trousers and platform shoes, and the remaining two band members on upright pianos. One was a young man, the other might have been his grandma. She had a jolly, chubby smile and was clearly loving every moment. Britain was used to women of about that age with jolly, chubby smiles tinkling away on upright pianos; there had been a few very popular ones in the fifties and one of them, stage name Mrs. Mills, had continued to appear on TV until very recently. "Is that Mrs. Mills?" was a question probably heard at least once in every household for the time that 'Mouldy Old Dough' was in the charts. But it wasn't Mrs. Mills.

The record begins with a marching drum pattern joined by a cute, four-bar melody played on a tin whistle that ends in a trill, a kind of high-speed warble. Then the pianos come in with the first round of the main tune. At first it's just plink-a-plonk, but gradually it unfurls into something surprisingly complex and engaging, culminating in the drummer growling "mouldy old dough" a couple of times, before the whole thing retracts to the drum intro and begins again.

Now, however, the piano arrangement has more depth, more harmony and embellishment, lifting the tune until it has forced you to like it. This time when it retracts, the drums are different; weary, calm; ambling towards the fade with the tin whistle playing the main tune soothingly alongside.

It had bang-up-to-date production, yet it managed to sound appealingly amateurish; fragile even, like it could all topple over any second. Topple, however, it did not. It crowned the charts for four weeks, giving a mighty finger to teeny-bop sensations, rock legends and glam aristocracy alike.

My grandparents liked it because it reminded them of tunes from years ago. My bearded teacher liked it because he could pick out the intro on the tin whistle he kept in his drawer, performing it for us as he rocked back and forth in his chair, eyes a-twinkle. I liked it because growling "mouldy old dough" was silly fun and referred to something smelly and yucky. Kids at school had begun to growl the phrase in judgement on anything dull or unwelcome, like a wet playtime or the appearance of a page of arithmetic. I heard an older boy responding to an admonishment from a dinner lady by growling "moany old cow" under his breath.

But in the main, it was simply taken as a charming tune and refreshingly different. The most negative anybody got was when kids screwed up their faces and said "But it's just *stupid*". Verdicts like this may have been influenced by older siblings; big sisters besotted with Marc Bolan of T.Rex or freshly aware of the intriguing David Bowie, big brothers who knew about bands like Led Zeppelin and Deep Purple.

These were artists representing a world out of reach to anyone who happened to be about nine, one with specific appeal to adolescents, a break with the frivolity of most chart pap. It just so happened that everyone in my immediate friendship group was an eldest child, so that influence never came to bear. There was one boy in my class however who did have older siblings. One day that autumn, when we were allowed to bring in records from home, he brought one that had come and gone from the Top 10 during Lieutenant Pigeon's chart run without me noticing it.

There was a huddle on the corner of the table beside the record player when it fired up. Grinding, snarling guitars, then a churning rhythm linking to a riff-laden verse with a manly vocal that meant every word, followed by a chorus so oxygenating I felt faint hearing it across the room. I sidled up and asked what it was. "It's 'Wig-Wam Bam' by the Sweet," said its owner, surprised that I had to ask. I imagine I went red. I was apparently the last to know about one of the most fantastic things I had ever heard.

When I was taken to buy it, the man in the shop had to go into the back to find a copy because it had dropped out of the charts. A few days later I knew its every detail. The Sweet had swapped di coconut tree for um totem pole. Publicity shots had them in all kinds of Native American paraphernalia including feathered head-dresses, with tribal symbols painted on their arms and faces.

The song tells of how Minnehaha couldn't get Hiawatha to put his arms around her, so to speak, until she took him to the Silver Stream and worked some squaw magic on him. Little White Dove had the same problem with Running Bear, but one Silver Stream visit later and all was well. Hooray. This narrative is much clearer than the meaning of the song's title. "Wig-wam bam" could be the aforementioned squaw magic; it could equally be an assertive figure of speech equivalent to "I do declare" or "Now look here". But neither you nor I should care. It's a terrific record; a clever, melodic pop tune that rocks.

For weeks it was the centre of my universe. So too now, was the band itself. I was a proper Sweet fan - committed, passionate and loyal. The boy in my class encouraged me. He taught me their names. He tipped me off when there was something about them in a magazine. One had a list of fan club addresses. I joined the Sweet Fan Club. It was run by two women whose names I can't remember. I sent payment in a stamped, addressed envelope and received a small bundle in return, including a postcard-sized, black and white photo of the group, which I've still got. I remember being disappointed by the rest but I may have been too young for it.

There couldn't have been a better band for a growing lad to be a fan of. Big, strapping geezers with eyebrow-level fringes, they looked a surly bunch: you wouldn't want to get into a fight with them but they looked great company.

Guitarist Andy Scott was reserved and moody; he might be about to tell a joke, he might be about to smash your face in. Mick Tucker was the drummer and therefore cool from head to toe, even before he started twirling sticks around his fingers between beats. Bass player Steve Priest was a pouting pantomime dame in a cape. In a run of singles beginning with 'Wig-Wam Bam' he was given lines of lyric to speak rather than sing, delivering them in degrees of camp ranging from broodiness to wide-eyed hysteria, providing their sound with one of its most distinctive features.

Finally, there was Brian Connolly, a fiercely handsome lead singer with the best hair in the world. It fell in heavy blond curtains from crown to jaw, then curled inwards at the throat, holding perfectly, a symmetrical statement of pop majesty, a frame for the place where that voice came from. I loved that voice. It was always strongly masculine: tender and sincere on love songs like 'Jeanie' (the B-side of 'Poppa Joe') but equally at home grating and yelling amid the riffs and thrashes of their later material. It was perhaps most effective as a mid-range hum, passing around dark messages in verses about the sinister doings of a song's protagonist. He also had a slight tremble on sustained notes, a must for good rock singers.

And it was a rock band that they wanted to be. They wanted to record their own songs too, but were only able to do that on B-sides. Their hits were all written by Nicky Chinn and Mike Chapman, a writing and production duo operating under the brand name Chinnichap, who, with some initial production help, enjoyed a highway of success stretching from one end of the 70s to the other. Some of this was with records that appealed to grannies. Some of it was with records that achieved the feat of being enormously pretentious and enormously vapid at the same time. If you don't believe this is possible, listen to 'Kara, Kara' by New World.

Some of it, however, was with records that galvanised young audiences, flew to the top of charts across Europe and beyond, and now stand as pillars of our heritage. This brings us back to the Sweet, who occupied one extremity of the Chinnichap domain: that of rock. But not merely rock – glam rock.

It has been suggested that glam took hold in Britain because of our tradition of pantomime. Men putting on make-up and flouncing around in women's clothes was something we had long been comfortable with. So when rock bands added eye liner and lipstick to their long hair, when they donned shiny costumes in gold, silver and red, and when they stopped their trousers just below the knee to expose striped socks going from the hem to the platform boot, nobody batted a powdered eyelid.

For a couple of years, *Top of the Pops* was a shop window for some of the most outrageous, often ridiculous, stage costumes imaginable. Entire suits were constructed in gold and silver, lewdly hugging the body, sometimes exposing chests, sometimes forming a choker collar, sometimes both at once. They might be skin-tight, they might be flared. They might have long sleeves festooned with dangling tassels, or rows of attached triangles like cartoon crocodile teeth. There were capes, often with huge, erect collars as if designed for a spoof Dracula. Some capes met the sleeves to make an all-in-one: flap it a bit and you could take off. Certain colour combinations made many look like superhero costumes. Some of them were matt, some of them were glittery, some of them shone like tin foil.

Make-up became not only commonplace on men but boldly decorative. Zigzag lightning flashes were painted on faces; if not black, then in layers of colour. There were stars, too, some arranged right around the eye, like a glam monocle exploding across half the face. Brian Connolly had two neat, gold ones, one under each eye, tinged with glitter. Many things were tinged with glitter; hair, cheeks, foreheads, painted symbols. There were themes attached. The Apollo moon missions were still going on, hence the silver, hence the stars; hence the idea, sometimes explicitly suggested, that the performers had actually descended from the cosmos to come among us.

Then there were the platforms. We're talking elevated soles and heels beneath shoes and boots, usually presented in pronounced, colourful layers of gloss and glitter. You assumed that as soon as they got more than four inches high you would struggle to stay upright on the things, but I suppose people practised. If any single feature of early 70s fashion truly deserves to be called iconic, it's got to be the platform.

Some have suggested that all this colour and costume was escapism in the face of the gloom, decay and strife of early 70s Britain. Possibly. But those of us who were about nine were protected from all that. For us, there was no need to question it, no need to put it into context, apart from: *This is how those blokes look who made that record I like.* Glam was certainly not street fashion. There may have been a few modest platforms peeping from the legs of flared trousers round our way, but nobody went round the Co-op in a silver choker. It was not for the likes of us.

It was for the likes of solo superstar Elton John, whose 'Crocodile Rock' was enjoying seriously heavy airplay at the time I bought 'Wig-Wam Bam'. He embraced glam wholesale, especially the platforms, which he wore rather high. One boy in my class was particularly taken with them. He would get a piece of paper, announce that he was going to draw "Elton John boots", then draw a pair right at the top and begin extending soles and heels downward, chuckling to himself all the way, until he had run out of space. He had drawn a pair of platforms with thirty or so layers; Elton John standing in them, but off the page from the shins up.

Elton carried off the glam thing effortlessly. Other unfortunate souls simply happened to be in a successful band at a point when this was what they were expected to wear, a coincidence they may later have come to curse. I had a friend for a sleepover when Chicory Tip appeared on *Top of the Pops* to perform their song 'Good Grief Christina'. The singer stood in a superhero all-in-one, clapping his hands above his head and mouthing the intro vocal. This position pushed his belly out and, as he sang, his mouth movements caused my friend to declare, through heaves of laughter, "He looks like a goldfish!" I liked the record, but this put me off it a bit.

The Sweet, of course, had no such problems. And things were about to get even better for them. A few days into 1973, they released a single called 'Blockbuster'. One morning, the Sweet fan in my class rushed up to tell me that it had shot up to number two and would be number one next week.

A week later, he rushed up again, grinning his head off, and told me it was indeed number one. Our favourite band was number one. I watched *Top of the Pops* and there they were – playing the last song in the show, outdoing all others, the climax of the proceedings. Wow. Being number one was victorious, an assertion of superiority and a claim to greatness. It was a big fat badge that said: *This has beaten everything else.* I got that now, suddenly and sharply.

The record itself I didn't get to begin with. It seemed to lack the cohesion of 'Wig-Wam Bam' and I found its success a little hard to understand. Its various hooks and gimmicks are, however, underpinned by a seriously heavy blues rhythm – *jun, jun, junga-lala; jun, jun, junga-lala* – delivered in a guitar sound with a shimmering veneer. Any rock band would have wanted a piece of it. It sets a mood that matches the theme: there's a nutter on the loose; malicious, cunning and a particular threat to women with long, black hair.

Its best detail is the cop siren, the one that begins the record with a twisting, turning wail, delivering the kind of instant and unique buzz that intros of all great singles ought to have, setting the scene until the first guitar appears, which it does, at just the right moment. Everything in 'Blockbuster' happens at just the right moment. This is British engineering at its finest and it crowned the charts for five satisfying weeks.

A few other singles that were near the top of the charts in those weeks deserve a mention. Former Beatle Paul McCartney had formed a new band with his wife Linda. They were called Wings and their new one was a double A-side: 'Hi Hi Hi'/'C Moon'. Double A-sides are curious things. They claim to present us with two tracks of equal status and yet one is always more popular than the other, often to the extent that fans don't know how the other one goes. Thing is, if you habitually checked out B-sides anyway, you would get to know the flip and make your own mind up, which leaves us to wonder about the whole point of a double A-side. But let's not wander off. I still have no idea what 'Hi Hi Hi' sounds like. 'C Moon' however, is a piece of light relief centred on piano and xylophone, whimsically pleasing to the ear. A good thing really, as it was on the radio rather a lot.

Former Beatles remained a big draw, but there was fresher stuff making its mark. David Bowie, for example. His new single was 'The Jean Genie', the most remarkable thing about which was that it had the same guitar riff as 'Blockbuster', albeit a little rougher at the edges. It was distracting and I got to know it well, but I didn't love it. It was with the older fans that Bowie's artistic expression and blurred sexual lines registered. He was for other people. But that's not to say that I was incapable or unwilling to visit unsettling places in my imagination because of a record: cue 'Ball Park Incident' by Wizzard.

Roy Wood was a former member of the Move and the writer of 'Blackberry Way'. He was a fan of the "Wall of Sound" made famous by producer Phil Spector in the early 60s and his new band set about creating its own version. Through subsequent 1973 singles, Wizzard became known for tunes of rich, booming texture, with Wood's gentle tenor delivering messages of love in classic melodies across the top.

But before all that nice stuff, there was 'Ball Park Incident'. Here was this gravel-voiced desperado, gripping the wire fence beside the school ballpark where he had found his girlfriend lying dead, slain by bullets from a hoodlum's gun, for what reason we can only guess. I pictured him stunted, misshapen, because of the voice; but it could just have been his slumped posture as he tells his tale. The complex arrangement creates an atmosphere of doom – sinister and gangster-ish. I listened to it from behind the sofa.

Many of the adults around me were more taken with Carly Simon's 'You're So Vain', a song about posh people doing posh things in posh places, sung by a posh woman in a posh dress. It elbowed its way past Wizzard in the Top 10 with a swish of its chiffon, smug in the knowl-edge that it was the talk of many a dinner party.

Yet the same might have been said of the final record in this little round-up: 'Part of the Union' by Strawbs. This is a real period piece, from a time when trade unionists were seen by many as the enemy within; hating the company, intimidating bosses whenever they flexed their collective muscle, getting whatever they wanted. All this was crisply and cleverly summarised by the lyric, and its oafish chorus might have been generated by a mob at the factory gates.

It was a fine lampoon but, like other fine lampoons, it was adopted as an anthem by its targets, perhaps believing it had been written in their honour but, more likely, flattered by the attention. There were several in my family. At any rate, it was a huge hit, number two for several weeks, a token of our economic circumstances, from which glam was reputedly a welcome diversion.

Three

Once upon a time, in a land not far away, a little single was released by its record company. It was a bright, lively single with a good beat, and after a few plays on the radio people began to notice it, feeling a slight sharpening of the senses whenever it came on. They mentioned it to their friends. A few weeks later, it sneaked into the Top 30, at number twenty-eight. This was good news, because now it could be performed on *Top of the Pops*, seen by millions of people, many of whom perhaps didn't listen to the radio much. At the same time, the artist began appearing in magazines and so, within the space of a few days, it seemed as though everybody knew about it.

That very weekend, thousands of them bought a copy while they were out shopping. Some even went out especially to buy that and nothing else. And well, well, well – when the new Top 30 was announced the following week it had leapt to number fifteen. Now it was on the radio all the time.

Children were singing it in gangs at school and arguing about it at playtimes, because we don't all like the same things, do we? Adults realised that they were humming it under their breath. Some of these thought to themselves, "Well, I might as well get it next time I'm out". And many did. Enough for it to have climbed even higher the following week – to number eight. No longer merely a record that some people liked, it was a proper big hit now – a Top 10 hit. The record at number nine was by one of the most popular groups in the world and had been number one just three weeks earlier. Now the newcomer was outselling it.

So, how high could it get? Lots of people, impressed by its progress and the excitement others felt about it, got their own copy so that they could join in. Its universe was continuing to grow. Its fans waited nervously until the next chart came out. It was now in a battle with other giant successes; a struggle to get as close to the top as it possibly could. The following week... number five! Another jump like that and it would be number two, banging on the door of number one! The week after that...number four. A climb of just one place. You couldn't help but be disappointed; you loved it so much, wanted so badly for it to be the number one, the toppermost record in the land. *Come on, keep on climbing!*

The next week, when you listened to the new chart being announced in its usual reverse order, you didn't want to hear its title; you prayed that the next record in the Top 10 would be somebody else's, so that yours – because it was your record – would be higher. *Come on!*

Then, suddenly, you hear it. Too soon. Far too soon. Number seven. It's gone down. *Down.* The next week it would drop further. The week after that, it would plummet. But by then it will no longer matter. You have been numbed. Anyway, there might be another one climbing the charts that has replaced it in your affections. Hopefully. Because you can't bear disappointments like that for too long.

This is fairly typical of the seriousness with which fans took the charts when they first discovered them, when their loyalty to the records they love was at its most untamed, most passionate and at its furthest point from any kind of perspective. This is the condition in which I learned of the progress of Sweet singles throughout 1973. It is also a fairly typical pattern of chart progress for a hit single – sorry, a Top 10 Smash. Because being in the Top 10 was a Very Big Deal, at least up until the 1990s. If you were in the Top 10 you had properly made it.

Everything is relative, of course: if an act that was always in the top three had a new single peak at number ten, questions would have to be asked. Such acts would expect to see their new release get to its peak position within three weeks. Never mind clawing its way up from twenty-eight: it would launch itself into the teens as a new entry. A few did even better - 'Cum On Feel the Noize' by Slade, for instance.

Slade were fun-loving lads from the English Midlands who studiously misspelt their song titles and knew how to groove. In Dave Hill, they had a guitarist ready to experiment with extremities of glam fashion, but the other three ploughed their own sartorial furrow. Most recognisably, lead singer Noddy Holder had out-sized sideburns and decorated top hats. He looked like Scrooge's hedonistic brother. His was another sore-throat voice, but the world's loudest: a grainy, joyful holler.

The group appealed to boys because their stomping beats and yellable choruses evoked the rousing atmosphere of the football terrace. They appealed to girls (a) because they were fun-loving lads and (b) because their first chart-topper, 'Coz I Luv You', was a song of romantic devotion with a violin on it. Between June and December 1972 they rolled out a trio of singles – 'Take Me Back 'Ome', 'Mama Weer All Crazee Now' and 'Gudbuy T'Jane' – which ranks among the finest runs of consecutive releases by anyone. People of all ages found themselves humming along with a tap of the foot. Now add these factors together: Slade were huge.

'Blockbuster' had been number one for five weeks, a fine effort by any standards, so there was no reason to grumble at the thought of something finally coming to knock it off. But the thing that came to knock it off was 'Cum On Feel the Noize' by Slade and it went straight in at number one. *Straight in.* It simply hadn't bothered with the rest of the chart.

At school I was surrounded by gloating twits wanting to make sure I knew that the Sweet had been royally booted out of the top position, emphatically deposed by a superior force: Slade. I went from self-assurance to extensive bruising in a matter of minutes. Bloody Slade. It was hard not to be resentful. I resented the ease with which they flew to the top of the charts; I resented the celebratory tone of their new record; I resented the great time they seemed to be having. *Straight in.*

The Sweet hadn't gone *straight in.*

This was, I realised, evidence that Slade were the winners. Going straight in at number one was incredibly rare; the reserve of true champions. The last record to do so had been 'Get Back' by the Beatles in 1969. After 1973, nobody would achieve the feat until 1980. Four records would do it in 1973, three of them by bloody Slade. One of these was 'Skweeze Me Pleeze Me', a record so insubstantial that you wondered whether they wouldn't have gone to number one that summer with three minutes of amplified arse scratching. These were the tense conditions under which I began following the singles chart.

The new weekly chart was announced on Radio 1 during the lunchtime show on Tuesday. It was featured on *Top of the Pops* two evenings later, with a final run-down of the Top 20 on Radio 1 at 6pm on Sunday. I had no idea about this. Every Sunday teatime I would settle down to stare at the silver mesh on the front of the portable radio, transfixed, believing that it was the first time these new positions had been revealed. The chart I was biting my nails over was five days old and news to very few.

Never mind. For now, this was my crunch time. Tom Browne was the show's host, the husky calm of his voice contrasting with the high drama that it was his duty to reveal; the progress of the cherished, the plucky and the loathed. I spent far more of it being anxious about the prospects for my favourites than I did enjoying the records, although, merely by sitting through it, I got to know sounds ranging from strutting soul to family pop, from turgid rock to tearful sincerities. Some of it was baffling, but it was all compelling. Varying your musical diet is good for the blood.

Unlike those in America, UK chart positions were determined exclusively by sales. The BBC had commissioned the British Market Research Bureau to gather sales figures from a shifting sample of record shops in a specified universe running into several hundred. None of the stores on the list knew from one week to the next if they would be called, making it more of a challenge for unscrupulous record companies to manipulate the system. It produced a chart of consistent patterns, providing rich pastures of conversation for the circles I moved in, allowing us to make wise predictions about next week's placings.

It was not the only chart. The music weeklies were at liberty to publish their own, and one of these, *Melody Maker*, began popping through our letterbox after Mum found out it had a folk section. Its pop chart had some curious variations with the BBC's. Tabloid newspapers would list Top 10s. The wall of local record shops displayed a Top 50 supplied by their preferred trade magazine. The world was full of charts. But the BBC's was the 'proper' one.

Like tens of thousands of Sweet fans up and down the country I was eager for the follow up to 'Blockbuster' and it appeared in the spring. It was new and it sounded like the Sweet. The pulse raced. 'Hell Raiser' is a striking time capsule of rock guitar; one eye on current patterns, the other on a future decades away, where metal bands would use dry, jagged riffs on tracks divided into contrasting sections. The song was about a lover so hot that when the guy touched her it burned his skin and cooked his insides. Presumably this was a metaphor covering her sex appeal, her libertarian dispositions and the emotional risks involved in being with her, but I had a mental image of a girl who was actually red and had horns.

It was disappointing that it went straight in at number four instead of number one, but four was still darned impressive. The incumbent chart-topper was 'Tie a Yellow Ribbon Round the Old Oak Tree', Dawn's skippity-dippity tale of wholesome parole, beloved of grannies everywhere. Its time was surely up. It did indeed drop to number three the following week, but then the shock: 'Hell Raiser' was leapfrogged. I had to contend with the crushing disappointment of it not getting to number one at all. I don't think I cried but I did a lot of sulking.

The leapfrogger was the new Wizzard single, 'See My Baby Jive'. Roy Wood had quit grimacing by the school fence and was now having the time of his life dancing with his adoring gal. The chorus is joyful, expansive and luxuriant; a tune like Momma used to bake. My Momma fell for it and so did my sisters, all of whom joined in regular, impromptu renditions for weeks on end. A copy was purchased for the house so that it could be sung along to, even when Tom Browne wasn't playing it. It was emphatically *our* copy. I didn't resent 'See My Baby Jive'. It is testimony to this fact that *our* copy is now in *my* record collection.

So I came to terms with 'Hell Raiser' peaking at number two. But, that autumn, the Sweet got stuck there again and this time it threatened my health. The release was 'The Ballroom Blitz', a glossy, tense, rich-sounding rocker with all the Sweet trimmings and a mighty, magnificent intro of drums, voices and a three-note rock riff to rank among the very best. This, surely, would slam its fist down on the number one spot and set things straight. It crashed in at number two and hands were rubbed in anticipation.

Meanwhile, a detective drama set in Holland called *Van der Valk* was playing on television. Its theme tune was an innocuous orchestral piece with a jaunty bit; catchy enough for an idle moment. It was released as a single by the Simon Park Orchestra and we discovered it was called 'Eye Level'. In the week after 'The Ballroom Blitz' entered the charts it went ballistic. The reigning number one was duly booted off, but when the dust settled, the Sweet were still at number two. My world caved in.

Who the hell was buying 'Eye Level'? Well I had a few clues. Almost everyone I knew was humming it, including some I had thought of as friends. There was even a running joke about it; people were humming the jaunty bit incorrectly, missing half a bar at the end of its first phrase, to the annoyance of those with a more musical ear, which of course meant that some began doing it on purpose. I noticed the error myself but I was buggered if I was going to pipe up in collaboration.

An orchestra – people in jumpers with a conductor – was keeping 'The Ballroom Blitz' from number one. Two weeks into this nightmare, when Tom Browne announced that the Sweet were still at number two, I felt violently sick. I remember resting my forehead on the dining table, hands over my ears, eyes screwed shut, Mum's kindly-meant condolences doing nothing to help. 'Eye Level' was probably the first thing I had ever encountered for which I felt savage, sulphuric hatred. And it had won. It stayed at the top as the good guys began slipping away.

If the Chinnichap boys were similarly disappointed by all this, they could console themselves with the success of two new acts they had launched into the charts, both on the RAK label. The first was Suzi Quatro, a leather-encased American who sang in a gravelly screech as she wielded a bass guitar bigger than she was, backed by geezers who looked like they would do your car if you said anything. Her debut hit was 'Can the Can', a song I dismissed as stupid. You could cup a cup and you could sandwich a sandwich, but would you really want to write a song about it? "Can" was a word meaning something with beans or soup in it; I was, as yet, unaware of its evening job as a collo-quial verb.

Even as a bit of slang it doesn't work; but then Chinnichap had a neat line in incoherent lyrics. Take 'Blockbuster', for instance. Why we should have to block Buster, rather than stop, catch or kill the scoundrel is a mystery; but the meaning is morphed until we have an explosive, single-word title to look brilliant in the listings. 'Can the Can' is obtuse at best, but here was another memorable title. Undaunted by my disapproval, the record went to number one at the start of the summer.

Their other new act was a group called Mud. One of my best friends was obsessed with 'Crazy', their first hit. What a brilliant, illicit name: Mud. It meant dirt, picking your nose and not washing your hands. With any luck, next week there might be a group called Poo. I liked their name more than their record; 'Crazy' used a tango rhythm in its chorus and seemed a bit smart-arsed. But the follow-up, 'Hypnosis', was much better, with a dark, spooky heaviness accompanying a lyric about a man intimidated by the effect a girl is having on him.

It was one of three singles I bought while on summer holiday in Scotland. Unable to play them until I got home, I spent long moments in the car, slipping them in and out of their sleeves to study the grooves and try to work out which part of those circular wiggles contained which part of the song. One of the others was '48 Crash', the new Suzi Quatro single. The lyric made no more sense than its predecessor but its energy was fantastic and I wanted a copy the second I heard it. I glossed over being told by Suzi that "a 48 crash is a silk sash bash". Well, quite.

I now had options for what I could play my records on. Dad had taken the Dansette when he moved out, but before he left, he built, painted and varnished a cabinet to house a turntable and radio, its speakers hidden behind grey mesh. It was a version of what would later be called a music centre, but without the cassette player (we were in our last few months of using reel-to-reel tape). This cabinet was in our lounge which, being a semi-detached, shared a wall with the lounge next door.

Up in my room I had a replacement for the Dansette, passed on by grandparents; a heavy box covered in red plastic with white polka-dots and a distinctive smell. Decades later I would encounter one in a musty junk shop and my first response was to sniff it. I was not disappointed. It was 1973 again for a few moments. I can't remember what make it was, but the arm and head were as proportionately heavy as the rest of it. The head was so big I couldn't easily see where the needle was and I worried that it was gouging important bits out of my records. Activating the machinery so that it played the record automatically was now beneath me, so I went through phases of keeping my new purchases downstairs, next to the new, lighter, more easily manoeuvred technology, with the added bonus that the lounge had more room to bounce around in.

It was during one of these bouncing sessions, when I had dared to raise the volume a tad, that I had my first complaint from a neighbour about noise. Mum answered the door and was taken aback. She quickly concluded that the stuck up so-and-so's had nothing better to do but complain about a child enjoying his music, but suggested I give it a rest anyway. It was a Sunday after all. In my defence, some records compel you to bounce. If you don't want to bounce, don't play the record. The one in question, for instance: 'Hello! Hello! I'm Back Again' by Gary Glitter.

I had initially heard of Gary Glitter due to his first hit, 'Rock and Roll Part 2' - a record that sounds as much like the early 70s as anything in existence – being on *20 Fantastic Hits vol.2.* I didn't take to it. It sounded like a gang of blokes hanging around on a street corner threatening people. When 'Blockbuster' was out, he had 'Do You Wanna Touch Me (Oh Yeah)', which was fun, bounceable and a bit rude, so I bought it. 'Hello! Hello! I'm Back Again' was next. The single after that was the other one I bought in Scotland: 'I'm The Leader of the Gang (I Am)', his first number one, with a motorbike engine intro and percussive hooks all over the place. He followed it up in the autumn with the slow-swinging 'I Love You Love Me Love'; the other record, apart from the three by bloody Slade, to go straight in at number one that year. It was massive. It was massively massive. On *Top of the Pops* he confirmed his pop-god status by being lowered to the stage on a giant, glitter-covered crescent moon. These overblown theatrics were instantly recognised as such and lapped up, even by us nine-year-olds.

Within a couple of years the big hits were gone, but he revived his fortunes in the mid-80s with a college tour, playing to rugby guys and lacrosse girls who had loved him when they were kids and could now love him all over again. I saw that tour, fifteen hundred people crammed into a university concert hall in an atmosphere you could dimple with your finger. It was the second-best gig I ever saw.

I can't offer more detail than this, not because I don't have it to hand, but because of what was to follow. In the late 90s, Gary-Glitter-real-name-Paul-Gadd received the first in a string of convictions for sexual offences involving children. So now we don't applaud the detail of those records, or go on about the *Top of the Pops* performances, or swap memories of that night on the university campus. All that has stopped.

In 2009 I heard a presenter on local radio in pain about it. If only, he anguished, there were some way of separating the man from the records, so that we could feel okay about them being so important to us; it doesn't mean we are sympathising with a paedophile. A brave thing to put out on air. I wonder what the consequences were. I have seen people saying similar things online: "Gary Glitter brilliant, Paul Gadd evil scumbag".

Music fans of about my age can go round and round in circles on this, wringing their hands all the way. But in the end it boils down to two questions. Were those records great? Yes. Can we breezily celebrate them despite Gadd's crimes? No. Let's move on.

Returning home from your summer holiday is sad in some ways and exciting in others. On the one hand you are no longer on that hot, sandy beach with waves that smash so wonderfully against your chest and capsize your lilo, or wading through the glassy waters of the loch beside your campsite to soothe feet made burningly sore from a walk that was three times longer than Mum had intended it to be. But to compensate for that, there is the reintroduction to all the neat stuff at home.

When we returned in August 1973 I had those three records to play, but among the regular neat stuff was picking up the phone and dialling 160. That was the number for Dial-a-Disc, a service run by the General Post Office, enabling callers to listen to a current chart hit on a loop. It played in real time, so when you called, you arrived in the middle of it. If you wanted to hear the whole thing from start to finish it would mean staying on the line for up to seven minutes. And there were no selections like a jukebox; what was on was what you got.

In the quiet of the back room, I put my finger in the number hole and hauled the disc round to the halting bracket, then let go so that it clicked back to the start position, before beginning on the next number. Telephoning in the olden days. I like to think I would have asked permission to dial first but I fear not. I dialled 1-6-0: through to music; new, yet, on this occasion, somehow familiar. I remember my confident, sneering response: "Nah. They're just trying to sound like Wizzard". 'See My Baby Jive' had been huge and so it had spawned imitators, eager to get a slice of the action. A decent instinct: I would see plenty of examples of precisely that in the years to come. Unfortunately, the record I was listening to was 'Angel Fingers', the new single by Wizzard.

This was one of a pack of records I associate with the end of that summer holiday, all of which are bound up in the memory of a scene in a street. I am standing beside my Dad's light blue Humber with my sisters: it is unlocked and we are climbing in and out, lounging on the back seat or pretending to drive, haring up and down the pavement and peering through the wire fence at the railway line running parallel to the road. It is a hot Sunday, early evening, concrete warm underfoot.

We've been to see relatives. Now we're waiting for Dad to come out of their house across the road. Something is holding him up, he's gone back inside, but we've got things to distract us; perhaps what I think Nan used to call a "lully bag", a package you could buy from newsagents containing an assortment of small toys, comic strips and sweets. Perhaps we had cans of coke – they cost about 7p then.

The one certainty is that the car doors are open and the radio is on. Tom Browne is doing his stuff. There's David Bowie's new one, 'Life on Mars'; as distant from me as other David Bowie ones, but grand and impressive. The same could be said of 'Touch Me in the Morning', Diana Ross' latest; grown-ups crying and trying not to cling, with a sound that sends tingles along the spine. These two may have grabbed me by the ears but I had no intention of spending my pocket money on them.

Neither did I spend it on a starry-eyed, finger-poppin' soul tune called 'You Can Do Magic' by Limmie and the Family Cookin', a record of overwhelming prettiness that somehow achieved no more than a week at number three. Anyone who says they don't like it is a liar.

Peters and Lee's 'Welcome Home' was continuing its descent from number one. Another grannies' favourite; everybody older than Mum loved it as far as I could tell. It said everything its title leads you to imagine it would say – *you're back at last, come inside and settle back beside me* - doing so in the gently swaying style of a Jim Reeves croon and, when you're sixty-odd, little could be sweeter. I hated it. I was, however, quietly fond of one of its competitors, by a group called the Carpenters.

It was the first I'd heard of them, and their sound was striking, due in huge part to the oaky richness of the singer's voice. She commanded a range from sullen depth to high alto tremor, every word delivered with care and accuracy, reassuring and trustworthy. You couldn't miss a shade of her meaning. This new song, 'Yesterday Once More', kept smiling at you until you smiled back.

In the lyric, someone was rediscovering how records are capable of making us feel, immersing themselves in hits from their younger days, becoming reacquainted with their every detail and their every effect. Their shalala-las and woh-wohos still shine. It's a fine hook. 'Yesterday Once More' climbed to number two and kept its slippers in the corner of the Top 10 for a month and a half.

But the song isn't just about hankering after old times and lost youth: the point is that the old records are *back*: the lyric says so explicitly. In this regard, it was a barometer of the times. One of the defining features of the early 1970s was the Rock 'n' Roll Revival, a loudly proclaimed reverence for the way things once were; the old rhythms, the old dances, the old clothes, which, thank heavens, were now back. This was not merely the wailing of Outraged from Little Minster; it seemed to represent almost everyone with influence over what went into the singles chart.

'Good Grief Christina', the Chicory Tip affair mentioned earlier, was typical: the guy is appalled that his girlfriend has neither heard of rock 'n' roll nor can dance to it, especially as he's had the good grace to take her to a show where its rhythms are played, where the old dances are performed and where the conventions of old song titles are observed. It's coming back, just like it used to be - if you can't join in there's something wrong. For two years, chart music referenced the trappings of old-time rock 'n' roll almost non-stop – the jive, the stroll, blue jeans, black leather, picking up my baby in the Chevrolet and taking her to the local hop. The phrase "Rock 'n' Roll" sprang up in song titles all over the place.

Rock 'n' roll was a 50s phenomenon that spilled over into the 60s a bit. Teenagers became a discrete section of the population in that period, distinguished from children and adults by their own styles, tastes and needs, and with their own money to spend on them. This happened first in America. Teenagers wanted music that reflected their concerns, songs they could identify with and dance to. They found it in rhythm & blues - black music marketed for a wide and growing audience.

Derided as "nigger music" in a segregated USA, it was a liberating force for youths of all backgrounds. An enthusiastic DJ called Alan Freed is credited with first coining the term rock 'n' roll: the name stuck and adventurous youngsters lapped it up. Its golden years are widely thought to have been 1956-8, when its aristocracy were in their rockin' pomp: Elvis Presley, Jerry Lee Lewis, Little Richard, Chuck Berry, Buddy Holly.

In 1958 it all started to crumble. In little over a year, all of these guys were either killed, publicly disgraced, recruited by the army, or recruited by Jesus. And that was it. But it had achieved huge impact, causing bands to form especially to play in its style and cater for audiences hungry for something wilder. A few of these got record deals and developed influential styles of their own. But they started with rock 'n roll, which retained its allure. If you were going to bring anything back in the early 70s, it had to be that.

So, in Britain, performers began wearing showbiz updates on the iconic garb of 50s bikers and teddy boys. Suzi Quatro performed in leather from head to foot as she sang about a disreputable venue with lines of bikes outside: a "dive" called 'Devil Gate Drive'. Alvin Stardust burst forth to enjoy a string of hits, the first three of which – 'My Coo Ca Choo', 'Jealous Mind' and 'Red Dress' – were excellent value for your pocket money. Sometimes he sounded like Elvis Presley, sometimes like Buddy Holly and, often, like Alvin Stardust. With his black leather garb, black leather hairdo and black leather stare, this sexy beast made shapes as he sang at you, like rotating stills from an old movie.

The Teddy Boys of the 50s, influenced by Edwardian fashions, had worn low-hanging drape jackets detailed with deep cuffs and long lapels, with tapered drainpipe trousers. Beneath these, crepe-soled suede shoes known, charmingly, as brothel-creepers – the chunkier the better. It was like having a bumper car on each foot. Teds creamed their hair, shaping the front into a protruding tornado known as a quiff, and the back into a horizontal meeting of the two sides called a duck's arse. Not often celebrated in lofty circles.

Anyway, in the early 70s, it was back. Mud went for it - at least the lead singer and bass player did - but this time the suits were clean, smooth and pastel-coloured, perfect for *Top of the Pops* and teeny-bopper mags. They gave the hairdo a miss; too greasy, too threatening. The following year, another group would cement this look. They won a TV talent show called *New Faces.* There seemed to be hundreds of them on the stage at any one time. They had the most unforgetta-ble name in the world. They were called Showaddywaddy and they would keep drapes and brothel-creepers in the singles chart for the best part of a decade.

The curious thing is that all this happened in the midst of glam's newness; its silver spacesuits, crimson capes and exposed chests. The contrast between the bumper-car shoe and the platform boot could not have been greater. And yet, both were part of the same whole. Both were about dressing up and cheering up. Both had early 70s strife as a backdrop. Depressed about the state of the nation? You've got two choices: emigrate to another star system or regress fifteen years.

There were also purely musical reasons for it. Extended rock man-tras had once represented the hope of eternal love and peace, but once flower power wilted, we were left with long, serious pieces for refined tastes. Terms like 'interminable' and 'self indulgent' became associated with these. For many, the idea of an energetic, urgent song about a girl (or boy), which did everything it needed to in under three minutes, had a contrasting and strong appeal. Audiences looked back. Survivors from the rock 'n' roll era including Chuck Berry, Fats Domino and Jerry Lee Lewis, toured the UK. Chuck Berry even had a first number one in 1972, albeit with the smirking smut of 'My Ding-A-Ling'. The first ever rock 'n' roll chart topper, 'Rock Around the Clock' from 1955, was re-recorded and launched back into the Top 20, and its performer, Bill Haley, crossed the Atlantic once more to see us.

At the same time, younger bands in the London area were getting back to basics on their own initiative, adapting rhythm and blues, playing with an authentic, aggressive edge, delivering thrills and frolics to those who felt un-catered for elsewhere. Doing its stuff in a network of small venues, this scene became known as pub rock. I noticed some of the names in the ad pages of Mum's *Melody Maker* and flicked straight past them. If you could get into a pub you were too old to like Mud. So I didn't know about pub rock. What I did know about was a soundtrack double-album called *That'll Be the Day*.

As far as I could make out, the movie it came from was about people fighting and trying to snog girls at fairgrounds in the early 60s. Fine. It starred David Essex, a new face with one hit to his name, a strange record called 'Rock On', full of Rock 'N' Roll Revival references but with a modern sound all of its own, almost an abstract; it made me think of purple blobs dripping steadily from the roof of a luminous cave. The movie featured records from the late 50s and very early 60s and its soundtrack album was a real treasure trove. It came out on Ronco, the label responsible for *20 Star Tracks*.

The TV ad was thrilling; a rampage of clips from what were clearly great records, all of high status, all waiting to be introduced to me. The climax, at the part when they summarise the proposition and tell you where you can buy it, was a blast from an instrumental passage; a minor-key melody racing around on goodness only knows what instrument, sounding like the loudest, most powerful, magnificent thing there could ever be. It nailed me to the chair. I had to have it. "Oh, yeh" some grown-up told me. "That's 'Runaway' by Del Shannon. Somebody nicked my copy". I went round asking people if they knew 'Runaway' by Del Shannon. Almost all of them said yes. For goodness' sake, I thought; why had nobody told me about it before? Why was it not routinely on everyone's mind?

Nan and Grandad bought me *That'll Be the Day* for my tenth birthday. 'Runaway', blistering and immaculate, was its star turn, along with something from my old friends Johnny and the Hurricanes, who came thundering back into my life bearing a gift called 'Red River Rock'. This is the last track on side two and because my pressing is slightly off-centre it oscillates annoyingly, especially at the end, but it didn't stop me playing it. It's a rocked-up version of an old cowboy standard called 'Red River Valley'. Giving the treatment to innocent standards is one of pop's best habits and Johnny and the Hurricanes turn 'Red River Valley' into a dirty, bug-eyed blare that makes it great to be alive. It's not as hectic as 'Rocking Goose'; it's steadier, sturdier, but every bit as mighty, every bit as mad.

Then there were the Everly Brothers. We have met them before, while remembering my mum's cousin's precious 78 of 'All I Have to Do Is Dream'. Mum liked the Everly Brothers, too. Her other cousins liked the Everly Brothers. Her friends liked the Everly Brothers. My aunts and uncles liked the Everly Brothers. My friends' parents – most of whom stared blankly at me if ever I asked them about pop music – also liked the Everly Brothers. The Everly Brothers had four songs on *That'll Be the Day*, one of them, 'Bye Bye Love', opened side one. This was a safe bet; a live version of the song was on *Bridge over Troubled Water* by Simon & Garfunkel, so it was already in everyone's house.

The Everly Brothers were actual siblings, Don and Phil. They sang convincing songs of sweet heartache in distinctive, crisp harmony and it seemed that the very mention of them was a balm for Mum's generation. Where their brow had been furrowed, the face relaxed; where their tone had been terse, the voice softened; where they had been too busy, there was suddenly time. They mentioned songs, sang a line or two, did a little dance; probably offering anecdotes connected to the tune in question.

Perhaps this was 'Bye Bye Love', maybe the cheerfully sentimental '(Til) I Kissed You', or the tense drama of 'Wake Up Little Suzy'. I had the latter's lyric explained to me. This young couple had fallen asleep in their car at a drive-in and woken up at 4am. Hmm. They've missed their curfew and disgrace awaits; harsh judgement from parents and peers alike – a ruined reputation. The adults describing this were, as they spoke, whisked away to the context of 1957 where this was heavy stuff. It was yesterday once more.

That'll Be the Day is a great place to start if you know nothing about pop before the Beatles. There are big-hitters from Little Richard and Jerry Lee Lewis - there are sentimental tunes for sweethearts, oddball novelties and energetic rockers by the less well-remembered. Buddy Holly is represented indirectly – his backing band, fronted by Bobby Vee, perform two songs that Holly is famous for, including the title track. There's no Presley, Domino or Berry, but this doesn't matter. It's a good, balanced snapshot, and three-quarters of it is of the highest quality.

However, then there's side four. This opens with 'Rock On' by David Essex. From 1973. The rest of the side is then mainly given over to one performer, Liverpudlian rocker Billy Fury, whose appeal I remain unable to fathom. I'm sure he was lauded in his day as a home-grown alternative to these distant Americans and he may have a part in the movie, although I don't know for sure as I still haven't seen the bloody thing. There are a few isolated gems on side four and I steered the needle towards them with tense precision.

For seven weeks that summer, *That'll Be the Day* was the UK's number one album and it kept selling for the rest of the year. It should be noted that it wasn't the first such compilation to get its brothel creeper in the door. A year earlier, *20 All Time Hits of the 50s* and *25 Rockin' and Rollin' Greats* on K-Tel had both topped the charts, the former for even longer than *That'll Be the Day*. Parents needed something to play on their new music centres, something better than 'today's rubbish', and many in the record industry whose youth had coincided with theirs were happy to help.

Legions of children fell under the influence. I was a typical example, loving the old tunes while favouring new ones that appeared to follow their blueprint, particularly the energetic rockers, and there were plenty of them on *Top of the Pops*, whether they were glammed-up old songs or draped-up new ones.

So there you had it: rock 'n' roll was now revived. Yester-hits were reissued and got back in the charts, some of them scrambling into the Top 10. A non-chronological list would include 'Let's Dance' by Chris Montez, loved for its sheer volume as much as for its pounding drums and distorted keyboard riff; it would include dance craze anthems 'The Loco-Motion' by Little Eva and 'Let's Twist Again' by Chubby Checker. It would include another record to turn an innocent tune into an instrumental freak-out - the march from Tchaikovsky's Nutcracker suite being converted into B. Bumble and the Stingers' ear-splitting 'Nut Rocker'. But, most satisfyingly, it would include a record which, over a decade earlier, had been a number one in the US but banned by the BBC: 'Monster Mash' by Bobby 'Boris' Pickett and the Crypt-Kickers.

I was invited to a party in the autumn. I can't remember if it was a birthday party, a Hallowe'en party or bonfire night but I remember a sizeable garden with banks, gullies and mature trees, lit at one end by the house, at the other by a blazing bonfire. Adults are standing round chatting and we are running between them, as well as into the house for more crisps and soft drinks. There's a rich smell of damp earth blending with the savoury tangs of the fire.

As we move through the house we pass a table with a record player, beside which is a small stack of singles. One of these is 'Monster Mash', in that London label company bag with its crooked, thick red spiral. A couple of us stop to investigate and our host's mum pauses behind us, checking that we're not damaging anything. We want to put 'Monster Mash' on but she declines with a groan: she's already sick of it. It's been in the charts for several weeks, getting as high as number three and, in their house at least, the novelty has worn very thin.

But what a novelty when fresh. The record opens with the creak of a coffin lid and the gurgle of laboratory experiments in some cold stone tower. A rhythm then kicks in on the drums, just enough to make you understand that this is not horror - it's going to be groovy fun. You instantly recognise it as old, early 60s, crisp and delicious. The drums have barely begun when the vocals start, a benign ghoul beginning his tale. Preparing one night to animate the monster laid out on his slab, he was surprised to see it get up by itself and begin to dance. A groovy dance, it soon caught on among various members of the horror community. The monster mash became a graveyard smash, right across the land, and the living were now being invited to join in.

Amongst the myriad dance crazes of early 60s America, this must have been a parody of renown, as well as an itchin' tune. The rhythm is hip, taken from a place where pop and rhythm 'n' blues exchange lingering kisses: exactly the sort used on very early Motown releases. You can only guess how often it had been played in our host's house prior to the party, there was no way we were going to hear it tonight.

His mum said we could put on 'Sorrow' instead if we wanted. This was the curious David Bowie newie, a cover of a Mersey-beat hit from the early 60s, about a girl with long blonde hair and blue eyes having done nothing but make him miserable.

It was perhaps an attempt to soothe the brows of parents, alarmed by their children being so keen on this half-naked whatever-it-was with spiky hair and hypnotic powers. *I'm going to be here for a while so let's be nice to mums and dads – here's a song you already like.* He might as well have knocked on your door wearing a suit and carrying a bunch of flowers. The production was modern lounge, offending nobody, and 'Sorrow' was a hit.

However, at the same time, there was another Bowie record in the charts; 'The Laughing Gnome', a novelty record he had made on his former label Deram in the late 60s and which was dreadful. Not even I liked it. A wafer-thin tale of a gnome who moves in with the song's protagonist to share a procession of puns on the word "gnome", peppered with embarrassing chuckling from Bowie. Deram had re-released it to cash in on the success he was now enjoying. It was in that same pile alongside 'Monster Mash'. I dare say our friend's mum would have given the same answer if we'd asked to hear that instead. In this case, good for her.

But back to *my* mum. We're in an electronics shop in Balham. I'm peering through the glass of a display case, studying gadgets and the various accompanying paraphernalia. The shop is crowded and has a slightly tense atmosphere, with people pushing past each other to peer and grab. I'm glad I'm away from the main scrum. It's Tuesday and we've got the day off school because it's royal wedding day: Princess Anne is marrying Captain Mark Phillips.

In the wall behind my display case a radio is playing. Tony Blackburn, who has moved from the breakfast show to late morning, is moaning live on air about not having been invited to the big do. He thinks he should have been; he is, after all, a Radio 1 DJ and as good as a pop star himself. A pillar of British entertainment, he's done his bit for the country. Although this was a whining bellyache, it wasn't unreasonable for its time, given the enormous regard in which those-

Radio 1 DJs were held by the public and the enormous regard in which they consequently held themselves.

But you've not been invited, Tone. It's tough titty. So shut up. Shut up and play a record. Play 'Dyna-Mite' by Mud. It's brilliant; my mates are all mad about it. We've got this thing where one of us just bursts into the chorus suddenly, for no reason, just because it's so funny and you just want to. You have to do it properly though, hold the mic and screw your face up. In school we bang the rhythm on table tops, in cubs we do it in the floorboards: bam, bam, ba-na-nam; bam, bam, ba-na-nam. It's not just the beat though, there are so many great bits to it. It makes your tummy feel funny, it makes you act stupid. 'Dyna-Mite' propelled Mud into the big time proper and remains their best record. In the weeks leading up to that Christmas, it was the most played 45 in my house by miles.

I don't remember if it was on Tone's playlist that morning, but I do remember why we were in the electronics shop. It would be my birthday soon and my main present was going to be a portable compact cassette recorder. This was too exciting for words.

Compact cassettes – "cassettes" for short – were a thrilling innovation in the use of tape. How fantastic it would be to have something that would enable you to record sounds, voices and music, then quickly play it back on something which you could carry around easily. Well, now you could. You didn't have to plug it into the wall; it could work on batteries, four of those big fat ones. It was about as long as your forearm and light enough to carry in one hand, leaving the other free to hold the microphone, a thing like a fat felt tip on a wire.

As already mentioned, we had used a reel-to-reel machine for years. Their chunky half-inch tape made you think of spy or sci-fi movies, where men in white coats with clipboards watched wall-mounted spools jerk back and forth. To use them, you had to put the tape on one spindle, feed the end through the reading mechanisms and on to the empty spool on the other side, wrapping it around until it was secure. You then pressed down the domino-sized play button, the spindles began turning and away you went.

But the compact cassette was neat and slick; both spools, of tape a few millimetres wide were contained within a case small enough to clasp in one hand. It slotted into its player in a single, fuss-less movement; a sweet little click, then play. If all that wasn't enough, the cassette had two sides. A C30 had fifteen minutes on Side A and another fifteen on Side B. Just turn it over, click it back in and go. A little rectangular window let you see how much tape there was to go. Fantastic.

So now you could record outside noises; birdsong, barking dogs and traffic. You could record television; listening to dialogue, sports commentary or theme tunes again, *after they had been broadcast.* You could tape people talking. As a family, we had previously recorded our memories of Christmas or summer holidays sitting around the reel-to-reel in the middle of the floor, taking it in turns to speak in very serious, affected voices into a microphone propped up on an awkward little plastic stand. All that formality was now redundant. The talker no longer had to come to you. Now you could follow them around, sometimes with their consent.

You could also, of course, record music. Some people had music centres, posh stereo sets the size of a suitcase, with a turntable, radio and cassette player all built in, which enabled you to tape records "direct". Our aunt and uncle had one. We mere mortals, however, had to try and tape records through the atmosphere, placing the cassette recorder close to the speaker and hoping that your sister wouldn't suddenly call out to Mum from the landing and ruin it. Something usually ruined it. The playback sound was useless anyway; thin and wispy compared to the full, rich sound of a record player or a "direct" recording.

You could get pre-recorded cassettes though, proper albums on tape, with the artwork, track listing and credits re-formatted for the inlay card that folded into the case. The sound on these was good. So now you could happily listen to *Bridge over Troubled Water* by Simon & Garfunkel under the bedclothes.

Another enticing possibility was becoming a recording artist yourself; perhaps strumming on a guitar and singing. If you mucked it up you could rewind and record over it. Sadly, however, this would always fall short of expectations. You could refine, rearrange and re-take as often as you wanted but the performances were never good enough and it sounded nothing like a record. It seemed so unfair. But at least there was now a world where such things could be attempted. It was a good one to be in.

I got two pre-recorded albums for Christmas: *Touch Me* by Gary Glitter and *Sweet's Biggest Hits*. During autumn half term, we had been in the record department of a huge branch of Woolworth's in Bristol, when I found the latter in the racks and almost combusted with excitement. How fantastic would it be to own a Sweet album? It was swiftly made clear that, at £3.15, I was not going to own this one today; I had £1 to spend on the whole trip.

Close by was a copy of *Rock Around the Clock* by Bill Haley and his Comets, an LP on Woolworths' own Hallmark label, priced at 75p. This was a few weeks before I would own *That'll Be the Day* and I was sold the idea of buying it as a collection of essential 50s rock 'n' roll by the guy who, according to Mum, had started it all. Her treasured 78 of Haley's 'Shake, Rattle & Roll' had been stolen and the memory still hurt. I had to decide between this LP and the distracting new Elton John single, 'Goodbye Yellow Brick Road'. Mum convinced me that ten tracks were much better value than two and I went for it. It would be almost 30 years before I would be swooning over my own copy of the Elton John song.

The Bill Haley album turned out to be re-recordings, inferior to the urgent, explosive originals, but I didn't know this when I took it to the counter. We couldn't find a B&B that night so Mum marched us defiantly into the foyer of the Dragonara Hotel and charged it to her new Access credit card. In our room, I spent the evening making paper 45s, copying onto their labels the titles of Bill Haley songs I had yet to hear. Both my drawing and my cutting out of circles were hopeless, but the strong urge was there to have them on single. I had the bug already; the album format would never quite compete.

So I got *Sweet's Biggest Hits* on cassette instead. The collection included all their singles up to and including 'Wig-Wam Bam' plus their B-sides; in other words, all their records, big or otherwise. I didn't have the full set of their pre-glam singles and so a lot of it was new to me. Its comparatively tame, jolly sound was curious, especially on 'Chop Chop', a song about a woodcutter going chop chop (woodcutter tributes are all too rare in popular culture). On the cover, the boys pose in jeans and t-shirts, like a bunch of everyblokes down the park; not a flash of glitter in sight. It seemed a bit odd so soon after 'The Ballroom Blitz'.

But never mind. I had my copy now and could play it on my birthday present. A new gadget meant fresh opportunities to explore and I poked it about, applying the 'play' and 'record' buttons without a cassette in, trying to establish how the music got from the tape to the speaker. I can't remember what conclusions, if any, I reached. I also, inevitably, played a form of Russian roulette with it, pressing play and record together over a pre-recorded tape – specifically, over one of the best bits of 'Wig-Wam Bam' - to see if it erased it. It didn't, but it turned it into an indistinct smudge of sound through which you could only just make out the tune. I didn't do this again.

On some portable cassette players, the operating button was a small, rectangular variation on a gear-stick; you levered it down to play, up to stop, and from side to side for the fast-forward and rewind functions. I never operated one of these. Mine had mini domino buttons, all white except for the red 'record' one. Our school had a gear-stick one. It also had a stupid black leather case with a shoulder strap, which didn't fit properly; the player slipped around inside it; it was covered in popper buttons and strap-endings that curled up, and the bit over the speaker was full of little holes that collected dirt.

One of the places to which you could carry your portable cassette player was the car. At that point we had a Mini Countryman, an estate with wooden trim, like a small, green, mock-Tudor outhouse on wheels. The ignition was a button on the floor that you pressed hard with your thumb. The hinges at the back were corroded, so the rear doors had to be held on with bungee straps hooked around whatever they could reach. This was the vehicle in which we had arrived at the forecourt of The Dragonara Hotel. It had a radio, which worked, if the wire coat hanger was positioned properly in the hole that had once hosted an aerial. But there was no cassette player. The idea of listening to whatever songs we wanted to as we drove along was exciting, yet a portable cassette player couldn't compete with the engine noise, especially not on the motorway.

Less than a year later however, we were able to buy a Ford Cortina. Now we're talking. Our neighbours, snobs to the last, breathed a sign of relief. Mum was all too aware of this and didn't like it. One of them was a nurse who bounded up to her in the local garage to congratulate her on having visibly gone up in the world. Mum was seething afterwards. The nurse used to reserve a parking space right outside her house by putting traffic cones and planks of wood in the kerb. We were sent to steal them, beginning a collection that clogged up our cellar for years. "She doesn't own the bloody road", Mum would say, stabbing the table with her finger. No, but neither did we own the cones and planks.

But we *did* own the Cortina. The Cortina had a medium wave/long wave radio in the dashboard and a proper aerial fixed in the right place, in front of the driver's wing mirror. Sadly, it didn't have a cassette player but it did have a quieter engine, meaning we could listen to the cassette player on holiday journeys. And what did we play on it? *Bridge over Troubled Water* by Simon & Garfunkel. Motorway long-hauls were how my sisters and I got to know it so well. My aunt and uncle taped it for us on their posh music centre. They may have taped their copy rather than Mum's. They could always have borrowed a neighbour's in an emergency.

They also taped a small pile of folk albums, specifically Irish folk. Mum now kept track of the folk scene through the weekly *Melody Maker* section, but this stuff had been in the house for ages, one particularly well-played album being *Isn't It Grand Boys* by The Clancy Brothers & Tommy Makem.

The cover shows four chaps in formal evening wear marching towards the camera with cable-knit jumpers over their arms: Celtic roots meet mainstream entertainment. Its songs had become standard fare at home. When the mood took hold, Mum would belt out the sea-shanty 'Westering Ho' like she was on stage in a glare of spotlights, rather than rummaging in a damp napkin-bucket by the light of a 60-watt.

That and others from the album were regularly sung to us and they are among the first songs my sisters ever got to know. I liked the title track because it had the word "bloody" in it, but the one I remember in most detail was 'Nancy Whisky'. This opens side one and is a cautionary tale about becoming reliant on the Devil's piss. The protagonist begins by enjoying a tipple, then by drinking more regularly in defiance of his mother's warnings.

The drink is personified in the lyric, hence the title – he kisses Nancy and her smiles return his love. Then one day he tries to rise from his bed and can't get up. I was fascinated by this situation: trying to get out of bed and not being able to move because of booze. I knew whisky to be one of those adult drinks that repulsed me to even sniff, but now I knew more. I imagined the room he was lying in: tattered curtains, grubby rug on the floor. A sense of seediness put into my head by what was, therefore, a good song.

Seediness brings us to the Dubliners. This earthy bunch were notorious for 'Seven Drunken Nights', a song about a man whose wife is having an affair right under his nose, but he is too shit-faced to notice what is going on. He sees a different piece of evidence every night - a horse outside the door, an unfamiliar coat on his hook and a strange pipe in his ashtray for example. But his wife confidently explains them away as various gifts from her mother - specifically a sow, a shawl and a tin whistle - adding that the reason he doesn't realise this is because he's drunk again.

There are only five verses on the version that was a hit in 1967: the final two are far too blue and would never have been played on Radio 1. In fact, I don't imagine that the rest of it got played, either. I didn't become familiar with this little ditty until I was older, but I did know its sibling song, 'Maids When You're Young Never Wed an Old Man'. As its spoken introduction states, its purpose is to warn young ladies against pairing up with mature gentlemen, as they have no "faloorum" and have lost their "ding-doorum"; compared, that is, to lusty, younger specimens. A fair point. Mum explained it to us in a very matter-of-fact way. We played the song to a teenager from a neighbouring tent one summer and he went away blushing.

This kind of folk was fun, tuneful and communal; a rancour of banjo, whistle and snarling, swaying voices. There were a number of Irish acts on our car tapes, but one band topped the lot. They had the tunes, the musicianship and an additional touch of class. They were called Planxty and their eponymous debut LP was special. For months, it decorated our lives like nothing else could.

The voice of lead singer Christy Moore was at once gentle, sad and assertive; he sang tenderly, yet on the brink of a menacing growl, as he rattled through lyrical tale after lyrical tale, a lady-o here, a gypsy-o there. The other defining aspect of their sound was that of the uilleann pipes, the Irish alternative to the bagpipes. There were two main differences: one, the wind for the uilleann pipes was provided by pumping a pouch with your elbow, and two, the uilleann pipes were far, far easier on the ear. I've had my ups and downs with bagpipes. Their sound is harsh and invasive and the idea that their original purpose was scaring the hell out of the enemy in battle makes absolute sense. Nobody could ever speak in such a way of the uilleann pipes. Planxty's Liam O'Flynn was, we were told, the piping champion of Ireland and some of the melodies he delivered could turn fearsome men to jelly.

The album's opening track showcases this superbly: 'The Raggle Taggle Gypsy' is a tale of forbidden love which races through verses and instrumental breaks until, abruptly and without any signal, the rhythm and mood has changed and we are in a graceful instrumental called 'Tabhair Dom Do Laimh' (don't ask, I can't remember) which unfurls gradually, the pipes carrying the tune on a bed of guitar and mandolin, its melody rising, falling, then rising further, until it has won you.

Just as you're recovering, up starts the second track, 'Arthur McBride', a tale of two fine fellows out for a stroll by the sea when they meet a sergeant, a corporal and a drummer from the British Army who attempt to enlist them. Within the cheerful confines of a cracking tune, we are told that they wield their shillelaghs quicker than the soldiers can draw their swords and deal with them decisively, which may or may not mean clubbing them to death.

Christy doesn't sing lead on this one; it's either Andy Irvine or Donal Lunny, I'm not sure which. Following this is another spine-tingling instrumental, 'Planxty Irwin', then the delicate 'Sweet Thames Flow Softly', and on it goes. Other treasures include the reel 'Merrily Kissed the Quaker', where the melody is repeated with a layer of instrumentation added each time, until it's a full-on party involving everything the band can hold at once. It rocks. In the car, we re-wound the cassette to hear this again and again.

Planxty represent another important milestone for me. My first gigs were Planxty ones. Mum was meeting folkie friends at clubs and concerts as often as babysitters would allow. Having reacted so positively to the album, I was taken along to venues such as Wandsworth Town Hall, which had a capacity of about five hundred and was packed to the gunnels with pissed-up Paddies. In terms of my life as a gig-goer, this was in at the deep end. It was noise and rowdiness, men clambering over seats rather than edging along rows, a constant throng of bodies in each aisle lugging drinks, a steady haze of cigarette smoke between us and the stage lights; many an "Oh, Jesus!" as an exclamation for any circumstance.

The crowd was boisterous enough to elicit reprimands from the band, gathered in dignified calm on the boards. I remember Liam O'Flynn, sitting on his stool, pipes under his elbow, leaning slowly towards the mic and telling some inebriated pest "I don't think you're addin' anything to the proceedin's at all", for which he received a huge cheer.

To be fair, there were probably huge cheers throughout; for Christy and his wonderful voice, Liam and his pipes, Andy and Donal covering vocals and a range of instruments including tin whistle, mandolin and hurdy-gurdy, playing us this fantastic stuff wearing jeans, t-shirts and cotton waistcoats and sporting their unclipped early 70s hair and sideburns. Donal would soon be replaced in the band by Paul Brady. All these guys are well-known to Celtic folkies. Christy Moore and Paul Brady are still touring as I write.

At the other end of the folk experience sat the Spinners. They were squeaky-clean and multi-ethnic, in black trousers and polo-necked tops. Each wore a different medallion to add character. They chatted pleasantly between songs and offended no-one. It was a studied image. In 1950s America there had been the Weavers, a massively popular group singing traditional songs enjoyed by ordinary folks, mixed in with modern protest songs. They took their name from honest-to-goodness proletarian labour. Because of this and their championing of good causes they became targeted by commie-bashing McCarthyite prosecutors, as a result of which they became significantly less popular. Weavers, Spinners: see the connection? At the start of the 70s there was also a soul act called the Spinners who, at the time, were recording on Motown. Because the folk group were so well-established in key markets – playing to packed concert halls, selling albums, being on television a lot – the soul group had to change their name to the Detroit Spinners.

The Spinners emphasised the English folk tradition but sang songs from around the world. They did that American one about little boxes on the hillside made out of ticky-tacky and all the same, which is a good observation of dull conformity, except that in the hands of these singing teddy bears it became a vehicle for dull conformity. They were the subject of a sneering send-up on a TV sketch show that I can't remember the name of, where the little boxes lyric was changed into a summary of their super-nice habits. I was taken to see them at the Royal Festival Hall, which was full of comfortably-seated, sober people breathing clean air and clapping politely. I heard no mention of a violently-wielded shillelagh or a two-timing lady-o, let alone an "Oh, Jesus!"

Speaking of whom, we were still going to church at this point. For Mum it was an opportunity for a bit of peace and quiet. I kept going until I started playing Sunday football at thirteen. Going to church was a chore but once there, I adjusted to its pace and atmosphere. The smells were different; rich wood and stone. It was a contrast. Also, some of the hymns were terrific. The sermons meant little to us; it was an exercise in staying still and quiet until the next song, or until invited into the Sunday School room for some colouring in. I don't remember doing anything else at Sunday school although I'm sure this is unfair.

I liked 'Praise, My Lord, the King of Heaven' for its shifting chords and melody, and its strong chorus of "praise Him, praise Him". For years I thought this was the hymn's title. There was another strong melody in one which I have recently discovered is called 'Praise to the Lord, the Almighty, the King of Creation', although I could never work out how all its syllables fit into the rhythm and still can't. Perhaps they don't.

But my favourite was an absolute belter: 'God is Love', the full title of which is apparently 'God is Love, His the Care'. I remember it more in school assemblies than in church. There was a retired lady with grey hair in a bun who came in to play the upright piano. She just seemed to magically appear whenever piano was required. One of the teachers strummed a guitar in assemblies sometimes, but whenever we needed piano, in came this lady. I don't remember her ever speaking, but she thumped the heck out of those keys.

'God is Love' begins with a sequence of seven descending notes that brought to mind feet stomping down stairs, the eighth step being the first note of the verse. She loved playing those seven notes; I remember the look on her face. They had a galvanising effect on us too, making us fill our lungs ready to get busy with this grand, percussive melody. We sang it better than anything else apart from 'Lord of the Dance'. The chorus went "Sing a-loud! Loud! Loud!" and finished with an all-guns-blazing "Praise Him!" Then that seven-note step-down again. Fantastic. Far and away the best hymn I ever knew.

In the mid-90s, a friend got married in the chapel at her old school and 'God is Love' was on the order of service. Weddings stir the emotions all by themselves, but when the organ fired up with those seven notes, in that setting, on that occasion, I utterly failed to sing straight.

I mentioned 'Lord of the Dance', which is a school assembly evergreen and was sung at least once a month in our primary. The song's status is well-deserved and it has permeated our culture sufficiently for it to have been adapted by football fans: *Fight, fight, wherever you may be; we are the boys from the Black Country*, etcetera. Not quite as fully in praise of Christ as the original.

It was the most famous of a number of songs written by Sydney Carter that were in our assembly song books; 'One More Step' and 'When I Needed a Neighbour' being two others. The lady on the piano enjoyed the latter because there was an emphatic *dun-dun-dun* with which to accentuate the end of each chorus: "And the creed and the colour and the name won't matter; were you there? *Dun-dun-dun*". Someone I met years later told me that his friends used to mutter their own extension to this, so that their version ended: "Were you there? *Dun-dun-dun*. Was I fuck".

Other assembly mainstays were a mixture of those I sometimes heard in church and others I never did: 'All Things Bright and Beautiful' and 'Onward Christian Soldiers' sometimes, 'Morning Has Broken' (by Cat Stevens, on *20 Star Tracks*) never. Another song very popular at that time was 'Streets of London', a portrait of lonely, forgotten people that we should think about instead of feeling sorry for ourselves. The verses painted vivid pictures of these poor souls which easily won our sympathy, but the song had a patronising tone that alienated many, including almost every adult I ever heard comment on it. It was nonetheless sung in many an assembly and its composer, Ralph McTell, took it to number two in the charts.

There remains another brace of these songs I should mention, if only for their strangeness. One was called 'I Lift My Eyes'. Its gentle tune was more of a meandering keyboard intro than a melody; it seemed to lack some vital ingredient to make it a proper song. It was "silent hills" that the eyes were lifted towards, making their owner consider the Lord as a source of strength.

The other was called 'Last Night I Had the Strangest Dream'. In this dream, men in a mighty room signed documents saying they would never go to war again, while outside, crowds were dancing in celebration on scattered weapons and uniforms, eschewing the opportunity to seize power during this temporary lapse in authority.

We went home singing all these songs and our various parents disagreed on their worthiness. Mum was appalled by 'Last Night I Had the Strangest Dream', saying it was so soppy it made her feel nauseous. I think I might have agreed. Mind you, the Vietnam War was still raging and various atrocities were being committed in Africa. It wasn't the loveliest of times. A bit of tissue-twisting sentimentality couldn't hurt that much, surely. The teachers organising our assemblies clearly thought so.

We followed the words to these songs on the overhead projector. This did not mean cricking our necks to gaze towards the ceiling. You wrote in marker pen on a rectangle of thick, clear film and placed it on a glass plate over a strong light. The writing was projected through a small window in a gadget above it, reflected and magnified, then thrown onto a screen for the audience. You focused it in the same way as a telescope. Two fourth-year children (Year 6 in new money) were given the job of overhead projector monitors. They set it up and operated it, then put it away at the end. Next year we would be fourth years. I did not aspire to be an overhead projector monitor. I aspired to be a music monitor.

These special ones got to choose music from the school's record box to play on the portable player at the beginning of assemblies as everyone filed in, then again at the end as they filed back out. And it really was their choice - I asked them. However, I soon learned that they had developed a sense of the acceptable. 'The Ballroom Blitz' would not have been acceptable, but certain orchestral tunes were; 'Morning' from *Peer Gynt* by Grieg, for example. This tune was as ubiquitous in our world as 'Lord of the Dance'; that floating flute and oboe melody seemed to be everywhere. Also acceptable: Handel. Some parts of *Firework Music* and *Water Music* are more than capable of captivating ten-year-olds – we heard 'Allegro, Alla Hornpipe' from *Water Music* a lot. Then there was 'Eine Kleine Nachtmusik' by Mozart: enormous, thrilling strings that grabbed you by the lapels and covered you with hard kisses, but a copy with a deep scratch on it. Even when I hear it digitally now, I know where the loud clicks come and where it starts to jump. The fourth year music monitors played it anyway.

At a time when boys' birthday treats would consist of a group of friends being taken to a First or Second Division football match via a Wimpy Bar, one of my best friends did something different. His Mum took five of us to see a ballet, *Swan Lake*, in Covent Garden. We were way back, up in the top circle, grappling with the binoculars that were fixed to the backs of the seats in front. I knew the main tune from somewhere, so I imagine I spent a lot of the performance waiting for it. But I can't remember how I felt about going in the first place. In those days, "poof" was an everyday term of abuse, one that you might have levelled at you for having moulded studs on your football boots instead of screw-ins, or spreading peanut butter too thinly on your toast, never mind watching a bunch of geezers springing about in tights.

However, apart from the giggly fun with mates, the one thing about the occasion that I can recall with clarity was the ending. In a heady swirl of dramatic music, with the dancers racing around in apparent chaos, a final, dramatic chord was played to signify the death in the story and, as it sounded, the dancers fell to the floor in the shape of a crucifix. I wasn't expecting anything like this. I was stunned, staring open-mouthed, my heart thumping. Absolutely brilliant. I've had a soft spot for ballet ever since and I can't say the same about opera. I raved about this to some of the boys at cubs. They said I was a poof.

1974 began with a new single from the Sweet. It was very good indeed, closer in feel to 'Blockbuster' than either of the two since, with the added ingredient of a fade-in apparently taken from a concert; a crowd of girls chanting "We want Sweet! We want Sweet!" in a rhythm which turns out to be in step with the guitar and drum intro that suddenly kicks in. Devilishly clever. It sounded great.

The song was 'Teenage Rampage', its lyric claiming that teenagers were taking command all over the land and would soon be in total control, so if you're the right age, join in or else. Where such a train of events would leave a ten-year-old I wasn't sure and I felt slightly alienated, but the rest of it was easily good enough to win me over. The Sweet fan in my class was particularly enthusiastic about its chart prospects.

Inevitably, it got stuck at number two. This was now getting ridiculous. The culprit this time was 'Tiger Feet', the new single by Mud, a record that everybody seemed to have heard before me. I turned up for school one day and the place was buzzing about it. Maybe I had missed an important *Top of the Pops*. Having paved the way with 'Dyna-Mite' they had gone the extra few yards with the next one and topped the charts. Bully for them, but it wasn't as good; a bit too fast and the lyrics were silly. That's right, that's right, that's right, that's right; that's neat, that's neat, that's neat, that's neat; he really loved her tiger feet. Really? What kind of girl has feet like a tiger? And what kind of bloke gets excited about them?

It didn't matter. If I was grumping about it, I was on my own. It was a huge dollop of silly fun underpinned by a cracking guitar line; the band were likeable and you could imagine them turning up at your door out of the blue, asking if the kettle was on. 'Tiger Feet' will be making people smile for a long time yet.

My group of friends must have done a lot of smiling that year; apparently we were exactly the right age. In a book I once read, a friend of the author was quoted, recalling how, at the age of eleven or twelve, he had been strolling through the summer countryside with friends when a thought occurred to him. He recognised that, for the last few years, life had been getting better and better; he now wondered whether this was how it was going to be for the rest of his life.

This is recounted knowingly, recognising that adolescence was lying in wait, with its harsh lessons, bewildering setbacks and periods of unproductive introspection. But at that special point, you have the best of everything: security, recognition, independence within your known world as well as glimpses of intriguing new ones, and the company of friends for whom simply being around you is enough. Comfort, satisfaction and excitement all in one, every day, for month upon month.

Not everybody has this precise experience of course; but it makes a valid point about a particular stage in life. This is where I was in 1974 and I wonder whether this is the key reason why records from that year sound and feel so brilliant. There are no negative connotations. They raise no threat, they are not downers even if they tell tragic tales. They gleam and shimmer in the merest of light.

For someone fifteen years younger than I am, it is entirely possible that the records from 1989 are all of these things when, for me, that was a year of anguish and struggle. That doesn't mean I resent its music, there are records from any year that bring me sunshine, including several from 1989. But there does seem to be a massive concentration of them in 1974. The dirty great secondary was still a year and a half away when I spent my pocket money on 'Teenage Rampage'. This was the start of my golden time. We each have our own 1974.

Mine was full of sounds that were bright and un-cynical, borrowing from glam and the Rock 'n' Roll Revival but aiming at a younger audience. Deadened drums, cute melodies, songs of romance. Many of these records were on the mighty Bell label which, between 1974 and 1976, was dominant in the UK singles chart.

Among its acts were the Drifters, a suited-up vocal group from the US who had been shuffling their line-up since the 50s. They sang about smooching with their baby in various places; at the club, at the movies, under the boardwalk, up on the roof, down on the beach, you name it. Love was a sweet, cuddly business and Johnny Moore was a sweet, cuddly lead singer, the oldest teenager in town. They signed for Bell in the early 70s. 'Kissin' in the Back Row of the Movies' was a big hit in '74: a tribute to sweet, cuddly nights out. They followed it up with 'Down on the Beach Tonight', a guy promising a heartbroken girl a sweet, cuddly recovery if she meets him there later. Their hits were stylish arrangements, with strings and everything; a touch of class.

Tartan-encrusted teenybop idols the Bay City Rollers were on Bell. With a "hi-de-hi-de-ho" and a "shoo-be-do-ay", their popularity exploded and eclipsed that of established heart-throbs like David Cassidy, who was also on Bell. Rollermania was a genuine phenomenon. Girls as young as eight came into conflict with the authorities in our school for refusing to remove tartan scarves from their wrists. I bought and enjoyed 'All of Me Loves All of You' and, in a moment of terminological giddiness, I told my drum teacher I thought it was "beautiful". He snorted and pretended the conversation had never happened.

Terry Jacks hit number one with 'Seasons in the Sun', a song about someone going around saying goodbye to everyone in preparation for his death. Perhaps he was going to top himself, perhaps he had some terminal illness. I don't suppose he would be wandering off visiting people if he was in police custody awaiting execution, but then again, he could have been writing letters. As he sang, he sounded like he was either about to cry or puke into a bowl. See, it must be a clever record; I'm still scratching my head about it decades later. Anyway, that was on Bell, too.

So was 'Guilty' by the Pearls, a female vocal duo whose records had an indefinable charm. 'Guilty' uses prosecution and imprisonment as a huge metaphor for falling in love, piling law-enforcement reference upon law-enforcement reference in a melody that springs a succession of nice surprises on you. It was one of my favourite records of the year. Gary Glitter was on Bell. So too were the Glitter Band, his backing group, who had a string of hits in their own right, starting with the intense, great-sounding 'Angel Face'.

Having won ITV's *New Faces* talent show, Showaddywaddy were signed to Bell for a terrific launch single called 'Hey Rock 'N' Roll' and its follow-up, 'Rock 'N' Roll Lady'. The drape and brothel-creeper floodgates were now truly open. There was also cherub-faced Barry Blue, who had five Top 30 hits on Bell, three of which - 'Dancin' On a Saturday Night' (from 1973), 'Miss Hit and Run' and 'Hot Shot' - are worthy of attention and full of 1974-ness. 'Hot Shot' is mental and has Cossacks on it. Honestly.

Olivia Newton-John was not on Bell. She was on Pye and also on TV a lot in the spring, because she was about to represent the UK in the Eurovision Song Contest. She was Australian, but born in Britain, so it was fine. The song, 'Long Live Love', was okay-ish, a board-level view of what made a good Eurovision entry - echoes of past UK successes with a bit of oompah-oompah thrown in.

But the previous two winners had set the bar high with strong songs and powerful vocal performances. In 1972 it was 'Come What May' by Vicky Leandros, a full-on, arms-out belter of a chorus to rattle the rafters and impress the voting juries. A year later, it was 'Wonderful

Dream' by Anne-Marie David, a distraught song of loss which had been the first record I ever bought on that lemon-yellow and black Epic label. It got right under my skin and I thought having the French version on the B-side was great.

Both had been the entries from Luxembourg; surely that teeny country couldn't make it a hat-trick? Mum invited two other mums round and a crowd of kids huddled together in the lounge with cushions, fizzy drinks and bowls of crisps, to cheer Olivia on. The mums drifted in and out to check on us, see what rubbish was on now and pinch crisps. 'Long Live Love' was on early, so then we had to sit through the rest.

Half an hour or so later, a group with the funny little name Abba came on. At first I thought they were Dutch because they had a cute blonde singer who reminded me of a girl on the cover of a Dutch phrase book we had. Actually they were Swedish. Within seconds of the start of their song, our allegiances had shifted. The lounge was full of wide eyes, straight backs and excited bouncing on bottoms.

This was, manifestly, miles and miles better than anything else we were likely to hear that evening. It was fast and loud and catchy and had enough energy to fly rockets to the moon. It was as if someone had taken the best bits from our favourite records of the past year and assembled them in just the right order, added a few flourishes of their own, then turned the volume up. It even had a little motif in it which featured in about half of all records released at that time – *duh-dun, duh-dun, duh-dun* – which signalled the end of a passage or phrase, seemingly to take the place of drum fills.

It was glam-era pop distilled, both in its sound and in its look. The guitarist had silver platform boots that came up to his shiny, silken knees. His instrument was a jaggedy silver star with strings. The cute blonde singer had her own silver platforms and was in blue sparkly stuff thereafter; a second girl singer beside her was more soberly dressed in caramel silks. Then there was a bloke with a beard on keyboards and a bloke with a moustache on bass. The song was called 'Waterloo' and, when the votes of the juries began to be collected, we cheered whenever it got high marks, all patriotism jettisoned.

The mums drifted in to see what the fuss was about: "We're doing well, are we?" "No, Mum, we want the other one to win!" And win it did, emphatically. When it was released as a single a few weeks later, it flew to number one and the world was a wonderful place. I now had my second single on that lemon-yellow and black Epic label.

Among the other number ones of the year were three from the summer. First, George McCrae's delicious 'Rock Your Baby', widely thought of as the first proper disco record; ecstatic falsetto vocals, shimmering guitar and keyboards. Next, 'When Will I See You Again' by American girl group the Three Degrees; a woman wanting to know where this relationship was going, polished into an epic by its orchestration. The final quarter is the best bit, the backing vocals turning the title into warm waves that wash over you repeatedly – you just don't want it to end. This is exactly the bit that DJs talk over if ever it gets played on the radio. Last: 'Love Me for a Reason' by the other big-league teen idols of the era, the Osmonds; their only really good record. Apart, that is, from 'Crazy Horses'; an electrifying nuthouse of a tune that you still can't believe was truly made by these disinfected bastions of the granny-comforting mainstream. Anyway, 'Love Me for a Reason' is a fine ballad.

I didn't properly appreciate any of these three at the time, but I mention them to give a balanced flavour of the year they appeared in. This balanced flavour is helpful in discussing a group that forms a bridge between the Rock 'n' Roll Revival and an act that was about to tear my allegiance away from the Sweet.

Four

Tartan scarves, as worn by the Bay City Rollers, were commercially available and easy to get hold of. Cotton hats, as worn by the Rubettes, were not. I never saw any in British Home Stores at any rate.

There are common misconceptions about Rubettes hats. Firstly, they were not cloth caps. Cloth caps were grey or mock tweed and went from crown to brow in one continuous slope, with the peak either stitched in or connected with a small popper. The Rubettes hat was a white cloth pancake with a matching button in the middle and a matching, unconnected, peak beneath. It was close in design to the classic Brooklyn cap, but shallower and not in sections, although the hem made it look like it might be. It was also more malleable. It looked best when worn off-centre, flopping over the side of the head.

I never had a proper one of my own. I got white hats in jumble sales that had the right shape, but never the right material. The Brooklyn cap was approximated in women's fashion, often in big, fat wool versions. I wore one of these in public once. It's not the sort of mistake you repeat.

Along with the hats, the Rubettes wore suits, like an American soul group; big shirt collars, flared trousers. Alan Williams had a cute little boy's face and his constant half-smile followed the camera as he sang. The camera didn't mind one bit. Paul Richardson was yer classic 70s clown drummer. He had speaking parts on their early records which he never took seriously in television performances, pulling silly faces as he mouthed the words – he was showing off like a kid and other kids thought this was great.

The rest of the band looked like a bunch of your dad's immature mates, goofing around down the pub while their marriages floundered. Like Mud, they were jobbing musicians, rescued from a life of sessions and club gigs by a songwriting/production duo, in this case Wayne Bickerton and Tony Waddington, who, for the record, did not go by the brand name Bickeriwadd. They were on Polydor, the same label as bloody Slade. Their first single was a huge number one.

'Sugar Baby Love' was a chunk of smooth, blue-eyed soul with a super-big, beautifully orchestrated sound. It began with a four-part harmony that built up, tantalisingly, voice by voice, over a rich, bassy beat, before exploding into the intro proper; a powerful, commanding falsetto singing "doobie-la-la" over sweeping strings and a "bub-shu-wally" backing vocal - cartoonish, yet manly. For the verse, the falsetto changed into an equally strong tenor. This bloke could sing.

It was a making-up song; they've hit rocky ground, he's been hurtful but he wants to love it all better. You believed him because of the record's heady atmosphere, helped along by those backing vocals, by strings that were soaring here, pizzicato there, by tubular chimes that marked a three-note descent between chords, an arrangement feature that sent tingles across your skin, one which Bickerton and Waddington would use again. It gave kids a taste of what being in love must feel like. It sounded like the best American import for years. Britain raced to the record shop. If you took the major hits of the year mentioned earlier – 'Rock Your Baby', 'When Will I See You Again', 'Love Me for a Reason', 'Seasons in the Sun', 'Kissin' in the Back Row of the Movies', 'Hey Rock 'N' Roll', 'Waterloo' – and whizzed them together in a giant blender, 'Sugar Baby Love' is what you would get. Grand, assertive, yet sweet and cuddly, it sounds more like 1974 than any other record.

Bickerton and Waddington recorded it using session musicians. It wasn't Alan Williams singing the lead vocal. That job was done by Paul da Vinci, who, having recorded that one song, turned down the offer of joining the group and never fronted them in public. He reappeared solo at the end of the summer with 'Your Baby Ain't Your Baby Anymore', a good record, rich in 1974-ness, that deserved better than a peak of number twenty.

The Rubettes, meanwhile, changed tack and became major standard-bearers for the Rock 'N' Roll Revival. Chewing their candy and sipping their soda pop, they leant against the record machine while staring at the girl in the tight blue jeans; soon they would ride to the high school hop, where they would do the jive and the stroll 'til morning light.

They told us of a dance called the juke box jive, which – trust them – had been all the rage back in 1955. They named a single after it, but gave us vague, unhelpful instructions in the lyric and didn't demonstrate it on *Top of the Pops*. It was all a matter of faith, the enjoyment of a world we could never truly experience. Their debut album, *Wear Its 'At*, opened with 'Way Back in the Fifties' a track whose lyric laid this world out before us in all its glory. At the start of the song, he tells us that he was in his teens in the 50s. My reaction to this was not "Urrgh! That means he must be over 30!" It was "Wow. He was *there*".

But I'm jumping ahead. I didn't begin to appreciate the Rubettes until 'Juke Box Jive' became a hit at Christmas. The main reason was that 'Sugar Baby Love' prevented one of the best records of the whole era from getting to number one.

Being in a family whose adults had grown up on cowboy movies, we got to hear various scraps of Western dialogue spoken in playful moments, one of which was "This town ain't big enough for the both of us – and it ain't me that's leavin'..." One Saturday morning, as I waited in the car for Mum, I heard a new record that, with minor modification, had this as its pivotal lyric.

It was built around a three-note keyboard motif which reappeared with a different arrangement after each chorus. The vocal sound was like nothing in my experience; tense, fidgety alto, slipping into reckless falsetto. And what was that accent? German? The bits of melody making up the verse barely, if at all, fit the chords they were being sung over. There was mention of "increasing heartbeat", then the short chorus "This town ain't big enough for both of us" and then, brilliantly, gunfire; the echoes of which dovetailed with "And it ain't me who's gonna leave", before the motif returned in a crashing blare of keyboard and guitar, bass and drums pounding. Bloody Nora.

I had no trouble remembering that it was called 'This Town Ain't Big Enough for Both of Us' or that it was by Sparks. The group's name seemed like an understatement. That afternoon, back at home, I heard it on the radio again. The next morning we went down the Walworth Road, the thoroughfare connecting Camberwell with the Elephant & Castle, to its neighbouring market on East Street. There were other reasons for us to go "down The Lane" but, on this occasion, there was only one that mattered.

A1 Stores was an electronics shop on the main road, whose frontage was dominated by elaborate household lighting displays. Deep in the back, like a cave, was a popular record department. On a wall behind its counter and away from grabbing customer hands, the entire Top 30 was stored, 15 or 20 copies of each, in order, waiting to be requested for purchase. In other record shops they were stored vertically on shelves, with tabs to separate them and mark their chart position. A1 Stores had custom-built wooden units storing them horizontally.

There was a lip at the front of each compartment to stop them sliding out, with a gap in the middle so you could lift and extract them. On each side of this gap were fixtures for slotting in squares of brightly coloured card; the title handwritten on one, the artist on the other. They were in order of chart position, so once a week everything had to be taken out and re-housed. A labour of love. Around the charting ones were others with cardboard stars telling you this one was "new".

The store had a small subsidiary outlet right at the crowded start of the market, catching both eye and ear as you edged your way towards the vegetables, fabrics and sarsaparilla, tempting you to part with 50p for that song you quite liked. On Sundays, a canopied wagon-stall with the same storage and labelling system did a similar job. This was where I got it.

It was the first single I had ever owned on the Island label and it came in a pink sleeve. Now, I was very much a boysy boy: racing car sets, toy soldiers and football, football, football. But I have a long-standing soft spot for candy pink and this may have been the start of it. The label design consisted of the word "island" moulded into a chunky little island shape, its first letter tall and crowned with palm leaves. From behind it, yellow sun rays fanned out towards white clouds. A thin pink circle went round the whole thing.

Apart from the RAK yacht, I had never seen so much colour and detail on a record label before. Label designs were still relatively plain, although, a few weeks earlier, CBS had gone mad and changed their time-honoured blood orange to a bright meld going from orange at the top to yellow at the bottom. It came in a speckled monochrome sleeve, making it look a bit like an orange gang and a yellow gang having a punch-up in a pepper shop.

The Island design added an unexpected dimension to my purchase. It was all very alien. Like the record itself. When I got it home, I found that the keyboard motif formed a long fade-in at the intro, sounding like a ghostly ice-cream van roaming the streets looking for you. Reading the label, I discovered that the producer was called Muff. It just kept getting better.

The song seemed to be about trying to meet a girl in town while there was a gangland war going on. Interesting enough, but then there was all this stuff about being grabbed by cannibals, about scary air stewardesses and rampaging mega fauna. Maybe it was meant to be mad. It certainly didn't spoil it, quite the opposite. The B-side was good, too; 'Barbecutie', presumably about a cute girl at a barbecue, had a languid, lolloping verse and a bright, poppy chorus. I played both, over and over. I felt different.

Soon afterwards, we saw them on *Top of the Pops*. The singer, with a dark mane of hair, juddered as he sang, leaning towards you with wide eyes, as if bursting into the room to tell you something unbelievable. The bass player, guitarist and drummer were in smart, inoffensive mid-70s garb, flares and wide collars, getting on with the job.

Then there was the bony-faced keyboard player sitting at the front. His hair was greased back and he had a little moustache that made you think of Hitler. He sat, lips pursed, motionless except for his fingers and slight, slow turns of the head and rolling of the eyes, in the midst of all this belting noise. Perhaps he was a cold-blooded killer. Perhaps he was mentally ill, unable to do anything apart from this. Perhaps, if you teased him, he might start crying. He wasn't normal. Everybody was talking about him the next morning, most of them pulling faces.

The boy in my class who had loved 'Crazy' by Mud had become the friend that I spent most time discussing music with. We swapped notes on new releases, things we had read, and lyrics that amused, baffled or embarrassed us. He was as keen on the Sparks single as I was. We watched as it flew up the charts, going to three, then two, but then staying there because of 'Sugar Baby Love.'

This was, of course, greatly disappointing, but then again the record was so different, so strange, that it was somehow understandable. It seemed a triumph of the underworld rather than a heroic failure. These people didn't belong anywhere, yet they had got all the way to there. And in any case, I was a dab hand at being stuck at number two.

We nevertheless pooled our disgust, consoling each other with the fact that we knew about 'Barbecutie', when most others didn't. This was good bonding because, in the course of our note-swapping, we came to realise that we didn't agree on much. That summer, he would be laughing and shaking his head at me for buying 'Judy Teen' by Cockney Rebel, a record that I felt very grown up for liking. It was about grown up people having grown up fun at a fairground thanks to this charismatic girl, its theme played on plucked strings in a re-freshing, grown up arrangement with an intriguing vocal. Do check it out. In the lyric, he mentions stroking her face, but there is a big delay between the 'f' and the rest of the word, so that it sounds like he's stroking her "ace". I'm afraid I leapt to grown up conclusions about that. But I got no credit from my friend.

His birthday had been a few weeks before Sparks appeared, and among the records at his party was 'Remember You're a Womble' by the Wombles, TV's furry litter-pickers. Their theme tune had already been a hit and this did even better, its folky fiddle making it ideal for dancing to with Granny. Beside it was the new Carpenters single, 'Jambalaya (On the Bayou)', an annoying cover of a tedious country standard. I didn't know what a bayou was, and initially wondered how anyone could have big fun on a biro; you'll possibly understand what I mean if you're ever unfortunate enough to hear it.

By contrast, he also had this ultra-heavy death record called 'Emma' by Hot Chocolate, which had clearly caught his imagination judging by the amount of time he spent talking about it. I couldn't stand that, either. His present from me was 'Seven Seas of Rhye' by a group called Queen, on that caramel-and-red EMI label, with a noble, galloping rhythm that seemed to fit their name, and a posh rendition of 'Oh, I Do Like to Be Beside the Seaside' at the fade. My memory is that the Wombles got played more than anything else.

He had never been particularly keen on the Sweet, but then most people were about to become a little less keen on them. Just as the summer holidays were beginning, they put a new single out. It was called 'The Six Teens' and it was difficult to like. I tried hard, I bought it early and played it time and again, encouraging it to enthuse me as it anxiously described the situations of three teenage couples and passed judgement on whether or not they were going to "make it", without a clue as to why it all had to be so bleak.

Its B-side, 'Burn On the Flame', was at least lively and distracting, and fires up a memory of being at Brockwell Park lido with friends from cubs, on a hot afternoon when we unexpectedly met a gang of girls from my school and had an unexpectedly great time with them. Well done, the B-side. The Sweet fan from our class was as puzzled and disappointed by 'The Six Teens' as I was. Sweet fans all over the country must have felt the same way. It struggled to number nine.

Hot on its heels came a follow-up by Sparks. 'Amateur Hour' had another striking keyboard motif, more of that big, reverberating sound and hooks all over the place; a solid chunk of gorgeous noise. It makes me think of being at a seafront fairground in Ayr, whose big wheel stood perpendicular to the beach, so that, as you came over the top, it felt like you were about to be slung out into the waves. Mum's terror was one of the reasons we enjoyed it so much. We also loved the ground-level attractions such as the Waltzer, which blared pop from grimy speakers to enhance the thrill of the ride.

Everybody has their favourite fairground record, one that represents velocity, flashing lights and a lace of danger, one that gets the pulse racing all by itself. 'Amateur Hour' is mine. Its lyric made me leap to more of my grown up conclusions: it mentions "one night stands" and "turning pro", and I casually told my grandad that it was about prostitution. I don't know what that did to his pulse.

I didn't buy it. I imagine I must have considered 'This Town Ain't Big Enough for Both of Us' to have been a glorious one-off, paying less attention as their second one came and went from the Top 10. Yet I remember that fairground, and Sparks remained a distraction.

I found an article about them in Mum's *Melody Maker*, in which two girls said they had been to see them in concert but hadn't really "got it" until they woke up the following morning. It made me wonder how that must have worked. In another issue there was a review asserting that "Dinky Diamond is brilliant". I assumed this was the name of a song; great title, typical of such an oddball group. I learned that the singer and keyboard player were actually brothers, respectively Russell and Ron Mael.

One Sunday, after Tom Browne had played that week's number one, there was a programme featuring an interview with them and clips from tracks. I held my cassette player next to the radio to record it. The usual poor quality was worsened by the fact that the radio signal was weak; too close to the radiator or something. When I played it back I couldn't make out what was being said, but got the flavour of the tracks, one of which I felt had to be 'Dinky Diamond', it just seemed to fit its mood: more of that intense tempo and chiming keyboard, with the vocal high and manic. Never had a diamond sounded more dinky.

The programme played out with the third single, which I had already heard Ed "Stewpot" Steward play on *Junior Choice*, a down-tempo song called 'Never Turn Your Back on Mother Earth' that pressed a whole different set of buttons. I rewound it a hundred times. I decided I needed to own a Sparks album.

Happily, it was early November, two weeks before my birthday. In the meanwhile, Dad took us to a bonfire night party at a tennis club. We drew patterns in the night air with sparklers, throwing their remains into the sizeable bonfire, getting as close to it as we dared. There was a disco in the clubhouse, a DJ doing his stuff in a corner, enjoyed by a crowd on the parquet dance floor rather thinner than the one at the bar. A few weeks earlier, one of Mum's youngest cousins had got married, and the reception had been a delirious blur of hugs, laughter and chicken drumsticks during, as well as between, long bouts of dancing. The DJ must have known what he was doing because the music had seemed to enhance it all wonderfully, as well as causing some of the excitement all by itself. I wanted more and here was my chance, with the role of the chicken drumsticks played by a hot dog with onions.

The music was loud and it swept me away, right into the thick of it. I was letting it do things to me, letting it direct me, feeling nothing but warmth from my surroundings. It was amazing. I didn't know anyone in this range of ages, but they were all friends. I might have been there for ten minutes; it might have been an hour.

Two records stand out from this. One had a lyric that I heard as "bring in the shopping" and made me think of a young man carrying the bags in through the door with less of a struggle than Mum often displayed. It had a laid-back beat in the tradition of 'I'm a Believer' and 'Sugar, Sugar' and I loved its sound. I wouldn't hear it again for thirty years, eventually discovering that it was 'Window Shopping' by R. Dean Taylor, a member of the Motown songwriting staff who managed a few hits on the label in his own right, one of which, 'There's a Ghost in My House', had made it big a few months previously, having been discovered by the northern soul crowd. 'Window Shopping' sounded very different and came out on Polydor.

Listening to it as an adult took the shine off the bonfire night memory a little. Its lyric is about walking along a beach ogling girls in bikinis: "You can take your pick, if you're quick," it suggests. This is bad enough in a youngster; coming from a man in his mid-thirties it's downright unpleasant. Nevertheless, for thirty years I cherished a memory of bouncing along to a song about carrier bags in the hallway.

People were watching and smiling, guys with pints were calling "Go on, son!" At the end of the record, the DJ looked straight at me, now almost alone on the dance floor, and announced: "I'm dedicating this next one to my little jumping bean." And he played 'Honey Honey' by Sweet Dreams, a record which, for that and other reasons, I will love until I die.

It's a powerful cover of an Abba song; its bass line a speeded-up version of the one from the Beatles' 'Ob-La-Di, Ob-La-Da', its melody kissed all over by a shrill and characterful female vocal, its pipey keyboard arrangement meaning that it must be somebody's favourite fairground record – made for the Waltzer, or at least for a tennis club bonfire disco.

When you're that age, dancing like that, there's no concept of policy, of following a set series of moves or deporting yourself in a set way. You just move, doing what the record tells you. There are endless lyrics about music as liberation, praising the act of dancing as sweet relief from pain and drudgery. But out here in the big, bad world, it takes a strong personality to give completely free self-expression in movement, while retaining status in the eyes of their peers. Such creatures are rare. Dancing to 'Honey Honey' was heavenly. It was probably the last, truly unselfconscious dance I ever had in public.

In the lead-up to my eleventh birthday, Mum warned me that getting an album that was not a "Best Of" might be a disappointment. It was not going to be like *20 Star Tracks* or *That'll Be the Day*, with every song a hit. It was an ordinary album; the other songs won't be as good as the ones that had got into the charts – I did realise that, didn't I? This was good advice, and in the years to come I would buy albums in good faith only to wonder why I hadn't just bought the other single instead.

However, the first non-compilation LPs I ever owned on vinyl were *Kimono My House* and *Propaganda* by Sparks, and normal rules did not apply. For, on my birthday, I got not one Sparks album but two, the new one with 'Never Turn Your Back on Mother Earth' on it having been released that very week.

Between them, they constituted a world I could disappear into for days on end, regardless of where I was physically. It was a dark, foreboding world with the odd sunny interval; anxious, tragic, sometimes just potty - but it sounded spectacular. Every track was at least good and at least distracting, bursting with ideas both musical and lyrical.

Getting them was a feast for the senses. In contrast to the Ronco, Arcade or K-Tel compilations, their covers were rigid and glossy; wonderful to handle. They had a great smell, the rich, heady aroma of factory-fresh printed matter and vinyl. I held my nose inside them for long, gently humming moments.

Then there were the images. The front of the *Kimono My House* cover had two girls dressed as geishas, one feigning alarm, the other hamming it up with a fan. All the text was on the back, alongside shots of the band bordered in green.

Inside, there was more. I was used to white inner sleeves with holes for reading the labels through. Sometimes these had a polyethene lining. Sometimes – often with ten-inch records – the inner sleeve was just polyethene: a transparent u-shaped bag. But the *Kimono My House* inner was made of card and had stuff on it; not the first, but *my* first. On one side, a big, serious picture of the Mael brothers. On the other, in tiny italics, the album's lyrics. Above these, pictures of the group standing around giant letters spelling the band's name.

The *Propaganda* cover had no text at all apart from its title on a small square sticker which, I discovered, you weren't supposed to peel off. The image on both front and back featured Russel and Ron bound and gagged, being kidnapped, once at the stern of a speedboat, once at the rear window of a car. The inner sleeve was similar to that of its predecessor.

Never before had I been able to listen to an album whilst reading its lyrics. I discovered that Ron wrote almost all of the songs. This made things even more interesting; he was the font of tune and lyric, not just a creepy adornment. That's all of the senses covered except taste. I did not taste them, although giving a record a kiss before returning it to its sleeve is sometimes a perfectly reasonable thing to do.

The aspect of these albums to really emphasise is their sound. The production is excellent. Well done Muff Winwood. The mix is just right, the reverb is just right; it's huge and powerful without being blary or overbearing. There is a lovely, leathery quality to the bass which I don't remember from anywhere else. It's a feature to rank alongside Ron's keyboard and Russell's Teutonic tones.

Side one of *Kimono My House* opens with 'This Town Ain't Big Enough for Both of Us' and 'Amateur Hour', then on into what for me was the unknown. Big drums, then a church organ with dirty pipes, rocking back and forth in waltz time as Russell begins singing a paean to selfishness and narcissism called 'Falling in Love with Myself Again', which, characteristically, is both worrying and funny.

Next, 'Here in Heaven', a harrowing monologue by a man in the afterlife whose lover broke their suicide pact and didn't jump. Blimey. Elsewhere, 'Talent Is an Asset'; a song about competitive parents molly-coddling a precious child and making plans for his precious future. Also, I discovered that Dinky Diamond was not the name of a song at all, but the name of the drummer. The song that I thought was called 'Dinky Diamond' was actually called 'In My Family' and, on reflection, I have to say that 'Talent Is an Asset' was dinkier.

Propaganda begins with its title track, which is feverish, *a capella* and twenty-two seconds long. The moment it finishes, 'At Home, at Work, at Play' explodes into action. It sounds as if it's all one song because the same beat is kept through the link. It's a stunning way to open an album. 'At Home, at Work, at Play' is thunderous, intricate and groovy all at once and it quickly became my favourite non-single.

Other winners included 'Don't Leave Me Alone with Her' which, had it been an instrumental, would have made a cracking TV detective theme. The song describes a man desperately trying to stop people leaving a party so that he won't be left alone with "her". Charming. Perhaps she was pestering him to stroke her ace. Then there was a hurtling, two-and-a-half-minute crescendo entitled 'Something for the Girl with Everything', about someone buying luxury after luxury for a spoilt young lady, becoming increasingly bitter as he does so. Its rhythms and atmosphere grew on me steadily.

This was the one that the Sparks fan in my class liked best. He had somehow also acquired both albums at about the same time and so we now had something massive to share, swapping observations and preferences like duelling croupiers. We felt special. If you were quoting lyrics like: "Who knows what the wind's gonna bring when the invalids sing la-las" ('Atchoo', from *Propaganda*), you had to have something going for you. We had our own passports for the Land of Sparks.

I spent a long time living there. Entire episodes of your life can come and go in a month when you're eleven. In that first month, only two other records intruded.

Queen had reappeared with something really special called 'Killer Queen'. In some ways, it was similar to the Sparks stuff; clever and eventful, full of great bits. It's about a sharp, sophisticated lady who, we were assured, would blow our minds. It was the first time I had heard that expression and I liked it. I also liked the sound of the lazer beams and dynamite being promised. Every tiny detail, from its click-finger intro to its outrageous coda, is either inspired or refined until just right. The number of times I played my copy is probably something to worry about. Where did it get to in the charts? Number two.

The other intruder was 'Apache' by the Shadows. Yes, that's right: the instrumental which topped the chart in 1960. This was a feature of November 1974 because of another double album of oldies I got for my birthday: *Alan Freeman's History of Pop*. I didn't know who Alan Freeman was, but he was obviously important enough for Arcade to release a double album of old hits on his say-so. The TV adverts grabbed my attention and Nan and Grandad forked out for it as they had a year earlier for *That'll Be the Day*.

This one wasn't as exciting. It covered the period from 1950 to 1969, therefore starting pre-Bill Haley. It ranged from big band singers like Kay Starr and Alma Cogan, to blues-mad sixties groups like the Yardbirds and the Animals, none of whom were any good as far as I was concerned. I liked 'How Do You Do It?' by Gerry and the Pacemakers, a stand-out from the advert; I was thoroughly entertained by Pat Boone's 'Speedy Gonzalez' and was drawn into the atmosphere of 'Johnny Remember Me' by John Leyton.

But they couldn't compete with 'Apache'. Huge, deep guitar, excellent tune, prominent drums, vast scale. It was the Wild West, but a peaceful, noble one. This was way better than any Western theme tune I'd ever heard. It made you like the Indians. Aged eleven, I had mixed feelings about them. Those movies usually made you want them to lose.

This temporal duality would continue. I was always to have a crop of new music in one pocket and something from years ago in the other. At our school fete that summer, Mum had volunteered to run a stall and I ended up managing the one next to it – I think you had to guess the number of marbles in the jar or something. I had money to spend, but I blew it on a particularly appealing cuddly toy.

The stall the other side of mine was bric-a-brac, made up mainly of donated jumble, amongst which was a big box of records. I had a flick through but didn't recognise anything. Before two hours was up, most people had drifted off and the clearing-up had started. The lady on the bric-a-brac stall said she didn't know what she was going to do with the left overs; Mum suggested I make her an offer for the records. Before I could say anything, she suggested: "50p?" Mum paid it on the condition that I shared them out with my sisters. We took the whole lot home; there must have been almost a hundred.

The albums ranged from motor-racing sound effects to comic monologues. We ended up liking a few of these, but the real excitement was caused by the singles. Going through them on the carpet beside the portable player was brilliant. We had never heard any of them before. They were all from the years between 1958 and 1966. About half of them were on the London label. There was a lot of Bobby Darin, mainly the kind of songs that our grandparents' generation sang around the piano - 'Hello Dolly', 'Baby Face', 'You Must Have Been a Beautiful Baby'. The latter had a good B-side called 'Sorrow Tomorrow' that we squabbled over.

We didn't actually know which were the A-sides and which were the B-sides, but I finally realised that each side had its own serial number, distinct from the record's catalogue number, and that the lower of the two had to be the A-side because that came first. This sometimes came in handy, honest. At the time, we just had to assume that the A-side was the one that was better.

Usually, we were right, as with 'The Wanderer'/'The Majestic' by Dion. Sometimes, as with 'Teenage Heaven'/'Cinderella Baby' by Johnny Cymbal, we were wrong. Actually, both sides of that were rubbish. Far from rubbish however, was 'Jeannie, Jeannie, Jeannie' by Eddie Cochran, a furious rocker that the Rubettes must surely have been fans of. There was also 'When' by the Kalin Twins, a 1959 number one thanks to its wood-block hook and cutesy-pie tune.

Perhaps best of all was 'What Can I Do Today' by the Swinging Blue Jeans. Don't be put off by the group name. The song is gorgeous, and turned out to be a B-side; the flip was the comparatively dull 'Don't Make Me Over'. There were loads more, all playable, with a few scratches that we didn't mind one bit. Some didn't have sleeves, some sleeves were worn, some didn't match. We sorted them out and straightened them up, with the odd, calamitous rippage. But what a haul. All those "new" records, all at once.

There was one more double album of oldies to appear at the end of 1974, and this one was huge. It seemed that every house in the land either owned a copy, claimed to own a copy, or were expecting to own one on Christmas morning. It was *Elvis's 40 Greatest*, a comprehensive round up of Mr Presley's major hits from the mid-50s to the end of the 60s, minus the Sun recordings he began with.

It's difficult to overstate the stature of Elvis Presley, his place in our culture or the impact he had. The gulf between rock 'n' roll and what had gone before was greater than any equivalent departure in music since. Those of my generation may well yawn when hearing, yet again, that it "changed everything" for the previous one, yet it's true. In a world of casual superlatives, it's hard to imagine the scale of it.

Likewise, the difference between Presley and earlier performers who had appealed to young audiences was shocking and, although nowadays he was lumbering up and down a Las Vegas stage dressed as a candied ice-cream, the shock waves were still being felt. Most chart performers aspired to be a version of him; to have a shard of his looks, a slither of his sound, a splinter of his effect. The release of *40 Great-*

est marked the climax of the Rock 'N' Roll Revival; its high point crowned by its greatest icon.

We got it at Christmas and it was the centrepiece of the celebration for our extended family. We sang along to it, danced to it, talked about it. There was something for everybody. Grandparents and their siblings liked the big melodies of 'One Night' and 'Wooden Heart', some cousins remembered the swoony 'Are You Lonesome Tonight' and 'Can't Help Falling in Love'; others preferred 'Heartbreak Hotel', which usually got the Elvis impersonations going. I found listening to this one more challenging. I'm still not sure how having your heart broken would drive you to "beck a salomie", nor indeed to "crabble", in the gloom or otherwise. I preferred the fast, rockin' ones: 'Blue Suede Shoes', 'I Got Stung', 'Jailhouse Rock', and one that seemed to have a sheen of particular quality, 'I Need Your Love Tonight'.

But my very favourite was '(Marie's the Name) His Latest Flame': great percussive arrangement, striking storyline. It painted a vivid picture of this heartbreaking, two-timing girl, with her jet-black hair, emerald eyes and permanent half-smile. I was really on the side of the poor guy, needing to stay calm and say nothing as his world collapsed. Brilliant.

An aunt spent two nights teaching us to jive; lots of one-more-goes and try-this-agains, all to Elvis, with a little bit saved for the Rubettes' 'Juke Box Jive' and a Wizzard single called 'Are You Ready to Rock' which was completely out if its mind. It was a fine Yule.

The following September I would start secondary school and so, for me, the first eight months of 1975 are kind of an extension of 1974. And yet the new year was different almost immediately. Now that the noise and clatter of glam had faded, pop had less of an edge. It all cranked down a gear, lost a chunk of reverb, took on a more sweetly sentimental focus. It was all about love, staring into each other's dilated pupils rather than going for a spin in the Chevy. That doesn't mean that there were no loud or lively records, just that they were the exception; they didn't fit the prevailing mood.

This mood is no better illustrated than by Bickerton and Waddington's new chart act, Mac and Katie Kissoon. I've always had it in my head that they were siblings but I may be wrong. Their song was 'Sugar Candy Kisses', a lovey-dovey lyric in a soppy tune, presented in a soft soul sheen. But whereas something like 'When Will I See You Again' sounded like you were listening to it in some grand, cavernous hall, 'Sugar Candy Kisses' sounded like you were sitting knee-to-knee with Mac and Katie in your living room. It was a piece of free-standing blancmange and it set the scene for the following months.

That spring, the Bay City Rollers finally had a number one, the first of their two, neither of which were as lively as their hits from the previous year. 'Bye Bye Baby' is a decent record in its own context but the trouble was, it wasn't in its own context. It was in the context of the absolute peak of Rollermania and anyone not in tartan was prone to involuntary retching at the very mention if it. It stayed at the top for five weeks.

The Carpenters returned, fully atoning for their sins with 'Only Yesterday' - a record so good that it made me spend accumulated Easter egg money on their *Singles, 1969-73,* a Best Of that had been selling by the skipload for over a year, containing, among others, 'Yesterday Once More'. The extended family approved, clearly relieved that I was listening to something other than "that horrible group", by which of course they meant my brilliant Sparks. The blancmange seemed to be winning. I didn't play anything on it it nearly as much as 'Only Yesterday'.

My Sparks friend celebrated his eleventh birthday in a similar manner to his tenth. Among the records this time was the Rubettes' 'I Can Do It'. The impersonal pronoun referred to dancing: from his head down to his blue suede shoes, he could really move. We were at the fag-end of the Rock 'N' Roll Revival, but the record was great fun. The album *We Can Do It* had a version of the second Mac and Katie Kissoon hit 'Don't Do It Baby', a hark-back to the heavier sentimentality of 'Sugar Baby Love', but much more in tune with the new style; more rounded, less attack. Both versions are good.

Also at the party was the recent one by Queen, 'Now I'm Here'. Its detached, other-worldly intro, where he's now here, now there, as a distorted guitar chugs with intent behind him, was an intriguing new departure. I didn't buy it. I remember feeling that it was adult in a way that I couldn't quite access; not something that fit my shoulders, yet it had a big, big sound worthy of substantial respect. My friend referred to owning it, but never to the record itself. The fact that I liked it, but didn't like it, if you see what I mean, bothered me. I asked him what he liked about it. He smiled and said "I dunno".

He was, however, able to talk enthusiastically and in detail about the song that had taken the Sweet back into the upper reaches of the Top 10: 'Fox on the Run' (not the Manfred Mann tune). He thought it was their best ever single. I didn't take to it, but they were welcomed back to number two with open arms for, as it turned out, the final time.

In keeping with the new mood, its sound was subdued and muffled compared to their earlier hits. Some of the reason for this may have been that Brian Connolly had suffered a violent attack in which he sustained severe bruising to the throat, affecting his vocal performance indefinitely. Also, it was written and produced by the band themselves. The Chinnichap boys had handed them the reins and gone off to play with new toys - inventive, charismatic pop-rock could scarcely have been further from their minds.

That summer, a new programme began broadcasting on BBC1 that brought blancmange to millions upon millions of screens. *Seaside Special* was a Saturday teatime variety show held in a Big Top at the seaside. A family audience, comprising at least three generations, sat with blankets on their knees as a parade of tepid light entertainment was conveyed before them. The knee-blankets were mostly metaphorical, but nonetheless ever-present.

The opening credits fooled you into thinking it was going to be good. Its theme tune, 'Summertime City', was catchy and had a giddy atmosphere, decent value for its chart peak of number four. It was written and sung by Mike Batt, who wrote and sung the Wombles records. When it beckoned, a rush of anticipation swept you to the sofa, but as you watched, your smile first froze, then gradually wilted, as it dawned on you that you were not only bored but strangely anxious and really shouldn't be there. It took weeks for this self-defeating behavioural pattern to change.

Pop acts often appeared on *Seaside Special*, occasionally current ones, leading to knee-blankets having to be repositioned in the wake of all that swaying and hand-clapping. This was the market that Chinnichap were going for with their new act: Smokie. Their string of hits would commit various crimes against civilisation but they nonetheless managed three good records, the first of which appeared that summer. 'If You Think You Know How to Love Me' was a tribute to the sound of harmonising hippie heroes Crosby, Stills and Nash. It had charm and worked well.

While it was moving towards the top of the charts, the latest one by Abba languished near the bottom. They were still trying to follow up 'Waterloo' and there had been another Eurovision Song Contest in the interim, won by Dutch group Teach In with 'Ding-a-dong' - the title referring to something that you either sang or did, perhaps in celebration of life, perhaps when needing to keep your spirits up. Thank goodness it was there for us.

The Abba song also had a ridiculous title: 'I Do I Do I Do I Do I Do'. Its review in *Melody Maker* is wedged in my memory: "Sorry kids, but Teach In are the champs now and there's nothing you're going to do about it with this one." It went on to reference arguing with Dorothy Squires in the shower, which was obviously meant for a set of experiences other than mine. I had no idea what the record sounded like, but if it wasn't as good as 'Ding-a-dong', then well, blimey. Poor little Abba. Yesterday's stars.

From a more distant yesterday, 1968 to be exact, came 'Stand by Your Man'. Its singer, Tammy Wynette, was well known to country fans, but it was the first time the rest of us had heard of her. Why the song rose to prominence in the middle of the subdued, un-thrusting 1975 is a story I've forgotten if I ever knew it, but rise it did, fitting the scene around it and causing quite a stir.

It tells us that your man should be stood by, even though he often does things that you can't quite get your little head round. This meant drink and other women. But remember: he's only a man, so give the poor thing a break. Put your arms around him, then he'll put his arms around you and everything will be fine.

By now, the phrase 'Women's Lib' was well-established and ridiculed by the mainstream in the same way that everything else that objects to the mainstream is certain to be. 'Lib' was short for 'liberation' and what many women wanted was liberation from the domestic servitude and relative lack of status that came with being wifey. It meant a change of expectation. It meant not putting up with any kind of crap from men. When 'Stand by Your Man' began climbing the charts, there was bound to be trouble. "God, that bloody record" I heard, from more than one trusted mouth. "Do you know what it's saying? Do you know what it *means?*" Well, yes I did. I guess, in my eleven-year-old way, I was taking an anthropological approach to the situation, just standing back and watching.

The disgust and anger were genuine, but this didn't set me against it. I assumed Mum realised I had bought a copy, I may even have waved it provocatively under her nose. When I played it, it was just me and a sentimental song, delivered by a voice of conviction and character; someone expressing their feelings. Yet the chorus does sound like a manifesto, a rallying cry for conservatives (with a small 'c'). It was not "I'm standing by *my* man", it was "You – yes, you dangling your bra over that bonfire – *you* stand by *your* man".

A few months earlier, Conservatives (with a large 'C') had elected a woman as their leader, someone who was in a rather different place to those spitting brimstone over this song. Now, I'm not saying that sending the record to number one was a political act, but the record reaching number one was certainly a political event. There was a clash of ideas and the conservatives seemed to win. A combination of anti-progressives, those for whom lyrics are merely a succession of syllables allowing there to be a singer, and those who made excuses for the lyric because the record had a seductive sound, scurried to the record shop and made it appear so. I remain in two minds over my complicity.

In a similarly uncomfortable vein, we have one more old friend to look in on. Di coconut tree, bless it, was alive, well and number one for a week in August, courtesy of 'Barbados' by Typically Tropical. This, for all its intrinsic faults, was a well-made and enjoyable record.

It starts with a fade-in of densely chirping crickets; then, in manly, all-purpose-Caribbean tones, Cpt. Tobias Wilcock welcomes you aboard Flight 372 to Bridgetown, Barbados.

The instrumentation builds around him as he speaks, until suddenly, "Woh!" We're in the arms of an unthreatening rocksteady rhythm and a mighty rush of a chorus. A man is going home to see his girlfriend among the palm trees in the sun, leaving the grey skies and swirling drains of London behind him. "Woh!" indeed. When it begins to fade at the end, your heart sinks; but then you realise that you can still hear the crickets. They linger, and you can feel the heat on your skin as you listen. Top marks for ambition and attention to detail.

Down a peg from this are the lyrics, with references to driving buses, being in Brixton and booking flights on Coconut Airways, which put the dodgy-ometer firmly in the red. But at least we can now be sure it's a black man we're talking about, just in case we're not clear about where Barbados is or can't quite place Cpt. Wilcock's accent.

We then, however, learned that Typically Tropical could not have been less so. They turned out to be two white blokes from Britain. It could be that a significant chunk of the record-buying public were put off when this became known, a chunk including all hitherto tolerant black fans. No doubt many were crying: "Aw, but it's just a bit of fun" while others turned their backs, embarrassed. It could be the reason why it was only number one for a single week. Pure conjecture; but a shame if it's true, because listening to it is great.

I didn't buy it that summer. I didn't buy much else, either. I was restless and hard to please, caught between the best of the sentimental sweeteners and the dwindling Rock 'N' Roll Revival. Sure, the Rubettes were still goin' down to the high school hop to really do it, but I couldn't be a Rubette. You couldn't get the hats. As the school year ended, they were somewhere mid-chart with 'Foe-Dee-O-Dee', an affectionate mess of drape and brothel-creeper action that the world around it seemed not to care about. It was over.

The situation was summed up by three other recent number ones. Cockney Rebel, responsible for the excellent 'Judy Teen' the previous year, were now Steve Harley and Cockney Rebel. They had 'Make Me

Smile (Come Up and See Me)', a song that Chinnichap might later have written for Smokie, a nice shoulder-rub of acoustic guitar and backing vocal. It was easy on the ear but had pleasingly odd flourishes, not least of which was Steve Harley's skilfully affected vocal. The *Seaside Special* crowd might have ruffled their knee-blankets to it happily if not for that funny voice.

Then there was 'If' by Telly Savalas, an old set of verses spoken by a middle-aged TV star over tame orchestration. There was also 'Whispering Grass' by Windsor Davies and Don Estelle, an old set of verses spoken and sung by two middle-aged TV stars over tame orchestration. They made 'Stand by Your Man' look like a towering cultural achievement.

At least the Rubettes were upbeat and a bit blary. Liking them was an act of quiet desperation. I had tasted excitement, I craved more. There was nothing new to rival the thrills, sophistication and grandeur of those two Sparks albums, yet even these brilliant things weren't cutting the mustard out there. 'Something for the Girl with Everything' had been correctly chosen as the second single from *Propaganda*, but had failed to make it into a Top 20 comprised, almost exclusively, of crap. It was vying to be near the top, battling for success among the knee-blankets and the blancmange, but it wasn't welcome. There was only one conclusion to reach: it was too bloody good for the stupid charts.

That summer, I lost patience. I needed something fresh, exciting, and safe from having its status dictated by chart announcements. I needed somewhere to turn, at least until the next Sparks album came out. Music was established as something that did amazing things, delivering knowledge and pleasure, both mindful and physical. There was no turning back. I had to find something different, something that was truly mine.

Well I did and I didn't.

David Essex had starred in a second movie, a sequel to *That'll Be The Day* called *Stardust*, in which his character formed a band, became a big star, then descended into drug squalor. There was another soundtrack album and another riveting TV advert to support it.

I didn't get it but it sparked a few new 60s interests. 'Do Wah Diddy Diddy' by Manfred Mann and 'I Get Around' by the Beach Boys sounded particularly exciting.

There were also a few Tamla-Motown tracks and two of them made it back into the singles chart as a result. 'What Becomes of the Brokenhearted' by Jimmy Ruffin is an indulgence in misery, to be enjoyed while stepping through mist in a black veil. It's the least offensive of his string of hits - painfully dull records which almost created their own genre, a kind of sub-blancmange. It got even higher in the Top 10 than it had done the first time round.

The other couldn't do this as it had already been number one. This was 'Baby Love' by Diana Ross and the Supremes, who, back then, had simply been "the Supremes". Motown boss Berry Gordy Jr. had decided that Miss Ross was going to be the big star of the company. He was already sleeping with her and, in 1967, he changed the group's name to feature hers. I didn't know about any of this; I just knew about the record. 'Baby Love' had been the single after 'Where Did Our Love Go' but I don't think I made a connection straight away. It came out again and climbed to number twelve. I heard it. I bought it. I played it. A lot.

Many people have written or spoken about the records which marked a turning-point in their young lives. They had been tootling along, liking this and that, when suddenly they heard something that jolted everything up to a whole new level. When they describe this event, a word that repeatedly crops up is "magic". This much-abused word, so often used lightly, isn't wasted here. It has proper meaning.

Until now, your world has been made up of things you could explain but this record seems beyond the craft of mere people, however grown-up, however musical, however talented. For it to do what it does, there must be some kind of sorcery involved. When this happens, it's enormous. It changes things. And the record responsible will be woven into your fabric for life. It could be by the Beatles. It could be by Pink Floyd or David Bowie, Kraftwerk or James Brown. Mine is by the Supremes. I spent weeks with 'Baby Love'; lying on the sofa; listening in a trance, feeling funny.

Music can be so many things; it can fulfil so many purposes, meet so many needs. So it could never be reasonable to call any one record the greatest ever made. But it would be reasonable to say there has never been a *better* one than 'Baby Love'. It does everything. You sing to it, you dance to it, you cry to it - you marvel at it. Its atmosphere is completely intoxicating. It drips with tears and there are sparkles everywhere. Not cheap sparkles, not those ones you can get in plastic tubes from card shops or by pressing a sound-effects button on a studio console; these are real sparkles from real spells. The intro is an explosion of them. Intros usually replicate part of the main melody, often played over the same chords. This one doesn't. Not uniquely so, but most strikingly, most memorably. It announces that something very special is starting. There's a vocal coo over the clip-clap from the previous single, then you're in and every internal organ, along with every inch of your skin, is grabbed at once.

It's the epitome of bittersweet, those sparkles and that song. The character is in the midst of an anguish that we all experience at one time or another: *Why don't you love me, when I love you this much?* She doesn't understand. Well of course she doesn't. Not yet. But we're right there wth her and the ache is exquisite.

You can quibble and say that the vocal jars in places, or the instrumental break is a bit half-arsed, or that drum thing in the second verse is just silly; but there's no beauty in perfection and this record is indisputably beautiful, as beautiful as anything there has ever been.

If any one part makes its sound above all others, it's the keyboard. I never really wanted to know what was making that miraculous noise, but in a weak moment of sobriety I reflected on it. There's probably some vibraphone mixed up in it too. No doubt there's a book or web page somewhere that could tell me. But I'm not interested in who did what. I'm interested in magic.

Back to my restless summer. It was early in the summer holiday and I was sitting in the car listening to the radio. Tony Blackburn was on. His first item at 9am each day was the *Golden Hour*, featuring a selection of records from a given year. You had to guess which one, but it wasn't a competition because an hour was insufficient time for sending a postcard.

Today, we were somewhere in the mid-60s. This record began, and I was bolt upright, heart thumping, breath short. The car was filled with sparkles. What a beat. What a melody. What a sound. And I recognised the voice, it was the same one from 'Baby Love'. I imagine Tone credited it to Diana Ross and the Supremes, since they had been back under that name less than a year earlier. The song was 'You Can't Hurry Love'. My mind was lost. I could think of nothing but how I was going to own a copy.

Various relatives had given us kids 50p each for our two-week camping trip, adding to the summer allowances given to us by Mum. It would gradually go on sweets, slot machines and amusements, perhaps beach toys from the bulging, colourful outlets along the seafront. Good budgeting practice. Perhaps some might be spent on singles. Every town, bar a few weird ones, had its own record shop. We found three within ten miles of our tent.

Down one stone-floored arcade, a man behind the counter responded to mention of Diana Ross and the Supremes by edging along to a rack from which he slid a big, fat silver cover. It was a compilation called *Anthology*. Across its three discs (*three* discs) were all their hit singles, plus a few early misses, plus other tracks recorded purely to please supper-club audiences. Mum knew one called 'Stop! In the Name of Love'. *Anthology* cost £5.50. My entire holiday purse totalled £6.00 and this was day two. I would put a 50p deposit on it and budget to save the balance.

This was an opportunity for martyrdom on an unprecedented scale. When my sisters went on fairground rides I would stand beside the grimy speakers and watch. While they were licking the melt-drips from a 'double 99', I would be savouring the tangy sugars of a hollow ball of bubble gum. As they flicked through their Bumper Holiday Special comics, I would be listening to the transistor radio and staring out to sea. Three pence a day, but 'You Can't Hurry Love' at the end of it. You just need the right motivation to do these things.

Being in my room with Diana Ross and the Supremes' *Anthology* is all I can remember about the end of that summer. Many of the songs remind me of different views of my old bedroom. The three discs were organised so that you could play the whole thing in order by stacking them on the spindle, then when side three had finished, turning the whole stack straight over and playing the rest: so the first disc had sides one and six, the second had sides two and five, the third three and four. Of course you follow.

Its casing folded out until it covered half the carpet. There was a booklet tucked inside, with colour pictures and a narrative. The pictures didn't match the images forming in my head as I listened to these songs. They were glitzy, slick, showbiz pictures, staged and unreal, whereas the songs were showing me teenagers from down the road, in cardigans and scuffed shoes, rushing towards, or crying over, boys who sniffed and didn't comb their hair properly. These feelings were amplified versions of the little flutters I knew from being beside the nicest girls at primary school. But I wasn't on the scale. I wasn't sure whether I wanted to be, and yet the emotional effects of listening to these songs were a high. Addiction was a serious risk. One thing was clear: love was trouble.

'Baby Love' we've already dealt with. 'Where Did Our Love Go' was cut from the same cloth; it's the same girl, bewildered, watching the guy walking away, unable to understand why. In 'Stop! In the Name of Love', a different girl confronts a two-timer. She wants him to do the right thing, hopes his better side will win out. We wonder. Her predicament is presented within a melody-and-chord interplay which brings the subject to life vividly and brilliantly, swirling and swooning as it dances along the spine within reach of every nerve.

The songwriting and production team responsible was Holland-Dozier-Holland, comprising brothers Brian and Eddie Holland and their partner Lamont Dozier; a trio whose legendary status would still be fully deserved if it was doubled. They oversaw all the Supremes' hits from 'Where Did Our Love Go' to the adult triumphalism of 'Forever Came Today' in 1968, when they left Motown. They achieved similar things in that period for the Four Tops. In doing so, they set quality standards for just about everything that followed.

One of their innovations was to bring into their arrangements aspects of classical music, using its chords and rhythms to imbue pop with new textures. In the case of one extraordinary Supremes single, it also meant tipping classical terms gratuitously into the lyric, to add a touch of gratuitous class. This was 'I Hear a Symphony', a piece of simpering candy-floss which, despite itself, steadily gathers momentum until it is hurtling through the stars under its own power, demanding your respect. You imagine that soon after it fades from earshot it simply explodes.

I recognised one song called 'The Happening' because an instrumental version of it was used in performances at my sisters' dance school. It was so catchy it almost hurt. I also loved the brainy moodiness of 'Reflections', an incredible track where the classical influence is integrated peerlessly. I became so used to it that it took me until middle age to realise what a grovel to psychedelia the lyric is, with its references to mirrors of the mind and distorted realities, not to mention the woozy, space-age sound effects at the start. At first, I was more concerned with Diana peeing out of the window after the second chorus. I know rock stars often behave badly when they go on tour, but why she couldn't just sling a telly into the swimming pool like any normal person is a mystery. Go on, listen to it.

When you sit through a chronology of hits from an act whose success was sustained over several years, you can hear the sound progressing. If your act goes from the start to the end of the 1960s this is particularly pronounced, because the evolution of recording techniques, songwriting and thematic styles was so dramatic. If you're listening to the Beatles, compare 'She Loves You' with 'Come Together'.

'Reflections' marks a turning point in the Supremes story. It was the first single to go out as Diana Ross and the Supremes. It also marked the end of a process of change in their sound, one replicated right across Motown's output; a move toward more rounded, sophisticated styles which took things in various directions, the way having been paved by Holland-Dozier-Holland on the 1966 records 'Reach Out I'll Be There' by the Four Tops and 'You Keep Me Hangin' On' by the Supremes.

Prior to this, the sound was raw, hectic and characterised by loud tambourine, handclaps and additional percussion that included crates, cooking pots and chains being slammed against the studio walls for effect; often by office staff, while their gifted house band played on around them. This was skilfully crafted, lovingly refined, progressive recording of pop songs, accompanied by clanks, crashes and smudges of distortion. But crucially, it was all on the beat and as loud as hell. You *moved* to it, by golly. The mods went nuts for it. The northern soul crowd went nuts for anything that reminded them of it. It is this sound, on records made between 1963 and 1966, that is The Motown Sound.

One of the strands within it came to be known as "stompers". Conventionally, where there are four beats to the bar, the rhythmic emphasis falls on the second and fourth beats; it is these beats that the snare drum sees to, while the bass drum sees to the first and third – *boom chack boom chack*. In a stomper, the emphasis is on all four beats and the snare plays them all, with the bass doing its thing somewhere underneath. 'Uptight (Everything's Alright)' by Stevie Wonder is a stomper, so is 'Nowhere to Run' by Martha and the Vandellas. Obviously, you can choose to stomp to records that do not do this, and records with this snare pattern do not have to be fast to be good, but let's paint the picture.

Other strands include high-octane hip-shakers like 'Take This Heart of Mine' by Marvin Gaye or 'First I Look at the Purse' by the Contours. Just as movable, and just as loud, are the finger-poppin' gum-chewers like 'You're My Remedy' by the Marvelettes or 'My Guy' by Mary Wells. You hear any of these, and *bang* – you know it's Motown.

Of course there are exceptions. Some, like 'Put Yourself in My Place' by the Elgins are purely for slumping to and reflecting on the pains of love; 'The Tracks of My Tears' by Smokey Robinson and the Miracles also falls into this category. Others, like almost everything by Junior Walker and the All Stars, are more soulful and less poppy; the swaggering 'Shotgun' points the way to funk, while '(I'm a) Roadrunner' is one of the grooviest records in history (you can hear its legacy in the outros of Oasis, decades later). Each of these acts recorded in a range of these styles.

A big reason for the unique character of all this is the drum sound.

The drums are subject to particularly crisp, resonant production and there are three or four fills which are uniquely associated with these records.

I keep mentioning drums. You may have detected from earlier comments that I had started taking lessons. Mum was driving me across South London once a week to see a hippy in a semi-detached with high ceilings. He taught me the rudiments of stick work but the second part of each lesson was playing along to repeated plays of a pop song he had recorded onto a reel-to-reel (some people are just so behind the times). There wasn't a record player in the music room but he did have a stack of albums. I was allowed to flick through them and to ask questions.

Obviously there was *Bridge over Troubled Water* by Simon & Garfunkel. He guessed that I wouldn't like Blood, Sweat & Tears or Humble Pie, but there was also an album with an intriguing cover, a pattern of silver shards shooting out from a central point, like an explosion in space, with the titles of songs down one side. On the reverse, the space theme was confirmed by an image of the lunar surface, the credits presented across it, white on black. It was a Motown "Chartbusters" album, the third in a series of LPs to gather recently-charting hits from the label, this one appearing in the wake of man's first walk on the moon.

I stared at the cover for long moments, watching its front shimmer as I turned it in the light. He asked me if I knew any of the songs. I sort of knew 'For Once in My Life' but none of the others. Not yet. This was before the three pence holiday. He double-checked that I didn't know a Marvin Gaye song called 'I Heard It Through the Grapevine'. I confirmed that I didn't. He shook his head, but not in response to my ignorance; it was at the effect the record had on him. He tried to express his feelings about it and struggled, shaking his mane, staring at the floor, muttering "...amazing... incredible... just... just fantastic". He was lost for a moment, but then had to snap himself out of it to teach me how to play something pathetically inferior. It must have been hard work for him.

I got to know 'I Heard It Through the Grapevine' in the course of the Motown odyssey I was soon to embark upon. I was helped by an aunt and uncle who had taken meticulous care of their 60s records. One of their Supremes albums was *I Hear a Symphony*, which took the classical theme in a twee, deflating direction simply by including megatons of strings in a succession of supper-club covers. You imagined the group being slowly elevated on a platform surrounded by the swirl of fountains and the trembling of ostrich feathers. Amongst this nonsense however, were a few new treasures that had The Sound, including the title track, which has already been mentioned. On the album that had followed it, *Supremes A' Go Go*, the singles were accompanied by a collection of danceable Motown covers, mostly very good. It introduced me to some important songs before I had heard the originals. The one after that, *The Supremes Sing Motown*, had fewer covers and a less stompy sound.

These were put on tape for me and I poured myself into them. I had found my thing. That black and silver Tamla-Motown label design was a guarantee of quality; its distinctive logo, which I soon learned to draw, a sign of class. Over the next few years, my album acquisitions would be almost all Greatest Hits by Motown artists. I went through the Four Tops, Stevie Wonder, Marvin Gaye, Junior Walker and the All Stars, Martha and the Vandellas, Smokey Robinson and the Miracles, as well as the Marvelettes. I recommend the Marvelettes to anyone checking this stuff out for the first time. Their chronology mirrors the evolution in Motown's styles particularly well and is riddled with absolute belters.

The Sound was over by 1967. The company became increasingly driven by outside influences and the desire to reach audiences beyond teenage ones. So it suited me that this is where most of these compilations stopped. They gave me the kind of home base I had been looking for. Between the ages of eleven and fourteen, this was a major part of what I lived on.

But there was something else. It took me to a world where everything was dictated by success or failure in love; where elation and pain were a whisper apart; where telling someone you loved them could be the gateway to paradise. Clever arrangements made it exciting, alluring, essential. We should be careful what we wish for.

Many years later, a band called Manic Street Preachers would release a single called 'Motown Junk'. I never listened to it closely, but I have always assumed that it refers to the unhelpful baggage we carry into our early relationships as a result of imbibing the lyrics of beguiling love songs. It's a point worth considering. And if that Manic Street Preachers record doesn't actually say that, they should perhaps make one that does.

Five

When we played football in the playground aged ten and eleven, one of the ways we organised teams was blacks against whites. Dark skins lined up on one side, pale skins opposite; then we would share out the others, which we all called "half-caste". One boy from a Caribbean family who happened to have fair skin was distressed at being lumped in with the Turkish kids. I can see him stomping up and down, wailing in frustration "But I'm coloured! I'm coloured!" I don't remember how we resolved it. There aren't many memories from childhood that make me so uncomfortable.

Birthday parties and teatime play-dates presented fresh opportunities to sniff out new piles of records. At black friends' houses the labels on the 45s were often curious. There were sometimes RAK ones, songs I didn't know by Hot Chocolate, but where was the Mud? There were sometimes ones on Bell that I faintly remembered being in the Top 20, but where was the Showaddywaddy? There were ones by Gladys Knight & the Pips on that lovely silver and black Tamla-Motown label; there were ones by the Stylistics with labels consisting of purple plastic rings, rather than printed paper circles.

Other labels were new and strange. One design looked like the dark blue Decca label but had 'Blue Beat' across the top. Another was yellow with a big red crab draped above it. Colourful and alien. I'd never heard of the artists. If I asked my friends about them, I might typically get "That's my mum's. Come on", then be ushered away.

A few weeks after my eleventh birthday, there was a tightly-packed crowd in a friend's kitchen, chatting and snacking, while a small black-and-white TV perched on the Formica began showing *Top of the Pops*. An older brother and his friend had taken up position before it and were passing loud judgement on each item: *Oh no, not this; the singer looks like* (so-and-so); *come on, who would dance like that in front of anybody; you know something, if I had a son and he even sung one note from this, I'd kick him out*. But then came the song they had been waiting for. *This is it! This is it!*

The noise level dropped; the room suddenly sounded empty, apart from strange drums coming from the other end of a tin tunnel and a male voice going "skanga, skanga" which then began singing about believing in love and feeling high, lazily, as if he hadn't woken up properly yet. The "skanga, skanga" then became "brunga, brunga" continuing over the lead vocal; finally, in a change of rhythm texture, it became "katika, katika".

He wasn't performing in the studio, it was a short film; just him and a plain background, his image suddenly reproduced in a line of shudders winding through the picture like an electronic snake. I was baffled. The brother and his friend watched it quietly, reverentially, occasionally turning to each other and nodding or chuckling. I asked my friend: "Do you like this?" He responded with a shrug. The record was a hit and on prime-time TV. It was 'Irie Feelings (Skanga)' by Rupie Edwards. I had just been introduced to dub reggae.

Of course I knew about reggae. I knew it was made by black artists. My aunt and uncle, in addition to the Supremes LPs, had a compilation of reggae tunes called *Red, Red Wine*, the cover of which showed a woman in silks, beside some red wine. I remember them liking a reggae song called 'Israelites' from around the time they got married. There were other records from the previous few years with similar rhythms that I just thought of as lively.

But I was beginning to recognise the bond between this stuff and the black people around me. A couple of months earlier, 'Everything I Own' by Ken Boothe had spent three weeks at number one. This was a sweet, heart-rending song of loss, supported perfectly by the sound of the singer's voice. He would give everything he owned, just to have her back again. This also had a short film to accompany it. In one scene, he was staring vacantly into a shop window when he suddenly thought he saw the reflection of the lost girl standing behind him. He spun round, but it wasn't her.

It seemed that every black kid at school was proclaiming this record, even quiet ones. Girls who barely said a word normally would take their place in unrehearsed performances, doing their bit with confident voices. Silences were broken by hummed extracts.

'Everything I Own' was a cover; white songwriter David Gates had originally composed it about the loss of his father. As a romantic heartbreaker, Ken Boothe's version worked wonders. It was the second time I had felt that a record belonged more to the black kids than to the rest of us. The first time had been a matter of weeks before.

There was a TV series called *Kung Fu*, in which a young man was tutored in the art by a wise, aged master, somewhere dusty in the Far East. It was mysterious and exotic. It was also the pretext for some brilliant fighting, very different from the boxing and punch-ups we were used to. It caught the imagination of black kids in particular, many of whose older siblings went to late night screenings of martial arts films, perhaps to watch the genre's star turn, Bruce Lee. If life is a struggle, you need warrior heroes. Lee wasn't black, but he wasn't white, either. He stood alongside boxing champion Muhammad Ali as an icon; our classroom was often the venue for passionate, ridiculous debates about who might win a fight between them.

As the language of Kung Fu began to spread, Jamaican performer Carl Douglas recorded 'Kung Fu Fighting', a classy, funky record with oriental flourishes which became a huge worldwide hit. Douglas performed it on *Top of the Pops* in a martial arts kit with a red bandanna. It inspired energetic dancing, but fighting shapes were an integral part of the deal.

The non-white kids claimed it immediately; those from black, Turkish and Asian families bonded, lining up in the playground to do the moves and sing bits of the song, particularly the intro with its mystical, rallying *Woh hoh-hoh hooaa* and three-note chromatic motif.

Either of these could turn up anywhere. Naughty boys in assembly would sing the motif as a final flourish of 'Kumbaya' or 'Shalom Chavarim'. Medieval guards in a class play might be allowed to go *Woh hoh-hoh hooaa* as they moved onstage. They made me laugh. Nobody was excluded. It just wasn't *mine* somehow.

We noticed these few divergences, we even spoke about race, but none of it caused friendship problems. There was no agenda. Ours was a progressive primary. Creative expression and experimentation, particularly in the arts, was fully encouraged. If you had put together a performance and wanted to show it in assembly, you usually could. We were known, valued and secure. I went from this atmosphere to a roaring comprehensive secondary of almost two thousand pupils where I was a nobody, arriving in my crisp, clean uniform with naïve choices of shirt and raincoat, on a site with quiet concrete corners and secluded brickwork spots. It was huge, unruly and largely unsupervised. It was also riddled with racial tension.

For years, racism had been both portrayed in, and stoked by, popular entertainment. Di coconut tree was the least of it. We may not have known about economic and institutional discrimination, but we did watch the telly.

TV comedy shows had been feeding us a vocabulary diet of "coon", "sambo" and "white honky" to play with, not that people were unable to come up with their own; one of my great aunts simply referred to black people as "coconuts". Men in jackets and bow ties came on screen to tell jokes – fully-formed, convoluted stories with punch-lines – about thick Irish fellas or dumb coloured fellas. TV adverts for sun-loving vegetable products would sign off with a grinning Uncle Tom declaring "Aah knows it, aah grows it". There was a campaign for the Condor brand of pipe tobacco, in which the satisfied smoker sighed "Aah, Condor". I was on a coach of football supporters as it went past a black man smoking a pipe and somebody called out "Aah, Coondor!" There were no black fans on mid-70s football coaches and this brought the house down. At my last cub scout gang show, a shy nine-year-old boy stood on the stage and told a joke about a lost dog, to which the punchline was "How would you like to walk round

Brixton shouting *Here, Nigger, Nigger?*" The black mums in the audience chuckled and clapped politely.

Little wonder, then, that there was resentment, mistrust and suspicion on the part of some groups of black youngsters moving around my new school, groups that could be intimidating when they were in the mood to be. Sometimes you feel that your only strength is in numbers. I didn't have such an overview when I was eleven; it was with good reason that I was wary of them.

But racism never made any sense to me. Picking on someone because of their colour, something they could do nothing about, was simply wrong. I liked my black friends. The lack of overt racism in my immediate family meant there was nothing tugging my opinions in the opposite direction. Also, I now had the Supremes and Tamla-Motown. It was *mine*, given to me by *them*.

I noticed black girls at school that had some vestige of Supreme about them; refined, pretty, smiling. Diana Ross, because of her solo album covers, was established in my mind as the very definition of womanly beauty. This was the era of the afro, the hairstyle achieved by letting naturally curly, springy hair grow into a smooth curve, kept in shape with an afro comb, a handle with a row of rigid prongs which you used by combing straight away from the head. It was years since anyone had straightened and smoothed like white folks. Diana had a fine afro. The rest of her looked alright, too. So, there you had it: I was firmly against racism on the grounds that (a) it offended my sense of reason and (b) I wanted to snog Diana Ross.

Now add this: during my final few weeks as a primary pupil, I had heard Jamaican patois for the first time. A boy in my class, who spoke in the same London accent as I did, had an older brother who was at the end of his first year at a different dirty great comprehensive from the one I was heading for. I remembered him as being quiet and reserved, but one sunny July evening he turned up as we were having a post-school kickabout in the playground, and quiet he wasn't.

He wore round glasses with thick lenses and I can see him now, perched on the wall above the football area in his uniform and talking, talking, talking, seemingly to nobody in particular; in a

monotone, but using vowel sounds and intonations that were wonderful to hear. I couldn't understand a word of it. I had heard the
accents of friends' parents many times, but this was something else.
I looked at my friend, his younger brother, who returned the gaze,
laughed, shrugged, then got on with the football. I couldn't – I was
rooted to the spot, hypnotised.

Before long, I had broken into giggles, which soon became uncon-
trollable. He peered at me, through those dense lenses, then looked
away again, not pausing for a second. I thought it was fantastic. There
were tears streaming down my cheeks. He could have been talking
about anything. He could, for instance, have been talking about this
stupid white boy who was giggling himself half to death in front of
him. I finally got myself under control, perhaps due to some slightly
overdue self-consciousness. My friend joined his brother, who jumped
down from the wall and they began walking home. He was still talking
as they reached the end of the street.

At my new school, most of the black kids spoke London most of
the time. But in moments of distress, anger or defiance, as well as of
mucking about, out came the patois. The rest of us began picking it
up, with varying degrees of authenticity and appropriateness, which
only helped it evolve. This kind of Brixto-Jamaican became a feature
of our lives. It was well dread, guy.

Versions of it would have been heard around the stands of English
cricket grounds during the summer of 1975, when we had hosted the
World Cup and the West Indies had put out one of their great teams.
Wherever they appeared, the air was filled with the sound of rhythms
played on empty drinks cans by thousands of black youngsters. They
were celebratory rhythms. As they danced and performed, they were
watching their heroes beat everybody to become champions of the
world. It was against the backdrop of all of the above, as I took my
first-form place among the Carols, Sandras and Traceys, the Pauls,
Dereks and Johns, that the general soundtrack humming away in the
background changed from glam-tinted pop, to soul and disco.

Did we know what these terms meant? Soul was black music that
wasn't reggae. Fine. And disco? Wasn't disco anything that was played

at a disco? The Three Degrees' 'When Will I See You Again' had been glossy soul, but their next big hit, 'Take Good Care of Yourself', was upbeat, so it was still soul, but was it disco as well? Was it disco *instead*?

Everybody used these terms, but I never heard the question being seriously tackled. Few would have disputed the point that there were some records that definitely were soul, but definitely not disco. Serious records. Maybe funk ones. Funk was an oft-coined term. But could something be funk and soul at the same time? Could a funk record be disco? If a funk record was played at a disco, would it be funk or would it be disco?

In practice, we avoided such headaches by talking about individual records and whether or not they were any good. I was now in an environment where there was more talking, by more people on more subjects, than I'd ever known. My most trusted guide in all of this was the DJ on the Radio 1 Breakfast Show. His name was Noel Edmonds and I thought he was the coolest bastard on the planet.

His reputation had gone before him, due almost entirely to the fact that his position was one of the most prestigious in Britain. Long before I became a listener, the name was synonymous with wisdom: *I heard it on Noel Edmonds; Noel Edmonds really likes it; listen to Noel Edmonds, he'll play it*. Noel knew, Noel provided.

His show delivered a similar diet to those of others: chart stuff, plus new releases and those bubbling under, plus a few oldies - plus the Record of the Week, the latter being a new release that the host was putting their name to, backing it for success or at least giving it exposure it might never otherwise have had. All the weekday DJs had one.

There were features peculiar to each show. Tone had the *Golden Hour*, big, formal and fanfared. Noel had running jokes and competitions born of his mischievous, ironic sense of humour, entirely in keeping with a time when humour was being defined by Monty Python and Spike Milligan. Among his popular prizes were garden gnomes, balaclavas with the holes in the wrong place and limited-edition stickers in the cartoony shape of a wellington boot. Pleasingly silly. He had an easy, uncontrived style which made me warm to him in the same way I had warmed to Leslie Crowther years before. Where other radio DJs were prone to sudden bursts of noisy enthusiasm in order to remind you what station you were listening to, or to tell you how many big Radio 1 minutes to the hour it was, Noel was just Noel: commandingly calm, funny, knowledgeable.

I trusted him to have impeccable taste in music. This was never actually proved, but I don't remember him ever seriously hacking me off. That would have been too big an event. What he did do was coo and gush over some of the smoother sounds, saying things like how they made him go all gooey, or turned him into a mushy puddle on the floor. He greeted the end of one particularly fine Gladys Knight performance with the whimpering groan "*Oh, Glad*". This was giving me vocabulary to latch onto whenever a record made me go funny. I took these things squarely at face value.

Best of all was the sheer amount of uninterrupted time I was now spending with new music. Between 7.00 and 8.15 every morning, cocooned in my bedsheets, I acquired knowledge, listening to everything over and over, getting to know every detail, including things I didn't like. Noel introduced me to them all.

Sadly, one of these was a re-issue of David Bowie's 1969 single 'Space Oddity'. This had initially been in the Top 10 immediately following the first moon landing. Then, it had at least been topical. But we were now in the autumn of 1975 and there didn't seem to be any reason for it. When it came on, my spirits slumped. Worse, it went to number one.

I suppose it's got an atmosphere. And it's got bits to like. People like bits to like. There's the "ground control to Major Tom" bits. There's the use of the word "helmet" which had some purchase among my peers. Then there's the stylophone bit. A stylophone was a nifty little hand-held gadget making an electronic organ sound that was unlike sounds made on any electronic organ. You played it by touching co-joined metal keys with a special pen. They were whizz-bang in 1969. There's a stylophone solo on it.

The narrative concerns an astronaut who gets into trouble and ends up floating off into outer space. So, dull *and* depressing. Excellent. Not as depressing as how popular it was in 1975. Its success could be partly explained by the fact that it was a "maxi single" – an RCA "Maximillion" to be precise – with two other re-issues on it, the first of which, 'Changes', is one of Bowie's best.

My main connection to 'Space Oddity' is through its powers of evocation; when I think of it, I think of dark, damp mornings, of wooden units in a maths room that need a lick of paint, of the view from a second-floor window down into the grey central yard, of being alone in an ocean of unfamiliarity and menace, of having the wrong colour shirt and the wrong kind of coat. My first term at secondary school.

Changes to my situation coincided with changes to the design and range of labels on the records we were buying. The red and black of Polydor was becoming a rarity in the singles chart, one reason being that Bickerton and Waddington had launched their own label for Rubettes and Mac and Katie Kissoon releases called State: pale blue, with its logo resembling a US licence plate. Elsewhere, RAK would continue without a change of appearance, but Mud had moved to Private Stock by the autumn, whose label was, for now, black and white with a bit of tan. The presence of Bell had peaked; it would disappear altogether in little over a year, subsumed into Arista along with its remaining hit artists, including the Drifters and Showaddywaddy. RCA had changed the design of its sleeve into an orange swirl on blue, but the label was pretty much untouched.

Alongside these were more recent arrivals. There was the tan of Jay Boy, with its bespectacled black cartoon bird, home to George Mc-Crae and horn-happy disco smilers KC & the Sunshine Band. There was the light blue of 20th Century, home to Barry White. Tamla-Motown had a particularly strong presence at this point, putting out quality soul and disco, but the genre's headline presence was that of Philadelphia International, whose olive green label, with its funny yin and yang-type magenta logo, had started to trickle into households due to Harold Melvin and the Blue Notes and the Three Degrees. It would never pepper the chart in the same way that Motown had, but its luscious output was becoming *the* sound of the mid-70s and the production duo that ran it, Kenny Gamble and Leon Huff, were heroes. Another new presence was that of GTO; contrasting blues, flecked with red on its Art Deco-style design. For now, its showing was down to the success of a stylish pop band called Fox, whose short list of hits are all worth spending time with.

That autumn, Island overhauled its look. Gone was the bright, clear rising sun and the small detail. Now we had a sunset scene, of strong colour and shape; silhouetted green palms before a red and orange sky and a blue sea. The pink bag was replaced by a black one. A bit more serious and grown-up. My first purchase of it was not a single but an album – *Indiscreet*, the new one by Sparks.

Or, to put it another way, *Indiscreet*, the deeply disappointing new one by Sparks. That rich sound, that explosive power, that warmth, that fascinating, brilliant dottiness: all gone. Instead; tinny treble, songs that were both shallow and hollow, instrumentation and rhythms that suggested we were somewhere in the 1930s. There was a song called 'Without Using Hands', about doing things without using your hands. It sounded like Russell should have been doing a slow tap-dance as he sang it. There was a song called 'Tits', about a man drunkenly bemoaning the fact that those parts of his wife which had once meant "fun and games" were now only there to feed the baby. The *Melody Maker* review called it "a silly song". You don't say. It didn't make you want to sing, it didn't make you want to play air drums, it didn't make you want to join them in their parallel world. What was the point?

Warning signs had appeared that summer. A single called 'Get in the Swing' had been a stark departure in style, but it could have been alright. The chorus was a parade march, the kind of thing that can be mantra-like if you keep it going. But it kept getting interrupted by passages that made you think they were trying to annoy you on purpose. One was about having a conversation with God about filling in a questionnaire, the subject of which wasn't even revealed. It was maddening.

I didn't buy it but I had faith in the idea of a new album. What a mug. The only thing that had anything of the flavour of *Kimono My House* or *Propaganda* was 'Happy Hunting Ground', a thumping thrash with a good verse and a decent chorus, but its sound was cold and my copy kept jumping as the track started, a problem I tried to fix by balancing coins on the head, then when that didn't work, pressing down with my finger, which only scarred the vinyl. My copy no longer jumped but it had patches of loud hissing instead. It was all going wrong. I had contrived to get a couple of days off sick and I lay on the living room floor in front of the electric fire in my dressing-gown, listening to this pile of crap and wondering what I had done to deserve being so let down; this, in addition to feeling so unsafe at school.

Inevitably, slowly, I began to calm down. I recognised that there was a different producer. Muff had been given the boot. Separately, I recognised the possibility that there may have been no intention of making another album like their previous two. A second single, 'Looks, Looks, Looks' was decidedly 1930s and initially alienated me, but it had made it into the Top 20 and I gradually acclimatised. It's a swipe at the haughty world of fashion; it works well and it's catchy.

I found scraps of merit in one or two other tracks. One endeared itself to me purely on the basis of something that happened at school. I was wandering around outside at lunchtime when I spotted a group of older boys gathered on a grass slope above one of the playgrounds. They were watching the performance of another boy, who was strutting up and down, giving air-slapping emphasis with his hands, half singing, half shouting 'How Are You Getting Home' from *Indiscreet*. My old Sparks friend was now at a different school, but there were clearly other Sparks fans and I recognised this one – he had been at our primary too.

The song is about a man trying to convince a girl to leave a party and get into his car, and the line that went down best with the grass slope audience was the one that mentioned her "independence - real *spunk*, real independence". It was delivered with gusto, amid laughter and applause. I must have stopped to watch. I may have been grinning. They became aware of me. The audience stared without returning the smile I offered, but the performer held my gaze for a second. There was a moment of recognition, then he looked away. I moved on.

Back in my tutor group for afternoon registration, I was approached by two other boys from the same year. This pair liked to amuse them-selves by putting me under pressure, telling me I'd got this this wrong and was doing that wrong – the shirt and coat were merely the tip of that iceberg – or that I was in trouble with someone because of something I'd said, whether I'd actually said it or not. Their soft voices made these experiences particularly uncomfortable.

They had seen me beside the grass slope and asked me what I reckoned. I had been laughing, so I must have thought it was funny; because they knew him, they could easily tell him. I think I must have made some clumsy remark about the clowning, because then it was "Right – we'll tell him you said that. You wait". But without hesitation I confidently replied: "I know him. He used to go to my old school". They asked me which school. I told them. They went quiet and pissed off.

This small turning point gives me something associated with *Indiscreet* to remember fondly. But I don't remember the album fondly. If there had only been two other things as good in their own way as 'Looks, Looks, Looks', I might have felt differently. There just wasn't. The front cover shows Ron and Russell beside the wreckage of a light aircraft in a residential street. Apt symbolism. I simply stopped caring.

I am guessing that I had been allowed to have the album as an early birthday present. I am also guessing that the two Diana Ross solo LPs I had acquired since the summer were as a result of stoically saving my pocket money and buying fewer 45s. This was something I needed to rectify. When my twelfth birthday came around, my vinyl credits were sufficient for five singles.

Each of the ones I chose were a big deal and have stood the test of time with distinction. One was 'Love Hurts' by Jim Capaldi, a con-trolled wail about love being responsible for nothing but pain and misery. I later found out that the Everly Brothers had done the song first. Capaldi delivered it with straight, wistful conviction. It could have been some bloke from down the road, telling you the truth as he stared into his pint.

Another was 'Right Back Where We Started From' by Maxine Nightingale; a jumpy, fidgety pop-soul tune, a lot more pop than soul, with a great percussive melody to its chorus. It also had little saxophone squiggles in the arrangement that reminded me of the Supremes. Extra gold stars.

I had felt sorry for Abba; the cruelty of that *Melody Maker* review had haunted me. So I was pleased when their next one did well. It didn't fit me at first, but there was something about it. It was called 'SOS'. I made it one of my five and, once I played it, all my reservations fell away. The melody, the classical piano arrangement, the morphing effects and the sound of the woman's voice combine in the verse to create a sadness that holds you with both hands. I can't believe how many performers sing a sad song without making any effort to put sadness into their voice. They just do showbiz. They should listen to this.

She's trying hard to understand what has gone wrong; you can feel her mind straining as her heart breaks. It's a plea for help, but the one person she wants to be able to turn to is the one person who is caring less and less. The big, sudden chorus confirms all of this; moving between a wall of adult cries and thumping despair. This atmosphere is sustained right to the end when the intro is repeated, descending piano notes slowing to a final, lingering chord. It's all the same notes as before; except that now, we know it really is the end.

The other two were both upbeat, with grooves I stuck my head straight into. One was by Roxy Music. I knew about this group mainly because of the number of times they were written about in *Melody Maker*. They had been there through glam, but not with proper songs and not in proper costumes. It was like nobody had told anybody else what they were going to wear before they all turned up. In some cases the top halves hadn't told the bottom halves. I thought hey were just stupid; they looked stupid and the singer had a stupid voice, like he was just mucking about instead of trying.

The only conversation I remember having about them was with our teenage babysitter. I thought our teenage babysitter was great. I stayed up after my sisters had gone to bed and got to talk to her about music. I was particularly excited when she reached that age so eulogised by songwriters, and asked her what it was like to be sixteen. "Useless", she said. "Can't wait 'till I'm seventeen." She didn't like Roxy Music much, either, but tried to explain why some people liked them, a broad view for which I wasn't quite ready. They weren't good enough to be like any of my favourites, so that was that.

Reaching the upper slopes of maturity that was twelve, however, made some small difference. I was at least open-minded when they released 'Love Is the Drug'. I learned that the singer's name was Bryan Ferry. It seemed he had stopped piddling around and got some proper clothes. He had also made a proper record. It starts with the opening of a car door; the bass pulses on a single note as the engine is started and, as the car roars off, the groove kicks in. I was right there. He's off to where there are red lights. Perhaps, if love is something he's hooked on, he's having to pay for it; elsewhere the lyric disputes that.

I loved that groove. It matched the picture in my mind of a darkened club where smart, well-off people lounged on leather sofas, impressing each other, laughing, preparing to slip away together. I was less keen on the bit where he goes *Ohhh, a-woh wohhh*. It made me think he was suddenly standing up in the middle of this place and throwing his arms out to sing it, with everyone edging away.

The last of the five, the other groovy one, was my first Hot Chocolate single. The idea of *not* liking 'You Sexy Thing' is ridiculous. I was slightly concerned about "sexy" being in the title – would I be allowed to have it in my room? Well I suppose I already had 'Tits'. The fact is, the record sounded so darn good and was so galvanising, even to the ears of protective parents, that one little word wasn't going to matter. Lyrically, it's an adult update on 'I'm a Believer'. A chronically single guy has been hauled off to the boudoir by the hottest of chicks and he can't believe his luck. Its joy is relentless. It's a fantastic, triumphant record and would have made a fantastic, triumphant number one. But dark clouds were gathering.

As autumn faded into winter, Queen released a very odd single. At first I thought the title, 'Bohemian Rhapsody', was a joke. Surely someone had made the name up in mockery of it. They hadn't. That precise title did indeed go with that record, the one that was creeping in everywhere.

There were three bits to it. The first, a slow bit with a piano, was when he's telling his mum he's killed someone and thrown his life away because he's now going to die. There was no justification for this killing like in other death songs; he's just shot some bloke. The second bit, his trial, sounded like an opera. Rather than "On the evidence you are guilty - what have you got to say in your defence?", it was "Galileo", "Scaramouche" and "Bizmilla", voices arguing back and forth in clipped phrases about whether they were going to let him go or not. The third bit was a rock bit with a complicated rhythm, which was just getting going when it stopped, everything slowing down to a reprise of the first bit. He said nothing really mattered to him. Then there was a gong.

I hated it straight away. I couldn't believe this was the same group that had made 'Killer Queen' and 'Now I'm Here'. What the hell were they playing at? It made my flesh crawl. What I hated most however, was the unquestioning reverence. Everybody was in thrall to it. There seemed to be no dissent anywhere. People sang the opera bit in silly voices as if to send it up, but without passing negative judgement. I told one or two people my age that I hated it, getting the shrugging response "Why? It's alright". People had laughed at lyrics from all sorts of records that I had liked, but "Scaramouche, Scaramouche, will you do the Fandango?" was apparently okay. *Psst! Bohemian Rhapsody is really good – pass it on.* There were terrific, lovely records all around us, yet this was the one considered the best in town. I fumed. I didn't know the word "pretentious" when I was twelve: "crap" had to do all by itself.

But in December 1975, what I thought mattered not one tiddly tad. The crap went to number one and stayed there for nine weeks. In a main assembly, our headmaster strolled across a bare stage to a portable record player and played 'Bohemian Rhapsody' while we listened in silence. The expectation was that we would appreciate it and be thankful. Collaboration was uniform. It was like living in an occupied country. If I'd spoken out too much I might have mysteriously disappeared.

Every Thursday night on *Top of the Pops*, we had it double-confirmed that it was still number one; then we had to watch the video. Many people claimed this was "the first video" but it wasn't, unless ones like Ken Boothe's a year earlier were "film" rather than "video". People went on about its innovative special effects, such as images being reproduced in a line of shudders winding through the picture like an electronic snake. Does this ring a bell? Rupie Edwards.

Amongst other bullshit flying around was "*It's the longest number one ever!*" No it wasn't. It wasn't even the longest number one of 1975 - 'I'm Not In Love' by 10cc was a good few seconds longer. But nothing made any difference. The country was on its knees before it and whenever it came on, they were in church.

That Christmas, a well-meaning family member asked "Has he got 'Bohemian Rhapsody'?" and was told "No, I don't think he has", instead of "Well actually, if you bought that for him, he might grab a hammer and smash it to pieces in front of you". I was doomed to having the blasted thing in the house.

But then, over that festive season, a light shone through the gloom. An antidote. Something else that was unlike anything around it. A piece of pure, crisp, catchy pop that could unblock nasal passages and clear dark clouds. What a sound. An energetic tick-tock of a beat, with xylophone and woodwind embellishments; a lyric about a girl whose guy is doing her wrong; she knows she has to end it but can't – there's a fire within her soul. When she bangs her fists in frustration, the arrangement flares up around her; when the feelings of love return, it's all pared back to the tick-tock. It's flooding through her and, just like before, it's winning: one look from him and here she goes again. The title, 'Mamma Mia', is her cry of exasperation. Abba were back, showing that they could do heartbreak immaculate as well as heavy. Hooks were laid throughout the arrangement like booby traps. Sparkles flew. To hear it was to be washed clean. It was in my house before it was in the charts.

Despite my railings earlier in the year, it was obvious that the charts did matter. There was no use pretending they didn't. The hit parade was central to our thoughts, as were the characters that populated it. My Birthday Five had all been big hits. It was okay to be excited about new announcements again, even if this included another week of 'Bohemian Rhapsody' being in the big place.

Having a record I loved go to number one seemed like something that just didn't happen. 'You Sexy Thing' had been kept at number two by the crap, as had Greg Lake's progressive Yuletide masterpiece 'I Believe In Father Christmas' (which I didn't get the point of at all), plus Laurel and Hardy's 'The Trail of the Lonesome Pine' a song peeled off some pre-war slapstick soundtrack and shovelled on to a 45 for the stocking-filler season. 'Mamma Mia' kicked its heels around the lower reaches of the Top 30 for a bit, then rocketed upward, arriving at number three and poised to go further. And oh, how badly I wanted it to.

The new chart was announced on Johnny Walker's lunchtime show on Tuesday. Noel then did his own run-down the next morning. I remember the gathering of things on the sideboard I was vacantly staring at when he revealed that 'Mamma Mia' was a non-mover at number three. Above it at two was 'A Glass of Champagne' by Sailor. Above that, well... It seemed immovable. Two weeks at number three almost certainly meant that Abba had peaked. The next seven days were spent trying not to care. I had been here before, of course. We don't often get what we most want.

But sometimes we do. I might have been staring at the same sideboard a week later, when Noel announced that 'Bohemian Rhapsody' was no longer Britain's chart topper, that Sailor were still number two, and there was a new number one – 'Mamma Mia' by Abba. I think I may have squealed. I may have yelled. I may have jumped around, making others in the house think the place was collapsing. I may have been told off for being ridiculous. But nothing would have spoilt that brilliant moment. To my elated mind, the beast was slain, chains were falling away. The last nine weeks had been like something approaching bondage - 'Mamma Mia' let me go.

Actually, things were improving gradually all round. It would be at least another year before I felt completely at ease in school; the sense of lurking threat remained a daily experience for now. But already, there was a change. I was getting my tie right now; an enormous knot, with one-and-a-half inches peeping from beneath. Any more was bookish; any less would look silly.

Then there was casual socialising. There were two ways of getting to school, by train or by bus, and I switched between them on a whim. Along from our bus stop, we gathered by a grimy wall with a low ledge which, inevitably, we stood on; a loosely-associated group of first and second years with one or two older brothers. Bus stop comrades.

I knew one from my primary school. As we waited, we talked about records. His older brother was into Led Zeppelin and Deep Purple and he was being influenced. Everything I liked, he sniggered at, or declared it "wally music", albeit with a warm smile that made him un-hateable. Others beside us showed more sympathy towards my picks, which made him snigger even more. Sometimes these sniggers would reach such a peak that they caused a single "Ha!" to burst from him, like a lid had been blown off. I mentioned Motown. "Motown! No!" he grin-cringed. It became a mission to find something that he might admit to liking, or that would get two "Ha"s out of him. I'm not sure I ever succeeded. The point was, this was comfortable; a little ledge-full of fun, to be enjoyed before the bus appeared and the various groups began drifting from unwashed walls and alcoves towards the stop.

Most importantly, I had begun to hold down a place in the school football team. This delivered status. We were a big school that was used to competing. I got to know cool, respected kids from right across the house system that I would never have known otherwise. When we warmed up before games, the white boys would kick about in one corner, the black kids in another, with me in the middle try-ing to pass to both. I'd hear "Get over here, don't stand with them". I stayed put. I amused everyone. I relaxed. I became less concerned when the available seat on the bus home was next to older black boys. I sat down, rarely hassled. I wanted to listen to them. I overheard con-versations like this one:

"So what you into?"

"Soul."

"Yeh? What, Al Green?"

"Hmm... deeper."

"Yeh? Isley Brothers?"

"Deeper."

"Stevie Wonder?"

"Deeper."

"Deeper than Stevie Wonder?"

"Hmm."

"Boy... Marvin Gaye?"

"Deeper."

"Boy, you're *gone*."

"Hmm."

They hadn't mentioned disco. But the term was in common enough use. One day, my drum teacher announced that he was going to teach me "the disco beat" on the kit. Actually, there were two disco beats. There was the Latin one – *chit ch'chit-bom, chit ch'chit-bom* – as showcased by the enduringly annoying 1974 hit 'Rock the Boat' by Hues Corporation. The one I was taught was a regimented four-to-the-bar, characterised by the hi-hat being loosened on the off-beat – *dom-tiss dat-tiss, dom-tiss dat-tiss.* Disco records were either one or the other, although some had aspects of both as well as variations thereon.

A striking variation on the regimented one was used in 'December, 1963 (Oh, What a Night) by Italian-American vocal group, the Four Seasons. This had a great arrangement: a thumping bass-and-keyboard riff intertwining wonderfully with the vocal melody, while snazzy detail popped out from all around to wink at you. In the lyric, a man is looking back on what we assume was his first significant sexual encounter – what a lady, what a night.

It's highly singable; most of us were singing and humming bits of it for weeks. As we have seen, ignorance of the words is rarely a barrier to this, and one line on this record was something of a minefield. It goes: "As I recall, it ended much too soon", but the syllabic emphasis is counter-intuitive, leading to interpretations including "As I recall, it ended my two shoes". Hearing this from a girl in my class made me relax about the fact that I had been singing "As I recall, it *emptied* my two shoes". Down at the grimy ledge near the bus stop, one boy was merely approximating the sound of each syllable, and when you put it all together, the English it most closely resembled was "His arm is cold, it emptied my goo chute".

The Four Seasons, it turned out, had been around for ages. Adults spoke fondly of their early 60s songs, none of which rang any bells with me. I discovered that the original version of 'Bye Bye Baby' was theirs. They had been part of the late rock 'n' roll era; now they had "gone disco" and bagged a number one. It was a good record, regardless of who liked it and who didn't, but those who remembered the group from the previous decade were particularly pleased.

They were pleased with other aspects of the new sounds, too. Disco didn't alienate older people to the extent that glam had. It seemed to have something for all ages. Its rhythms weren't too strenuous to dance to and you could usually sing along to it. A dance and a sing-song – who doesn't like a bit of that? Also, it was smart. On TV, we saw singers in stage suits and dresses, performing in the smooth, choreographed style audiences had been used to for years.

Apart from the odd exposed belly and glittery trim, none of it was too far from the clothes parents might wear for special occasions. You could imagine a grey-flecked uncle approaching the reception dance floor with a shoulder shimmy, grinning through a mouthful of vol-au-vent as 'December, 1963 (Oh, What a Night)' flew from the speakers. With all those nice strings and hardly ever a grunt, the sounds were airy and unthreatening. It was as gleaming and streamlined as the cars your neighbours washed in the kerb on Sundays. It was modern. It was comfortable. It was also, to a large, visible degree, reassuringly white.

Tina Charles was a nice London girl with a bang up-to-date wardrobe and a voice that could blow the hat clean off your head at twenty paces. Her biggest hit, 'I Love to Love (But My Baby Just Loves to Dance)', used the Latin beat and had a very disco theme. He's off to do his stuff under the glitterball instead of staying in and doing it under the bedclothes. Poor Tina. You see, dancing was the thing. Dancing got in the way of normal business. Dancing won.

Our little crowd, huddled on the grimy ledge, had no idea of the significance of disco for gay people, particularly American gay people. Our understanding began and ended with how the guy in the song had to be a poof if he didn't want to shag Tina. On the grimy ledge, that amounted to insight.

'I Love to Love (But My Baby Just Loves to Dance)' knocked 'December, 1963 (Oh, What A Night)' off the top of the charts and stayed there for a week longer. As she sang it on *Top of the Pops*, she looked just like one of your mum's friends from work; popular, lively and big-eyed, talking a lot and giggling noisily at the merest of jokes. A disco record had replaced another disco record at number one. Both were by acts that the older generation in our family would happily have put out the biscuits for.

The dance thing and the smooth orchestration thing were ever-present in disco, but within its range there was great variation. There was heavily soulful disco; there was airily soulful disco; there was poppy disco with good tunes; there was poppy disco with useless tunes. There was also disco blancmange. Ladies and gentlemen, I give you 'The Hustle' by Van McCoy and the Soul City Orchestra.

This was the record that gave disco licence to be sappy. It invited all kinds of undesirables in off the street. It was a triumph of blandness; a slow, string-section melody, a flute playing an unbroken sequence of pips over a chuggidy-chuggidy beat and excessively tidy chord changes. Excited voices meanwhile encouraged us to do the dance of the title, because the Hustle was a dance; a series of moves to learn and perform in formation – heaven forbid you might be inspired by music to produce any of your own.

It didn't sound like a proper record at all. It was more like a piece of backdrop music from a television programme; an accompaniment to sweeping shots of gleaming marinas, Pacific beaches and cruising Ferraris. It was going on somewhere in the background from the middle of 1975 until well over a year later.

The releases coming from Philadelphia International were much better; they had drive, they had throb. Noel played 'The Soul City Walk' by Archie Bell and the Drells, 'The Love I Lost' by Harold Melvin and the Blue Notes and 'I Love Music' by the O'Jays, a group remembered for their global brotherhood anthem 'Love Train' a few years before.

On the 20th Century label, Barry White, a growling expanse of manhood brilliantly monickered "the Love Walrus", had enjoyed his golden medallion moment at the end of 1974 when 'You're the First, the Last, My Everything' had clambered to number one. Now he was having a purple patch with the consecutive releases 'Let the Music Play' and 'You See the Trouble with Me'; inventive, swashbuckling string arrangements to frame urgent songs of passion and heartache.

By contrast, there was 'Get Up and Boogie' by Silver Convention, a repetitive plod that was on the radio far too often. If a record was going to persuade you to boogie in addition to getting up, it should at least have something energising about it. The Stylistics had had their quality moments, but they obliterated the memory of these with a disco cover of Elvis Presley's 'Can't Help Falling in Love', sounding like a party made entirely of sticky sweets and congealed cola.

Infinitely better, was 'More, More, More' by Andrea True Connection, a breathy female vocal making grown-up promises over an intriguing, laid-back rhythm; a blast of fresh air. Tamla-Motown had been in on the act, too. The Miracles, now minus Smokey Robinson, issued 'Love Machine (Part 1)', to shake the icicles from the guttering on a cold winter's morning. This began with a chiselled, metallic guitar riff, some hairy-chested beast growling *Hoo-hoo-hmm, yeahh*, then flung itself into a lashing, belting blend of falsetto vocal and concerted riffing. 'Love Machine (Part 2)' was, you'll be pleased to hear, on the B-side.

The previous December, a matter of days before the horror of 'Bohemian Rhapsody' began to unfold, I read that there was a new single by Diana Ross. In an act of proud faith, I got it without hearing it first. The man in the shop had to scrabble around to find a copy. As I brought it indoors I had no idea what to expect, but I was hoping for sparkles. On the label it grandly said: "Diana Ross sings Theme from Mahogany 'Do You Know Where You're Going To'". At first, I was disappointed. It was all adult and orchestral; someone strolling alone, moodily, probably in a long coat, at some big junction in their life. Yawn. No drums until the chorus, which wasn't even a proper chorus; just a break from all the delicate stuff.

But I adjusted. It's centred on a melody, used by the vocal in the verse, and which floods instrumental passages elsewhere, achieving the delicious trick of changing key each time, without you realising it's happening. It's highly effective and not in the slightest bit wearing because, firstly, no two arrangements of it are the same, and secondly, it's lovely. It seemed I was the only one who bought it.

Except that, in the middle of the following spring, there it was, climbing the charts and getting to number five. I was proud as punch. The album, uncontroversially entitled *Diana Ross*, was standard showbiz fare, albeit of decent quality. But amongst it was something called 'Love Hangover'. The hangover in question is the sweetest thing: she doesn't want a cure.

There are two bits to it, a slow bit and a fast bit. The slow bit gives us the dreamy meaning of the lyric, the fast bit is a disco freak-out, centred on a guitar riff that boings up in the air then settles like a bouncy ball in the bottom of a barrel before starting off again. Here, the vocal switches between frivolous and woozy. Love has made her high. It goes on for ages. As 'Theme from Mahogany' slid down the charts, 'Love Hangover' moved up, peaking at ten. On the album, the slow bit is twice as long, which makes it better, but the fast bit made the difference between ordinary good and surprising good. Diana was back in the limelight on merit.

This was big news in our house. But, on balance, the bigger news was that Mum was getting married again. He moved in. It worked out. We merged furniture. The house gained a brown imitation-leather swivel armchair with a brown imitation-leather swivel footstool. Also new, was a black and white space-age TV – curved white plastic with the screen in a bubble at the top, standing on a single leg which fanned out into a circular stand. There was a join half way up the leg which was loose, meaning that it leant creakingly to one side and was in constant danger of heaving over. However, I had this in my room, so it was great.

As well as furniture, we merged albums. So now we had two copies of *Bridge over Troubled Water* by Simon & Garfunkel. And we had something new to play them on. The cabinet built by Dad went, replaced by a wide shelf that filled its alcove, on top of which sat a Sanyo Super Music Centre, housing a turntable and horizontal cassette player with a tinted lid to cover the whole shebang and a radio tuner fitted at the front. For the first time, we had a record player with external speakers that you could move wherever you wanted as long as the leads were long enough. It was well flash, guy.

It also provided the facility of recording "direct" from turntable to cassette without the intrusion of surrounding noise, which was very exciting. It put us in the same league as the aunt and uncle who had recorded our holiday tapes and those Motown albums. There was even a duster arm. Dusting records is sensible; it's also part and parcel of fussing over your vinyl and, therefore, an entirely reasonable thing to do.

This thing dusted during play. It was a clear plastic strip, at the end of which was a fuzzy red roller for collecting the dust and a tiny sheaf of down-turned bristles for keeping it moving across the record in a similar way to the needle. You fixed it on a spindle beside the arm rest and took it off to remove any dust. I was seriously impressed. I now felt like a proper record owner.

Indeed, under the influence of certain adults, I began to look after records more carefully. From *Anthology* onwards, I returned albums to their inner sleeves, which I had never bothered doing at the time of *That'll Be the Day*. Singles had once been left out of their sleeves and strewn, mixed up in piles of bedroom detritus. They may have been stacked in horizontal piles. A current favourite may simply have been left on the turntable until superseded. Now they were diligently returned.

My new dresser had a raised, square-fronted drawer at each side. The portable player fit neatly on the surface between them, so the drawers would have made perfect homes for my singles. I was quite excited when the thought occurred to me. I cleared out the forgotten stationery and bits of now-useless toy, only to find that they were not quite seven inches across. I put them in there anyway, but they lay at uncomfortable angles, looking sad, impossible to flick through.

This frustration temporarily abated when I got a record rack. This was a row of wire dividers just over a foot long, which you could zing with your fingers as if playing a harp. Numbers were arranged in a zigzag along a strip of card glued beneath them, so you could index the contents. If you were so inclined.

The main drawback was that the records tipped out with the slightest nudge, making it impossible to carry it, despite the encouragement of handles. Another was that it left dents in the bottom of the sleeves where they rested on the wire. Obviously, having vowed to care properly for my records, dents in paper sleeves were not going to do. My aunt had donated a sturdy singles carrier with a fat handle, robust lid hinges and a clip lock. Once I decided to ditch the rack, my system was to keep the most recent ones in the carrier, and stack older ones – vertically and side-on – at the back of the wardrobe shelf. Much better.

In the meanwhile, life's Noel-approved soundtrack rumbled on. I trusted him to present us with a comprehensive spread of what was happening out there and, as far as I could tell, this is exactly what he continued to do. Some records he played most days. Others he played only a couple of times ever. Did he influence my taste? I don't think so. However much he played 'I'd Really Love to See You Tonight' by England Dan and John Ford Coley, a classy adult love song in a Californian jumper, I didn't want to buy it. It may have been one of the records that turned him into a mushy puddle, but it did nothing for me. If I'm fond of it now, it's only because it reminds me so strongly of snuggling under the bedclothes on dark, autumnal mornings, not having to get up yet, absorbing my broad and varied soundtrack.

Something I was swayed by however, was the use of the term "classic" with regard to certain records. Some did indeed have a bigger, more significant sound and feel to them, in addition to being good. But whether radio DJs applied this empirically, or merely to hits they happened to like, was open to debate. I probably considered each use of the term on its own merits, but I wanted to be able to identify a new "classic" for myself.

I also grappled with the term "*big* number one". Wasn't every number one big by virtue of being number one? Or were some number ones bigger than others? If the latter were true, was this merely due to the number of weeks spent there? Or did it hint at some other status understood by those with sufficiently developed senses? I cared about these things.

Noel was far from the worst offender, but I think he may have dabbled, perhaps from beneath the cloak of irony. Meanwhile, I was happy with my soundtrack. Disco was the glue that bound it all together. In between were the records we spent most time talking about - novelties and great pop.

A novelty first. At the start of the year, we had learned about Citizen's Band radio, or CB. This was a frequency for folks to communicate on via radio handsets. It was bit like the telephone, except that you weren't wired into a wall; you were mobile, so you could, for example, have it in your vehicle. American truckers used it to keep tabs on each other, to share news about places to eat, weather conditions, or the location of police speed traps. They spoke in euphemistic code and each had a CB identity which they called a "handle".

For a few weeks, the media was full of features on this underworld and its language, all because of a record called 'Convoy' by CW McCall. Truck convoys were prohibited on US roads, but here was one, formed in defiance of police harassment and vindictive tolls, speeding and crashing gates, their strength in numbers. The handles of the main protagonists were Rubber Duck and Pig Pen. Over a bluegrass march, Rubber Duck delivered the narrative in cavernous tones, while a huddle of southern belles jiggled a tribute to this truckin' convoy in the chorus. It sounded great, good buddy. It was fun. We cheered it on to number two.

In the same weeks, Smokie released the second of their three good singles, 'Something's Been Making Me Blue'; a simple pleasure with a tune too strong to deny. There was also 'Low Rider' by War, another of those records that made you feel very grown up when you found yourself enjoying it so much. For all I knew, this was the heaviest, darkest funk available; edgy, rhythmic hooks that strode across the landscape. Indeed, it always makes me think of fields and hedgerows. Maybe this had been the view from a coach window as we were first talking about it, winding through some Surrey backwater on the way to a rugby field. The visual associations held by records are sometimes strange. Fields and hedgerows, with urban funk and me from South London. Like, crazy.

Having fallen so in love with mid-60s Motown, I would have self-flagellated to hear anything with similar intensity and crispness coming from Noel's cueing finger, but I was beginning to accept that it was over and gone. Motown was now disco, not pop, which was fine: the best of the new sounds were easy to live with. And yet, suddenly, almost unbelievably, there was 'Love Really Hurts Without You' by Billy Ocean – straight from the good old days via courier and in bubble-wrap.

It was the first new release I had known to deliver the thrills of the Motown Sound whilst clearly being not of it. Its pace was exhilarating. Its arrangement was flawless. There was nothing about it that wasn't great. Its lyric of frustrated desire was delivered with straightforward power, without stylistic grunts or soulful slurs: Billy just belted it out like a good 'un.

Also, it was the first record I knew to use the word "fancy". Talking about fancying someone was what the likes of us did. Nobody on the grimy ledge ever spoke about burning, yearning feelings or being together for all eternitee: we said "fancy". Some wonderful people, who I had never met, had taken the trouble to make this record just for me. Or rather us, because there it was, haring towards the top of the charts. The only people who said they didn't like it seemed to be doing so on some kind of self-defeating principle.

And if that was exciting, then get this – the UK, having spent years stuck behind the Monacos and the Luxembourgs, finally won Eurovision again. The song was 'Save All Your Kisses for Me' by Brotherhood of Man; a cute, dinky tune to sing with bright faces, accompanied by a cute, dinky, up-and-down dance that required no energy whatsoever. Perfect. He's asking her to save her kisses for him while he's away working, but there's a cute, dinky twist. Right at the end, it's revealed that he's actually singing to a three year-old. Aww – it was Dad all along.

The words and tune were piddle-easy to remember, and with a little co-ordination, you could do the dance. It won the song contest at a canter which, of course, was worthy of celebration. Day after day, patriotic consumers waited their turn at the record counter. It was an example of buying a record because you felt you ought to. Standing in the queue, many may have been struck by the distinct absence of genuine enthusiasm – shortly before being struck by the distinct absence of 60p. It was the biggest-selling single of the year. It held 'Love Really Hurts Without You' at number two.

It was now pretty much the case that, when I looked down the chart listing, I knew how everything in it went, whether I liked it or not. This was true even when reading the funny version in Mum's *Melody Maker*. But there beside it was a list whose contents were a complete mystery: the Reggae Chart.

I was fascinated by this, gazing in wonder at the titles and the artists' names. Virtually none were known to me then. If I were to speculate on which ones I had read, I would, I fear, be influenced by what I have discovered in the years since. So I'm not going to. One however has stuck in my mind: 'Natty Dread a Weh She Want' by Tapper Zukie. It might be 'Wants' rather than 'Want', but please don't be silly about it.

Those familiar with the output of Uncle Tapper will know that he often uses the term "natty dread" to a quite extraordinary extent. This phrase, among many others, was a familiar one, although "cool Jamaican bloke" was probably the closest my imagination got to its actual meaning. Us white kids were often left guessing. We guessed that "ballhead" meant someone with short hair, but we didn't guess that it signified the opposite status to having righteous Rastafarian locks. "Buku-head" remains an enigma. "Butty" was easy, particularly if you heard the word as you were getting kicked in yours. There was a theory that "bomba claat" had something to do with the Jamaican Air Force. One morning, we walked into a maths room and there, in beautiful script in the middle of the chalk board, was written "rastamabumseed". No point looking that up in the dictionary, either. Tcha.

Crowds of black kids would often begin chanting what I assumed to be something from a reggae record, one or two breaking out into a passage while others laughed and egged them on. There must have been an aspect of improvisation to these sessions, judging by some of the gleeful responses. Much of the language was sexual. Those were probably the bits I understood most easily. Make of that what you will.

Occasionally, it seemed designed to intimidate. One girl in our class was fairly hostile to whites, although never physically. I don't remember hearing her speak in anything other than patois. Her attitude may simply have been a response to our levels of maturity, but she puzzled even some of the black boys, who sometimes berated her in patois themselves. Once, it was because they were fed up with her endless rendition of Tapper Zukie's 'MPLA', a single that made it into the pop chart at the end of the year and which, to my unacclimatised ears, made 'Irie Feelings (Skanga)' sound like a pub singalong.

This type of stuff was a far cry from 'Everything I Own', or the 1975 number one by Johnny Nash 'Tears on My Pillow (I Can't Take It)'; a piece of Jamaican knee-blanket action that would have fit neatly between grinning plate-spinners and somersaulting budgerigars on *Seaside Special.* Something of a half-way point between these was achieved by a single which appeared that spring: 'Dat' by Pluto.

We bloody loved this record. It was performed entirely in patois, but the fact that we could make out few of the words didn't seem to matter. The very sound of the language, added to the humorous feel, made it a joy. We knew that somebody called Ossie was in a market, having a farcical conversation with an increasingly irate butcher and not buying anything. We caught a few familiar phrases and a line that might have been about bomming his belly and pulling his pipe. But that was pretty much it. We didn't care. We thought it was brilliant.

The situation in the song is actually this: Ossie is a Rastafari who wants to save enough money from his grocery budget to buy some ganja. But times are hard, and in order to do this he has to buy the cheapest meat available – pork, which Rastas are not supposed to eat. He speaks cautiously to the butcher, scared that his Rasta brethren might overhear, referring to the pork only as "dat ting dere". But the butcher doesn't twig, and keeps suggesting alternatives while Ossie's various excuses for not taking any of them drive him steadily up the wall.

The British public were meanwhile being driven steadily up the wall by 'Save All Your Kisses for Me'. It had been number one for six weeks and the novelty of the Eurovision triumph had well and truly worn off. Any mention of it now met with groans, tuts and the occasional snarl. Enough was enough.

Once again, it was Abba who came to the rescue; it seemed they had a lance and a galloping steed on standby. This time, they liberated us with a song about fighting for freedom. 'Fernando' dealt with comradeship in the Mexican Civil War, or so I came to believe. I got the idea from somewhere and was comfortable with it although, even today, I'm not certain that there was ever a civil war in Mexico. I could always look it up.

The record was a bit stodgy, but my debt to Abba was such that I chose to overlook it. A bit of stodge sat perfectly well with many others, however. In the video, they sat around a handsome camp fire with guitars; earnest and cosy, despite the shadow of "gunce" and "cannonce". A broad audience clutched it to their collective bosom. It was safe and sounded traditional, like something from an old musical, or a folk ballad given a modern makeover.

Speaking of revivals, old-time rock 'n' roll was still capable of the occasional twitch. The previous autumn, I had caught a music show from the Tyne-Tees region, featuring an energetic performance by the group Shakin' Stevens and the Sunsets doing a song called 'Jungle Rock'. This was a load of old bunkum about wild animals jiving and jitterbugging, but it did the trick for me.

Months later (ironically while the Rubettes, having left the high school hop for the final time, were in the lower reaches of the chart with a fine effort called 'You're the Reason Why') the 1958 version of 'Jungle Rock' by Hank Mizell caught on like bushfire. It was a blaring bundle of energy in the style known as rockabilly – wild, jittery, box-slappin' stuff from the southern hills. Elvis Presley had rockabilly credentials; listen to 'Blue Suede Shoes' for an example (Chuck Berry and Little Richard, by contrast, had definitely been of the city).

There were rockabilly fans at school, with delicate quiffs flattened at the top, carrying 45s without centres by artists I hadn't heard of. One in my tutor group spent long, patient minutes telling me about them. I admired his passion and expertise. I'm not sure what he thought of 'Jungle Rock'. Perhaps he was sightly embarrassed that it had made it to number three, and that dance troupe Pan's People were prancing around to it on *Top of the Pops* in zoo costumes.

If you looked around, there was plenty of evidence that, now the Rock 'N' Roll Revival had slipped away from the charts, it had all settled into an ongoing underground scene for the truly dedicated, where teddy boy fashions were the norm. There were brothel creepers kicking around our school. Some boys wore lace ties fixed at the throat by wolf-head brooches, authentic detail adhered to by Showaddywaddy.

Our school had a thriving music department with a good dance orchestra. They played in the assembly hall on Friday lunchtimes for anybody who happened to be there, and a favourite turn was the theme from US cop drama *Hawaii Five-O*. When they fired this up, junior teds would pounce, thumbs hooked in belts, bouncing around like puppets on the end of a plank, ankles working overtime. You had to do *something* to the theme from *Hawaii Five-O*. I probably sat at the side, drumming on a table. There were black teds as well. Our school had two; older lads with quiffs fashioned from afros like topiary. Fantastic.

'Fernando' set up camp at number one for a month, then was ousted by the sickly sentimental 'No Charge' by JJ Barrie, which mercifully was only there for a week. It's about a kid presenting his parents with an itemised bill for all the jobs he'd done. Mum responds by presenting a list of her own, of all the things she's done for him since he was born, out of love and free of charge. It makes him think a bit. A worthwhile anecdote. Tell it at a dinner party to get everyone smiling and nodding. But please, please don't make it into a record; it couldn't possibly be anything other than horrible.

Its removal was celebrated the length and breadth of the land. The record responsible was a Noel-endorsed novelty, one before which other novelty records of the era bowed low. 'Combine Harvester (Brand New Key)' by the Wurzels had *oo-ar oo-ar* backing vocals, a banjo and euphonium accompaniment and was sung in a cider-soaked west country burr with rosy cheeks and glazed eyes.

It was a re-working of Melanie Safka's late-hippy winner 'Brand New Key'. She was apparently flattered. The Wurzels had taken a subtle, risqué song about teenage desire and dunked it cheerfully in pig swill. The lyric was a grand tour of farmer mythology; you kept expecting Harry Cart from the Diddymen to walk in. This fellow's gleaming new harvesting appliance meant he was now worthy of asking for her hand. They were getting on a bit; it was about time they put their acres together.

Be in no doubt as to how loved this record was. Noel was elated and proud when it got to the big place and there was nothing but encouragement from the rest of us. A silly idea, fleshed out cleverly, executed with style. Top marks to all concerned.

But if anyone was wringing their hands in despair at the state of pop because of JJ Barrie and the Wurzels, they had only to wait a matter of days. By the end of June, the number one was 'You to Me Are Everything' by the Real Thing; a sweet, soulful song with a cracking arrangement. This guy has got it bad. Love has seen perspective off but he's able to declare himself with sincerity while throwing the ball smartly into her court. It's easy to believe that she will respond.

It was an excellent pop record and had real cred. These were not seasoned Americans with aerodynamic lapels; they were young black guys from Britain – Liverpool to be exact – standing in a line on *Top of the Pops*, singing their heads off in clothes which they might, at a pinch, have bought down the road. Young black Britain loved it. Britain in general loved it.

With it in the upper reaches, and meaningful in a different way, was 'Young Hearts Run Free': upbeat soul, hard wisdom, and the clear, distracting voice of Candi Staton. She's bogged down in an unhappy relationship and longs for the freedom she fears she will never know. She's stuck. She has been for years. She pleads with youngsters everywhere to avoid her fate and fulfil themselves. In the meanwhile, she's going to get on with putting herself first more often and making the best of things.

The song was able to strike various chords with various people. Whether it was sad and claustrophobic more than it was uplifting and optimistic, was something we each had to decide for ourselves. It was substantial stuff for a disco record, in any case.

Far less substantial, was the recent single by the Carpenters; a niggling, pointless cover of a sappy 60s song called 'There's a Kind of Hush'. The only reason I mention it is because of our end-of-year school concert. The first part of the programme was to be a series of recent, family-safe hits, played by the dance orchestra and sung by a choir consisting of first and second years standing on a raised platform behind the stage. Music teachers had guided us through rehearsals with the backing on a cassette; now we had to do it with the band.

The band leader was good-humoured and patient. The head of department, watching from the side with his hands clasped behind his back, was not. In 'There's a Kind of Hush', part of the lyric states that the only sound during this hush will be "when I whisper in your ear 'I love you'". We were singing it well, if a little lazily; we certainly wanted it to sound good on the night. The head of department, however, was in no mood for cutting slack. Part way through another attempt, he strode into the middle of the stage, waving his arms wildly to stop the band, then positioned himself to bellow: "It's when I whisper in your *ear!* Your *ear!* Not when I whisper in your *rear!*"

Rarely has a chap's own grave been so thoroughly dug. The thought hadn't even occurred to us. It had now. From then on, few of us had any intention of singing "ear". "Rear" was stressed knowingly; some were singing "when I whisper in your *arse*".

The man may have realised very quickly that his intervention had done far more harm than good. To be fair, he may have tried it as a tactic, enjoying a rude joke before letting us get it out of our system and thereafter pronouncing the lyric more crisply. If so, the gamble didn't work. For members of that choir, the Carpenters may forever be associated with the idea of whispering into somebody's bottom.

The summer of 1976 was uncommonly hot and dry. Temperatures, especially in the south-east of Britain, went above 30 Celsius towards the end of June and stayed there. There was no sign of rain for week after week. Reservoir levels, already low, fell further. There was alarm. Regulations were introduced. It was to become known as The Drought. The authorities and media panicked, as they do every time we have weather.

Our school's response was to begin each morning an hour earlier at 8.00, and end the day at 1.00. So now we started three hours before the point at which teenagers are able to function rather than two, and were sent out of the building when the sun was hottest. Well done everyone.

Still, there were advantages. The new hours did not apply to my sisters' primary school, so I had the house to myself when I got home. Each day I filled a pint glass with orange squash and wedged it in the freezer until a thin layer of ice formed on the top. I then carried it out into the garden for a spot of sunbathing and to listen to the David Hamilton Show on Radio 1. The early start meant I got less of Noel's breakfast programme, but 'Diddy' David Hamilton's playlist was the one that most closely resembled it and was good compensation.

I sunbathed to the classy soul of Lou Rawls' 'You'll Never Find Another Love Like Mine', and Dorothy Moore's 'Misty Blue'; I sipped iced squash to the granny-friendly adult pop of 'A Little Bit More' by Dr Hook, and the driving blasts of Bryan Ferry's solo single 'Let's Stick Together'. There was also a new 45 by Queen, 'You're My Best Friend'; a tumble of chord changes and accentuation so pleasing that I almost forgave them. There were many other distractions on this summer soundtrack; those that were good, those that were noteworthy, as well as those that were both. But the record that dominated the airwaves as well as the top of the chart that summer was a duet between Elton John and Kiki Dee called 'Don't Go Breaking My Heart'.

Many would have rolled their eyes at this. There would have been groans, tuts and the occasional snarl. A video was recorded for *Top of the Pops*, which we saw a lot of. For those used to Elton's flamboyant, high-glam persona, this was something of a transformation. He and Kiki stood in a studio booth, dressed down, exchanging twee glances and pantomime smiles as they sang, sometimes with their arms across each other's shoulders like marshmallow-toasting chums. At one point, Elton leant forward to place a chaste kiss on the flap of Kiki's dungarees. Granny thought it was smashing.

It's a straightforward, brightly catchy love song; a nothing lyric, a "gave you my heart right from the start" kind of thing, but with 'Young Hearts Run Free' on its tail, heavy was there if you wanted it. This was not heavy. It was meant not to be. It was a highly successful piece of mainstream pop, with its greatest qualities in the orchestration. Just listen to the arrangement, just listen to the string parts. These are clever, passionate people who know what they're doing. Kiki Dee recorded her earlier solo hit 'Amoureuse' on Elton's label Rocket and you should check the orchestration out on that, too.

These arrangements – and we should include 'Love Really Hurts Without You' in this – were not thrown together in a thrice as an insult to our intelligence; they were poured over, re-written, tested and adjusted. And if they weren't, then by golly those people were in the right job.

Abba were no slouches when it came to arrangement, either. They had mastered a range of styles across their hits to date. As if to celebrate this, they released a shockingly premature *Greatest Hits* album, over half of which needed to have their claims to the status of "hit" put before a jury. The title *Greatest Hits* strongly implies that there are some hits that have been left off, i.e. the least-great ones. All of the evidence points to their English being good enough to understand this, but they ploughed on regardless and sales were vast.

They then came to the matter of what the next single would be. So far, they had gone from glam thrash to tear stains, to shimmering pop and then ethnic folk. What could they do now? Well perhaps they could go disco.

'Dancing Queen' came out at the end of the summer holiday. It had started raining again by then but it was still bloody hot. The last straw for my zinging record rack came when I discovered that a breeze had blown the curtains across it, dislodging a few of its contents, one of which, the new Abba single, had come to rest on the window ledge in the blazing sun. By the time I found it, it had warped magnificently, like a kid's drawing of a rollercoaster. I had to find funds for a second copy. I felt noble about this, as if fate had handed me an additional role in getting it to number one. But it wasn't needed. My extra copy was a tiny drop in a seething lemon-yellow and black ocean.

For, in a year of long-reigning number ones, here was another; a record which has since been examined by musicologists at great centres of learning, their papers describing its wonders in scientific detail. None of this is inappropriate, and such attentions enhance the status of pop, which is to be celebrated. Listen to it again: find something the matter with it.

Apart, that is, from the lyric. Look out – there's a teenage girl on the pull; she wants a king; he needs to be able to dance to rock music, which means he'll probably have to go to different club, but her self-assurance is such that she'll surely work something out. She's apparently jiving in the disco anyway and clearly doesn't care. Maybe they're playing 'Jungle Rock'. I didn't like it anywhere as much as 'SOS' or 'Mamma Mia'. I was pissed off that they'd gone disco with the common herd. But I was still proud of them.

The fact that 'Dancing Queen' existed proved how powerful the gravitational pull of disco was. You weren't in entertainment if you didn't have a bit of disco going on; it completed the stardust spectrum. Take, for example, Leo Sayer; a British entertainer who presented like a restless kid wanting to finish his lessons quickly so he could run off and look for conkers.

He had first appeared in an early 1974 chart dressed as a clown, singing 'The Show Must Go On', a banjo scratch with jazzy vocal detail that had its merits. He went from there through fidgety, middle-of-the-road narratives – one of which, to be fair, 'Long Tall Glasses', was about dancing - until, in the autumn of 1976, having established himself as a chart regular, he went disco. He got himself a crisp suit, had his curly hair bouffed up into something close to an afro, and strutted up and down doing 'You Make Me Feel Like Dancing', complete with falsetto vocal. Wifey and hubby had something with which to entice each other onto the dance floor. Groans, tuts and the occasional snarl. But it was a huge hit, as well as – and I still can't quite get my head around this – a number one in the US.

In the UK chart, it rubbed shoulders with the Richie Family's tame 'Best Disco in Town', which included a medley of danceable oldies, the kind of record which is always profoundly annoying, and 'Disco Duck' by Rick Dees and his Cast of Idiots, about a bloke who finds himself being transformed into a duck as he dances, to the delight of all around. The duck boogies and says groovy disco things as the backing girls coo his name. Seriously. This too, was a US number one. I mention these to provide some context, not to slag off disco or say how awful it all was, because it wasn't. Disco records could be electrifying, inspirational, essential. But goodness me, there was some poxy shit as well.

I thought 'Mississippi' by Pussycat was poxy shit. This was the record that finally booted 'Dancing Queen' off number one, then got rather comfortable there itself. It's a knee-blanket singalong *par excellence*, one to really sway in your seat to. Roll on, Mississippi, until the end of time; I'll remember you whenever I hear this song. When I was almost thirteen, it made me want to smash furniture.

But I no longer think that it's poxy shit. There are two reasons for this. Firstly, I came to realise something rather wonderful about its success. It is a country song. It has a country feel, is full of country instrumentation including pedal steel guitar, and is a sentimental tribute to a mighty American river. It is deeply and unctuously country, from top to bottom, inside and out. Except it isn't. Listen to a country record from the USA and you'll realise it sounds nothing like one. Pussycat were from Holland. Not Holland, Texas; but Holland, The Netherlands, Europe. Their record was number one just about everywhere except, well, guess. It topped the chart in Canada, France, Australia, Austria, Spain, Norway, New Zealand, Sweden, Switzerland, Ireland, Germany and Britain. But not America.

I would love to think that it was because the Yanks were sulking over a bunch of Europeans having made a fake-country record that was more charming than any anything country that they could manage. It made sense; look how they objected to our supersonic Concorde aircraft because they hadn't managed one of their own. The fact that it did so well in Canada lends credence to this lovely idea.

The second reason, however, is less fanciful. The older I get, the more 'Mississippi' appeals to me. In my forties I sought out a well-preserved copy of my own. When it comes on, my senses sharpen. I often scroll down play-lists looking for it. This is hardly surprising, since it was people my age that made it number one in the first place.

But before I changed enough to be middle-aged, I changed a bit less, to become an early teen. This happened just as dramatic, unwelcome changes to the soundtrack threatened to erupt rudely all around us.

Six

There is a question which floats into my mind every now and then: is the Electric Light Orchestra a light orchestra which is electric, or an orchestra named in honour of the invention that knocked the stuffing out of the candle industry? I like this question. Resolving it would achieve nothing.

It's likely to have first occurred to me in December 1976, when their single 'Livin' Thing' was the most played thing on the radio by miles. The group had been around for years - their first line-up had included a pre-Wizzard Roy Wood - and they were now settling into a trademark sound of big string arrangements over warm guitars and crashing beats, a straining tenor lead and neatly-clipped falsetto backing vocals. It was an accomplished, reassuring frame for widescreen songs of emotional fancy.

'Livin' Thing' was everywhere in December 1976, and its powers of evocation remain great. The darting, gypsyish violin intro reminds me of trudging through another wet morning on the way to the train station. The shaded cries of someone apparently thinking of dying, puts me in a street market, looking at Christmas trees in the drizzle. Its measured stomp of a chorus takes me to the draughty stand of a certain non-league football ground, watching an uneventful evening game with bellyaching peers. If ever I need to re-live the sensations of being cold, damp and in the dark, all I have to do is listen to 'Livin' Thing'.

I wasn't keen on it. Neither was I keen on the new single by Abba. This was called 'Money, Money, Money' and was about somebody wishing they had lots of money. It was both smug and unimaginative, sounding like the least interesting part of some stage musical. When it came on I turned the radio off. Its release was followed a week later by the new album, *Arrival*, the cover of which presented the group in jump suits of brilliant white, both in and around a high-specification helicopter. Up, up and away – Abba were now a full-blown global phenomenon.

We already knew they were Agnetha, Bjorn, Benny and Anni-Frid, their initials making up the group's name. With this release, they reversed the first B, to create a logo; making their name not only a palindrome, but a symmetrical palindrome. Abba was now a brand. The lemon-yellow and black Epic label design was replaced by a brash orange with thin white rings. I felt like something was being dragged away from me.

Logos were increasingly common on label designs. One group taking this option, with a flamboyant crest of feathers and rampant beasts covering the entire label, were Queen. They were busy blotting their copybook again with 'Somebody to Love', a record remarkable only for the number of ways in which it managed to be both dull and annoying in the space of four minutes. Many felt it was cut from the same cloth as 'Bohemian Rhapsody', but it defied categorisation; it wasn't quite opera, it wasn't quite music hall, nor was it quite jazz and certainly not pop. But it *was* horrible.

The fact that it rose to number two suggests that not everybody thought this. One of those who didn't was Mum's cousin, who came for tea on Tuesdays, bringing the newspapers from her office – the *Daily Express*, the *Daily Mirror* and the *Sun* – so that I could read about the football, find articles about music and look at anything else that caught my eye; women with bare breasts, for example.

I was still young enough to want to discuss new records with adults, especially since so many of them were Noel-goers. Mum's cousin liked Queen because of Freddie Mercury's voice. "I like a strong voice", she told me. "I could listen to him sing anything". I didn't get this, but we found common ground talking about Queen songs that I *had* liked, and I consoled myself with the fact that at least 'Somebody to Love' had been held from number one; as, for that matter, had 'Money, Money, Money' and 'Livin' Thing'. This was all greatly comforting. Mighty deeds had been done in the name of all things decent. The heroes responsible? Showaddywaddy.

'Under the Moon of Love' was, simply, a very good pop record. They took this sort-of-hit from 1961, updated and improved its sound, then unleashed the bastard. The whole thing is built on a swaggering saxophone riff that you can *dun da-dun dun* to; and we all did exactly that. There are thunderous percussive hooks throughout, and the title refrain is the biggest hook of all. It's comfortably-paced; drunken revellers could step up and down to it with their arms round each other in safety; you could – and did – rock around the Christmas tree to it with Granny. Granny would probably have done it without you. Bashing an old rock 'n' roll tune into modern shape was a formula that would maintain the Wad as Top 10 regulars for two more years, but they would never achieve quite this standard again.

Its release coincided with that of an album of instrumentals by British guitar guru Bert Weedon. The TV adverts for his *22 Golden Guitar Greats* did the same job as those of *That'll Be the Day*, three years before. They were almost all covers; a fresh injection of old tunes to please still-hungry audiences. I loved 'Wonderful Land' and 'FBI', both hits for the Shadows. I remember the black teds at school, marching up and down the corridor going *dun da-dun dun* to a galvanising tune called 'Diamonds'. The reaction was typical and widespread. Just in time for letters to Santa. It sold shedloads. Thanks to Bert Weedon and Showaddywaddy, old time rock 'n' roll ended the year on a high.

But then, a low. A new issue of *Melody Maker* came through the door and the image on the cover made me feel sick. *Melody Maker* covers were usually a pile-up of blotchy photos and text beneath the white-on-red logo. This was different. It filled the whole page. It was a black and white cartoon drawing of a scrawny Christmas tree. It may have been completely bare of needles. At the end of each branch hung a disposable razor blade. Beside it, an equally scrawny figure sat smirking; his nasty, ratty features exuding satisfaction. There was possibly a scrawny, ratty caption alongside it.

Christmas was not like this. It was rich green and red, with tinsel and glitter that twinkled in candlelight; it was chubby plastic snowmen in top hats sitting on the mantelpiece; it was decorated baubles that cracked and shattered if you were not gentle. It was 'Santa Claus Is Coming to Town' by the Crystals and 'Frosty the Snowman' by the Ronettes. I worried and I seethed. It was the razor blades. It was the satisfaction on the face. It was the idea that this version was better; or, perhaps, simply, that Christmas was shit.

At that point, I already knew that the figure depicted was called Johnny Rotten and that he was in a group called the Sex Pistols. This was horrible enough. You couldn't have a group called the Sex Pistols. I didn't get why anyone would want to. They were becoming notorious. I heard they had sworn on TV. I couldn't say too much with the language I was using these days, but I still didn't like it. Over the next few months I would discover more. I heard the term "punk rock" at some point – don't remember when. It stood for all of the groups that were suddenly there, making blary, nasty, sneering music for the benefit of fuck knows who. The Sex Pistols were simply the best-known.

That Christmas tree cover put me off *Melody Maker* for a long time. Instead, I got my information from the papers. I wasn't the only one. We talked about punk rockers at school, swapping notes on what we'd heard. Our sniggering friend at the grimy ledge had now settled on a rock band called Thin Lizzy as his favourites - "proper music", he called it. He pulled faces at the mention of punk rockers. "Load of wallies", he said, looking just a little uncomfortable.

From the newspapers and from each other, we heard that punk rockers wore bin liners and dog collars to shock people. There were pictures in the tabloids to back this up. Their clothes were ripped, or badly fitting; some had what looked like Terry's nappies hanging from their trousers. They spiked their hair up. They got drunk. They went to dingy clubs to see blary, sneery punk rock groups and thought it was good. They danced by doing the Pogo, going straight up and down with rigid bodies, without necessarily being in time with the music. And get this – they spent the whole time spitting at each other. They spat at the groups as they played and the groups spat back. This was a sign of approval. I read this in a paper. If you played in one of these places and got completely covered in gob from the audience, it meant they liked you. The more gob the better. And the rougher the better. It was part of a good night to get slashed with a broken beer glass or whacked with a bicycle chain. You'd lose teeth and think it was part and parcel. They didn't care. Gob, blood and pain. They wore safety pins – through their cheeks. Opened the pins up and stuck them straight in, through and out the other side, then did them up again. They wore razor blades as earrings, scraping and snipping at their necks. The papers told me the lot.

It wasn't what I wanted to hear. Things were nasty enough already. Darwinian rules applied all day long. At school, you could me mugged for your dinner money anywhere. Your face could be the target for someone simply experimenting with how high they could get their foot. A favourite pastime for the older kids was coming alongside your class queuing outside a room, and heaving at your head so that it cracked against the wall behind. The first you knew about it was when you were being picked off the floor, shaking and in tears. I saw a girl, rumoured to be pregnant, being harried down the street by a baying mob; punches aimed at her face, kicks at her stomach.

Days when there was suddenly more violence than usual, we called "nutty season". Gangs would rampage through the buildings and the outside areas, relieving you of anything that you had and they didn't. They steamrollered down the corridors, punching, kicking, mowing down anyone in their path. Some corridors had no windows, just classroom doors on either side, and the light-bulbs were routinely smashed. Kids had their arms broken in stampedes. Teachers were viciously attacked. If you heard a rumble in the darkness up ahead, you turned sharpish and legged it. At the most popular bus stops at home time there was constant conflict; kids battling to be first on the open rear platform long before the bus stopped, pushing away anyone smaller, making it their business to brush aside sappy notions of waiting your turn, defying the authority of transport staff, however much the conductors stood up to it. The poor sods had to think about their own safety.

But once it was over and you were home, whether you had been caught up in anything or not, you had your records. They were an antidote, presenting a different world; affording indulgences in sentimentality. You were flexing your emotional muscles, responding to lyrics and atmospheres, balancing out harsh realities by imagining what it would be like to be in love and to be loved right back. Song lyrics told you that somewhere out there was someone special just for you, maybe just one perfect love in the whole world.

In contrast to your daily experience, this world was classy, soothing and affectionate. Cherry-pick records from any month of any year from the mid-fifties onwards, and that's what you could have. It was reliable.

In December 1976, I was able to rely on 'Love Me' by Yvonne Elliman. It brought me soft, warm lights; it brought me visions of adulthood; it brought me peace. I played it over and over. It was the first single I owned on the RSO label, with its funny little cow logo in the midst of all that tan. There would be more. The song used a slowed version of the Latin disco beat as a backdrop to the chronicle of a breaking, pleading heart. Its sound was rich and subtle. It was gorgeous. Punk rockers would have sneered and gobbed on it. They would have wanted something blary.

It wasn't that I didn't like blary music; half the best things on *That'll Be the Day* were blary. It wasn't that I didn't like new stuff, either; new stuff was great, as long as it was good. But it was the vocal delivery. It was the sneering. They weren't even trying to sing properly; it was anti-singing. It was the sneering and the cockiness and the gob. And it was *them*. Because I knew all about *them*. I had been coming into contact with their kind for some time, often being left with nothing but trembling, nauseous insides and fantasies about having a gun, a gang, or special powers. And now their day was coming. Everything would be handed over to those that never had anything positive to contribute; who could only slag off, slash, and obstruct; who never laughed with you, only at you; who never helped or constructed, only mangled; who were never joyfully amazed by anything. The future was theirs. What would there be for us? The papers didn't tell me that.

I already understood that things change; that change begins with something new that grows and spreads, regardless of how you feel about it; like a dad "living somewhere else for a while" or a grandparent "not coming to us for Christmas this year, just for once".

Punk rock was the new thing. The things we liked were "boring", "old" and "rubbish". Most adults dismissed it as horrible, but others, many of whom I respected, seemed quite excited: "They want to wipe everything away and start again, see off everything that's past it". Things change; and here they were, changing.

I remember one particularly pointed remark: "Abba's exactly the kind of thing they want to get rid of". I was shaken. I was furious. They were coming to get us, and they were gathering support. It might be that we were in the final days of a dying soundtrack. Clear everything away and start again. Shit. Why?

There was no one to answer that question. I never saw any punk rockers. Despite my fears about bumping into some at the bottom of our road, I never did. I didn't see any at football. There were none at school. In time, there would be one; a black girl in a studded dog collar and spiky make up, with a small chain of safety pins on her school shirt – our token punk rocker. But that was months away. Their threat remained distant. There were reports that they were being attacked in the street, often by teds. Good old teds. Yet "out there" they remained, growing in influence, spreading in numbers, mustering for assault.

For now, life continued as normal. Noel played Leo Sayer, Showaddywaddy and Billy Ocean. I moved further into the Motown catalogue, going from the Four Tops, to pre-1967 Marvin Gaye, Junior Walker & the All-Stars, Smokey Robinson & the Miracles and Stevie Wonder.

I bought fewer singles in the first few months of 1977 – what I most wanted to do was save up enough to get on a bus and head to the salubrious HMV store on Oxford Street, the biggest record shop in the world, so I was told; where albums were stacked upright in plastic wrapping and everything smelt wonderful, where the lights were dimmed and the atmosphere was scholarly, where customers revered the goods. There were few people my age in there. You went up and down stairs, through doors and between aisles, and there always seemed to be more.

How different from the little local shops, whose albums were tucked away behind the counter in their inner sleeves, while their covers suffocated in over-stuffed racks, spines broken in several places by the brash flicking and rifling of browsers. I loved the HMV store. There were no punk rockers there, either.

I've no idea how I imagined they were going to "get rid" of Abba, but the threat felt real. I was years away from understanding how easily vacuous tripe can torrent, both from lazily un-informed adults and determinedly un-informed newspapers. I was easy to rattle. I was downcast. Once again, it was a record that came to the rescue. Once again, it was Abba that came to the rescue. If they had indeed been under pressure, their response was decisive; they released as their new single a track from *Arrival* called 'Knowing Me, Knowing You'.

Had I not been on such a huge Motown trip, I may well have owned a copy of *Arrival* and understood that it was the obvious choice. But I was, so I didn't and I couldn't. When Noel said "... and this is the new single from Abba..." it was the first time I heard it. Straight away, everybody seemed to accept that it would be another number one – a *big* number one. We spoke in terms of when, not if, it would get there.

The reason for this was, simply, the scale of its quality. It was more than good; it was magnificent. It had grandeur; it had power. It shone, shimmered and throbbed right from the ringing strums of its intro; a blend of somehow familiar sounds we had heard nowhere else.

It was about an adult break-up. They've moved their stuff out; now she's tearfully touring bare rooms where there was once laughter, where there were once children playing; she hears echoes of what is now gone; it's horrible, but they can't stay together; they just can't. The sound and the arrangement elevate this local agony into something vast, super-brilliant, oozing class; pop savvy draped in velvets with a generous ermine trim. It had big number one written all over it. Tone fearlessly made it his Record of the Week.

It was quite normal for a second or third single from a successful album to be a huge hit, even though the album had sold well. Album sales had now overtaken those of singles, so you might wonder how this was happening. If you had *Arrival*, would you get 'Knowing Me, Knowing You' on a single as well?

Well there are various reasons why you might. Maybe you were a "completist", someone unable to take their own enthusiasm for an act seriously unless they had everything they had ever done. Perhaps there was a track on the B-side that wasn't on the album – you'd have to have that. You might simply want to "support" your favourites; having the album, but wanting to do your bit to get the singles up the charts by buying them, too. This was an act of devotion and also faith; it was unlikely that, as a mere punter, you would know which shops were being selected by the British Market Research Bureau in a given week, although I assumed that HMV in Oxford Street always were. The third possibility was that you were a big fan of the act and there-fore had the album, but generally preferred the single format and so bought the 45s automatically. Over the next few years, each of these definitions would repeatedly apply to me.

But the most populous category of single purchaser was probably that of those who didn't have the album, were not particularly keen on the band, but loved the song. Good singles, whoever they are by, have merit in their own right.

In the spring of 1977, I bought singles by funky soul groups, supper club divas and airy Americans because I thought they were good, or at least interesting; but I would never have bought their albums in a million years. It was the appeal of that one record.

Many in this category went out and bought 'Knowing Me, Knowing You'. It's worth noting that, however eagerly fans had been waiting for the new album at the end of November, *Arrival* spent its second, and far longer, stay on top of the album charts *after* 'Knowing Me, Knowing You' had been the number one single. The army of existing devotees had been joined by legions of gob-smacked new ones. Abba were the absolute overlords and overladies of the music scene, and the world seemed quite content.

Except the bits that contained punk rockers. There were no punk rock records in the charts yet, but there surely would be; and as soon as the first one appeared, there would be more, and the sneering gobbers would have their justification and would swarm in everywhere, doing what they wanted, wrecking everything of value and laughing while they were doing it. They'd have to let them on *Top of the Pops*. They'd have to let them be DJs on Radio 1. Wait until other, more local, sneering gobbers realised what fun they could have by joining the fray. All the nice things, all the nice people, would just be kicked to pieces.

This analysis ignored two things. Firstly, I was no simpering innocent. When in the mood, I could sneer with the best of them. I sneered at my sisters; I sneered at teachers; I sneered at certain football teams and their supporters.

I could also gob. I envied those around me who appeared capable of gobbing semi-professionally. Conjuring up a good furry one and expelling it with a clean *thoot* towards a target, was greatly satisfying for a thirteen-year-old. I tended not to do it in front of people; if you mucked it up you got sneered at. But the second thing was this: all the sneering gobbers I knew were either soul fans or loved Rod Stewart.

Rod Stewart had been a superstar since dominating the autumn of 1971 with 'Maggie May', a record good enough to lift a sordid tale of sexual convenience to the status of British folk standard. In the following years he turned his hand to everything from the sedated sea shanty 'Sailing' to the slow swingin' smooch of 'Tonight's the Night' with a few surprises in between; and the glue that held it all together was his compelling figure – he cut quite a dash.

He might have enjoyed being a hairy-arsed rocker when it suited him, delivering lyrics like "You're breaking my heart 'cos you're stealing my tart" when fronting his band the Faces; but he could, and did, appeal to everybody. He was a showman, filling the stage with his strutting and shape-making, inverting his mic stand, leaning towards, stretching away, grimacing as he hit and held those special notes, generously providing long, have-your-fill glimpses of his backside. There was a twinkle in his eye, there was a promise on his lips. His chiselled looks were his trademark. He dressed posh, he dressed glam, he dressed international; sometimes he barely dressed at all. His hair was incredible, like a shop-front for all style. It was almost feathered, cascading in perfect layers; on top, it had begun to spring forth from a crown just above the forehead. This was the prototype for the later, un-revered style known as the mullet, but Rod was not yet being tittered at in the same way; no one was sneering.

Some of the toughest kids I knew wouldn't hear a word against Rod. You could say what you liked about his records – they could always listen to them in secret – but never about him. He was what they wanted to be. "I ain't queer or nothing", I was told, "but don't you think he's good-looking?" It didn't seem reasonable to say no, not least because such sincerity, even in a sneering gobber, was impossible to crush.

But I wasn't really sure what good-looking was in a bloke. I thought the best-looking man on TV was possibly Harry H. Corbett, from the rag-and-bone comedy *Steptoe and Son*, because of his strong, dark looks; but that was just my opinion, and testament to how you can warm to people in all sorts of ways if they make you laugh.

For many of the girls around us, the latest pin-ups were David Soul and Paul Michael Glaser, stars of the American cop show *Starsky & Hutch*. Neither was particularly handsome or pretty; but they were irreverent, tough, well-dressed and in possession of an excellent car. Well, there you go. David Soul had recently launched a pop career and taken the oh-so-sensitive 'Don't Give Up on Us' to number one.

His name belied his musical style, but the soul genre itself was chugging along very nicely. Stevie Wonder's new double-album, *Songs in the Key of Life*, was a mainstream sensation; memorable tunes and themes for all the family, with jazz detail to delight the musos. Some sneering gobbers may have liked its curves and polish, but many would have recoiled from the doting parental anthem 'Isn't She Lovely', as well as other bits that made it all a bit too cosy.

Both of its hit singles - 'I Wish' and 'Sir Duke' - were early releases on a new, re-designed label for Motown recordings. The Tamla-Motown label was suddenly gone, that refined, silver-on-black replaced by solid spokes of blue light; perhaps it was an explosion, perhaps you were looking down a tunnel. It was possibly the brashest, most shocking label makeover there would ever be. It felt like a death in the family.

Thelma Houston was on its roster. Her dance hit was 'Don't Leave Me This Way', a good song with a haunting verse and a shouty chorus. A rival version, from Harold Melvin and the Blue Notes on Philadelphia International, was in the charts at the same time. There wasn't much between them in terms of quality, but Harold made it to number five, Thelma to thirteen.

Not far from these, was 'Car Wash' by Rose Royce; a cheerful, finger-poppin' tribute to how much fun it was working at the car wash. It came out in the spring – see if it's as much fun washing cars at the end of the autumn. It had a patterned handclap intro, which football fans experimented with for a while.

These records had the accomplished American sound that we had come to regard as standard for soul and disco. But there were other sounds. At the start of the year, there had been 'Daddy Cool' by the curiously-named Boney M; three girls and a bloke – they stood still and rolled their shoulders as they sang, while he shuffled and twirled busily around them like a ten-year-old trying to impress the judges. Straight away we were told that they were German, as if to excuse its strange, not-quite-right sound (the lead singer was actually British but I wouldn't discover this for years). It was European disco; in the same way that 'Mississippi' had been European country.

There were assertive strings, throbbing bass and uh-huh saxophone detail, all of it percussive, all of it benign. She was crazy like a fool, for her Daddy Cool. The lyric didn't expand beyond this; the spoken part in the middle said the same thing with minimal alteration. Everything was purely functional; big-sound disco by numbers; as if 'Get Up and Boogie' had been wisely scrapped and a better job made at the second attempt.

Its B-side was 'No Woman, No Cry', a song written by Bob Marley, the handsome, enigmatic Jamaican who had emerged as the global star of reggae music; his Rasta message woven into songs commanding wide appeal. 'No Woman, No Cry' was downbeat and reflective; Boney M's cover was mid-tempo, perfect for doing the washing up to.

If you liked it a little funkier, there was 'Boogie Nights' by Heatwave. Apart from one American band member, this was an entirely British effort, and the best home-grown soul yet. A swirling, dreamy intro featuring jazzy guitar and harp, leaps into a tight, edgy groove, with backing vocals delivering the title like a repeated *chang ga-chang* rhythm-guitar lick. And that was just the first thirty seconds. Wicked.

Even funkier, though not quite as good, was 'Ain't Gonna Bump No More (With No Big Fat Woman)' by Joe Tex. This was about the perils of doing the Bump, a dance involving you bumping hips with a partner, when that partner's hips were capable of sending you flying into a wall. Joe had been rather keen on this big fat woman, but she kept knocking him over and he had come close to serious injury. Why he didn't simply suggest a different dance, is something we were left to guess at. An alternative reading is that she was following him around the dance floor to get him for calling her big and fat. Joe sang in hoarse, southern-state tones with the occasional shriek. You might imagine that these were shrieks of fear – she's found him again; hips at the ready, vengeance on her mind.

No such images were conjured listening to 'Free' by Denice Williams, a gently atmospheric record that reached number one in May. It was full of jazz harmonics; its backing vocal went *bup buddup-bah*, and warm vibraphone notes floated around like fuzzy confetti.

Usually when jazz had sidled into pop, it had a traditional, big-band-and-posh-clothes kind of vibe. This didn't – it was less showbiz; it was less old. Soul would increasingly sound like this. The girlish, powerful lead vocal performed warbling acrobatics of the kind that would in time become the norm, to the extent that anyone not delivering them would be deemed not to be a proper singer. Here, it was merely a striking embellishment at the end of a lovely, refreshing song. When 'Free' was mentioned, most girls smiled and said they liked that one; most boys shrugged and said "'s alright".

So, soul was not necessarily for the dance floor. Slow ones could be for smooching to, but 'Free' wasn't a smoocher. Neither was 'Show You the Way to Go' by the Jacksons. They had once been the Jackson 5; spangled Motown superstar heart-throbs, with cute kid brother Michael in front and a concentration of Berry Gordy's keenest studio talents behind, performing pop songs of intense quality like 'I Want You Back', 'ABC' and 'I'll Be There'. Now they were older; they had grown up a bit; Michael was a fascinating teenager; they had moved to Epic and forged a more mature sound. 'Show You the Way to Go' was smooth, laid-back and resolutely hookless. Somehow, it too went to number one, little over a month after Denice Williams had been there. Lots of soul, but no party. In the interim, Britain had staged the biggest party for many a year, and punk rock had stolen a big chunk of the limelight.

The occasion was the Queen's Silver Jubilee. Elizabeth II had been on the throne for 25 years and it was to be marked grandly, with receptions, parades and street parties, scheduled for early June. Bunting was put out. London buses were re-painted silver. There were union flags everywhere. Jubilee Days were declared – extra national holidays. The popularity of the monarch, together with the various strains of patriotism among the population, came together to produce a major event throughout nation and Commonwealth.

It was a celebration of the establishment. It was something to cheer. Hooray for the queen. Hooray for the flag. People happily conformed. All eyes were on it. An opportunity, therefore, to grab attention by not conforming. Especially if you were able to not-conform rudely, and with blaring amplification. For punk rockers, it was tantalising.

Few of them, however, were in a position to do more than sneer and gob from the sidelines. Those who were, did so because of Malcolm McLaren. He was an entrepreneur who owned a shop on the King's Road in west London called Sex. It was a fashion outlet. He considered himself able to spot youth trends ahead of the game. He was happy to shock. Hence the name of the shop. His partner, Vivienne Westwood, was a designer with similar instincts. She began using forms and imagery connected to fetishism, bondage and Nazism; anything that would conduct anger; anything that would ruffle the feathers of the onlooker.

Those that were prepared to wear them were those for whom they were absolutely right. If you put that stuff on, you wanted to alarm and offend. It was deliberate, the mark of a distinct and separate identity. It was dissent. Those that hung around Sex were natural outsiders; misfits and rejects. Some were smart and thoughtful, some were downright unpleasant. A few of them had formed a band and McLaren began managing them. They were called the Sex Pistols. There was a young audience absolutely ready for something like them; appalled by some of the world, bored by the rest of it. The country was in the doldrums. There appeared to be no future; there appeared to be no fun.

Having begun to gain their notoriety from playing in London, they started touring. They had gigs cancelled on the orders of outraged local promoters. They were banned from towns. Matriarchs in head scarves stood before TV cameras saying we don't want them here. They were harried and harassed, while those who were dying to see them were left frustrated. All this served as publicity. They had been signed by EMI, releasing the single 'Anarchy in the UK' in honour of the political anti-system they purported to be in favour of; words associated with it included "chaos" and "destruction", things that punk rockers said they aspired to anyway. It reached number thirty-eight in December. I never heard Noel play it; it might have meant having to leave out 'Livin' Thing' for a day.

Unhappy with their reputation, EMI dropped them. They then signed to A&M, making them stablemates of the Carpenters. The next single was to be 'God Save the Queen', whose core, sarcastic purpose seemed to be sticking two fingers up at the Silver Jubilee. Any broader meaning in the lyric was always going to be lost against that backdrop. They were gobbing at Her Majesty with the nation's Jubilee Days in sight. Terrified, A&M sacked them before it was released. It seemed that the establishment was winning and would squash them.

But, then, along came Richard Branson. This was the entrepreneur's entrepreneur; a grinning beard on legs who saw an opportunity in the Sex Pistols. He had been selling records to rock fans via mail order; he had then launched a record label of his own, which he named Virgin. To it, he had signed a multi-instrumentalist called Mike Oldfield, whose progressive album *Tubular Bells* became one of the most successful LPs of the decade. He took these hippy credentials and set them at the service of Malcolm McLaren, a man associated with the slogan "Never trust a hippy". The Sex Pistols signed to Virgin. 'God Save the Queen' was released in the last week of May.

My memories of the Jubilee include sitting at a long table surrounded by red, white and blue bunting at a crowded street party just off the Walworth Road. There were cuboids of jelly on paper plates. There's a photograph of me waving a small union flag on a plastic stick, with something close to a smile.

My soundtrack had the glossy rock chug of 'Lido Shuffle' by Boz Scaggs – whose name sounds like something you put ointment on – and 10cc's distracting bag of tricks 'Good Morning Judge'. It didn't have the Sex Pistols. 'God Save the Queen' was, inevitably, banned from the radio. This did not stop it racing towards the top of the charts, supported further by publicity stunts engineered by McLaren, which included a Thames cruise at the height of the celebrations, with the band performing and their entourage partying for as long as it took the police boats to intercept them.

The incumbent number one was a double A-side that I *do* know both sides of very well – without liking it, I hasten to add: 'I Don't Want to Talk About It'/'First Cut Is the Deepest' by Rod Stewart. Strong rumour has it, backed by anecdotal evidence from the distribution company that handled both records, that the Sex Pistols comfortably outsold The Gorgeous One during Jubilee Week. Yet, when the chart was published, Rod was holding them at number two. I might have been more enthusiastic if he'd done it with a record that didn't send me to sleep. I simply ignored the whole thing and went back to the Four Tops.

I can't remember when we stopped calling it "punk rock" and started referring to it simply as "punk". If I guess, I could be months and months out. People were already calling them "punks" rather than "punk rockers", but I'm not sure how widespread this was. For the sake of this narrative, I am going to assume it was not until at least the following spring, when there was a crisis in my record box.

In the interim, the inevitable punk rock invasion of the soundtrack and of the singles chart began. We're talking one or two a month at most, but I still hated it. Already, at Crisis in the Record Box minus nine months, there was 'Sheena Is a Punk Rocker' by the Ramones, which was un-shocking and uninspiring. Punk rock could now add dull to its list of sins.

Then there was 'Peaches' by the Stranglers – the most intentionally nasty band name yet, aside, arguably, from the Damned. 'Peaches' was in the charts for ages and got into the Top 10. A grating but compelling bass riff accompanied the theme of strolling along the beach, ogling girls in bikinis. We've been here before. Some in my circles were excited about the lyric containing the words "shit" and "clitoris". It only got played on the radio after they re-recorded the vocal with these words taken out. Ogling girls in bikinis was clearly okay, as long as you didn't swear.

My only other encounter with punk rocker sexuality had been through the tabloids that Mum's cousin brought round. Sneering gobbers in my circles spoke about sex and female body parts with icy aggression, and it would be reasonable to assume that punk rockers shared the habit. But my reaction to one particular shocking exposé took me by surprise. It was claimed that when propositioning for sex, boy punk rockers went up to girl punk rockers and asked them if they wanted to go outside, and: "A good punk girl would say yes".

I pictured black make up and bin liners, people taking a break from pogo-ing to quietly sneak off for a bit of the other, and it struck me as highly unlikely. I just didn't buy it. Why were they trying to make us angry about sex when the rest of it was bad enough? It was the first time it had occurred to me that a newspaper might be telling us something that they had made up. It made me uncomfortable, not because my faith in adults had been damaged, but because I was showing a glimmer of sympathy for punk rockers.

Their genre may have been gathering pace, but the world was not yet coming to an end. There were balancing factors. Two features of the late summer stand out. One of these was a concentration of instrumental chart hits, the like of which had not been seen since the days of the Shadows and Johnny and the Hurricanes. Crisis in the

Record Box minus eight months: Emerson, Lake and Palmer, famous for albums that gave the progressive rock treatment to revered classical pieces – a far cry from B. Bumble and the Stingers – entered the singles chart with a re-working of Aaron Copland's 'Fanfare for the Common Man', full of powerful, inspiring rhythms and organ blurts that sounded great. It made number two.

It was followed into the Top 10 by a pair of real electronic gems: 'Oxygene (part 4)' by Jean Michelle Jarre and 'Magic Fly' by Space; distinct from each other, but equally hypnotic and melodic. Both of these records appealed across every barrier you could think of and thoroughly deserved to do so. Electronic sounds had been around for a long time but here was a fresh crop - Donna Summer's revolutionary disco number one 'I Feel Love' had recently showcased them. An alternative future was on full display and had apparently stolen a march.

But before we start getting all highbrow about it, there was also 'The Crunch' by the Rah Band; catchy and almost as electronic, but low-slung and goofy, with plenty of room for the silliest dances you could dream up. Good fun. For a few weeks, the early 60s were back, only this time with more dials and wires.

The second event touched just about everybody. Crisis in the Record Box minus seven months: I was with my dad on a football terrace at an August pre-season friendly, when a rumour started spreading through the crowd that Elvis Presley had died. My aunt, at home, called out to my uncle; her distressed voice brought him hurrying down the stairs. She told him Elvis was dead. "Bloody hell," he said, "for a minute I thought it was something serious".

Many, however, thought it was very serious indeed. The King of Rock 'N' Roll was no more. There was a sense of collective mourning. Blokes with quiffs and tattoos took the fags out of their mouths for the cameras, to wipe away tears and say that they couldn't believe it. His new single, the upbeat, moody but unremarkable 'Way Down', was number one within a fortnight. A sentimental tribute, 'I Remember Elvis Presley' by Danny Mirror, left slime trails around the charts for a few weeks. It was the drugs that killed him, we were told; drugs that were helping him with his weight. We heard that he was found dead on the toilet, but woe betide us if we started giggling about it. The King is dead. Blimey.

Crisis in the Record Box minus six months: my fears were being realised – increasing punk rock chart success. A new Sex Pistols single, 'Pretty Vacant' had come and gone, now there was 'Do Anything You Wanna Do' by the Rods. Their name had been shortened from Eddie and the Hot Rods, one I was familiar with from *Melody Maker*. It was thrashy and blary and I just lumped it in with the rest, which was unfair for many reasons. This was a record I would grow to love deeply, but during the weeks when it was zig-zagging up and down the chart in ungainly lurches, I wanted nothing to do with it. Then came 'Looking After Number One' by the Boomtown Rats, a convincing punk rock name and title alongside a sneering, finger-jabbing lyric that got lots of airplay.

Each of these tunes had bits which, annoyingly, got stuck in my head. Considering I had just discovered the Marvelettes and had their Best Of on heavy rotation alongside Smokey Robinson and the Miracles' Greatest Hits, they were doing very well to be grabbing so much of my attention, curse them.

A better target for my hatred might have been 'Gimme Dat Banana' by Black Gorilla, a nasty little record in the guise of a jolly romp about jungle animals; in the lower chart at a time when the far right National Front were marching through our cities, parading the same flag we had been waving in the Jubilee Days. Racists at school latched onto it straight away. Perhaps di coconut tree's darkest hour.

Crisis in the Record Box minus five months: speaking of darkest hours, disco was threatening to become a parody of itself. The upper reaches were being taken over by cute European accents talking off ze boogie-voogie and panting about how much they liked the disco sound – hey! 'Yes Sir, I Can Boogie' by Spanish duo Baccara, took its kitsch and (possible) irony to number one, while French act La Belle Epoque took a mirrorball cover of the 60s hit 'Black Is Black' to number two. Both were knee-blanket disco; un-threatening, happy with any kind of backdrop and any kind of audience, but each a good old singalong. The only way either act would have upset Granny would have been by winking at Grandad.

And if you thought the Americans would come galloping to the rescue, you could think again. Their response was 'Star Wars Theme' by Meco, a disco re-working of excerpts from the soundtrack of the new space adventure movie *Star Wars*, due for release in late December and awaited with unfathomable eagerness. This drivel was the closest many could come to a preview.

At the same time, also linked to the space theme, was the worst Carpenters single yet: 'Calling Occupants of Interplanetary Craft', a narrative about an extra-terrestrial encounter, painful to listen to, even before you realised how far up itself it was.

Not far from it however, was the third and final good single by Smokie; a robust cover of the twangy 60s favourite 'Needles and Pins'. Well done, Smokie. And that, dear reader, is that promise kept.

Crisis in the Record Box minus four months: my fourteenth birthday. I got the last Motown "Best Of" I would ever acquire on vinyl. The remaining act I was interested in was Martha Reeves and the Vandellas; I knew 'Heat Wave' and 'Jimmy Mack', both of which raise an enthusiasm among other Motown fans which I have never quite understood, but I was keen to check out the back catalogue. I got their *Anthology*, a single disc on the new, blue spokes Motown label. My favourite discovery was 'Love Bug Leave My Heart Alone', a gripping melodrama; mid-paced, well arranged, with fuzz guitar providing depth to its effect. A wonderful surprise.

There had been another Motown-related surprise recently. A new compilation, *Diana Ross and the Supremes – 20 Golden Greats*, had spent most of the autumn on top of the UK album chart. It contained all the singles from their *Anthology*, minus the very early ones and those with the Temptations. The UK had gone nuts for it; the word had spread. It was a good feeling.

Crisis in the Record Box minus three months: older boys had been wandering around school singing a punk rock song called 'Orgasm Addict'. I didn't know who it was by. The title's suggestion was intriguing, but although I spent a few moments pondering it, I had picked sides and therefore thought it was disgraceful. I also thought it disgraceful that many girls were wearing synthetic sandals – shallow, shabby-looking things they called "plastics" - instead of proper shoes. Sneering with the feet.

Another sign of creeping punk rock popularity was the appearance, on the boys' toilet wall, of the logo for a band called Jam, with the last bit of the 'm' curling back underneath. Who were these cowards sneaking into the bogs to scrawl this filth on the walls? I had seen pictures of Jam. The fact that they were wearing suits meant nothing. They weren't proper suits anyway; the lapels were too thin and they didn't have waistcoats. Just punk rockers. You could tell from the hair, the shades and the expressions. I had heard a recent single, 'All Around the World' and felt pleased that it was rubbish.

Within a year, this band would release a record that I liked. I would then summon the enthusiasm to recognise that their full name was *the* Jam, a name with credible resonance and nothing to do with fruit preserve. For now, they were the enemy.

Also, there was a new Elvis. As soon as Elvis Presley died, someone called Elvis Costello appeared; Noel had played a single called '(The Angels Wanna Wear My) Red Shoes' which I had liked but didn't buy. It obviously wasn't punk rock; it sounded like a punk rock group had got into the studio but decided to do something nicer at the last minute. It didn't get anywhere.

His new one was 'Watching the Detectives' which was bloody great; a sinister atmosphere in keeping with the "detective" theme, created and sustained by the whole band over well-spaced reggae. The lyrics were delivered with an aggression which I somehow didn't mind. This guy might be able to sneer and gob, but I instinctively felt that he wasn't going to do it at me. I raced out to get it, along with others sufficient in number to put it in the Top 20. I kept putting the needle back to the start after it faded, often just for its incredible drum intro. It was on a label with a grey design called Stiff. I liked that, too.

The other two I will mention here are ones I bought during the Christmas holiday and would have been more cautious about mentioning. 'Love of My Life' by the Dooleys – most of whom were members of the same family – was safe, living-room friendly, disco-ish pop for white folks. The lyric was standard splodge about forever and always, but there was something in the sound that made me like it. Good quality, perhaps. We have not heard the last of the Dooleys.

By contrast, Scott Fitzgerald and Yvonne Keeley had just released what would be their only hit. I hooked on to it ages before it got into the charts. 'If I Had Words' was an extraordinary and unique record; its melody taken from an organ piece by classical composer Saint-Saens, its lyric worshipful, its rhythm a gently chugging reggae beat. It was a single verse, repeated over and over again, each time building on the last; initially by switching the vocal between Yvonne and a some-what comical, cod-gospel Scott; then by adding a children's choir; then more strings; then more vocal embellishments; then church bells; then more noise from everybody. It sounded like the coolest Sunday school outing ever. Not once have I turned down the chance to hear it again.

Crisis in the Record Box minus two months: out with the old, in with the new. Following 'C Moon', Paul McCartney's band Wings had produced some really good singles before falling into sentimental dis-repute at the expense of those who trusted him because he used to be in the Beatles. Now, they were at number one with 'Mull of Kintyre', a swaying tribute to the area of Scotland where his family now lived, complete with lashings of bagpipes. It was actually a double A-side, its flip being the rock fidget 'Girls' School'. If the latter had been played more, we may not have minded so much. If the single had been num-ber one for two, maybe three weeks, we may not have minded so much. But it was there for nine weeks, through Christmas and into the New Year.

It was finally replaced by a reggae record so rickety that it sounded like it was held together with sticky tape. 'Uptown Top Ranking' by Althia and Donna was a joyful bundle of frivolous patois, peppered with the phrase "and ting", sung by two girls who, when performing it on *Top of the Pops*, giggled and forgot the words.

It was a perfect antidote and the mood of celebration was wide-spread. It certainly made our school happy, uniting disparate tribes in grinning nods of satisfaction. The links between the punk rock scene and that of reggae are well documented: their outsider status gave them common ground and they shook hands regularly. So there was enormous meaning in 'Uptown Top Ranking' seeing off the cosy international polish of 'Mull of Kintyre'. It was arguably the most punk moment of the punk era.

Crisis in the Record Box minus one month: Abba's absolute peak. They had finally followed up 'Knowing Me, Knowing You' deep in the autumn with 'Name of the Game', which also, obviously, went to number one. It had been worthy and accomplished, as impressive as anything they had done; a stately procession of pop power. But I never raced to listen to it.

Their new single, 'Take a Chance on Me', was another matter entirely. This was the sound of the world's greatest pop group at optimum swagger. It was like they were standing on top of the world's tallest mountain, with the world's biggest megaphone, going: "Attention all recording artists. This is Abba. Listen to our new single, and understand that none of you can make pop music as good as this. You may cry for a bit, then kiss our arses and fuck off".

The record was a big-sky sparkle display, existing completely on its own terms: singable, danceable and optimistic. The accompanying video, shot in the snow, with tasteful cavorting and suggestive glances from the girls that came crashing out of the screen at you, justified every positive thought you had ever had about them.

A new album swiftly followed, called *The Album*. Its title caused a few under-awed eyebrows to be raised. After school one night, in the week it was released, a classmate led me across his estate to another house, where we were ushered up the stairs. There seemed to be a queue forming outside one of the bedrooms. It soon became clear that this was the overspill; the small room was crammed, with kids sardined into the bunk beds and hip-to-hip along the walls. This girl had just bought *The Album* and was about to play it for the assembled. We could just about see the record player on the cupboard surface if we craned our necks. I was surprised how loud it was when it began.

The sound immediately brought visions of enormous space, an American desert, rock stacks, orange light and heat. The song was called 'Eagle' and the bird was part of the scene – I can't remember if this was by virtue of the title or simply the sound. I can't remember at which point I learned the title. But I can remember the stunned silence in which it was listened to at the top of that house; by everyone including me. This was even before the vocals started, which wasn't long; they only made it even better. Like every other Abba LP, *The Album* had significant flaws, but nobody there was picking fault. The first two things on it were 'Eagle' and 'Take a Chance on Me'. It's the kind of start that pushes flaws into quiet corners.

Then came the Crisis in the Record Box. Hand-wringing, self-abhorrence, wavering on the threshold of betrayal. I fell in love with, and bought, a punk single. Having recognised that some punk records had bits that made me hum along, or pause to reflect, or make me think "That's interesting – they should put it in a *good* record", I was perhaps beginning to realise that one would eventually appear with a full merit card, worthy of anybody's 75p. And, then, along it came.

It was raucous and blary, but just raucous and blary enough, plus a bit more; it made me want to leap about, play air drums, splash energy; but it was also cute – a song about sweethearts who hold hands; it reminded me of things I had heard from the early 60s (it was indeed a cover of a song from that era but I didn't know that yet). Punks doing cute things, the devious, evil bastards. Sealed with a loving safety pin. And with a bit of French thrown in.

There was a girl singer, which made it a gentler landing. She had a straightforward, unglitzy, not-trying-too-hard-voice that I warmed to. I warmed to all of it. I loved it. I had to have it. Punk rock had produced a great fairground record. The group was called Blondie and I soon learned that they were American. The song was 'Denis'. It came in a picture cover, only my fourth to date. The credits and image were red on a plain white background. It used bleak typewriter lettering which, along with blackmail letter symbols, was standard punk presentation. The singer arched herself beside it; in a jagged punk fringe, with a sneering punk stare, dressed in a very punk leopard skin.

Having it in the house took some getting used to. I really couldn't decide how to feel about it. I worried about what it made me. Then, one morning, Noel opened his show with it, and all that stopped. It became just another bloody good record, alongside the bloody good disco, the bloody good progressive rock and the bloody good studio novelty resting against it in the record box. Who had made it, what they looked like and what they told interviewers, didn't matter one bit if it was a bloody good record.

Seemingly all at once, friends at school who, like me, had distanced themselves from anything to do with punk, changed their tone. If 'Denis' was punk, then punk could be okay – we could step inside a little, we could pick and choose. The classmate who had taken me to the recent Abba unveiling loved it and fancied the singer. Loving it and fancying the singer was normal. 'Denis' was the bridge to a new pasture. I felt more grown up. I started to look down my nose at things.

One of these things was 'Come Back My Love' by Darts, a group whose creed it was hard to pin down. There was essence of drape and brothel-creeper, essence of lunatic clowning and essence of *Seaside Special* knee-blanket all in one pipette. They were older, multi-racial, a mixture of hairies and going-balds; they stood in rows and snapped their fingers but were studiously unsynchronised. There was much in this to like, but the Rock 'N' Roll Revival was over, and anyway, their first two singles sounded too clean.

'Come Back My Love' was the second of these and a particular memory is attached to it. On one of our lunchtime wanderings, the classmate and I were invited to the house of another boy who wanted to show us his new music centre. There in his bedroom was the gleaming item, huge and fabulous, with futuristic patterns on the turntable mat, racy lettering on the cassette player and buttons and lights everywhere. He lifted the smoked-brown lid right off and placed it on the bed cover to show us round it, taking long moments to guide us through every detail. We asked him where the records were. "Oh, I've got one here", he said, and tossed it down in front of us. He had all this equipment and one record: 'Come Back My Love' by Darts. We laughed ourselves stupid.

Darts were clearly striking a chord, but they were simply there. If you hadn't crossed Blondie's bridge to new pastures, they were a place you could go to escape all that nasty new stuff. In my circles, we were now at a point where, having skirted carefully round the big, bad world, we were increasingly a part of it, experiencing the intense ups and downs that came with the package. This intensity had tone; emotions mirrored by the blary, thrashy, growly and yelling sounds that many records provided; a musical representation of what was swirling in the head and churning in the stomach - pile-ups of energy, desire and uncertainty. In other words, truth.

At this point, artists who expressed themselves in such a way might have been lumped in with the punks, but they didn't need to be Sex customers to be genuine. The punk scene had, at its core, a crowd that had donned its uniform, but there had been many other crowds gathered around them that didn't; the pub rock crowd, for instance, plus others who felt that there was little for them in the mainstream, but who were there for their own reasons, who had their own ideas and their own purpose. They didn't want to wear nappies or gob on their fans; they just didn't want to look like the clean, smart conformists they could see on *Top of the Pops*. They rejected that uniform but they rejected Sex's punk uniform just as instantly. In fact, they were a bit like us.

'Denis' peaked at number two. But hating the record that held it there was difficult, partly because there was no category you could toss it disdainfully into. 'Denis' by Blondie was punk gone pop; but what in tarnation was 'Wuthering Heights' by Kate Bush?

Noel had started playing it during the Christmas holiday, and the impression it made was mainly to do with how different it was. That was it, to start with. Nobody bought it for ages. First you got tinkling, restrained piano; then, suddenly, this voice; high – I mean right up there – clean and pearly, and strikingly *English*, singing with uncommonly dramatic intonation about one of those dusty books that had been made into films and TV series. The band's sound was straightforward, but what they did wasn't. The verse was full of disquieting harmonics, right where the vocal expression was as its densest; the chorus sounded like a chorus, but there were funny things happening to the time signature. It was all a bit unusual.

You forgot about it, then it got played again and other things oc-curred to you about it, things that hung around your mind. It began to haunt you. Well, it was about a ghost - Cathy appearing to Heath-cliff, shivering at the window. We didn't usually hear names like these in choruses. People brought it up in conversation. All sorts of people; gigglers and wise goats alike. Once we got used to the idea that it wasn't going back to its own planet any time soon, copies began to shift. It finally entered the chart in February. Three weeks later, it was number one.

Watching her on the telly, I wasn't sure if I fancied her or not. Now, I can categorically say that my fancying the singer has absolutely nev-er been a prerequisite for liking a record. Deciding whether someone is pretty is an automatic response to seeing them for the first time; it's normal. It's only if you start pronouncing these judgements out loud that it becomes naff.

Unfortunately, teenage boys are all too often in this habit, in hud-dles and frequently amidst much sneering and gobbing. It's a defence mechanism. They are experiencing the power of feminine allure, something without which the world would cease to turn, and are withering before it – they need their mates around them to shrink it and make it manageable. In time, they will recognise that girls are not impressed by this; they will learn to keep their own counsel and be nicer.

In the previous year, young men had drunk in the feminine allure of three Americans playing the main roles in a detective show called Charlie's Angels, which was much more a vehicle for feminine allure than it was for gripping detection. It was pretty much obligatory to choose which one you fancied most and talk grubbily about her to other boys in secluded spots. But they were actors. Singers were giving us something far more important than looks.

This is not to say that I have ever been above having my head turned by a shapely ankle. Yet there was a conventional attractiveness among performers, one that I tended to respond to: clean, smart, smiling, and in contemporary threads. The punky singer from Blondie didn't con-form to this. Neither did Kate Bush.

On *Top of the Pops* she moved around as if impersonating animals in a Music & Movement session, over-articulating, with unkempt auburn hair and un-subtle make up, in clothes she had grabbed from the dressing-up cupboard with two minutes to go. I wasn't being critical, just noticing, just being unsettled.

The performance was another aspect of 'Wuthering Heights' that required audience adjustment. Here was something different, strange, and clearly good – if only we could decide how. It was a welcome and contrasting part of the soundtrack. You might wonder how she was going to follow it up. The B-side, 'Kite', an enjoyable and clever piece of play-school reggae, didn't seem to be much of a clue.

While it was number one, I was at a tense, important football match. The two sets of supporters were noisily baiting each other in the lead up to kick-off, as records blasted out of the tannoy system. When 'Wuthering Heights' came on they stopped, going from gruff chants to wailing falsetto in an instant; thousands of lads, all at once, united in parody, their rivalry tucked away in recognition of that voice.

One lad in my class dealt with it in a different way, by associating the name Heathcliff with any behaviour considered less than masculine, as in a disapproving: "He's a bit of a Heathcliff, 'n' ee?". It was an experiment, driven by necessity. We all had to deal with it somehow.

I loved 'Denis' and would have been thrilled to see it at number one, but it was not to be. When Kate Bush dropped to number three, 'Denis' was above it, but only to spend a final week at number two. Above them both, was 'Matchstalk Men and Matchstalk Cats and Dogs' by Brian and Michael. 'Matchstalk Men and Matchstalk Cats and Dogs' by Brian and Michael was a sentimental song about the artist J.S. Lowry, featuring two guys on acoustic guitar and a row of school children going "alley-alley-o". Glossing over it is the solemn duty of every last one of Her Majesty's subjects.

Nobody I knew had a bad word to say about that Blondie single. It was, more than any other, the record that brought this new wave of bands – which, indeed, was already being called New Wave – into the warm. When tens of thousands of kids carried 'Denis' through their front door, parades of bin liners, queen-baiting t-shirts and drools of blood-stained gob did not necessarily follow. In fact, nothing happened apart from having a great new record in the house. But there was, perhaps, something else; there was, perhaps, the picture cover.

Other kids may by now have accumulated more than my own total of four, but they were still a rarity. The first I had ever seen was for 'Lady Rose' by Mungo Jerry, which Mum had bought years before. My first had come with 'Juke Box Jive' by the Rubettes – bright blue with a full colour image of the band. I was amazed by it. Then there had been Bryan Ferry's *Extended Play* EP. Like the EPs from the 60s, which had had their own chart, it had four tracks and a glossy cover, just as *Twist and Shout* had done.

I didn't see another until I got 'Turn to Stone' by the Electric Light Orchestra (who we were now referring to as ELO). This one had a gleaming logo and credits only – no image of the band. Their next one, their magnum opus 'Mr Blue Sky' - in the Top 10 at the same time as 'Denis' - came in another; this one with the faces of the group blended into a thematic image. Lots of people I knew had it. These covers slowly became talking points in their own right. As well as asking "Have you got it?", we began asking "Did you get a picture cover?"

It was assumed that only the first few thousand copies of a release came with picture covers, if it had them at all; so you had to buy them early, or be lucky. For now, having one handed to you in the shop was an exciting result.

Coincidentally however, regular sleeves were now becoming more colourful. My copy of 'Wuthering Heights' came in a caramel-and-red EMI sleeve that matched the design of the label; it hadn't been long since all my EMI singles had come in plain white bags. Disco hits on Atlantic, such as the excellent 'I Can't Stand the Rain' by Eruption featuring Precious Wilson, came in a sleeve with the various logos of its parent company arranged in colourful rings around the view hole. The tan of RSO, the orange of Epic, the olive green of Philadelphia International and the array of square logos on the Phonogram sleeves, were all on regular display. Plain white sleeves became less normal; by the end of the following year, you would feel distinctly short-changed if you got one.

1978 was when picture covers took off. They went from being a rare treat, to something hoped for and, eventually, to something expected. They were quality items, made of sturdy cardboard rather than print-ed paper; if you bent them they would be ruined. Striking and sub-stantial containers, for striking and substantial things. Also, from the record company's point of view, an additional printed area on which to advertise albums.

All this added an additional dimension to entering record shops. To the possible disappointment of their being sold out of the one you wanted, might now be added the disappointment of not getting a pic-ture cover. But there were other stresses on top of these.

I often went to Superdisc in Herne Hill, a little cube of a shop at the Brockwell Park end of Railton Road. I bought 'Take a Chance on Me' there. My copy came with one of those new squiggly replacement centres, the horrible ones. The cut was clean, there were no signs of the original centre having been pushed out, that would have made it seem second-hand; but it took out some of the lettering from the title. This pissed me off. Why cut out the centre at all? It looked shoddy and incomplete.

But that's not why I took it back and asked for a refund. The reason for taking it back and asking for a refund was that it jumped; three or four times over the first thirty seconds. Okay, so I was playing it on a music centre with a pretty flimsy arm, the adjustable balancing weight of which I just couldn't get the hang of, but the other records I played on it didn't jump. It was incredibly frustrating, especially since I loved the record so much. I wanted my money back so that I could buy it somewhere else.

But the Superdisc man, hunched on his little stool behind the coun-ter, wasn't having it; he said there must be something wrong with my record player and wouldn't take it back. He played it on his turntable and of course it didn't jump. He put it back in its sleeve and thrust it towards me. Blushing and defeated, I took it and trudged home.

The more I walked, the angrier I got. I played it again. It jumped again, in all the same places. I tried other records, more than I had before, and all of them were fine. I had been right. I went back to

Superdisc and this time I wouldn't budge – it must be the record, so I want my money back. Finally, angrily, he returned the 75p and was muttering things as I headed for the bus stop and A1 Stores, feeling rotten all the way.

It was far from the only confrontation I ever had at record counters. The man in the record department at the Elephant & Castle WH Smith refused to accept that I could insist on there being nothing on the vinyl but the music; that if there was hissing or crackling on a new record than the product was faulty. But was I going to accept surface noise as part of the deal with buying vinyl? Was I bollocks. I had grown accustomed to immersing myself in the effects of different kinds of music and the wonders of synchronising them with different moods, and I wasn't going to allow clicks, sizzles and jarring jumps, happening in the same places every time and never on the beat, to get in the way.

Unfortunately, I was inconsistent with my Super Consumer act. If I got up a head of steam I could take on anybody anywhere, but some records hissed and I didn't take them back; some records jumped and I kept them, solving the problem by weighing the stylus down with coins; some records were pressed off-centre or had labels coming loose and, instead of becoming Mr Truth & Justice, I became Mr Make-Do & Mend. I often ended up seeing these blemishes as part of the unique character of *my* copy.

I didn't return to Superdisc for well over a year. When I did, it was because I was desperately looking for a copy of a record I had once eschewed; 'Do Anything You Wanna Do' by Rods. They had one. Thrilled, I told the same guy that I had been all over the West End looking for it, which was partially true. "There you go", he smiled, "You should always try the local shop first".

I was pleased; I liked Superdisc, they were often just mucking about in there, making people laugh. If you squeezed through, there was a staircase leading down to a tiny cellar with boxes of old singles; here I unearthed treasure from my primary school days. Back upstairs, I one day found what proved to be a rare Marvin Gaye album, *In the Groove*, the one 'I Heard it Through the Grapevine' first appeared on, for £1.99. Bargain.

So why did I want that Rods single so badly all of a sudden? Well it was because I had become conscious of the power that records had to bring back smells, views and feelings associated with past events. This amazing facility is available to all of us; the penny had suddenly dropped with me. Once you get a sniff of it, you're away. Days when certain things happened, when I had a particular new song in my head, could be revisited by hearing it again, sometimes with incredible clarity and strength. I have, in my time, hunted down records that I would never have bought otherwise, just to be there again; even if it's for suffering a crushing disappointment, because the feelings attached to it are so strong. It's exhilarating. It's the closest thing available to time travel, and it's real. When DJs say "Let's go back in time", they're not lying – some listeners will disappear from the present.

Given the choice, a time traveller might go back to the sack of Rome by the Visigoths, or the sack of Napoleon by Wellington. I went back to when I almost asked out the girl with the freckles; the richness of all that sentimentality and anticipation, then of all that hard, jagged disappointment and shame – it was like having super senses; being able to smell the soil under the hedge in the background. The Rods helped. The fact that 'Do Anything You Wanna Do' is also a fabulous feast of noise and rhythm guitar's finest moment, is a bonus. Learn the chords and strum through it. I can't sing along without welling up.

But we've jumped ahead. Back in the spring of 1978, following 'Denis', I had acquired two further picture covers; the most recent being that for Elvis Costello and the Attractions' mesmerising collision of rhythms '(I Don't Want to Go to) Chelsea'. He was now on a label called Radar, a rich green with electronic signals going across it. The image on the cover was that of the band, seemingly startled by an interruption to a rehearsal in somebody's front room.

The cover was a top-loader, rather than a side-loader – it's important to gauge this quickly otherwise you'll find your records rolling out towards an unforgiving floor surface – and within weeks the opening had curled back, meaning that, ever since, extreme care has had to be taken when extracting and returning the disc, so as not to tear the lip. This would annoy some people.

The other one came with something by the Bee Gees. We last met these chaps in a 1972 moment of syrupy sentimentality. They had ditched all that now. These days, they were the hottest boys on the sun-baked sidewalk; stepping to the beat, wrapped in golden orchestration. Their turtle-neck jumpers had been swapped for silks and bare chests with the sole purpose of resting medallions on. Their voices had been re-set to trembling falsetto. Whether this sounded manly or ridiculous was something that would remain a matter for debate, but it was a crucial part of a grown-up package and instantly recognisable as the Bee Gees sound.

They had gone disco, massively so, creating a mainstream strand for adults, a market which they were to hog. Their crystalline look was right there on the cover of the new single, 'Stayin' Alive', which was just bloody great; big, infectious beat; big, infectious guitar riff; hooks strong enough to hang giant mirrorballs on. The lyric was all swaggering defiance; I'm great, even though I'm downtrodden.

It was taken from the soundtrack of a movie called *Saturday Night Fever*, which was about the New York disco scene, but a palatable version of it: poor boy near the bottom of the ladder, in a slightly tough family, with a slightly rotten job, in a slightly rough neighbourhood, who becomes a king when he hits the dance floor, making shapes that would become synonymous with a genre that had been building its own traditions in relative secret for years.

It starred John Travolta – markedly white and heterosexual – who was suddenly the biggest pin-up in the world. He had a dimpled chin and blue eyes bright enough to redirect air traffic. Girls at school were swooning and nattering about how they were going to try and get in to see it even though it was an X certificate. They were welcome to it – I was happy owning this excellent single. In America, these re-imagined Bee Gees were already unassailable. In the UK, for now, they couldn't quite mix it with Kate Bush and Blondie, but 'Stayin' Alive' was right up there.

It would have been interesting to see John Travolta and the Bee Gees strutting around the playgrounds and corridors of our school with as much confidence. You tended not to get away with strutting unless you had back up. But our status was developing. We were third years now and no longer the little guys. We were turning fourteen. Our emotions had developed and our soundtracks changed to mirror it all; just enough to reflect what was happening to us.

If you were black and turning fourteen, this could mean a fresh understanding of your identity and culture; it could mean new ways of dealing with a racist landscape. Some of our black friends were having decidedly militant moments. *We might have been playing football with you lot yesterday, but today, we don't like white people.* In knee-length camel hair coats, leather moccasin shoes and impeccably kept afros, a gang could strut all it liked.

Their soundtrack was, as ever, reggae that Noel never played; but now there was also Bob Marley & the Wailers, which he *did* play. At the start of the year, their 'Jamming' had been in the Top 10. When the camel hair coats and moccasins sauntered in, this was the song that might be on their lips, particularly the bit from the middle, which, if done in a certain way, could translate into a conductor of threat. The lyric in this section was actually "Holy Mount Zion", but I first heard it as "owner leave for Zion". Others believed it to be a slightly more credible "Whole heap of Zion". Whatever it was, on some days it was like an air raid siren. It's a shame that such a positive, bright song is something I associate with impending violence.

As a result of one of these moments, I got into a vicious fight which went on in sporadic bouts for a couple of weeks. Successions of sneering gobbers sidled up alongside, to tell me they had heard I was having trouble with the niggers. I ignored their implied offers of help, and sorted it out my own way, which, even given some additional bruising, ultimately won me more respect and better friends.

Typically for boys, my nemesis and I were firm buddies by the summer. We would sit on walls, long into the evenings, somewhere, talking about anything. He confided in me all sorts of thoughts and feelings, those on race included. It was touching. I asked him about the sort of reggae that Noel never played. He said he didn't really know any. I said: "What about Tapper Zukie?" He laughed and said it sounded like a new type of bubble gum.

He did however know about Boney M, because everybody did now. They had kept their echoey Euro-disco up for over a year, taking us through Chicago gangsters we had never heard of ('Ma Baker') and, puzzlingly, troubled cities that we definitely had ('Belfast'), before arriving at slavery and black identity with the Rastafarian lament 'Rivers of Babylon', a song adapted from psalms and recorded by Jamaican group the Melodians in 1970. In the hands of Boney M, it became a polished, mid-tempo stroll with a strong sound, which only elevated the status of its subject matter.

The message was not diluted one iota and black kids flocked to it, whatever their other tastes might have been. It went to number one in late spring and, as it began descending the chart five weeks later, attention was drawn to its B-side, a three-minute Caribbean kids' party called 'Brown Girl in the Ring'. This got airplay on its own merits and the single went back up, reaching number two in late summer. It was biggest-selling seven inch of the year.

A successful, award-laden US television series called *Roots* had recently told the story of a young West African sold into slavery in the 18th Century. It was told from the African's point of view; the first time a big series had dealt with slavery without pulling punches or smoothing things off. Its impact was huge. Understanding your roots was something that was suddenly important. It made sense of a lot of stuff for a lot of people. Basically, if you were black and in the Caribbean, you were in the wrong place.

Babylon and Zion now had context: ditto banging on about Africa when your family was from the West Indies. Being resentful towards white kids in the recreation areas was perhaps a response to more than the coon jokes and the habitual muttering.

If it made some white kids think about their own roots, they might have dwelt on Celtic links, if they had any; I knew that ancestors of mine had arrived from southern Ireland some time in the late Victorian period. But the roots of our cultural comfort zone seemed, still, to be the rock 'n' roll era.

Perhaps the most popular TV series of the time was *Happy Days*. Every week, its finger poppin' theme song heralded a disinfected feast of preppy cardies, bobby-socks and ponytails. Homage to bygone days had been the preserve of tattooed old-timers and their loyal offspring; now even David Soul fans could join in. It was the kind of show where the main characters generated wild applause from the studio audience just for walking on. Watching it was a weekly communal event. It stayed close to the top of the television ratings for about as long as Showaddywaddy stayed close to the top of the singles chart. I never watched it. Like, I mean for a few minutes a few times. I knew it would annoy me. It was like getting a whiff of a bag of sweets that you knew would make you sick if you ate it, when everyone around you was gleefully tucking in.

And suddenly, in the summer, there was a big-screen equivalent called *Grease*; same audience, same candy-coated dreamworld, only this time with a few good songs. It was a musical, so it was a non-starter for me anyway, but its songs came out as singles and everybody got to know them. In the lead roles, as high school sweethearts from opposite sides of the tracks, were the thoroughly post-teenage but appropriately cute Olivia Newton-John, who had maintained greater success in the States than the UK for the last few years, and – oh looky here – megastar of the moment John Travolta.

The mainstream public lost its collective mind. People I knew boasted about how many days on the trot they had been to see it, and how far round the corner the queue had stretched. Many didn't seem to step outside its bubble for months.

It was launched on a clip that kind of gave away the twist, where the goody-goody girl turns into a made-up, fag-smokin' vision of lust in leather, confronting the Travolta character at the fairground and making his day. The song that went with it was 'You're the One That I Want', and this was excellent: two and a half minutes of characterful rush. It was number one for nine weeks. There was another duet from earlier in the story, where each character, in concurrent but separate scenes, de-briefs to their friends about their first date. This was 'Summer Nights' and is almost as good. Number one for seven weeks. Clever bastards made these. You can keep the film, though. I've still never seen it.

Saturday Night Fever remained big, and the singles from the soundtrack, most of which were written by the Bee Gees, were still climbing the chart. Their own 'Night Fever' had been number one, and Yvonne Elliman's terrific 'If I Can't Have You' was now high in the Top 10. Alongside it were Friends-of-*Happy-Days*-and-*Grease*: Showaddywaddy, with 'A Little Bit of Soap'; harmless, catchy Wad-fodder; and Darts, with 'Boy from New York City'. This was much better than their first two, a big, powerful sound for a cracking tune. But 'You're the One That I Want' was top dog.

If all this retrospection was a surprise given the advent of punk and the unstoppable march of disco, it was nothing compared to the shock of the announcement made in the spring: Noel Edmonds was leaving the *Breakfast Show*. It had not been long since punk had threatened to remove all comfort, a change I wanted the world to resist with all its might. But this was more than mere threat. At first, I wondered if it was going to be one of his pranks. But newspaper reports confirmed it repeatedly and, by the end of April, he was gone.

He had already begun to spread his wings, hosting a TV extravaganza on Saturday mornings called *Multi-coloured Swap Shop*, a magazine format centred on the purpose of viewers swapping something they no longer wanted for something they did, with someone who no longer wanted that, but wanted what the other person no longer wanted, if you see what I mean. Special guest stars brought in something signed or limited-edition, so that they could join in with the swapping. They sat self-consciously on soft seating, speaking to shy viewers on plastic telephones that looked light enough to float away. It was easily watchable, but it now had a wistful edge - Noel had deserted my school mornings. His replacement was Dave Lee Travis. He used to be on at tea-time. I had listened to him there sometimes, but never for long.

Seven

Back in January, while on tour in America, the Sex Pistols had fall-
en out and split up. The black girl with the spiky hair and dog collar
was in tears walking down our school corridor on the day the news
broke. 'Denis' came out shortly after that. Add these events together
and this new wave was a lot less threatening. We had not been over-
run by punk rockers and some of this new stuff had good things to
offer. There was still violence, still an atmosphere of lurking, indis-
criminate thuggery, but the sneering gobbers I most feared had not
become gangs of rampaging punks. They had become gangs of rampaging skinheads.

Skinheads had appeared towards the end of the 60s as a stylistic
working-class riposte to the prissy, precious mods, whose fashion-ob-
sessed vanguard were now in frills, paisleys and floppy velvets. Their
contrasting look was ugly; plain, poorly-fitting and industrial, with
jeans riding up the shin to expose the laces on long boots, and shorn
heads to contrast with the flowing locks on Carnaby Street and the
King's Road. It was a tough look.

Their music was the tight, juddery sound of rocksteady reggae. So
closely were they associated with it that records like 'Skinhead Moon-
stomp' were dedicated to them, along with compilations of 'Skinhead'
reggae such as *Tighten Up*. Jamaican performers were heroes; when
they visited the UK, it was the skinheads who protected them.

All this was news to me. The skinheads gaining in number while I was fourteen were just thugs; cold, cynical thugs. Or thug wannabes who began adopting the manner as soon as they adopted the uniform. If ever there was anything positive, constructive or plain lovely, a gang of skinheads would be there, sniggering and yelping, to kick it down and, preferably, you with it.

Plus they were racist; meetings of the extreme right were occasions for thuggery and, therefore, a perfect environment for them – *What you gonna fucking do about this Nazi salute, eh?* Thuggish politics, thuggish followers, thuggish attendants. Skinheads took thuggery with them wherever they went. It was their natural, default state; their badge of being. Youthful energy, distilled and focussed on kicking someone's head in.

Everybody had some harrowing experience of this and I was no exception. Skinheads could appear at the door if you were having a party; they could flood the top deck of the bus when you were having a laugh with your mates; they could come round the corner of a street where you were having a quiet walk by yourself. They screwed their faces up and swore in spikes; terrorising, destroying, blocking out the sun. Elite sneering gobbers got an all-over grade one and swapped their sneers for scowls. It had been almost a year since Sunday football had put a final end to my regular church attendance. But even if I had been a profound believer, buried in scripture and married to Christian purity, I might easily have suffered a crisis of faith over why God had allowed these cunts to exist.

I was sitting on the grassy slope below the big posh house at the top of Brockwell Park. It was a hot Saturday and I had taken my transistor radio out, letting my mind drift listening to music. The smell of new-cut grass was in the air; a motorised mower had just dumped a trailer-load in a huge pile behind me. I was on my own, relaxed, thinking fourteen-year-old thoughts; legs stretched out, gazing down the hill.

I noticed a group moving up the broad path from the main gate. They were not strolling, they were hurrying, striding. As they came closer I recognised them as skinheads; three blokes and a girl, perhaps a couple of years older than me, stomping the path as they came. I hoped they wouldn't notice me. The path wound away from where I was positioned and, if they kept to it, they would steer clear. But I was alone, visible, clearly enjoying myself: a preferred category of victim. They looked up and stopped. They spoke to each other, then left the path and headed my way.

Relaxation drained from me as if my legs had been cut off. As they neared, they broke into a trot, and their sniggers became audible, their glee visible; this was going to be fun; I can still hear the girl's high-pitched ninnying. I knew about taking a few punches when it was pointless fighting back. I accepted the situation. I was going to get beaten up and my radio smashed, my nice time terminated simply because someone had noticed it. Their boots thundered and stampeded, the leather, the braces, the tight muscles all blurred; I steeled myself for the first crunching thud.

But it never came. They rushed past me as if I wasn't there. When I finally de-frosted and turned to look, they were diving around in the mountain of mown grass; wrestling, stuffing handfuls down each other's shirts, laughing their heads off. This was wrong, of course. It wasn't their grass. Someone had put it there for a reason. You can't just help yourself to it. Who was going to clear it up now? How terrible. Still.

For that and other reasons, and despite the occasional bits of unpleasantness that teenage boys always attract, I remember that summer as being a good one. Summers would not always be good, but that one was fine. There had been an addition to the family – Mum's new marriage had produced a baby girl. We loved having a baby sister. There was also reward at school. When the big summer concert came round again, I was invited to join the stage crew.

This was a privilege reserved for fourth years; I was a third year, but in my house master's good books. The rest of the crew were a brilliant laugh, infused with the kind of ironic humour I was increasingly taking to, and they welcomed me in. Their leader was a tall, swaying lurch of a lad who spoke in evenly-spaced syllables: *We got ta pack u way the cay siz next; I'm die yin fur a drink a wor tah.* He had a mature philosophy of work first, play second.

Like countless others, he was in the habit of approximating John

Travolta's dance moves from *Saturday Night Fever*, the most famous of which being where he points up and down cross-laterally. On the posters and the album cover he is frozen in this position, one hand up, the other down, right there in his white suit with his arse sticking out. An iconic pose to rank with the best of them. "Watch me do my John Travolta" was a challenge you heard about every five paces that summer; someone, somewhere not very far away, was about to do it – a little disco smudge of roly-poly hands and shuffling feet, then the pose. Our stage crew leader would orchestrate mass rehearsals of it behind the wing curtains. We all had to line up and have a go.

On the night of the concert, as he returned from removing the chairs and music stands of the string quartet to make way for the majorettes (I'm guessing this detail, my memory's not that bloody good) he beckoned me over and said in a hushed voice: "'Ere, d'you dare me to go on and do my John Truh vol tuh?"

Before I could reply, he was back through the curtain, moving a third of the way across the stage before launching into his routine, which lasted several seconds. The hall was full of between-item murmuring and it went largely unnoticed, but there were splatterings of applause and one whoop. He came back into the wings, blushing deeply, but dare fully met. Good lad.

I hadn't been buying records recently. Since February, my only single had been 'Baker Street' by Gerry Rafferty, a piece of serious, unpretentious adult pop whose merits are quite rightly recognised to this day. I had started doing odd jobs for people, earning 50p here, 50p there. Indeed, this was my hourly rate at home for major tasks like clearing out, cleaning and re-ordering the contents of kitchen units, which sometimes meant crawling in on my stomach to rescue cobweb-covered pans at a stretch. In fact, it rarely involved anything that didn't involve cobwebs and contorted body shapes. My earnings went into a plastic toilet bag hanging from a nail above my bed. By June it was heavy, with pound notes peeping from the top.

I had got it into my head that I wanted to buy ten singles in one go. The most I had ever done previously, and only as a result of record tokens, was five. I was excited. I would include records that were now sliding down, or had left, the chart; I had made myself wait to get them.

One Saturday morning, I drew up my final list carefully while sitting up in bed listening to the Adrian Juste show, which I liked because he played collages of comedy dialogue between records and interjected with only the briefest of comments before firing up another current hit. It was fast-paced, slickly executed and free of the self-indulgence that was all too common elsewhere. In that context, 'A Little Bit of Soap' by Showaddywaddy was made to sound like an essential purchase.

The chosen outlet for this extravaganza was the Elephant & Castle WH Smith. Apart from the aforementioned Wad single, I got 'Boy From New York City' by Darts, the only one of the ten that came in a picture cover, with a sweeping shot of the group performing on stage which seemed to match the big sound of the record. I got 'Night Fever' and 'You're the One That I Want', which was the current number one. I got 'Davy's on the Road Again' by Manfred Mann's Earth Band, a curiosity with a pleasing *chug cha-chug* of a rhythm, and the sentimental 'Run for Home' by electric folkies Lindisfarne.

The football World Cup was on, hosted by Argentina, with matches finishing at unholy hours of the night; the theme tune for the BBC coverage, which I also bought, was the jangling instrumental 'Argentine Melody' by San Jose – AKA musical theatre impresario Andrew Lloyd Webber - which had enough charm to do the job, even though its similarity to the tune of a two-year-old Drifters hit called 'Hello Happiness' was a distraction.

Blondie had followed up 'Denis' in late spring with '(I'm Always Touched by Your) Presence Dear', and blary punk rock it certainly wasn't. I had sort of liked it but it grew and grew on me until it seemed to be healing the whole world before my very ears. It sounded like it had been thrown together casually, even haphazardly; yet every note, every beat and intonation, contributed something to its glorious effect. It was now fairly common knowledge that the singer was called Debbie Harry. I now also noticed the drummer, whose long fills in the final third of the record were warm tides for floating on.

Next: 'Airport' by the Motors. Some of the stage crew were in a gang that hung around the dining halls at lunch time, laughing themselves stupid about one thing or another. They had running jokes on top of running jokes. 'Airport' gave them a means of re-establishing order when things descended into chaos.

In the song, the airport represents the break-up of the relationship because his lover left on a plane. The upbeat arrangement is straight-forward but it has a sizzle about it and there is a major role for the backing vocals, which *dut-dut-dut-derr* through the verse before snapping out the song's title in the chorus, while a keyboard riff drifts around them. When the dining hall gigglers needed to calm down, someone would suddenly call "Airport!" and the others would stop to sing the riff in an immediate, unified but disharmonious falsetto re-sponse, to tears of stomach-twisting laughter from onlookers. Genius. Every body of men needs good discipline.

The last of the ten would certainly not have been last on the list. Kate Bush had released a follow-up to 'Wuthering Heights'. From the impression I had of her so far, reading its title, 'Man with the Child in His Eyes', led me to imagine a lot of mystical prancing about. But it was a surprise. It was a love song; huge, warm, richly orchestrated, calming. For the short time between its dream-like, spoken intro and its final, lingering chord, you were transported. Having it as part of the soundtrack was like turning a corner on a busy high street and finding yourself in the middle of an enchanted wood. And that voice. The B-side, 'Moving', opened with whale song; then gradually unfold-ed, each chord change going somewhere surprising but reassuring; the melody following as if there were a thousand records like this. A sud-den vocal harmony in the second verse made your insides go funny. There was a lily in her soul that was being crushed. Blimey.

In one sense, its chart peak of number six was ridiculously low. In another, it was just right. A big hit, yet not everybody *should* get this. 'Wuthering Heights' had been several parts novelty. There was no novelty here. I thought: better get the album.

Soon afterwards, there I was, in the living room, sliding *The Kick Inside* from the shop bag. It was all golds and browns, oriental-style fonts, the seemingly greased-up singer hanging from a giant kite in a top corner. My step father groaned: "Oh God, we're not going to have to listen to that bloody voice all summer, are we?" My reply was immediate, monosyllabic, and in the affirmative.

The striking thing about that list is the lack of any evidence that punk rock had succeeded in wrecking anything. There were still records that we said were punk. There were still people that we said were punk. We still referred to it and them on a daily basis. But their records were now sitting alongside mainstream pop on mainstream radio and were being assimilated.

The Stranglers' 'Five Minutes', a deafening ditty about rape and murder, was a shocking exception for being in the Top 20. 'Denis' was the real signpost. Because of 'Denis', the alternative had been edged forward. Because of 'Denis', we were able to indulge, then accept, then enjoy 'The Day the World Turned Day-Glo' by X-Ray Spex, featuring a lead singer called Poly Styrene who yelled her vocal and sported a look that gave the finger to cosy mainstream expectations to a far greater extent than Debbie Harry. You weren't supposed to fancy her. You were supposed to get off on the energy of the record. You did just that. The alternative had edged forward again. There had been some big changes since the early shock of punk rock, but wholesale wreckage there was not. There remained alternatives to the alternative. The dust was now settling.

Poly Styrene was a stage name that represented a different strand of the new wave. Johnny Rotten, Sid Vicious and the Stranglers evoked nastiness and menace, but polystyrene and day-glo fluorescence gave us an over-clean, anti-organic future we wanted to avoid just as much. Punk images began to include narrow, wrap-around plastic shades, chunky plastic jewellery and skinny plastic ties to go with the plastic sandals. Instead of filth and fury, we were all going to die in a vortex of synthetic.

Except that we weren't, of course; it was simply a backdrop for bouncing and yelling the chorus. And if this was true of the plastic vortex, it could also be true of the rest of it. Safety pins through the nose could still look scary, but it very much depended on whose nose, and blary guitars with unpolished production could be deployed anywhere. Punk had delivered an opportunity to the pantomime tradition. It all became something of a cartoon sideshow and it happened very quickly.

In late spring, there was Plastic Bertrand, who was Belgian and a punk on the grounds that he looked like one and made a stompy record with droning, blary guitar. 'Ca Plane pour Moi' was sung mostly in French to add to its novelty and it became a hit. Its main hook was the vocal going *oo wee oo woo* at regular intervals, in high clarity contrasting with the rasping vocal elsewhere.

Two girls in our class were known for performing versions of whatever had taken their fancy on the radio that day, clicking their fingers and rocking from side to side at the back of the room. They were tolerated because it annoyed the teachers so much. Underachieving in French did not put them off having a go at 'Ca Plane pour Moi'. One teacher called to them: "You only like that song because of the *oo wee oo woo* bit". They looked at each other, shrugged, then carried on.

At the end of the summer there was 'Top of the Pops' by the Rezillos, the blary guitar sound condensed to within an inch of its life. This was the plastic vortex in full animation – check out its picture cover – singing about having a hit record and being on the show of the title, which they duly did and duly were. Singer Fay Fife was in plastic from head to toe. If there had been a fire, she would have shrunk to scale like a crisp packet.

With it in the charts was a record using blary guitars, unpolished production and plastic vortex moves by backing performers in a tale of kitchen-sink heartbreak with its tongue firmly in its cheek. This was 'Jilted John' by Jilted John; a bellyaching lad from down the road, singing in studiously untrained tones about chip shops and bus stops and how his girlfriend packed him in to go out with a cool, good-looking bloke called Gordon, leaving him to nurse his broken heart by hurling insults at them both. Some of these insults were more okay than others, but "Gordon is a moron" became one of the best-known refrains of the era. Full of teenage resonance, 'Jilted John' was sweet and funny and got to number four.

If, at this point, there were debates to be had about what was punk and what wasn't, or what was new wave and what wasn't, in addition to the old one about what was good and what wasn't, there were increasing numbers of seriously-minded kids in our peer group to have them.

The school team goalkeeper had announced that he was taking music more seriously by parading his copy of a double A-sided single by a group called Sham 69, 'Angels with Dirty Faces'/'Borstal Breakout', both of which I got to know just because of the number of times he and his mates boorishly sang them. Their renditions turned out to be pretty accurate. By the end of the summer, Sham 69 would have taken their stompy chants of laddish togetherness into the Top 10 with 'If the Kids Are United', which was hardly off the radio during the holiday.

Another boy, with whom I had had my first ever secondary school fight three years earlier, was now part of a group that spoke in hushes and passed around 45s. He told me about them in knowledgeable detail, bands I had never heard of and can't remember the names of now. He said they were brilliant. I could only nod and smile.

None of these guys wore anything like the Sex uniform. They wore lace-up Dr Marten boots and army surplus trousers, maybe an army surplus overcoat; perhaps a Harrington jacket, which, depending on the colour, is where they might have crossed over with the skinheads. But lots of crowds liked Harrington jackets. I had one for a while. They didn't spike their hair, but they pushed it up, away from the forehead.

This was becoming the street fashion. I never had the army trousers – wearing jeans, rather than cotton trousers, was still a novelty – but I did love my 8-hole Dr Martens. That's eight holes up *each side*, you understand. One day late in the summer, my old primary chum, the one whose tenth birthday party had rocked to the sound of the Wombles, turned up at the front door, looking very different. "What d'you think?" he grinned. "New image!"

I don't remember what he was wearing beneath the waist, but I do remember the vest: a plain, white cotton vest, a well-fitting version of what my grandad wore, and I had stopped wearing ages ago. It struck me as rather punk. The hair was now swept back and up, kept there by some lotion or other. It was quite shocking; but actually, he was simply joining in, and clearly very excited. He was full of talk about new music, mentioning a few things that I responded to with screwed-up expressions and funny noises; but at some point, he uttered the magic words 'Hong Kong Garden' by Siouxsie and the Banshees, and that made everything alright. For here was something we could certainly agree on.

Few acts from the original punk scene managed to sustain their momentum on anything other than a small, jobbing scale. The Sex Pistols were already gone and a final album of collected recordings would be aptly titled *Flogging a Dead Horse*; the Stranglers would evolve into uncles and enjoy chart success into the 90s; knockabout nutcases the Damned had found a snug fit in punk, and later found mainstream respectability as lovable veterans; the Clash were high-profile, sloganeering punk originals with attitude but, as such, they were more performance art than music, and in any case quickly became a radio-friendly rock band contributing to the dull fug emitting from car speakers on US freeways. If I've missed anyone out, the most I will do is shrug; because the point of all this is to get to Siouxsie Sioux.

She was in the original Sex crowd and took part in that Bill Grundy TV interview with the swearing (look it up). She was there because she was bored with old stuff and had the stomach to express herself in the face of whatever hostility tradition and the mainstream could throw. There were other such women in that scene, but she was the one to go furthest, forming a band and, eventually, getting a record deal – with Polydor.

For the next seventeen years, Siouxsie and the Banshees would be in and out of the charts with a succession of powerfully atmospheric - often outstanding - records, within which she was able to express wonder and anger in equal measure, and with undiminishing strength. Pantomime it was not.

'Hong Kong Garden' was built around a brisk, four-bar riff that sounded Chinese. This starts on a xylophone, with a harmonising guitar joining in before the vocal picks it up. Nice and simple. The bass plays four different notes in the whole thing. It stomps and bounces brilliantly.

I've never looked too deeply into the lyric, I suppose in case it spoils an overall effect I have loved for decades. It's difficult to get it all anyway, but some phrases leap out; one about crashing cymbals and another about chicken chow-mein and chop suey, as well as one about selling your daughter. Or so I have always thought; I have no plans to check. Siouxsie sings in tune, but is almost shouting, and in an accent. It's a suburban London shout, which, you could say, was punk in a nutshell.

Its long, final section features a virtuoso performance on rhythm guitar which raises the excitement even further, then it all ends abruptly with a gong. Not a 'Bohemian Rhapsody' gong; a good gong. A Hong Kong gong.

The picture cover showed an image of a woman wrapped in bandage, or perhaps work overalls, or perhaps sheets from a Chinese laundry, but with her face enshrouded as well. We associated the word "bondage" with punk and knew it meant various things, so it could be that. But it was unnerving, and, against a pale background with jagged lettering around it, ghostly. 'Hong Kong Garden' was, and remains, a special record.

It got to number seven as we were settling into our new school year. There were lots of changes. The kids we already knew were changing. Also, there were different kids. We were in classes with people from other houses that we may never have spoken to before. Streaming meant that we were now in the groups that would take 'O' levels and CSEs together.

Music oiled the wheels as we got to know each other. The humour was beginning to mature, too. Some spoke with ironic pride about how many times they had been to see *Grease*, laughing at themselves, letting you know they weren't taking it too seriously. Others were clearly not being ironic about it, but we'll swish past those.

Ironic humour proved a great bonding agent and helped these new friendships along. This brings us back to the Dooleys. Now let me be clear from the outset: the Dooleys were an old-fashioned variety act. They would have slotted nicely into the running order on *Seaside Special* and, for all I know, were on the show several times. They were awash with conjured grins and showbiz razzle. But they did make a few memorable records, ones with a feel and an atmosphere which, sometimes, you could do with. Their best records were as listenable as anything around them and I will mention these in due course. Their new single that September, which is not one of them, was the none-theless insistently catchy 'A Rose Has to Die'.

A few of us from the new maths group had, in the throes of clowning around, been adding the Dooleys to the list of things we approved of and, one day, this other kid was listening in. He knew the group but hadn't heard their new song. It is, actually, a sentimental notion about flowers wilting whenever a lover betrays you. But we convinced him that they had gone punk and made a nasty record called 'Rose Has to Die', that they had bleached and spiked their hair, and that the music papers were full of speculation about what this Rose character had done to incur such wrath.

It didn't take long for our victim to rumble us, but the Dooleys thing gathered momentum and before long their name was being applied to anything good. When one of the guys fell for this girl, she was his "little Dooley". When someone returned from the tuck shop satisfied, it was because they had just had a "well Dooley cheese roll". You get the picture.

Darts were high in the Top 10 again, with a weepie called 'It's Raining', which was solidly retro and solidly good. They were on an upward trajectory that would continue for a further two singles. This was when I also bought my first 45 by the Jam, a double A-side led by the radio-friendly 'David Watts', an amusing bellyache about a boy at school who is brilliant at everything; I later found out it had originally been done by the Kinks.

When you flipped it over, you got '"A" Bomb in Wardour Street', which I ended up playing much more. It was the kind of aggressive, explosive noise that I was turning to increasingly; noise that sounded the way my anger and frustration felt. Having strong feelings mirrored in records I could listen to loud was a balm. It soothed the rage. I would make use of more like this. In another two years, I would be buying the Sex Pistols' only studio album, their 1977 number one *Never Mind the Bollocks, Here's the Sex Pistols*, to have buckets of it. Anger and frustration were moving in; they were going to have to be managed.

There's an arguable link from this topic to the next item, which I will refer to only subtly. There. Already done it. Knocking on the door of the Top 20 was an accomplished, prurient novelty, which certainly did not get played on the radio: 'The Winker's Song (Misprint)' by Ivor Biggun and the Red-Nosed Burglars, a cheerfully fulsome tribute to, shall we say, booking a table for one. It was good and funny, done somewhat in the style of mid-century ukulele twanger George Formby, and news of it spread like wildfire.

They happened to be playing it in Superdisc, in hushed hysterics behind the counter, when Mum walked in to look for something. They became self-conscious and apologised, but never for a moment thought about taking it off. Its picture cover features a drawing of a dedicated "winker", his face displaying the madness to which his dedication has driven him, holding open his dirty raincoat, from which, at groin level, protrudes the arm of a guitar. An unforgettable image, far more disturbing than the song.

But if you wanted disturbing, all you had to do was reflect on the success of 'Lucky Stars' by Dean Friedman. A man, seemingly made entirely of candy floss, proving how sensitive and smart he was by claiming at various points that he was neither sensitive nor smart, in a song which included toe-curling dialogues with his lover and the most annoying vowel sounds America had yet produced. Turning on the radio while it was high in the charts was like playing Russian roulette.

If you were fortunate however, you might happen upon a good soul tune; perhaps 'Now That We've Found Love' by Third World, with its unusual, intriguing, jiggly beat; or the sumptuous 'Love Don't Live Here Anymore' by Rose Royce, a record kept from number one only by 'Summer Nights'. It featured a new percussion effect, that of the syndrum; an electronic pad which responded to the drumstick with what sounded like the falling call of a robotic owl – *bauw ba-bauw bauw*. In the wrong hands it could be tortuous, but Rose Royce's were safe. This was their second sumptuous hit of the year; the first, 'Wishing on a Star', had been sending people into swoons while 'Take a Chance on Me' was number one.

But for me, the biggest change was to radio schedules. I was trying hard to acclimatise to Dave Lee Travis. Because of his big, dark hair joining his big, dark beard and big, dark moustache in a continuous mane, he was known as the Hairy Monster and, when he started on the breakfast show, he began alternating between this and Hairy Cornflake. From his clutch of new jingles, the one I remember easiest was the one about the Hairy Monster comin' atcha through the cornflakes, complete with an alarmed screech and the sound of breakfast cereal being trampled underfoot.

There was no subtlety about it and, however we may have hoped that subtle, irreverent humour might follow, it didn't seem to. It was all a bit abrupt, all a bit angular. Noel was just too hard an act to follow.

I tried to adjust. I've still got a half-printed, half-typewritten invitation to "be part of the DLT Breakfast Show", something I had to apply for. You were supposed to ring between 7.00 and 9.00 any weekday in September, to take part in something or other; possibly a quiz. Anyway, having to get ready for school and then leave by 8.20, my opportunities to ring were limited and I never got through. This only compounded my deflation.

Not everybody shared these trials, because not everybody listened to Radio 1. Large numbers of my school and football friends were devotees of Capital Radio, London's commercial station. I couldn't imagine why anyone would want to listen to a station with adverts on. You'd have fewer records. Also, their chart was different, and if wasn't the BBC one, then it was being wrong on purpose. But about half the people I knew loved it. We used this split as an occasional way of sorting out sides for playground football.

I gave it a go here and there, and must have done so that September because I think of Capital when reminded of '(You Make Me Feel) Mighty Real' by Sylvester, a disco record that seemed to raise the stakes; it was urgent, wired, and sung in an assertive falsetto, suddenly making other disco records seem lethargic.

It sounded like the future, as for different reasons, did its co-charter 'Supernature' by Cerrone, an excellent record that my memory links to dealing with cobwebs for 50p an hour while listening to Radio 1. This was pure science fiction: a set of alarming, futuristic images drawn by sound manipulations and droid-ish vocal delivery. It could easily have been naff, but it very definitely wasn't.

Another Radio 1 change that autumn was that the station was moving frequencies. Big publicity campaigns and long, convoluted jingles announced that it was moving from 247 metres medium wave, to 275 and 285 metres medium wave. Your geographical location dictated whether your best signal was going to be from 275 or 285 – we London types were going to be 275.

Radio was on one of three frequencies: long wave, medium wave and VHF. Long wave was for the shipping forecast and listening to cricket on Radio 4. It was occasionally fun for exploring late at night, because you could pick up foreign stations and find out what they were playing, while despairing at how you were ever going to pass French or German 'O' level. A cricket-free version of Radio 4 lived on medium wave, along with virtually everything else broadcasting from Britain during the day.

But moving slickly between its stations wasn't easy. On your radio was a dial that you turned to move a pointer up and down a strip. When you got near 250, you knew that Radio 1, at 247, was close, and you had to twiddle with tiny movements to adjust it to the best reception, otherwise there'd be all sorts of nasty noise and you wouldn't be able to hear the Dooleys so clearly.

Even then, depending on the time of day, you might have to alter the angle of the radio, or the aerial, or both. The third frequency, VHF, was for God knows what, but it finally became FM. America was already familiar with this, and one day the UK would move everything to it.

The other change was straightforwardly exciting. The singles chart was going to be a Top 40 rather than a Top 30. Those records that were "bubbling under", or *just outside* the chart in some unspecified position, were now going to be in the chart instead – these non-hits would be hits! It was going to take ages to count it all down. And would they have to make the Sunday chart show longer? I'm sure they'd thought of all this, and decided they could manage. But they sold it to us as something to get excited about and, by gosh, I got excited about it. Never mind that the top seventy-five was on the wall of every record shop I went into. This was on the radio. It was different.

I did, however, also think about a couple of boys at school, who spent lunchtimes copying out the chart on lined paper in felt pens, giving each position its own style of lettering and its own colour scheme across two or three lines, perhaps dictated by its musical characteristics; a real labour of love. They did it in quiet corners, rummaging with gentle clacks through pencil cases to find the right colour for representing Third World or the Jam.

One of these boys had been in my maths group the previous year and had let me copy his answers, which was why he was now in the top maths group and I wasn't. As I edged between the backs of dining area chairs one day, I spied him and stopped, peering over his shoulder to see. He became aware of me, paused, hunched his shoulders, then cautiously turned, reddening madly.

The smile of reassurance I gave him was one of the things I am proudest of. To him, I was a loud, oiksome football lad; but to me, he was something of a kindred spirit. I wondered how long it was going to take him to do forty instead of thirty.

Assuming he continued with this for a while, he would, in mid-November, have written out a chart giving a fairly balanced picture of how this whole punk/new wave thing was settling down.

Some of it was going artistic. Its main figurehead had dropped the moniker Johnny Rotten, reverted to his real name John Lydon and formed Public Image, Ltd., which was definitely not Sex Pistols mk2, although he still sang funny. Their debut single, 'Public Image', was a deep, driving beat with squally guitars and Lydon's voice swirling around it. It sounded like noises gathered from different records which just about hung together. It was a statement. It was interesting, but you didn't listen to it for pleasure. It got to just inside the Top 10.

Some of it was going cuddly. The group responsible for 'Orgasm Addict' a year earlier were called the Buzzcocks. Now, a few singles on, they were doing good business with 'Ever Fallen In Love (With Someone You Shouldn't've?)', a blistering, thrilling frame of fuzz and distortion for a song about real feelings, which was loved by a striking range of people and only slightly spoilt by its frustratingly blunted production. It was Jilted John's less cartoonish cousin; cute, but more believable. The opening line, "You disturb my natural emotions", had a feel which forced you to sing it spontaneously and often, not always in appropriate situations. You could be on a crowded train, at a first meeting with your girlfriend's parents, it didn't matter. You thought of it, you blurted it. It got to just outside the Top 10.

Just as believable, but somewhat less cuddly, was the new one by the Jam, 'Down in the Tube Station at Midnight'; thrashy here, measured and thoughtful there – another step forward for a maturing band. It was about being down in the tube station at midnight. And getting your head kicked in. Probably by skinheads. I had never been down in a tube station at midnight, but I didn't need to be – that kind of shit could happen at four o'clock in the afternoon. It got to number fifteen.

The new one by Blondie was about to roar past it on the way to number five. 'Hanging on the Telephone' was their most upbeat A-side yet; a defiantly poppy blare, as cool as a fish. They were clearly gathering pace, and Debbie Harry was overtaking both Olivia Newton-John and Agnetha from Abba as top blonde.

The same month saw the launch of a new pop magazine called Smash Hits, aimed at kids too young for, or unimpressed by, the established music press; kids who wanted to buy records, learn the words, and cover their bedroom walls with colour pictures of stars who told you what their favourite breakfast cereal was. Kids who wrote the charts out in felt tips at lunchtime. Its first issue had Debbie Harry on the cover.

And if that was something, which it was, then how about this: in the same month, punk had its first number one single. The Boomtown

Rats were becoming refined, serious punks. In the summer, they had signalled an intention to leave all that thrashy, 100mph stuff behind them with 'Like Clockwork', a particularly well-crafted record which tasted punky but threatened no one.

Their new one was 'Rat Trap'. It was a bleak tale of no-hoper kids, its narrative decorated by saxophone licks, by laid-back finger-clickin', and by the vocal performance of front man Bob Geldof; sometimes sung, sometimes spoken, occasionally screeched. It was well sophisticated, guy. Like other punk, but glummer, and in sentences that had been marked by the teacher. Geldof was a convincing punk because he looked like he genuinely didn't give a shit and would sneer at the toast for popping up.

'Rat Trap' impressed more and more people until, one November day, it was outselling everything, knocking 'Summer Nights' off number one after seven weeks. The triumphant *Top of the Pops* performance began with a picture of John Travolta and Olivia Newton-John being torn ceremoniously in half. It felt like an occasion to celebrate, and many around us were indeed grinning and giving the thumbs-up, even if, like me, they knew 'Rat Trap' in every detail without particularly liking it.

For some people, punk was an ethos, a state of mind and a style of expression that wanted nothing to do with *Top of the Pops* or *Smash Hits*; whereas new wave was all those bands that wanted a different kind of pop stardom. Really, Bob Geldof wasn't a punk in a million years; he had used the new scene to launch himself, and good for him.

But arguing about definitions and authenticity is almost always a waste of time. The important thing was that people our age were now listening to new types of music and idolising new kinds of pop star. The confident individualism of Debbie Harry was a healthy influence on girls, just like the sensitivity of the Buzzcocks was a healthy reassurance for boys. Blary, thrashy, angry stuff was now on the menu and available for soothing life's rages, perhaps alongside lyrics describing the world as we saw it. It is to be hoped that every generation gets to taste some of that. Nobody I knew was wearing bin liners and safety pins; but the hair was now different, trouser legs were narrower, and ties were now stretching several inches down the chest. Flares and the giant knot had been consigned to the bin.

My transistor radio, by contrast, had not. Happily un-smashed by skinheads, it was available to be taken to school – sliding around in the bottom of my vast Adidas bag along with two small books and a pen – and carted around at lunchtimes, as our little band of brothers idled its way from bakery to grocer to confectioner. I don't suppose I brought it every day, but Tuesdays were a must, because that's when the new chart was announced on Radio 1; at 12.45, (following *Newsbeat*), by Paul Burnett, who had replaced Johnny Walker.

He played the new numbers five down to two, then counted down the whole Top 40, causing various groans and curses, before confirming the number one, which often led to the radio being switched off in disgust. We listened intently as we drifted past bramble and brick, with only these outbursts to break our pious attention.

Whenever I hear 'Hanging on the Telephone', the time machine sends me on one of these mid-day walks, alongside the rusting diamonds of a British Rail fence close to school. The same scene conjures up the record with which Boney M followed up 'Rivers of Babylon/ Brown Girl in the Ring'. Having gone through murderous Chicago gangsters, sectarian killing fields and slavery, what was now left for them to address but the collapse of Imperialist Russia? Elsewhere, the disco world was all dance-dance-dance and boogie-oogie-oogie, but not for these lunatics; they were instead giving us decadence and death in the saga of 'Rasputin'.

School corridors everywhere were soon ringing to outbursts of *rah-rah-Rusputeen*, from a chorus that had something of the football chant about it. Having said that, it did have lots of sex. The eponymous hero shagged just about everyone, including the Empress, before the nobility did for him with poison and bullets.

Boney M made a mad party out of it all, and the guy, who we now knew as Bobby, did his most berserk dancing yet, spinning and swirling in a blur of limbs, looking at various points as if he were trying to drill a hole in the stage with his toes. If not for 'Summer Nights', it would have been another number one.

But if Bobby thought he was going to have the field all to himself, he was very much mistaken. The general public, having now been made to feel comfortable with disco due to *Saturday Night Fever*, wanted to know who the real dance kings and queens were. Thames Television were happy to oblige, by inaugurating the *World Disco Dance Championships*, hosted by David Hamilton, where representatives from each of the independent television regions did dance floor battle with each other, as well as with overseas competitors who, one was at liberty to suspect, had been press-ganged from various corners of the British catering industry. It was television's way of showing Granny what disco looked like.

The segmented flooring flashed colourfully in time to the music, just like at the club featured in *Saturday Night Fever*, while the contestants grinned and twizzled soullessly, making the viewing audience feel perhaps inadequate, perhaps puzzled, perhaps merely anthropologically informed.

The record they did all this to was 'Instant Replay' by Dan Hartman. It was played pretty much on a continuous loop throughout the broadcast; I don't remember there being anything else. It was a big hit and is memorable for its ten-to-one countdown intro, a jazz bit in the middle which delivered the cartoonishness, and its association with the *World Disco Dance Championships*.

The lyric was vacuous. It was one of these more urgently-paced dance records with sharper production, a far cry from the classy, easy-going disco sounds of Philadelphia International. Many people would think of it when being reminded of that explosion of disco awareness, perhaps ahead of anything else that wasn't on the *Saturday Night Fever* soundtrack.

There may yet have been some who thought that disco wasn't cartoonish enough; that it was still too much of a credible, homogeneous scene with cultural coherence and dignity. If so, Rod Stewart was on hand to help. He released a single called 'Da Ya Think I'm Sexy?' Rod had gone disco. There was a variation on the *dom-tiss dat-tiss* rhythm that went *doom chugga-doom chugga-doom*. There was a blurry keyboard riff. There was some kind of narrative in the verse. The chorus was a come-on to some woman to grab him if she liked his money and the cut of his jib, but it could have been an invitation to the whole world.

You could look at it another way, seeing it as Rod's self-deprecating dig at his own celebrity. Nobody would ask anybody "Hey, do you think I'm sexy?" unless they were a complete tosser. Perhaps that was the point; perhaps we were supposed to laugh. But I wasn't going to ponder it. I didn't spend any time at all thinking about it. It actually hurt to remember it existed. In a shameful act of vulgarity, the British public sent it to number one for a week.

Rod was attempting, at the far end of his decade, to be like one of those hot young dance things in silvery tracksuits and sweatbands. He was succeeding, through overt sexiness, to be embarrassing. Younger dancers lithely doing the same thing were somehow less so. A dance troupe called Hot Gossip had recently risen to prominence on a new TV show fronted by the notoriously loony DJ Kenny Everett. Their steamy moves and stares made the current dancers on *Top of the Pops*, Legs & Co., look like nice aunties. They had blokes, too – black blokes. Getting hold of those white girls in such a way added another layer of, shall we say, *interest*.

Sadly, any good they had done by shaking things up a bit was undermined when, as Sarah Brightman and Hot Gossip, they reached the Top 10 with a single called 'I Lost My Heart to a Starship Trooper'. No, I did not make that up. Sex, disco and *Star Wars* in one go; shouty and full of lazer-gun sound effects. To be fair, they may have been trying to follow in the footsteps of the excellent 'Supernature', which they had writhed along to on the first *Kenny Everett Video Show*. If you want to give them the benefit of the doubt, there's your excuse.

Then there was the classy stuff. There was 'Le Freak' by Chic; smooth strings and *bob-bob-bobbing* bass, hand claps and a duet of female voices, carefully layered, measured and cool. Le Freak was apparently a new dance craze. We hadn't had one of those for a while and this one certainly had a bit of promise. We weren't told how to do it, but the record promised to show us. On the radio.

It had an extremely long instrumental middle section. This was where we had to freak, still none the wiser as to what it should look like. It kind of didn't matter. The song was all about having a good time and so, if you clearly were, your freaking style would probably be fine. I was imagining all kinds of monstrous body shapes to go with the name, ones which jarred with the smoothly racy sound of a record I found myself playing rather a lot.

It was an anchor, a reassurance; a reminder of what things could sound like when they were being okay. It was needed. In December, we began hearing 'YMCA' by the Village People, a public information announcement about an accommodation facility, done in song form and in the latest "disco" style, so that young people would pay attention. There were a couple of YMCAs in London. As far as I was aware, they were cheap hotels for young men passing through, but the Village People could offer more detail: patrons could have a rest, freshen up, then maybe have something to eat. Sounded well Dooley.

Of course, the truth was that it was a song knowingly in praise of an environment where nice young chaps could spend time together without interruption, if you get my drift. But I was innocent of this. I just found it puzzling. I thought perhaps they would put out a song about the Post Office next.

I was further puzzled by its success. It went to number one just after Christmas and its popularity would endure to an inexplicable extent. In time, there would be a dance to go with it, much to the relief of those who would otherwise be left to move in ways inspired by the record (I've brought this up before and I'll be doing so again). In this dance, you use your arms to make the shapes of the letters in the title, as you step from side to side. It's dance floor blancmange. The fact that we know how to do this but were never shown how to do Le Freak is a cultural catastrophe.

But then came a reminder of why, despite everything, disco was worth bothering with. One of the best things about buying singles was the spontaneity. Nobody had money to burn, but if you were near a record shop or a record department and the possibility arose, you sometimes found yourself thinking "Actually, I think I'm going to buy *that* one", when you hadn't previously imagined you would. One such spontaneous decision that holiday was one of my very best.

I was in the HMV store on Oxford Street, spending my Christmas record tokens. You didn't get change from record tokens; if it was to the value of £5 and you spent £4, they took your £5 token and that was it; so it made sense, if possible, to "go over" and add the difference in cash, which was possibly the point. Anyway, I had accounted for all but 50p or so of my tokens and there was nothing else I was particularly dying to get. The shop was busy and I think I was being put under pressure by family to get a move on.

In the middle of the floor was a revolving wire rack on coasters, like the type you get postcards in. It seemed out of place in these haughty surroundings but there it was, stuffed with 45s and catching the eye. I needed to choose something fast and I saw 'In the Bush' by Musique, which, when it had popped up on the radio, I had merely heard. Something made me grab it.

It's possibly rude. Make that probably. Connotations for the word "bush" were few, as indeed were horticultural references in disco lyrics. The record featured tumultuous groans which were certainly nothing to do with floral cultivation. So, even if the Village People were planning to follow up their Post Office tribute with a paean to the Garden Centre, it's probably rude.

But whether it was or wasn't, whether it did or didn't, 'In the Bush' is fantastic; full testimony to how good disco could be. Intense, breathless and dizzying, it rains hooks on you relentlessly. You can't count them all – it won't give you time to. It leaves you knackered, fit for nothing; and wanting to do it all again straight away. The idea that it shares locker-room space with 'Instant Replay' and 'YMCA' seems ludicrous.

Variations on *dom-tiss dat-tiss* were everywhere, and now beginning to appear in the repertoire of new wave acts, giving their rhythms the space to be danceable if you wanted them to be. Although this wasn't strictly disco in the sense we had come to understand, distinctions became blurred. The intention was left open to interpretation; pop pickers could opt for rolling their eyes and thinking "There's another lot gone disco".

But the benefit of the doubt was easily awarded to one such record climbing the charts. This was 'Hit Me with Your Rhythm Stick' by Ian Dury and the Blockheads. They had scored the previous spring with 'What a Waste', a good record whose bubbling arrangement matched its lyric of comic regret. The new one was better still; quite unhinged as its title suggests it ought to be; lyrical wordplay for all the family; a comforting London growl pondering a list of exotic locations over the *dom-tiss dat-tiss*, augmented by busy bass and keyboard off-beats that gave the whole thing a delightful wobble. It single-handedly boosted national morale. When it went to number one for a week in January, the sky seemed to fill with fireworks.

And then Blondie went disco. Yeh, I know. But they did. It was what it took to get them to number one. The song was called 'Heart of Glass' and, however brightly some things about it shimmered, however authentic a part of the band's backdrop disco was, the event annoyed the hell out of me.

For *Smash Hits* readers, however, it was a dream come true; Debbie Harry under a mirrorball, singing a sparkling disco song in a chiffony disco outfit and a sleek disco haircut, invading unattainable territory and beckoning you to follow. In the video that we saw on *Top of the Pops* during its four-week stay in the big place, the band fell into role effortlessly, only without the grins and exposed flesh. A cool new wave band doing disco, right in your face, with every encouragement from the public.

It was what we would come to call a cross-over, and one of those number ones that was definitely bigger than others. I was learning to get a sense of the latter without some DJ having to tell me. Inevitably, I became curious about other big number ones that were too far in the past for me to remember; perhaps something played on the *Golden Hour* or elsewhere, that I thought might have been a big number one, if it had been number one at all, if only I could find out.

I had been listening to a Sunday afternoon programme called *The Double Top Ten Show*, which played two old Top 10s straight through. It was hosted by Jimmy Savile, white-haired Radio 1 veteran who had been the first ever host of *Top of the Pops*. As far as we knew back then, he was distinctly and defiantly odd, but worthy of respect. Following his death in 2011, revelations would re-classify him as a sexual predator of monstrous proportions, a violator of the innocent with a trail of crimes stretching back decades. But this was back then. It was on this show that I first heard the Hollies oldie 'Look Through Any Window', a fantastic twangy guitar thrash from 1965.

Savile awarded points for knowing the answers to questions he would pose every few records; questions about follow-up singles, band membership, or subsequent chart-toppers. As far as we knew back then, it was okay to get points from Jimmy Savile. But this would have been tantalising offered by anybody. I wanted to get points. Who wouldn't want to get points? Who wouldn't want this knowledge? For now, my point totals were low and I didn't like it.

I wanted to know about important old records. I wanted to know about successions of singles by important acts; what they contained and in which order. Typically, if you listened to the radio a lot, you knew the big names and were familiar with some of their songs, many of which felt big indeed, given either the raucous enthusiasm of the DJ, the effect it had on you, or both. But what number had it got to? If the DJ didn't say, you wouldn't know.

Ask an adult? *Oh, I'm sure it was number one* – thinking they were being kind and telling you what you wanted to hear, but breezily dismissive; they weren't even taking it seriously. They were similarly unreliable on what they had followed it up with – an important detail given some of the puzzling follow-ups of the present. Also, if it *had* been number one, what had knocked it off? And if it hadn't, what had been holding it down? There was an urge to know and a solid wall of frustration to deal with.

Well not any more. Because now there was the *Guinness Book of British Hit Singles*. When I found out that it existed, and what it promised to show me, my levels of excitement were quite ridiculous. The first edition had just been reprinted. I got one for Christmas and, for a good chunk of that holiday, I heard nothing that was said to me.

Any act that had ever been in the British singles chart from 1952 to 1977 was there, in alphabetical order, with their own section

under a fat red heading. Each of their singles was listed chronologically beneath, with the date of its first chart entry, its catalogue number
(corresponding to the mysterious numbers on the side of the label – I
checked), its highest position and the number of weeks it had spent
in the chart. Top 10 hits were prefixed with black dots, number ones
with red dots, so you could see at a glance where the big hits were and
study the pattern of a top act's success. The appendices included a
list of every number one, in order, with the date and the number of
weeks printed alongside.

It was like a lovely dream. I could see the order of the Beatles singles;
I could discover where songs on *That'll Be the Day* had got to; I could
check my memory of records I had loved or hated while at primary
school; I could discover, and be shocked by, how many of my favourite Motown songs had got nowhere. I could check the listings for the
Seekers, the Hollies, Donovan and others, to find out how well those
records had actually done. Suddenly, wonderfully, all this was mine. If
I heard an interesting oldie on the radio now, I could just go and look
it up.

Thus did I begin to build up knowledge. I wanted to be quizzed. Also,
I wanted to have some of these important old records on a single. It
was fine having a *20 Golden Greats*, such as those of the Shadows – a
recent best-seller – but instinct drove me to desire their best tracks on
45 which, to my mind, would mean having them properly. It was the
most pleasing format and people had, after all, bought them on 45 in
the first place.

At A1 Stores, I got 'Look Through Any Window' as a re-issue on
the caramel-and-red EMI label, with two other early Hollies songs
squidged onto the B-side; I also got 'The Tears of a Clown' by Smokey
Robinson and the Miracles, on the silver-and-black Tamla-Motown
label but in the new Motown sleeve that went with the blue spokes,
carrying two good tracks I had never heard before on the reverse.

'The Tears of a Clown' was an intensely atmospheric 1967 stomper,
discovered by clubbers and DJs who forced Motown's UK people to
put it out in 1970, whereupon it climbed to number one, repeating
the feat in the US soon afterwards – a fine effort, UK clubbers and

DJs. This re-issue had recently made it into the lower chart without me noticing.

Of course, I dreamed of having original copies. But I knew from my own early care of them, that they were all probably scratched, discarded or spoilt by children. My aunt and uncle had a box of them from the 60s, cared for and undamaged, which they treasured and were reluctant to let me even breathe on. But I was allowed to look.

I loved the range of label and cover designs. I could register a beat and a loving blare just looking, without the faintest idea as to how they sounded. I assumed that original 45s were either tucked away carefully or pulped in waste disposal. If my 1972 copy of 'Poppa Joe' was now so blemished as to be unusable (not that I was pining for it these days), what chance did records from the decade before it stand?

And yet. On one of my various routes home from school stood a row of grimy shops; an electrician's, a laundrette and a few others. They all looked like junk shops from the outside, but one of them actually was. Through the exhaust discharge and algae on the glass, you could make out items of wood, brass and china, alongside piles of books and clusters of bannister rails. The very fact of wondering why anyone would want to step inside, made me do so.

I entered silence. On a shelf above an ancient sideboard was a record. One record. Not a box of them, but a single single, lying flat between a perfume bottle and a wooden elephant with a missing tusk. It was 'Mama Weer All Crazee Now' by bloody Slade; on Polydor but in a Page One sleeve. Time had softened my stance on bloody Slade and I bought it, giving 20p to someone who had eventually and reluctantly appeared from the back.

At home, I carefully wiped the dust away and began getting to know one of British music's most stunning achievements. Weeks later I returned and found 'Rag Doll' by the Four Seasons, from 1964 on Philips; wonderfully clanky and sweet. I had collected two originals in great condition.

I was fascinated to find that the B-side of 'Rag Doll' was 'Silence is Golden', a bewitching, tearful 1967 number one for the Tremeloes – those of 'Helule Helule' fame – that often got played in oldies slots, making me think that this is where they must have pinched the song from. The Tremeloes had improved it. More knowledge. Exciting knowledge. I returned to the shop here and there but never found another interesting record. I maybe passed up some good stuff because my knowledge was only developing.

Paul Gambaccini was an American who presented programmes on Radio 1 which I never listened to. However, one day I happened to hear an interview where he revealed that he had a standing order with his local record shop to put by a copy of every single that got into the Top 10. Every one. Wow.

It struck me that this was a collection worth having. I had recently turned over another new leaf in record care, updating my storage to cardboard crisp-boxes, adapted and reinforced so that they (a) held 45s snugly with a little leeway on either side, and (b) made it easy to flick through their contents. I insured against them being bent under the weight of the stack by placing hardback books at each end. A relative had offered me an unwanted cupboard unit and, before accepting, I made sure it would hold several such boxes in a way that made them simple to extract. Current singles still went in the record carrier with the fat handle, but "oldies" went in the boxes.

This, allied to the meticulous care with which I handled the records and their sleeves, made it unlikely that anything would ever get scratched, bent or ripped. All well and good. But imagine being able to say that, within your wicked and dread storage system, you had a copy of *every* record that had got into the Top 10. It wouldn't be just about the bragging rights, it would be about history. Your collection would be *the* history of the Top 10. Talking to friends about what you had, and showing them your latest picture cover was one thing. Watching the countdown on *Top of the Pops* and bettering the usual "...brilliant, alright, shit, alright, shit, brilliant..." by saying "...got it, nope, nope, got it, nope, got it...", was a second thing. It would be quite another to *have the Top 10*, for whichever week of whichever year was under discussion.

The problem, however, was that there were records at the top of the chart that I didn't want anywhere near me. This was not to be compromised on, so I solved it by inaugurating my own Top 10, writing them out each week in an exercise book I had stolen from school, and counting them down on my bedroom turntable every Friday teatime, for an audience of one (I had to double-up as audience).

The performance of big records in my Top 10 didn't differ too much from those in the real one, maybe a few by one or two places, but the shit was left out completely. No shit allowed. I didn't write them out lovingly in felt pens; just in standard block caps, making it neat, like in the newspapers, with last week's positions in brackets. But now there was a Top 10 in which I had a copy of every record. I kept this up for a length of time that I really ought to keep quiet about.

We were well into 1979 now and, among other things, the presence of the picture cover was growing. Little over a year ago I had got only my fourth ever, but of the twenty-eight singles I bought between Boxing Day and the end of March, a total of eight had them. A mere eight others had come in plain white sleeves, although one of these was stiff white card rather than paper. My experience was probably representative because I was buying from a wide range of outlets: HMV, A1 Stores, Superdisc and WH Smith among them.

Adding to these was Harlequin, which had branches dotted around the West End that were furnished like school foyers. Their racks of back-catalogue oldies were often worth exploring and I bought several new releases from them in Haymarket or Leicester Square. There was also a place at the bottom of the steps leading down into Brixton tube station, where a quietly grinning middle-aged man sold chart singles and imports in a harsh brightness that made the shop seem like a cleaner's store room.

Department stores all sold records; I was a regular visitor to Woolworth's. Even Boot's the chemist had a record section; it was in their Regent Street shop that I got a cartoony punk 45 called 'King Rocker' by Generation X; raucous, buffoonish fun with a good sound, using what people called the "jungle beat", the one pioneered by 50s performer Bo Diddley; *dun ga-dun ga-dun, ga-dun-dun-bom*. It was being discounted even before it left the chart. I got it for 39p. In a plain white sleeve.

So, as I flicked through recent singles in my new storage system, the visual experience was becoming more interesting and this trend would continue. In the same Boxing Day/end of March period the following year, twenty-three of my thirty-seven new singles would have picture covers.

But now there was something else, too. The previous autumn, I had bought a hard-not-to-like ELO single called 'Sweet Talkin' Woman'. I was pleased to find that it came in a picture sleeve featuring a concert stage made from a space ship emitting lazer beams. But then, when I slid the single out, the vinyl wasn't black. It was purple.

I froze, wondering what to do. Was it a mistake? Would it play okay? It then dawned on me that I had heard about coloured vinyl somewhere. It had seemed to be some kind of specialism; but now here was one in my hand. It played fine. I had my first coloured vinyl. The following spring I got 'Cool for Cats' by Squeeze, which was candy pink. The image on the sleeve was mainly pink, and the design of its A&M label, usually faun and beige, had a pink tint. It had gone out of its way to be pink. Coloured vinyl was now an additional feature of the landscape. By the end of the year, I would also have it in yellow, violet, blue, green and white.

Squeeze were a bunch of cockneys who were new wave but not particularly punk. They were loud and thrashy on occasion and, of their two vocalists, one performed in a guttural sneer. But much of their sound made it seem as if they had been trapped in the orchestra pit at a kids' TV studio and decided to make the best of it: the *chuffa-chuffa* rhythm section, the keyboard with a distinct *boi-oing* to it.

Their subject matter was kitchen-sink romance and laddish sleaze, capable of being mildly shocking, funny and, often, moving. I remembered their galloping, windswept 'Take Me, I'm Yours' from the previous summer, but it was 'Cool for Cats' that carried them to the high table. In an atmosphere of growling frivolity, it told of discos, pulling birds and getting nicked, with female voices from the plastic vortex roughly cooing the title at the end of each verse. It had fast-burning charm and went to number two.

I bought it in A1, shocked to find that singles were now 90p. That was up 15p in less than a year, for fuck's sake. Where would it end? I promised to limit myself to one per week from now on, a promise I would break in no time; but I was angry. I was somewhat soothed by the gorgeous smell of the pink vinyl and the inside of the glossy picture cover. I had my nose in it for much of the bus journey home.

Beside it in the bag were two other new wave singles; a communal bellow called 'Into the Valley' by the Skids, a record whose lyric was stylishly difficult to decipher but whose energy was galvanising, and 'Lucky Number' by Lene Lovich, an odd, strikingly rhythmic love parable whose main hook, in an echo of 'Ca Plane pour Moi', was a four-note vocal phrase like a malfunctioning robot – *er oo ar or* – jarring with its surroundings in a way that was fun.

These sounds were just right for me; tough, challenging, yet comfortable. They sounded like I felt. Not goody-goody-nice-nice, but not a steel toe-cap to the bollocks; neither an apple for the teacher, nor a flob on their windscreen. They soothed rages; they made me want to go out and do things. Just right.

I was fifteen, and the soundtrack was a monsoon of distractions across every style and genre. I will offer highlights, but I'm twisted in frustration at what I have to leave out. I must, however, mention this. Ask someone who Barry Manilow is. They will groan, make some reference to a big nose, then, as their hands become fists, paint pictures of fake palm trees and row upon row of over-excited mums. Not Dooley. So listen to that, and then go and listen to his single 'Could It Be Magic', which is stunning. There have been various cover versions, two of which were big, uptempo hits, but all of which are cheap mockeries of the grand original. A good record is a good record, no matter who makes it.

Elvis Costello had his biggest hit yet with the barnstorming 'Oliver's Army', which was about mercenaries, contained the phrase "white nigger", and spent three weeks at number two. He followed it up with 'Accidents Will Happen', which wasn't nearly as big, but which I played obsessively because of its chorus. The UK release had a picture cover which was issued inside-out. Well, accidents *will* happen.

I didn't get one because my copy was on Columbia, not Radar. It was an import copy. I hadn't yet learned to question what I was being passed in return for my 90p. I realised that record shops were habitually selling import copies – mainly from France and the USA – in place of the regular UK issue. I imagined that this was because they were cheaper to buy in, but this may have been unfair. Singles sales reached an all-time peak in 1978-9 and so perhaps they needed to supplement their stock to cope with demand. The guy at Brixton tube station was certainly at it. I got my copy of 'Rat Trap' there and it was French. When I realised this, I felt ripped off. At the time, I had thought that the reason for the plastic ring being silver – rather than Ensign's usual green – was that it was "special". Mug.

But if I felt hard done by, there were, as is usual in life, strokes of good luck to compensate; although not often as big as this next one. One day in the spring, my longest-standing mate (hereafter abbreviated to LSM) rang to remind me about the foreign holiday that his family were taking at Easter. Unfortunately, the dates meant that they couldn't after all go to the Kate Bush concert at the Palladium, which his sister was distraught about because she was probably the biggest Kate Bush fan in the world. They wondered if I would like the tickets, and suggested another friend of ours – who had likewise spent long weeks in the arms of *The Kick Inside* - to go with me.

I had never been to a concert by a charting pop act before. Her new single, 'Wow', was okay, but had left my reactions in neutral. I went out and got it that day. I had bought 'Hammer Horror' the previous autumn, a single of good ideas let down by a useless chorus. The B-side, 'Coffee Homeground', was much better.

But the most striking thing about it was its cover, the front of which was filled with a crisply colourful shot of her face, surrounded by masses of hair, with no lettering. The feminine allure emanating from it was almost off the scale. It had made me try harder to like the record.

The Palladium, just off Oxford Circus, had a rich history of top-notch variety, weekly television broadcasts and world-conquering musicals. I felt a bit like an intruder as we trotted up its hallowed steps, but anticipation was high; this was going to be a night unspoilt by skinheads. At Planxty and the Spinners, there had been seats. There were seats here, too. The audience behaved like Spinners fans and sat on them nicely. We were about half way back, dead centre. Perfect. As we waited, a girl drifted down the aisle who looked just like Kate Bush; I mean *just* like her, with the crimped hair, the make-up and everything. Then I looked up and there was another one; I looked around and there was a third. I didn't get it.

The show, in keeping with its venue, brimmed with variety: the scenery and costume changes were almost non-stop. Most unfamiliar songs were from the new album *Lionheart*. One instant favourite was wistful homage to Albion 'Oh England My Lionheart'. Another was 'Symphony in Blue', a seemingly perfect vehicle for that voice.

She was impressive. She wore raincoats, parachutes and leotards, while sitting at the piano, interacting with the scenery or performing with dancers, using a microphone fitted to a discrete unit that she wore around her head so that she could sing with both hands free and while upside down. It was a concert rather than a gig, although I was not experienced enough to make that distinction at the time. If anyone had tried to point it out they would have been given short shrift.

The effect was as follows. I bought *Lionheart* the next morning and listened to it right through at least twice a day for weeks. I had money set aside for two end-of-season away games; I gave it all to a pavement ticket tout so that I could get in again for the final Palladium date; £15 for a £5 ticket – I didn't think twice.

My position this time was three rows from the stage, but right on the outside so my view was sharply angled. However, during the final encore – 'Wuthering Heights' – I left my seat and marched up, across and down the middle aisle, just as others were leaving their seats to scramble forward, and got to the front. To mark the final night, she left the stage during the long play-out, reappearing with her arms full of carnations, which, with a "Thank you London, you're amazing!", she hurled into the fevered crowd. I got three. As I made my way toward the exit, I was glared at enviously. One guy, who must have been twenty at least, begged me tearfully to let him have one – *just one*. He was disappointed.

Within days I had joined the Kate Bush Club and bought, among other trinkets, a lump of wax in the shape of a heart, with a lion's head covering half of it. It was advertised as a badge but was more like a brooch. I was never going to wear it. Once I'd calmed down a bit, I stopped sending them money that could be better spent on a single by someone other than Kate Bush, but I kept up the membership for a few years. And the carnations? Two I pressed and still have. The other stayed in a glass next to my bed until it disintegrated.

If you've been wondering what had happened to Abba, I can tell you. They had been brought down to earth with a bump the previous September, when 'Summer Night City' only got to number five. Reaching number five made something a big fat hit, but normal measures had ceased to apply to Abba some time ago. 'Summer Night City' was stodgy, with little sense of purpose apart from saying it was great fun being at some leisure resort (that few of us were likely to visit) and, in the chorus, it sounded for all the world as if they were singing about "fucking in the moonlight" (about which the same could be said).

The following winter, they came up with 'Chiquitita', which was instantly recognisable as sentimental slush. Because we first heard them doing it on telly at some Unicef event, it made us think they were getting us to furrow our brows about poor Mexican kids; they had form with Mexico and the title seemed to fit.

But the more you listened, the more you came to realise that the song was actually about a friend helping another to recover from a serious down and, on later occasions, I would imagine how it must feel to have a friend give that kind of support. You'd cry a bit more, but you'd feel better sooner. Whether or not you were in Mexico. I won't hear a word against 'Chiquitita'. It got to number two, held there by 'Heart of Glass'.

In the summer, they released the album *Voulez-Vous* which, song for song, is probably their best; yet there's nothing really great on it, merely the absence of crap. Their 1979 singles all went into the top five. But events seemed to be overtaking them.

Among which, was a genuinely big hit from the Dooleys. 'Wanted' was instantly catchy and its chorus had one of those descending chord sequences that are always good for a punt. Many a tight-lipped moanie had to admit that they quite liked it. It went to number three and it seemed their moment had finally come.

But sadly not. Although their follow-up, 'The Chosen Few', also went Top 10, it was for reasons that remain a mystery to me. It's actually quite painful. If the single after that, the ultra-poppy and well loud 'Love Patrol', had followed 'Wanted' instead, history may have been different, but the momentum had been lost. Another good single, 'Body Language', quietly sank. I would like to describe the sullen atmosphere in our maths class at this turn of events, but nobody actually gave a shit.

Squeeze proved more adept at following up a big success. They reached number two again in the summer with 'Up the Junction', a first-person narrative telling a tale of love and ambition being stifled by poverty and alcohol. Stilted rhyming contributed to its melancholy and it broke tens of thousands of hearts at a stroke, despite its production making it seem like you were listening to it through a wall.

It would have been a triumphant number one, if not for 'Are Friends Electric?' by Tubeway Army, a bleak and dour slab of synthesizer sound with a bleak and dour vocal. I hated it for holding Squeeze down but had to admit in the end that it was good; its impressive scope and weight helped me adjust. It came from nowhere, but there was clearly an audience waiting for something like it. Bleached front man Gary Numan was immediately a known figure; not a typical pop star at all, but with legions of admirers appearing from the shadows; people around me who I couldn't remember having expressed opinions on music before; making me think: "So this is the kind of thing they like".

Roxy Music returned, increasingly smooth, with a song of recovery called 'Dance Away', a good record, which got stuck at number two behind Blondie's follow-up to 'Heart of Glass', the tepid 'Sunday Girl'. Also number two in those weeks was 'Pop Muzik' by M; a lively piece of electronic pop which, as such, felt lemon-fresh. With lyrics like "boogie with a suitcase", it was always going to find a happy home in the record box. It encouraged us to talk about pop music, so it had confirmation going for it, too – perhaps their next one was going to encourage us to eat crisps.

There was a lot of this electronic stuff, now. Tubeway Army came several weeks after M, but with it in the summer were a couple of gems that didn't make the chart. One was 'Memphis Tennessee' by the Silicon Teens; smudges of driving synth with no reverb whatsoever and somebody singing a cute tune in a nasal whine. It turned out to be an old Chuck Berry song.

The synth sounds in the other one were topped with a fantastic xylophone part (possibly electronically generated) which took over between verses, and a lyric about how great electricity is. Fittingly, it was called 'Electricity' and was by a band with the wonderful name of Orchestral Manoeuvres in the Dark. Of the two, this was the one I had to get, and in HMV I found it, in a cover that was almost like rice paper, which appeared to be plain black until you turned it in the light and its design became visible. *Woooh.*

I heard both of these on the John Peel show, which I listened to in bed. Radio 1 went off air at tea-time, and between then and 7am the next morning, you had whatever was on Radio 2, except for between 10pm and midnight, when Radio 1 flared up again for John Peel.

This was everything that daytime Radio 1 wasn't. It eschewed the mainstream entirely and his style was the antithesis of the DLTs and the Tones: no gratuitous jollity or nudge-nudge quipping, no big minutes, no Dooleys (but we'll gloss over that); in fact, the pop charts were rejected entirely, in favour of anything new or different that interested the host.

It became a haven to those looking for an alternative to what *Top of the Pops* or *Smash Hits* offered, and who didn't particularly want to snigger and guffaw at Kenny Everett. He played reggae, punk and the avant-garde; as well as this electronic stuff. I dipped in and out. I quickly lost interest if nothing good came on within a couple of records, perhaps farting around with the dial to get Radio Luxembourg instead, which, given its fluctuating signal, was always a pain in the arse, but worth it if I could leave some unfathomable dirge behind in favour of one of the better pop hits of the hour. However, John was proving to be worth the gamble, as long as my dipping occasionally coincided with a 'Memphis Tennessee' or an 'Electricity'.

One band he certainly favoured was Siouxsie and the Banshees. Their new single that summer was the tortured 'Playground Twist'; squalling guitars, cemetery bells and a desperate, wailing vocal, in a waltz time that went with its macabre imagery. I was amazed that it barely scraped into the Top 30.

Some way above it and having been as high as number seven, was 'Babylon's Burning' by the Ruts. Now then. Let's just consider this. If, in some parallel universe, the multitude of events that constituted punk rock had been organised just to enable the making of this record, it would have been worth every last splinter of bother. It's a two-and-a-half minute crowning glory of some damn thing, that's for sure. An unholy racket, yes; but one of passion, craft and economy. Nothing is too much or too little; no part of it is found wanting.

It is, essentially, an urgent riff played on every quaver over four bars. There was something clever about it. It sounded like you'd heard it before; perhaps in some detective or spy theme; it was a bit like the incidental music from the *Inspector* cartoons on *The Pink Panther Show*. The blaring guitars and blaring vocals all blare to exactly the right level for whatever you need them for and, towards the end, it all starts to build to a climax, additional layers of noise and percussive purpose driving it up and up until it's the best trance you've ever been in, flooding every neglected corner of you; hugging, nourishing, justifying - and then four emphatic blasts of clean conclusion: *duh-nu-nu-nun!* Fucking fantastic. It is that rarest of things: an utterly satisfying listen.

The fact that it got no higher than number seven tells you that not everybody felt the same way about it. Plenty in my circles were loud in their adulation, but I was amazed how many people didn't know it at all. Many of them said it had to be reggae because it had 'Babylon' in the title. This was somewhat understandable. Most of us had at least a cursory idea of Rastafarian tenets, maintained in no small part by the fact that there were several reggae hits of quality that year, including the rootsy 'Cool Meditation' by Third World, which I loved.

But they were all trumped by Janet Kay's 'Silly Games'. This was from a strain of reggae called lovers rock, which gave it licence to cover affairs of the heart just like soul music did, at a pace ideal for serious slow dancing. Girls in particular were mad on it, but, apart from seasoned rednecks, almost everyone around us liked 'Silly Games'.

It had a gentle sway and a restrained, upper-register vocal, with a set-piece high note at the end of each chorus which, in a comedy movie, would have shattered glass cabinets. It wafted around us on warm summer days, distributing calm and contentment like a garden sprinkler. It seemed that every few yards you would hear someone singing it, daring themselves to have a go at the high notes.

Janet Kay appeared on *Top of the Pops* in a purple gown and a sparkly head scarf that made her look like a genie. The only reason I didn't kick back and enjoy it as much as others did, was that it had a manic hi-hat part that I couldn't imagine playing comfortably and which seemed to jar with the general feel. Once you've noticed something like that, it can balls the whole thing up for you.

Speaking of seasoned rednecks, across the pond in Chicago, large numbers of them were holding an event which achieved notoriety although I didn't hear about it at the time. At the White Sox baseball stadium, they staged a "Disco Demolition Derby", where piles of disco records were burned and a massive crate of them blown up, amid scenes of wild celebration and chants of "disco sucks". It was part of an orchestrated backlash against the chart dominance of disco – an empowering force for homosexuals, women and blacks – which wasn't as marked in dear old Blighty; but no doubt many of our own rednecks raised a glass.

The target for much of their ire was of course the Bee Gees who, it has to be said, hadn't done themselves any favours with their most recent single, the aptly-named 'Tragedy', in which they appeared to be lampooning their own sound. Towards the end, there is a silly quivering cry which sounds like a parody of their usual silly quivering cries; outsized, as if it had been punched in by a piss-taking DJ or a Chicago baseball fan. But it hadn't. It therefore follows that the Bee Gees had chosen to put it in and leave it there to sound shit for all time.

Given this, it is perhaps ironic that 1979 was a golden year for soul and disco, with the breakthrough pop success of funk group Earth, Wind & Fire, as well as the launch proper of Michael Jackson – which we will come to later – and exciting, fresh-tasting sounds all over the place, including 'Contact' by Edwin Starr, 'Keep on Dancing' by Gary's Gang, 'Knock on Wood' by Aimee Stewart and 'He's the Greatest Dancer' by Sister Sledge.

Brits got in on the act, too; the Real Thing did excellent business with 'Can You Feel the Force', an example of a brisk, top-heavy funk native to the UK (doing *Star Wars* over a year after the movie's release was not considered odd or stale in the late 70s). In the summer, there came a joint effort by Earth, Wind & Fire and the Emotions called 'Boogie Wonderland', which is often held up as one of the era's very best; it was on the radio endlessly, alongside one of the last big hitters from Philadelphia International: 'Ain't No Stopping Us Now' by McFadden & Whitehead.

There was also Anita Ward's perky 'Ring My Bell'; a record featuring the syndrum heavily; way too heavily in the opinion of many. The lyric, delivered in a breathy, ultra-girly voice, can be summarised as: "We're mad about each other, which is lovely, and you're going to do the business for me in bed just as soon as I've finished tidying the kitchen".

Within the broad church of disco, its sound stood out and, from the moment it first appeared on the radio, it made people smile and sing. Cute, fun and laced with sparkles, it quickly removed 'Sunday Girl' from number one. I loved it and I still do.

Then ELO went disco. Okay, so they already had a string section. But they were a big, chunky band making a big, chunky sound, only occasionally veering into the gratuitously catchy; disco just didn't seem to fit. That summer, they bombarded us with singles; the first being 'Shine a Little Love', which simply shoved all the elements of their trademark sound under a mirrorball, installed *dom-tiss dat-tiss* and put falling *wooooh!* vocal sounds on top. Its chorus defied belief. If, before this, some cynical type had made a piss-take of what ELO would sound like if they took the inconceivable step of going disco, it might have been identical.

They do, at least, deserve credit for the variety they delivered across their four 1979 hits. In September, 'Don't Bring Me Down' appeared to be a cover of an under-appreciated Beatles track, with big, chugging beats and little to offend apart from an over-arching dullness. At the end of the autumn, they gave us 'Confusion', which, aptly, was one of the year's best records of any kind: great song, great arrangement, great atmosphere. Bingo.

But before these, there was 'The Diary of Horace Wimp', the ballad of an everyman tootling along until a voice from on high tells him to get a life: whereupon he meets a small, pretty girl who accepts his almost immediate proposal of marriage. Just like that. Clearly bollocks. Almost everything in the arrangement was annoying. It was on the radio endlessly during the summer holiday, the *doo-be-do-wow-wow* backing vocal floating from car windows on the seafront to put you right off your ice cream. You cried out for 'Wanted' to be on next and make it all better. Well I did.

And that was the point. Why did everybody seem to be calmly putting up with it? However tongue-in-cheek it might have been, listening to it was like punishment for the wrongly convicted. Some daytime DJs may have sniggered or shaken their heads, but I don't remember them doing so. It reached the Top 10 and ELO's share price was clearly unaffected. When I asked footballers down the park, they just smiled and shrugged because they liked ELO. They even began singing the chorus. I began to wonder: *Does this mean they don't understand why other records are good?*

To soothe my brow, I tried to imagine a gang of skinheads at a performance of it, hoping to see ELO's audience shaken from their cosy reverie in a blur of boots and expletives; but instead, getting a picture of grinning, ironic enjoyment, akin to stuffing shirts with newly-cut grass.

This only added to my anxiety, and skinheads were already good at making me anxious. Anti-fascists divided their energies between events such as Rock Against Racism and reasoned argument. Skinheads put their energies into thuggery. I saw this pretty much whenever I went out. The street was where their strength lay.

But then two records appeared which gave far cooler audiences different kinds of strength just about everywhere else.

Eight

It was an extravaganza. At 11am each summer weekday, the *Radio 1 Roadshow* would broadcast from a seaside venue somewhere in the UK, providing games, frolics, a famous disc jockey and the current soundtrack. You could ask for no more. The leading DJs did a week apiece and, since they were still among the best-known personalities going, thousands would pack whichever beach, esplanade or car park they pitched up in. Some of the crowds were huge. They saw the Mileage Game, where contestants guessed the *Roadshow*'s mileage. They saw Bits and Pieces, where contestants had to identify short clips from ten records. Winners got Radio 1 mugs, t-shirts, badges and key-rings. Everyone else had to queue at the Goodie Mobile and buy them.

Nowadays I was a regular *Roadshow* listener, but I had actually been to one in 1977. It came to our favourite seafront while we were on holiday and the host had been none other than Noel. The family went to the beach, leaving me to plunge into the crowd. I plunged about ten yards. Between me and the stage lay a solid mass of picnic blankets. I couldn't get anywhere near. It was crap. There was nobody to talk to and people closest to me were moany and not talking about music. I watched with envy as distant figures were hauled up to be on Bits and Pieces. Noel was great, but he would have been better closer. I didn't queue to get his autograph afterwards. Neither did I line up at the Goodie Mobile. The experience was all a bit deflating. But I wanted to go to another one. And be closer.

Since then, I had merely listened, competing with the Bits and Pieces contestants and usually beating them. I did this habitually while we were on holiday in 1979, often in the same seafront car park where Noel had appeared two years earlier. Each time the programme finished, I imagine I drifted off to the beach for a bit. Then I imagine I went to the family pub across the road because they had a Space Invaders machine. This was the summer of Space Invaders, a rhythmically juddery digital game played on a monochrome arcade console; you took pot-shots at bomb-dropping aliens from behind barriers which, as the bombs hit, eroded until you were fatally exposed. You were usually killed as the pace increased, by a bomb that you ran into while escaping another twelve. Then you would put more money in. I was dangerously close to addiction. It was probably the threat to the record budget that saved me.

That, pretty much, was the summer holiday. The soundtrack, as usual, held a few horrors, a few welcome curiosities and, here and there, occasions for genuine excitement. Then suddenly there was 'Gangsters' by the Special A.K.A. It came flying from the radio as an instant new best friend, grabbing me by the head and sending blancmange squelching for cover. It was made of fast reggae with a distinctly white, un-showbiz voice over the top, minor chords, sporadic yelled threats and bits that sounded Egyptian. Recent reggae had been smooth and laid-back. This was groovy and pissed off. The sky changed colour. 'The Diary of Horace Wimp' could no longer hurt me.

Back in London, my hands on a copy, I was further smitten. The only thing wrong with it was the ending. It had an organ coda that would've been one of the best things ever if left to fade right out, but it stopped abruptly during the fade, which was bollocks. I had to twiddle the volume knob to fix the problem every time I played it.

The B-side wasn't by the Special A.K.A. - it was 'The Selecter' by the Selecter, a moody reggae instrumental with a mesmerising bassline. It was on a label called 2-Tone; black and white lines of check, blended with the logo of a gangster in a suit, hat and shades, leaning against a doorway. Fantastic. I kept flipping it; playing one side, then the other, over and over. It got to number six.

As it was slipping down the chart, 'Don't Stop 'Till You Get Enough' by Michael Jackson, on the far more familiar orange of Epic, was zooming up. This was the moment for launching Michael as a grown-up, fully-fledged megastar, and it was a huge departure.

Earlier that year, the Jacksons' Top 10 hit 'Shake Your Body (Down to the Ground)', had used a blend of funk, Latin and extra thrust which galloped and gyrated and was a bit wilder than usual. The new solo single took this feel, but whereas the Jacksons record was linked to disco and to family-friendliness, 'Don't Stop 'Till You Get Enough' was a clean break.

Disco never brought black people together in the way this did. Its intro was like a storm, a cyclone of strings and percussion. Michael's new falsetto was raw, edgy and indecipherable; you couldn't get much of the lyric apart from the title and "get on". It was speaking to those for whom it was meant. This clearly wasn't me. I couldn't understand the words and I was bored by the last minute and a half – there was no build to it and little variation; it just kept repeating itself. But making a great pop record was perhaps not the point.

It has always conjured a symbolic image in my mind: an outdoor scene, with a drifting crowd of kids from my universe; there are black kids and white kids, but all the black people I know are in it, every last one. From the opening "Ooooh!" of this single, they were Michael's people. They might have been into reggae, chiffony soul or electronica; but here, now, was something they could rally around.

Soul was reaffirming its right to go its own way, meeting the needs and expectations of a new audience. Soon, "disco" would be a term of derision. In the years to come, none of my black friends would ever hear a word against Michael, not once, not under any circumstances, no matter what. He would never make another record like 'Don't Stop 'Till You Get Enough'. It got to number three.

These singles were like a pair of starting guns. From this moment on, soul music was different. From this moment on, there was a whole other scene taking its precedent from the mod era rather than the rock 'n' roll one. Soon, new soul sounds would rule; funkier, jazzier, more assertive, more spacious; a good, jazzy example from the end of that holiday being 'Street Life' by the Crusaders. Soon, we would learn that the figure on the 2-Tone label design was a rude boy, a member of a Jamaican toughies cult from the first half of the 60s whose music was ska; an early, up-tempo form of reggae years before the term "reggae" was ever coined. The mods had been into ska.

Mum had once told me that mods and rockers were rival gangs who fought each other in the 60s. Rockers liked original rock 'n' roll, wore leather and rode motorbikes, whereas mods dressed smart and followed "modern" music.

My aunt told me stories about going to hip mod clubs. Whenever I subsequently mentioned a mod record from the era, she not only knew it but gave me details; where she had danced to it, who with, and which moves they had in certain bits, like making a gun with your fingers during 'Ride Your Pony' by Lee Dorsey.

She had been at Clacton when "the first trouble" happened, which, the way I heard it, wasn't trouble at all, just an everyday scuffle involving a few bored youths on a bank holiday by the sea when everything was shut. Mods and rockers were there together. Locals, intimidated by these alien crowds, moaned to the press, who livened up a nothing story by reporting it as aggravation between the two tribes. The result was that on the next bank holiday a load of yobs travelled to the seaside for the fighting. Mods and rockers violence was born. Well done, the press.

During the summer of Space Invaders, a mod revival which had been taking shape over the preceding months was given *Quadrophenia,* a movie about 60s mods that featured plenty of fighting. It was based on a double album of the same name by the Who, a band from the height of 60s mod chic, honed by their manager to be an integral part of the scene as well as the epitome of youthful energy and rebellion. Their best records, particularly 1965's 'My Generation', were cool, angry and explosive all at once.

They adapted to survive the hippy years, but 1973's *Quadrophenia* was a homage to mod-dom and its cover showed a young man in a fish-tail parka (preferred mod overcoat) sitting on a Vespa motor scooter (preferred mod transport). The movie followed its narrative.

If you were young and needed a scene to belong to, here was one, straight off the peg. It revived good stuff from the 60s – which, importantly, included Motown, something my peers were largely scoffing at not long ago – and put it at the top of the cool list. I thought it was great.

Back at school in September, I noticed a few kids with the classic mod look of neat hair, button-down collars, slim ties and parkas, as modelled in the movie; tough kids that I didn't know. Gradually, more appeared. By Christmas there were loads, groups of mates who all became mods together and steeped themselves in mod-lore. Some of them were sent to me on recommendation to ask about Motown. They sported the union flag, because The Who had used it, as well as that Royal Air Force target symbol – a mod badge for reasons I still don't quite understand: sometimes it was a patch sewn onto the parka sleeve; sometimes it was massive and covered the back, with "the Who" or "mod" written across it. The best parka I remember along our corridors had the rude boy from the 2-Tone label going from collar to fish-tail. It looked brilliant.

It was there because 2-Tone was busy following up 'Gangsters' with a string of releases in this "ska" style by a succession of ultra-cool, youthful bands of mixed race, touting punk and Jamaican influences in roughly equal measure. The new mods loved them. *Smash Hits* readers loved them. They roared up the charts.

This was thrilling. Firstly, the records were loud, energetic and good – almost all of them. Secondly, it was all on one label with a charismatic design and its own sound; I had been born too late for Tamla-Motown, but now here was 2-Tone doing pretty much the same thing. Thirdly, it provided a scene for blacks and whites to share in explicit defiance of the rednecks; a common understanding, a common platform, a common cause for celebration. I was typical of a type of youngster for whom this was pure vindication. Our excitement must have been visible before we came round the corner.

But then there were the skinheads. 2-Tone's Jamaican rhythms spoke to their tradition. Its energy did, too. This was a potent, irresistible cocktail. But the new skinheads were racist. 2-Tone was about racial togetherness. Plus, mods were a ready-made rival tribe for applying fist and boot to, and these new mods were madly into 2-Tone. The net result was angrier skinheads. Oh goody.

Before we gallop on however, there are other records from the start of the school year that need to be mentioned. The Police was a provocative name for a band, associated as it was with something both dull and oppressive – coppers mistrusted and mistreated us because we were young, and our black friends because they were black.

The band in question were a three-piece, which was similarly unusual. The Jam were a trio, but we were used to groups with four, perhaps five members; occasionally more. Three was gimmicky. They too used reggae rhythms, taking the familiar, clipped, chang guitar off-beat and doing all manner of things with it. The drummer used the classic reggae pattern I had been taught by the hippy, but played as if he were trying to break his sticks.

The main thing about the Police was that they looked great; three chiselled lads with lively blond hair staring straight at you. The lead singer was called Sting, the name of an elf sword in *The Hobbit*. They had an air of maturity about them. Indeed, the guitarist, alarmingly, was over 30. But they were so good-looking that it didn't matter. They became instant favourites with *Smash Hits* readers.

They had already had two sizeable hits, both of which were annoying. 'Roxanne' was a hectoring, moralistic song about a prostitute; 'Can't Stand Losing You' was about someone who was going to commit suicide because his girl was leaving him; its chorus drove you up the wall and its unpleasant picture cover had a figure hanging from a noose while an electric fire melted the ice block under his feet. It reached number two, which baffled me. But Sting was in *Quadrophenia*, playing the part of a particularly stylish mod. His stock could scarcely have been higher. It all had an "about-to-have-a-number-one" feeling about it.

Thankfully, their next single, which did indeed rocket to number one, was the brilliant 'Message in a Bottle': a galvanising sound, boss guitar riff and high sparkle count, unspoilt by the fact that its lyrical *denouement* was worryingly close to that of 'Tie a Yellow Ribbon

Round the Old Oak Tree'. There was something here for everybody. They were on A&M, who remained keen to stress their coloured vinyl credentials. Their number two had been on blue; this one, thematically, was on green and its picture cover showed the beautiful boys gazing at us through broken green shards with the title written on crumpled paper.

This single was some package. Just thinking about it was exciting. I remember a girl from our maths class producing it from her bag during a lesson to show friends, blushing and giggling uncontrollably as she did so. This must have been a common scene. The Police were beyond hot.

One of the 'O' Levels I was going to take was called Economic and Public Affairs, an odd mixture of British Constitution and Politics. There was a very different crowd in here; thoughtful, serious kids who were into Monty Python at a time when *Life of Brian* was barely three months old, and were more open-minded about music than the tribal hoards in the corridor.

There was a tall boy who lived beneath a curtainous fringe and spoke in low growls, sitting next to a girl with a huge, breezy laugh who crossed her legs confidently and was the first person I had ever met who said they were going to vote Liberal; beside them was the quiet boy from my old maths class who had copied out the charts in felt tips. Then there was me and the LSM. An eclectic bunch, but united by a common enthusiasm for a new record called 'Video Killed the Radio Star' by the Buggles.

Their name suggested they might be chubby little things toddling around Toytown, but they sounded bright, sweet and tuneful. The song was about music media; a wistful reflection on the passing of the old ways, giving the impression that these were jolly decent people thinking jolly decent thoughts, and capping it all with a jolly catchy chorus.

Our enthusiasm began as semi-ironic, but this was a good record. Lots of other people thought so, too. One week that autumn, enough of them bought it to get it to number one, replacing the Police. They really did. Two brilliant number ones in a row. Wonderful things do sometimes happen. We drank those heady days in, with little idea of the horrors that were to follow.

For wonderful things do not last. Seven days after the Buggles got to the top of the charts, they were booted off by a country singer called Lena Martell. It's only now, as I write, acknowledging the need to mention her Jesus-bothering record 'One Day at a Time', that I am spending my first traces of mental energy considering it at all. The fact that it knocked 'Video Killed the Radio Star' off number one was like a boot in the guts. Our fire had been stomped out by the Salvation Army and I was blinded with anger. *Some desperate old misery holding her trembling hands out to Jesus – who the fuck needs that?* Everybody who bought it, that's who – an underground army of people about whom I was swift to leap to conclusions.

Having now finally considered it in my capacity as a calm and thoughtful adult, I do see the purpose of the lyric. Life can indeed be relentlessly, exhaustingly dispiriting. I'm not without empathy. But that can be dealt with in any number of ways. 'One Day at a Time' must not be accepted as one of them.

When, after three harrowing weeks, it fell from number one, it was only to be replaced by 'When You're in Love with a Beautiful Woman' by Dr. Hook. These had once been cowboy stoners, then they went all lovey-dovey; now, having wormed their way into your living room, they went disco. Suburban tales of jealousy and swishing netties, performed by characterful hairies swinging their hips with eyebrows aloft and maracas having at that Latin beat. It was part tongue-in-cheek, part bawdy, overwhelmingly horrible. Once Lena Martell fans got a couple of sherries inside them, they raced out to buy it.

A good thing, then, that there was all this other stuff going on. There was 2-Tone. There were mods. With these new mods, came new mod bands, who stared at you moodily from suits. Early autumn saw the appearance of Secret Affair, on the very mod-sounding I-Spy label. Their visual and lyrical imagery was all about action and direction. Their logo was a keyhole, reminiscent of 60s spy thrillers, but there were arrows, too. Arrows represented action and direction. I remembered that the picture cover of 'David Watts'/'"A" Bomb in Wardour

Street' by the Jam the year before had arrows all over it.

It was now becoming clear that the Jam were a mod band, it had been their game all along; hence the suits with the thin lapels, hence their own lyrics about action and direction, and hence the arrows. Mods loved arrows. Those target symbols often had arrows pointing from them, providing action and direction for their parkas.

Secret Affair's hit, 'Time for Action', was a crisp homage to being out and looking good. It was an announcement – the mods were here. There was a good organ sound and oafish backing vocals sounding like a gang of lads bouncing up and down together behind the goal, or re-enacting a sea-front scene from *Quadrophenia*. It got to number thirteen. I played it a lot.

At the same time, a second 2-Tone single appeared, by a band called Madness. The song was 'The Prince', a tribute to early 60s ska hero Prince Buster, which used a great rhythm but had a flimsy sound and I didn't find myself playing it much. Its B-side was a cover of a Prince Buster song, 'Madness', which presumably gave the band their name. It sounded like one of the less appealing songs my grandparents would sing around the piano when I was little.

But the important thing was that here was another 2-Tone single in the Top 20. I was slightly disappointed that the label was a plastic ring rather than the paper one that 'Gangsters' had, but then 'Gangsters' had come in a plain white sleeve and 'The Prince' had a 2-Tone company bag, with the rude boy figure going down the left-hand side like a giant Buddha in the side of a mountain. Most of my 2-Tone copies would have this bag plus the plastic rings.

Next came the Selecter, liberated from B-side duty to put out their own single; with vocals by a black girl in a suit and a narrow-rim trilby hat. 'On My Radio' was high-octane, clapalong ska, a song about a bloke enjoying the radio his girlfriend had bought him, with a strikingly odd chorus that we all quickly acclimatised to. It got to number eight.

The Special A.K.A had changed their name to the far zippier Specials for their second single; to be precise, it was the Specials featuring Rico, an imported Jamaican trombonist. The new song was a laid-back chug called 'Message to You Rudy' which, I later discovered, was a cover; not particularly exciting, but loved. It was a double A-side with 'Nite Klub', a fired-up ditty about being unemployed and trying to have night out on watery lager and not being able to pull a bird; a song with its arm across the shoulder of most of its listeners. It reached number ten.

The album *Specials* soon followed, demonstrating that, although everybody said 2-Tone was ska, it was actually a showcase for a whole range of Jamaican styles married to punk attitude. Old-time ska had been born through a misinterpretation of the New Orleans rhythm made famous by performers such as Fats Domino. This had gone *dun ga-dun ga-dun ga-dun*, but the Jamaicans played it as *nn-cha nn-cha nn-cha nn-cha* with the emphasis squarely on the *cha*. Except that they said *ska*. This was much more fun to dance to (listen again to Millie's 'My Boy Lollipop', a bona fide ska hit).

As Jamaican music evolved through rockesteady to reggae, this off-beat accentuation was retained and developed. By adding the punk ingredient, 2-Tone gave right angles to ska's rounded bounce, so that the off-beat could yell "ska" regardless of whether the frame it sat in was rock, pop or anything else.

So there was indeed a new sound, a distinctly 2-Tone sound, most consistently illustrated in the output of the Selecter. But between them, 2-Tone bands played in each of the available styles and referenced them lyrically. The Specials' album featured them all.

'Gangsters' wasn't on it, but there were things here that were as good. 'Do The Dog' was a concentrated blast of adrenaline, a plea for a long list of disparate youth and political tribes to recognise their differences without kicking the shit out of each other. The gentler 'Doesn't Make It Alright' said something similar, but more subtly and with specific regard to racism. This had real context; skinheads were going to 2-Tone concerts and, twisted by their conflicting purpose, were causing plenty of trouble. Front man Terry Hall once sang 'Doesn't Make It Alright' acapella in a hail of missiles after the rest of the band had been driven from the stage.

But the best track was on side two: 'Too Much Too Young', a lament about teenage motherhood; she got pregnant and married instead of having fun, now there's another hungry mouth for someone to pay for and she's stuck. The song is both angry and miserable, done in a low-slung reggae tempo, a long way from ska.

One night that month, John Peel opened his show by saying that, as we knew, he wasn't in the habit of playing records from the hit parade: "...but in this case, I'll make an exception". And he played 'The Eton Rifles', the new single by the Jam. It was edgy, aggressive, laced with resentment and righteous aggro, dealing defiantly with class privilege and arrogance; soothing the rage better than most, filling voids left by our own injustices. Plus, you could sing along to every last bit. It made you feel brilliant.

Front man and songwriter Paul Weller, barely in his twenties, was now a revered figure and beginning to be treated as a spokesperson for his generation. He may not have been completely comfortable with that idea, but this single was like he was saying: *You're right to think I'm fucking great; cop a load of this.* Having it start the John Peel show on the week it entered the charts was saying the same thing in the third person. It would storm to number three and the new mods now had a genuinely great record of their own.

Another week passed, and into the chart flew a second Madness single. This one was bang on the money. 'One Step Beyond' was a mad, super-loud instrumental of growling saxophone; the title ringing out intermittently as the pace blistered and you threw yourself around in as close to a beat as you could manage. But it wasn't on 2-Tone. Suddenly, with only their second single, they had absconded to Stiff. The label design was bespoke, the artwork burgundy, reminding me of grandads, and making me feel extremely comfortable. Indeed, they dressed like grandads waiting for a bus in winter.

Also, they did this thing like a deranged conga, chugging forward in unified stomps, groins spooned, knees and elbows in controlled co-ordination; a beast with twelve legs that we learned was called "the nutty train". Everybody immediately wanted to be in a nutty train. They were having a blast and so were we. 'One Step Beyond' got to number seven, with the nutty train on its cover.

Then, another Secret Affair single: 'Let Your Heart Dance', with its rumbustious, bassy beat; less of an anthem, but it did the trick and deserved more than number thirty-two. It got there as more mods than ever were drifting down our school corridors, looking cool, looking like mods, calling out mod-ishly, or rehearsing in relative hush with a pump of the fist: *Mods! Mods! Mods!*

Ours was a mod and soul school, not a skinhead school. Skinheads were out there somewhere. I don't know if there was such thing as a skinhead school. Mods and soul kids dressed smart, adapted the school uniform rather than defied it. The soul kids were less keen on ties, but the authorities were not alarmed.

Mods would emerge from shadows next to the cinders pitch where our Sunday team trained. They would neaten their hair for a bit, then thrust their hands deep into their parkas. Some of them had classic side-partings. I had stuck resolutely to my side-parting through punk rock's spikes and disco's curly perms which, like disco itself, had infected a large chunk of the population. I thought they all looked fucking stupid. Now, the mods had caught up with me. Or at least the ones not trying to look like Paul Weller had.

Beside the cinders pitch, they engaged me in conversations about Martha and the Vandellas' 'Heat Wave', or other tracks from *20 Mod Classics*, a new compilation of old Motown stuff that mods would have liked back then which, because it was for mods, came on the black-and-silver Tamla-Motown label rather than the blue spokes. Had to be authentic. With the target symbol on the cover. And an arrow sticking out. Action and direction for Motown at last.

They also spoke about 'Green Onions'; a sassy, organ-based 1962 instrumental by Booker T. and the M.G.s, featured in *Quadrophenia*, which had been re-released on Atlantic and was climbing the chart. They told stories about going to venues that were putting on mod nights, and encounters with skinheads. Exaggerations were few. They were cautious and wary, with a hint of resignation.

Another new 2-Tone act began climbing the chart at Christmas. The Beat used a sweetened, rounded "tighten up" rhythm for a cover of 'The Tears of a Clown', which went down a storm. They had an old guy called Saxa in the line-up (playing the saxophone, you'll be shocked to hear). Because I knew the original, I couldn't help but compare it and found it flimsy.

But it was a double A-side with 'Ranking Full Stop', which causes involuntary bouncing on my part to this day and was a showcase for their sharp, silvery guitar sound and overlapping vocals which meant the action never let up. Or the direction. It got to number six in the new year.

At the same time, came a third Madness single; 'My Girl', a mild domestic drama, a lad sincere and uncertain. Girls swooned, boys were taken aback. They'd had the car-park party of 'The Prince', the explosion of unadulterated energy that was 'One Step Beyond' and now 'My Girl'. We thought: *Blimey, if they can do all this...*

There was an album, *One Step Beyond*, another nutty train on its cover, which had about a hundred tracks on it on a mad range of styles and rhythms, but was truer to original ska detail than *Specials*. These were lads like the ones we bumped into at bus stops, who you could have the most brilliant laugh with – if you got on.

It had a ska-ed up version of the theme from the *Tarzan* TV series, which they called 'Tarzan's Nuts' – the sound of one of those most brilliant laughs. They did something similar with the "theme" from *Swan Lake*, called 'Swan Lake', which I didn't realise had been done as reggae before and would, in time, inspire me to finally get the orchestral album.

It was all excitingly familiar. As if to underline this, the inside cover featured a huge collage of pictures of fans, people from their world, many of them photo-booth shots; people exactly like us, mucking about, having a laugh. The band were on the outside, the fans on the inside.

The Specials did something similar with their new single. The cover was an image of fans at a concert, taken from the front of the stage; a sea of happy, sweaty heads, with the band nowhere in sight. I didn't get one, mine came in the 2-Tone company sleeve. This was a live EP – *The Special A.K.A. Live!* - featuring 'Too Much Too Young', but a frantic, yelled version that wasn't as good as the one on the album.

Still, if you had been at the concert you probably wouldn't have cared.

Clearly, few people cared in any case. The EP became 2-Tone's first number one in January and the excitement squeezed your cheeks. The other four tracks were covers of old skinhead favourites and there was another cover on the B-side of the new Selecter single, ska-ed up version of the James Bond Theme called 'James Bond', with a snarling voiceover going *James Bond, di killah!* The A-side, 'Three Minute Hero', was more of the Selecter same, but a bit different, which is exactly what we wanted. It got to number sixteen.

Into all of this came UB40, a band with a great song in a more conventionally modern reggae style called 'Food for Thought'; moody, reflective and political, as was its paired A-side, 'King'; a lament about the loss of Civil Rights momentum in a world still suffering from racism. They were on the hitherto unknown Graduate label, but they fit right in and went to number four.

Another new label was Go-Feet, one formed by the Beat, who, like Madness, had left 2-Tone after a single single. To the 2-Tone rude boy was now added the icon of a dancing girl in a pencil skirt and an Alice band, allied with a sound that was already recognisably theirs. 'Hands Off – She's Mine' was an everyday adolescent heart-pang drama, but its B-side, 'Twist and Crawl' was serious business that made you feel like you could lift a truck. Number nine for that one.

Then another new mod band, the Lambrettas, named after the other brand of Italian motor scooter favoured by mods, made the Top 10 with a cover of a 1959 song by the Coasters, 'Poison Ivy'. The singer performed in a mid-Atlantic drawl until his spoken part which was all lord-luvva-duck-gawd-blimey, to the delight of seasoned piss-takers everywhere. It was neutrally remarkable but did extremely well.

The phrase "extremely well" was then given a different meaning. The eighteen new number ones in the year leading up to the end of March had taken a mean average of 3.6 weeks to get to the top. Six of them took a mere two, putting them in the category of "unstoppable". But then there was the anticipation surrounding 'Going Underground'/'Dreams of Children', the new double A-side from the Jam. When it was announced, tectonic plates began shifting. Suddenly, the anticipation was over and it was out. British youth poured itself into record shops and, seven days later, it became the first record since bloody Slade to go straight in at number one.

'Going Underground' was in the same ballpark as 'The Eton Rifles', but frightened, putting a brave face on panic; and in keeping with its time, it had context. We were in the midst of the Cold War and, due to events in the middle east, tensions between the USA and the Soviet Union had heightened to the extent that nuclear weapons could be deployed. This is what we were told, by newspapers and television reports, as well as public information films and leaflets advising on how to give yourself the best chance of surviving a nuclear attack. They were very clearly not joking.

Blondie's recent, "unstoppable" number one had been called 'Atomic'; its cover featured Debbie Harry preening herself before a huge, fire-filled mushroom cloud. So 'Going Underground' made us think about descending into a bunker, containing as it did lyrics about bodies freezing when listening to the news; about shouting, about screaming; the need for escape.

This was the climate. It was like living with a spear continuously wedged through your stomach. No matter where you were, you felt it grind against your insides whenever you heard an aeroplane overhead, all intention forgotten, all activity suspended, because it could be a nuclear missile; that's what they would probably sound like. As far as you knew. You couldn't check – who could you ask? Someone giving an unconsidered, unbalanced answer because they were as scared as you were?

Kate Bush released a single called 'Breathing', about a baby in the womb suffering from nuclear fallout. Listening to it was an ordeal even before you heard the backing vocal telling us "We are all going to die". Thank fuck for 'The Empty Bullring' on the B-side. In the summer, a group called the Piranhas would storm the Top 10 with 'Tom Hark', the sprightly adaptation of a 1958 record of the same name based on the African "kwela" beat, rendered ska-like and given new scenery. Its cover featured cartoon minstrels cavorting at the seaside with a mushroom cloud going off in the background. The lyric opened with the protagonist's hope that he would squeeze his holiday in before the bombs started.

War of a different kind was in the air whenever mods and skinheads came into contact. My first two concerts by charting acts had both been Kate Bush. My third, that spring, was the Selecter at the Lewisham Odeon. Tense and a little rough round the edges it might have been, full of mods and skinheads it might have been, but war-like it actually wasn't.

Cavernous, frayed and dingy; this was a typical public space. The stalls were divided by walkways including a main one parallel to the stage, half-way back. The LSM and I were just behind this and could see everyone coming and going; braces, parkas and Harrington jackets; spikes, crops and side-partings all milling around. It seemed to be mainly mods on one side, mainly skinheads on the other.

There were lots of button badges. The small, round design, less than an inch in diameter, had made badges desirable. All sorts of band names, logos and mottoes featured on these. Most of us had a little cluster on display somewhere, perhaps along the collar or beneath the lapel, as a snapshot of our tastes. Mods had targets and arrows. I had an Elvis Costello one and a Squeeze one. The LSM had 2-Tone ones. They were cool.

So too were my shoes, black loafers with tassels on, part of the 2-Tone uniform. I had narrow black trousers and, possibly, white socks; but prior to 2-Tone, white socks had been for virgins. I wanted a proper trilby hat but wasn't sure where to get one. Had I found one, I may never have worn it. In any case, I topped whatever I had with my denim sheepskin bomber jacket and I wasn't taking that off for anybody. I had it on that night.

From our vantage point we could scrutinise not only the behaviour, but also the dancing. 2-Tone bands, like other new wave acts, did a lot of bouncing. They bounced conventionally, leaving the floor, but their fans made their bodies bounce while keeping their feet relatively still. Hips, knees, elbows and fists did the bouncing; elbows bent to bring alternating fists up to the chin, sometimes in paradiddle patterns, occasionally accompanied by skips, twists and drumming toes, like cartoon characters preparing to scarper. It was mad grandad dancing, the solo version of Madness' nutty train and, when it was executed smoothly, it looked brilliant, even if it wasn't quite on the beat.

Its masters were all linked to Madness. Their biggest fan, Chas Smash, had constantly invaded the stage during their early gigs to dance in his own space. In the end they let him join, to showcase the style. He was good at it.

Some in the Lewisham Odeon looked like they were pumping water from a well. Others were doing it in such minute movements that they seemed about to implode. A guy close to us had his jacket off the shoulders and half way down the biceps, a straining muscularity beneath cropped black hair that would have looked better if there had been any rhythm to it. Perhaps bouncing was, after all, the best way to express yourself to this stuff. I was way too self-conscious to attempt the nutty dance but the LSM had an honest go. I just gripped the seat in front and lurched to the beat. I was a drummer; whatever I did, it had to be to the beat.

That springtime saw the peak of the mod revival and 2-Tone scene. The Selecter's new one, 'Missing Words', was a particularly good single. Madness had the *Work, Rest and Play EP* in the Top 10, featuring the robust 'Night Boat to Cairo' from the album, alongside the nutty freak-out 'Don't Quote Me on That' which was new. On the radio, an act called Cairo performed 'I Like Blue Beat', breathing in Cockney about liking the 60s import label for Jamaican releases that I remembered seeing at friends' houses; meanwhile, Graduate gave us 'Elvis Should Play Ska', an encouragement for Mr Costello to join the fray. He was, actually, already involved, having been the producer on *Specials*.

Both acts supporting the Selecter at Lewisham were on 2-Tone; the Swinging Cats kind of made up the numbers, but the Bodysnatchers were just outside the Top 20 with 'Let's Do Rocksteady', a piece of shameless bandwagon-jumping in strained patois; a nursery-school action song minus the good bits. Because it was on 2-Tone, I bought it unquestioningly.

Jamaican acts from the 60s had usually featured horns, sometimes a line of them, sometimes a lone trombone, so 2-Tone acts had them, too. The last of the charting ska acts to appear on the scene followed this trend, although they were not on 2-Tone but on Magnet, alongside Darts. This act was Bad Manners, fronted by a huge bald-headed bloke called Buster Bloodvessel who had a massive tongue. If you could imagine Darts returning over-enthusiastically from two weeks at a Jamaican theme park, they would have looked like Bad Manners. They, too, had a logo: a fat, cheerful chappie grabbing a microphone, in nothing but boots and a jock-strap held up by braces. Lovely.

Their single was the clownish 'Ne Ne Na Na Na Na Nu Nu', a series of instrumental vignettes linked by the yelled title and a singalong motif, perfect for football fans to go der-der-der nuts to on the terraces. Bad Manners had lots of horns. So did Dexy's Midnight Runners, who weren't ska, but more influenced by southern-state soul. They dressed in black donkey jackets and black bobble hats with the bobbles removed, like they were off to build a motorway. Their single was the stodgy 'Dance Stance'. Because they were in black and had horns, they slotted in with Bad Manners, UB40 and all this other stuff. Soon they would release 'Geno' and slot into number one.

People our age were all in this together. Even the soul boys could join in with 2-Tone; they just weren't Jam fans. Friends from my Sunday team liked it because of its punk elements, but they were mainly punk kids in army trousers, boots and Harrington jackets; into Stiff Little Fingers from Belfast and 999 from just down the road.

We swapped thoughts on all these records, as well as stories about aggro. These were threatening days. Violence loomed constantly, often just because we were teenage boys and other teenage boys were out looking for fights. A drifting gang might come up to you at a bus stop, one of them holding his jaw, accusing your friend of having punched him and now they were going to get you back. These situations were often de-fusable, but just as often they weren't. I once had to lock my arms around a lamp post so that I couldn't be dragged away. I wasn't prepared to run. A lady walking her dog screamed at them until they pissed off.

A new, excellent Ruts single was an aggro narrative called 'Staring at the Rude Boys', an expression of righteous defiance in a sea of yobbery. These were the days before football hooligans achieved the relative respectability of only looking for fights with other recognised football hooligans. Anybody was fair game. After a local derby that month, I saw a car waiting at traffic lights, containing fans in rival colours happily sharing a ride home, while a skinhead tried to punch his way through the window to get to the one he disapproved of.

Drifting thug skinheads. Drifting thug soul boys, jumping off football specials at Euston to rush home and listen to *Soul Spectrum* on Capital Radio, while getting ready to go out and shag some bird. Me, wondering if I was going to get home in one piece when upcountry supporting my team. Me, wondering if I was going to get home in one piece when round the corner getting a paper. Aggro-thirsty yobs and nuclear bombs. My memory associates all of this with Madness, Bad Manners and the Bodysnatchers.

The memory of others, of course, might be different. Having now sat through two *World Disco Dance Championships* as well as shaken a saucy leg to 'When You're in Love with a Beautiful Woman', Granny had decided that she quite liked disco. To cater for this burgeoning market, disco turned to the Nolan Sisters. These were a cabaret vocal act from Ireland, smiley and reassuring, with co-ordinated moves and co-ordinated trouser suits, made for Saturday night variety shows.

Their next career step was to synchronise their disco credentials with those of the BBC Concert Orchestra and, re-branded as the Nolans, they prepared to assault the pop charts with 'I'm in the Mood for Dancing'. If anyone between the ages of fifteen and thirty liked it, they kept quiet. To my ears, it was a malevolent test signal. It was for those who could declare themselves to be in the mood for dancing without actually then getting on with it; like a couple who told each other, once every week, "We must do something about that shelf". Perhaps a bit of upper-body twisting with angled elbows, then back to the biscuits.

But for others in the tribe who wanted to move more vigorously, there was soon Liquid Gold; twice as hectic, twice as energetic, just as horrible. They were taking their single 'Dance Yourself Dizzy' to number two just as 'I'm in the Mood For Dancing' was slipping down from its peak of three.

This was disco now. Safe, toothy, less a scene than an idea – one of lights, razzle and a dance you could get away with while chomping on a cocktail sausage. Good pop songs to its beat would be just pop. *Dom-tiss dat-tiss* would pare down to *dom chack, dom chack* and be accessory to heinous crimes. Disco's life blood had left it. Its soul was now elsewhere, and was simply soul.

Defining a musical era by its decade is an artificial, lazy and misleading construct. So it is pure coincidence that 'And the Beat Goes On' by the Whispers appeared in January 1980. When you think of "80s soul", you think of some of the coolest, most inspiring and often euphoric things you've ever heard. 'And the Beat Goes On' was therefore a fitting way to open the account. For years to come, these sounds would be reaching for us – wondrous textures to engage every sense. You could put the needle in the groove and make all the grey in your world vanish.

'And the Beat Goes On' was as clear a break from the recent past as 'Don't Stop Till You Get Enough' had been, but warmer, richer, more roundedly well-crafted, with a more subtle kind of power. It reached number two, in the same Top 10 as 'Too Much Too Young' and 'My Girl'. Its chorus contains the phrase "Just like my love – everlasting" but it is not always delivered cleanly. The casual rendition of somebody at school made it sound like "Just like my love, and my pasty". The contrast between this streamlined piece of classy soul and a flaky dollop of cholesterol was enough to induce long moments of giggling in our History class when we should have been concentrating on the Industrial Revolution. The fact that it only sounds like "and my pasty" in one, less well-delivered chorus made no difference whatsoever.

Other records worth mentioning from these months include 'Underpass' by John Foxx. This seemed to crystallise all of the keyboard-based sounds of the previous year into one huge, bleak slab of concrete, with an almighty lazer riff in the chorus against which the singer called "Underpass!" in mid-Atlantic tones which, obviously, left the door open for people to cry "Underpants!" instead.

I'm afraid I was one of them. This was an outstanding but challenging single and the association with Y-fronts gave us the excuse to back down from proper engagement with it. It stalled outside the Top 30 and deserved much, much better. Some dismissively said he was just a carbon copy of Gary Numan, but there was easily room for two of them.

New electronic sounds had recently taken a gentler, more easily digestible form when mixed with guitar, in 'Living By Numbers' by New Musik, one of a number of records using the word "digital" in its lyric as a mark of being up-to-date. It charmed whole swathes of my peers at the start of the year, particularly the Buggle-fanciers. It was, simply, a great tune; disarming, welcoming and rewarding; like us, when we weren't chucking expletives at enemies or clinging for dear life to lamp posts.

Then there was Genesis, who I remembered having an unbearably odd song called 'I Know What I Like' when I was at primary school and who kept getting in the way when I was flicking through *Melody Maker*. Two years earlier they had taken 'Follow You, Follow Me' - a proper song – into the Top 10. Their new one, 'Turn It on Again', had funny time-signature things going on but a fantastic chug at its core, one which fired up at the intro and reminded me a bit of Queen's 'Now I'm Here', making me want to listen to that again.

So it was good news all round. I loved it. It was clever and gritty, like a messy-haired mathematician in jeans and a sweatshirt; very different from the showbiz glitz and nutty grandads that surrounded it. It conjured up a look that was no look at all. I thought of men washing their cars on Sundays. 'Turn It on Again' is also a highly efficient time machine; I can vividly revisit the ups and downs of being sixteen when I hear it – impending violence and nuclear Armageddon.

And if all that wasn't challenging enough, I was about to take my 'O' Levels. Chances were, I would do okay if I pulled my finger out and revised properly. Nobody in my family had ever been to university, but I was expected to start 'A' Levels afterwards.

As they began looming, the Beat released their best thing yet, 'Mirror in the Bathroom', with a searing pace and a riff that came from deep in the earth. I was sure it would be a number one but it peaked at four. As the revision gathered pace and the pressure grew, the Specials went to number five with 'Rat Race', a song about what a waste of time it is passing exams. Not helpful. But the two best records from exam season were both soul ones.

Modern soul, to me, was clean, smart and sophisticated. It gave poise and maturity to those that belonged to it. I knew I wasn't one of them. So it could be a little intimidating. I had loved 'And the Beat Goes On' for its poise and maturity nevertheless. But I had no idea that soul was going to be as exciting as 'You Gave Me Love' by Crown Heights Affair and 'Behind the Groove' by Teena Marie.

These sounds were simply colossal. The former had jagged bass, grinding rock guitar, fattened and distorted keyboard, chiming bells and all manner of whooping and leaping about in the chorus. Full blast and full tilt. You could happily forgive its weak lyric. The latter was built on an outrageous rhythm which everything else – including the belting lead vocal – supported and augmented in a blur of joy. Its lyric worked: there was something for you too, behind this groove, just get up and grab it. *Yes, Teena – I'm coming.* Listening to these two records burned calories by the hundred. God only knows what I looked like moving to them in my room.

It wasn't all like this, of course. Michael's people were busy worshipping at the altar of his *Off the Wall* album which had some decent tunes but was, by comparison to how soul was capable of sounding, a neatly-presented helping of blancmange. On the one hand, this served to make 'Don't Stop 'Till You Get Enough' sound even more vital but, on the other, it didn't matter a fig because it was a whole album by Michael – its success was always likely to be out of proportion to its quality, which is perhaps being a bit unfair to its quality, but not by much.

When you stretched out the gate-fold sleeve, there he was, against a wall – which could easily be your wall - in a crisp going-out suit and medium, wet-look curls that were soon appearing on heads the length and breadth. There was yet life in the perm. You too could be a bit like Michael.

As far as I could make out, soul boys had been into 'Don't Stop 'Till You Get Enough' but kind of drew the line there. We could all join in with loving Michael, as long as the loving was unconditional. Soul boys were not used to unconditional loving. I had been taken to an estate youth club, where the atmosphere was tense and the soul-spinning DJ was a sullen lad from our school who scowled the second he saw me approach. My experience did not yet encompass smoothing such paths, so my impression remained: small brains and big fists.

One soul lad from school who was also in my Sunday team alternated with strict regularity between buddying up beside me and ruthlessly winding me up. One way of achieving the latter was to mention his supposed membership of the British Movement, a far-right organisation who seemed to be rivalling the National Front, referenced by the Ruts in 'Staring at the Rude Boys'. Casually racist soul fans were commonplace. It was the kind of thing that threatened to make your brain explode and this guy acted as if he understood that perfectly.

In one of his better moods, he invited me back to his house to listen to records and dropped all his bravado. Kids our age were starting to choose the twelve-inch single format favoured by club DJs because its grooves were deeper and therefore, in theory at least, the sound was better; plus, it made the tracks significantly longer. We'll come back to twelve-inch singles.

Anyway, this lad produced one, tentatively, slightly bashfully, saying that he absolutely loved it; thought it was the best thing in the world, even though it was a couple of years old. It was 'Shame' by Evelyn "Champagne" King which, to my ears, was over-smooth and twiddly and lacked percussion. But I was touched by his openness and, for an hour or so, I warmed to him. He had said he had some old stuff to get rid of and I paid him a pittance for 'Barbados' by Typically Tropical. He was back to being a towering tosspot the next day, but without reference to me wanting 'Barbados'.

My money was now coming in monthly chunks; an allowance given in return for diligently undertaking specific household tasks and conforming to behavioural boundaries. Tcha. It meant that I had a week to enjoy the novelty of the pile of singles I had bought, then another three to build the list of the ones I would get next. I reckon I was getting between twelve and eighteen a month, plus others I would pick up from bargain bins, market stalls and the bedrooms of tosspots.

Suddenly I was getting all my new releases from one place. My stepfather had mentioned to a work colleague that I bought "loads of records", and this guy happened to be friends with the owner of the record store at the Camberwell end of Coldharbour Lane – which I still think was called Page 39 – the one where, as a four-year-old, I had got 'The Ballad of Bonnie and Clyde'. He introduced us with the suggestion that if I bought everything there I would get a discount, taking the price per item from 90p to 80p.

The owner surveyed me with suspicion, perhaps feeling under pressure; I don't ever remember him smiling, but perhaps I didn't smile much, either. It was all a bit uncomfortable, even though the other guys hanging around were friendly. This was another store where French and American copies were sold in place of UK ones; I got 'Behind the Groove' on the maroon Gordy label instead of UK Motown's blue spokes; the 1980 hits by the Detroit Spinners came on the black-and-red Atlantic label instead of the expected green, white and orange.

The arrangement worked for almost a year, until one day the price went up again because, he said, gruffly, I wasn't buying enough; so I went back to A1 Stores and the West End. It was a relief. I suspect it had all been a misunderstanding over the phrase "loads of records". I wasn't a bloody DJ; I was just a punter.

Anyway, it was through this little network of contacts that I heard of the need to find someone to dress up as Buzby for the local junior school's summer fair. Buzby was the annoying mascot for British Telecom's ubiquitous advertising campaigns and, perhaps in return for some promotional goodies, the school had got hold of a full-sized costume, including rubber feet, yellow-feathered body and fibre-glass beak, for someone to squeeze into. Oh, and red tights.

Full of exuberance at having finished my exams, and having checked that the costume covered absolutely everything from head to toe, I put myself forward.

For TV viewers, Buzby did little apart from flutter around encouraging everybody to phone someone up and make them happy. Few would ever have thought they might one day see him on a crash mat, dancing to a steel band at a school fair with a maraca at the tip of each wing. But this was the fate of the fete.

Once I began to truly believe that nobody had a clue who I was, it became something approaching fun and I embellished my movements with high kicks, jumps to the side and components borrowed from the Charleston. Kids cautiously came forward, then beamed and ran away when I waved. Some stood firm in pairs, a little braver, saying "Hello, Buzby"; disappointed when all they got in return was a cheerful maraca gesture.

Then, I noticed a group of boys, maybe eight or nine years old; playground hoods, staring at me side on, narrow-eyed and pouting. If I had been eight or nine I would have resigned myself to imminent attack. But I was twice their size and surrounded by witnesses; surely I was safe. All the same, it was discomforting.

They were muttering to each other, then turning back to stare; clearly planning something. Suddenly, one of them was marching forward. He grabbed my beak and peered inside. His shoulders slumped. He turned and began walking back. "Nah", he moaned. "There's a man in there".

Before getting into the costume, there had been time to stroll around. At one stall, a cluster of adults were rifling through two large boxes of singles. I can't remember how much they were asking for them. There were a few current and recent hits in there but nothing I wanted.

When they were tidying up at the end they put the remainder into one huge box and a woman carried it inside to where, now back in my normal clothes, I was sipping tea and getting my breath back. She asked if I wanted to make her an offer. It was an echo of my own school's fete six years earlier, but these were all new and recent releases, donated by a parent who was a reviewer and got sent mountains of stuff. I ended up with the whole lot for three quid, carrying this massive box home through the park with aching arms.

What a result. It brought me into contact with records I never would have known otherwise. A few I might have heard on the radio if I was lucky. A small number have become lifelong favourites. Some are simply extraordinary. One band was called Pointed Sticks. I was amazed by that. I can't remember their song. There was a heavy metal band called Samson, who I thought were just comical. A girl I knew from school would tell me the next term that she loved them. I couldn't imagine it.

There were a few releases on Stiff. One of these was by Any Trouble, a group led by Clive Gregson, who looked like he might be Elvis Costello's older brother. They had had a minor hit a few months earlier with the busy 'Yesterday's Love'. Their new one, which I found in the box, was a good song with an expansive chorus called 'Second Choice'. Its recent *Melody Maker* review had been particularly keen on the live cover of Abba's 'Name of the Game' on the B-side.

Also on Stiff were Dirty Looks, who were a little bit ted, a little bit blues, and enormously never-heard-of. I kept two of theirs; strong sounds called 'Lie to Me' and 'Let Go'. On the Cocteau label, was 'Do You Dream in Colour?' by Bill Nelson, with its steam-pump beat that seemed to use a funny time signature but actually didn't. I liked this a lot. I would find out that he had been lead singer with Be-Bop Deluxe, another *Melody Maker* name who, to this day, I have never heard a note by.

Then, on Dindisc, the new home for the increasingly successful Orchestral Manoeuvres in the Dark, were Bardi Blaise, with 'Trans Siberian Express'; a song about a girl who goes on holiday to the Soviet Union, loses her train ticket and is persuaded to offer alternative forms of payment by a lusty train guard who speaks innuendo in a costume-shop Russian accent. The backing vocal in the chorus goes "She lost her ticket, then her dress – wooh, wooh!" Dizzy blondes, cossacks and some interesting ideas about the relative geographical positions of Siberia, Moscow and the Ukraine. You've got to hear it to believe it.

You can say the same, with several knobs on, about 'Hazards in the Home' by the Portraits, on Ariola. This cheerful ditty warns about the dangers of electrical appliances, broken crockery and just about everything else in the death-trap behind your front door. It almost, though never quite, sounds like a cautionary feature on a kids' magazine programme. It's either totally sincere or totally ironic, but there's no way to tell.

To stop my head spinning, I turned to 'Why'd Ya Have to Lie?' by the Sweat, on Double D records; thrashy guitar pop about betrayal and heartbreak – engaging and really rather good. I also turned to 'Back on the Road' by Joe Egan on Ariola, an oasis of calm which lowered the pulse and reassured. Then there were two on the nasty light green of the Gem label; jumpy, urgent records both – 'Causing Complications' by sort-of mod group the V.I.P.'s, who I would seek out more by, and 'Modern Love' by the Indicators, a piece of junk elevated by its sheer nerve into something genuinely enjoyable. I kept all of these and a few more, but not Pointed Sticks or Samson.

If history had somewhat repeated itself with school fairs, it repeated itself in similar style at our favourite beach, because the *Radio 1 Roadshow* returned, almost exactly three years after I had seen Noel. This time, I was ready. The DJ was weekday lunchtime host and demon chart-revealer Paul Burnett. I got very close to the front, wearing a Radio 1 t-shirt and holding a placard which read: "Paul Burnett is fab – I wanna go on Bits & Pieces".

When the time arrived to choose potential contestants, I was simply too animated to ignore and I found myself on the stage with a handful of others, being introduced, then being put through the humiliation of a qualification challenge which involved crossing the stage with a 10p clutched between the knees, with the aim of dropping it into a distant Radio 1 mug, as the DJ barked a commentary from within his Radio 1 flight jacket and the crowd yelled Radio 1 encouragement. The tension was heavy but I managed it. If anyone else dropped theirs early I think they were probably let off.

We then had to sit on chairs and don headphones, ready for the contest, with a sheet on a clipboard to write the answers on. They fired up the Bits & Pieces theme which, uncontroversially, was an excerpt from the 1963 hit 'Bits and Pieces' by the Dave Clark Five, before we were played our ten clips. I guessed one, didn't know the last one, so reckoned I had eight, which was probably good enough to win.

Paul Burnett went into the booth to mark them himself and as he saw me watching, he smiled and winked. My guess had been good and I won with nine out of ten, with the clip I hadn't known being the final chord of ELO's 'I'm Alive', which I had at home. Tcha.

I received my applause, stood to take a bow and soak up the adulation, such as it was, then left clutching a bag of Radio 1 stuff from the Goodie Mobile. Job done. I had won on the *Radio 1 Roadshow*, broadcast nationally. Nobody I knew at home heard it. Nobody. Not one person.

A package of additional stuff was sent on because my score was the highest that week. More Radio 1 goodies, plus the current number one album, *Flesh and Blood* by Roxy Music, whose two singles that summer, 'Over You' and 'Oh Yeah (On the Radio)' were both gorgeous. If they got any smoother they would slip straight off the sofa. The following week, an Irish bloke got a full ten. I tried not to be pissed off.

Other notable events from the summer included this: Abba had their first number one in two-and-a-half years with 'The Winner Takes It All'. This was cause for celebration, even though listening to it was like wading through treacle. It was like a soliloquy song from a stage musical, a vehicle for the leading lady to make us all sniffle over her break-up. Sparkling pop it wasn't. Still, we owed them so much, it was good to see them back on top; and the B-side, 'Elaine', was okay. I remained, intrinsically, a loyal servant.

Also back and soliciting similar responses, was Diana Ross. She had been disco before, but now she went mega-disco, with the guys from Chic producing her album *Diana*. The first single from it was the tiresome 'Upside Down', which went all the way to number two. I found it harder to be pleased for her than for Abba, even though 'Upside Down' was more listenable than 'The Winner Takes It All'. It's a contradiction I have yet to resolve. Subsequent singles from *Diana* would be better.

She got away with disco in mid-1980 because she was Diana Ross. Elsewhere, the evolution of soul gathered pace. One of the summer's best sounds was 'Funkin' for Jamaica' by Tom Browne. Hearing it still makes me want to reach for the shades and apply the sun lotion whilst smoothly swaying my hips. I hope you never have to bear witness to this, but such is the power of some records.

It had a great female vocal, but also a half-arsed "rap" bit in it; like some guy was having a go at "rapping", quickly realising that he was useless at it, then saying anything, anything at all, to use up the remaining syllables so that he could stop. It was probably what would happen to most of us if we had a go at "rapping". The fact that it had been left on the record contributed to its charm.

We knew about "rapping" because of a record that had been at number three the previous December: 'Rapper's Delight' by the Sugarhill Gang. They had taken a Chic bassline and put "rapping" over the top. We had learned that rapping was rhythmic, rhyming talk; fast and jam-packed. There was no singing at all. It was three blokes taking turns to tell us how great they were at rapping, at dancing, at owning all the best stuff and at impressing the foxy ladies. I knew guys like this at school; geeky, softly-spoken chatterboxes bragging away with smiles fixed to their faces and girls nowhere to be seen. Those on the record were gamely labouring in much the same way. I felt quite sorry for them.

Anyway, the novelty caught fire and everybody had to decide how well-equipped they were to be a rapper, in the same way that, a few years before, they had had to decide how much of a CB-talker they were when they heard 'Convoy'. Capital Radio ran a competition offering huge prizes for being able to perform the whole thing right through, including getting all of the "boppity-bop-bop" bits absolutely spot on.

Eight months later, there hadn't been a follow-up; but the half-arsed rapping bit on 'Funkin' for Jamaica' seemed to represent our experience of it quite well. The smooth, jazzy feel that governed it was shared by 'Give Me the Night' by George Benson, whose grinning spotlessness would make him a poster-boy for this kind of sound.

In the coming months, it would be all but obligatory to name-check George Benson.

But new soul was a broad church. There was also 'Oops Upside Your Head' by the Gap Band, which was closer to a circus than a cocktail lounge. It had a sturdy, down-tempo beat that was rock steady – more so than rocksteady – within which was room to wiggle and shake your thang all you wanted; across the top wafted a sweet breeze of acoustic guitar, then the backing vocal, which switched between a mantra chant of the title and a refrain about not wanting to get up and dance, topped with the lead – a reverb-soaked MC conducting and cajoling the whole thing like a cackling gargoyle. It had jazzy breaks, it had rude nursery rhymes. It was mad and fantastic. It got to number six and hung around the chart for ages.

The 'O' Level results came through. They were a mixed bag, but there were more ups than downs. I signed up for the sixth form, which put me back at the same school, minus uniform but plus a spacious common room with its own student-administered kitchen.

One of the most enthusiastically talked-about records when we started back was 'Babooshka' by Kate Bush, which had been climbing the charts at the start of the holiday and had been on the radio throughout. It had only just dropped out of the Top 40.

This was a good tune with a big chorus, smart and intriguing, telling the story of an ageing woman testing her husband's loyalty by posing as a mysterious admirer. The title referred to a Russian name for a matriarch. The *Melody Maker* review, which I cut out and kept, said it was "more accessible than the one about babies in a womb with a view" and that, once the chorus arrives, "tills begin to clink and the heavens begin to open". They seemed to like it. As did armies of others. The publicity shots that went with it were incredible; Kate as some kind of mystical warrior woman: something for boys and girls alike. So why did it stall at number five?

I asked a new friend in the sixth form what he thought, someone who seemed to have informed views on music. He kind of screwed his face up. "It's alright, it's good, but, I dunno, it's a bit *tame*". When I listened to it again, I could hear "tame" right through it. Despite its eastern flourishes and distracting effects, its overall sound was conservative. It could have done with racing the pulse a little more, perhaps by being a few beats-per-minute faster.

I kept coming back to the subject. I fantasised once about it having Wild West saloon piano jangling away on the chorus. No thematic relevance there of course, but that's the kind of thing it needed; a bit of hurtling, an additional layer of sparkles to take it to the next grade up. It felt like the chance of a second number one had been blown.

But no matter. She was soon number one in the album chart. When *Never For Ever* came out I took my £3.99 to Woolworth's in Camberwell and bought it on the first day of release. The day after this, she was scheduled to be signing copies in the Virgin Megastore, at the Tottenham Court Road end of Oxford Street, which had opened the year before as serious competition to HMV and a retail showcase for Richard Branson's expanding Virgin empire. I bunked off school early, raced home to get my copy and headed for the West End.

The queue snaked through a labyrinth of barriers inside the store and then out onto the pavement, stretching west, half-way to Oxford Circus. There were rockers in denim jackets, studious Kate lookalikes and small clusters of friends-and-family. I waited quietly, while voices all around me eagerly discussed who they were going to get her to sign it in dedication to, and a pair of skinheads marched along the line growling "Kate Bush is a slag".

I don't know how long I queued. Two hours. Maybe more. It didn't matter. Inside the store. Around the barriers. Then to a line of tables in front of a screen with a cluster of people, in the middle of which she sat, smiling, talking, scribbling. The exchanges were uniform, like the drip of a tap. *Can you sign it to..?* No, she had to say – she was sorry, she could only sign "love from". Over and over, nearer and nearer. People before me surely heard all this as clearly as I did, but it didn't stop them asking the same bloody thing.

The idea was that you took a copy from a pile, she signed it, and you paid for it on the way out. I, however, had my copy in a Woolworth's bag. When it was my turn, she smiled and asked if I had been waiting long. I can't remember what I said, but it was something plain. I was determined not to be a smart-arse and, above all, not to ask for any favours. At the bottom of the opened gate-fold, she wrote "Lots of love, Kate Bush", and put three kisses.

As she handed it back, I said "Thanks", adding "and good luck with it". And, as she thanked me back, I got another smile, a different one; one, I like to think, of gratitude at hearing a good wish instead of a demand; one, I like to think, of warmth. It followed me as I walked away, right up until the point at which I had to turn around to avoid bumping into something.

Up until now the results of my talking to nice girls had been mixed. So I was glad that my one chance to talk to Kate Bush had gone well. And I bet there were a hundred other young men from that queue with a very similar memory. But I don't suppose many of them had the additional one of being roughly grabbed by security on suspicion of trying to steal a hot new album and having to produce a Woolworth's receipt to prove their innocence. Tcha.

Never For Ever was either the first album by a British female solo artist to get to number one, or the first album by a female solo artist from anywhere to go straight in at number one in the UK. I can't remember which. The event was brilliant, but the album didn't get under my skin the way the previous two had. In fact, I don't think I listened to much of it after a couple of plays.

It was, as my informed friend had put it, a bit *tame*, in contrast to the promise of the cover, where a darkly atmospheric illustration showed her stretching on tiptoe, a river of myth flowing from beneath her dress. 'Army Dreamers' was a skilful lament about teenage boys joining the army and getting killed. It became the next single. I had been looking forward to a track called 'Violin' which had featured in the Palladium concert, but the recorded version was disappointing.

The one really good thing was a tense, wonderfully arranged song called 'The Infant Kiss', which was about falling under the spell of a young boy, and which was decidedly sexual. I am writing at a time when the merest suggestion of any sexual response to a child is unthinkable, but back then, I just thought of it as Kate being bold and interesting.

This is uncomfortable ground. Days later, the new number one single, going straight in, was 'Don't Stand So Close to Me' by the Police, a song about a teacher having an affair with a teenage pupil, given texture by the fact that Sting had previously been a teacher. It was considered no more than risqué and, as he pranced about on the video in a Beat t-shirt, nobody suggested lynching him. The Police were unassailable - the most recent single by the Jam, the defiantly derivative 'Start', had taken a slovenly three weeks to get to number one and had been knocked off a week later.

Speaking of unassailable, in our sixth form common room, you didn't question George Benson. You just didn't. 'Give Me the Night' stood as sacred text in a world without acne, farts or chewed fingernails. Similarly revered was Stevie Wonder, about to unleash his *Hotter Than July* album and sporting columns of beads on his tightly-woven locks; strongly ethnic. So was the resonance in the funky lyrics of his funky single 'Master Blaster (Jammin')', which I tried hard to like but never quite managed to. I kept this safely to myself.

I turned instead to Randy Crawford, lead singer on the Crusaders' 'Street Life', who now had a grandly delicious solo single at number two called 'One Day I'll Fly Away'. Loving this enabled me to fit in alongside girls in pastel cardigans who sat up straight and told you in calm voices that they liked George Benson and they liked soul. There was room for no other opinion and you were calmly placed under an undesirable heading if you deviated.

But there were other types of soul fan. I knew energetic people with spectacular smiles who had medium-tight perms and wore vests with light jackets over the top. They went to all-nighter soul parties featuring DJs from Capital Radio and Radio London and were always happy.

Disco suddenly seemed a long time ago, even though 'D.I.S.C.O' by Ottowan, a cathedral of candy floss and kiss-me-quick made from a single, gigantic knee-blanket, was doing excellent business including three weeks at number two.

Queen, who had remained a harmless part of the chart furniture for the last four years, chose this moment for a better-late-than-never conversion to disco and released a single called 'Another One Bites the Dust', which Queen fans liked a lot. It was a bit embarrassing. As if to ram home the point, the Nolans repaid their debts to society with 'Gotta Pull Myself Together', a piece of pure, quality pop that didn't need disco bunting. They would produce the equally good 'Attention to Me' the following spring. Even they had moved on.

If Granny was disappointed by this, she soon cheered up when Blondie went to the top of the charts with 'The Tide Is High', a reggae-lite party record of Olympian dullness which cemented the group's universal acceptability. You could, and did, hear it anywhere. You could, and did, watch it extracting compliance from just about everybody, with 'D.I.S.C.O' waiting on the next turntable. It sent a shiver down the spine. It broke the heart. The brilliance of their 'Dreaming' and 'Union City Blue' singles had been only a year ago.

And the Specials didn't help with their new one. The lyric of 'Stereotype', was a good, damning observation of reckless young pissheads, but it was presented in a hissing bossanova that took the wind out of your sails and, overall, the feeling was one of being whined at. The B-side, 'International Jet Set', was curious and odd; woozy piped sounds that fit the image of an airport lounge and could have been incidental music from a 60s spoof. It all felt like one huge mistake.

'Baggy Trousers' by Madness, however, certainly did not. This was their next step up, an intense, aggressive declaration of nutty creed: *School was rubbish, I didn't take it seriously and I was fine, my memories are all of mucking about and breaking stuff – don't waste your chance to copy me. It's not being irresponsible; this is life.*
The video we saw on *Top of the Pops* was a celebration, every bit as much as the record called 'Celebration' that appeared at the other end of the autumn; the one by becalmed funksters Kool and the Gang which, ever since, has been rolled out on the flimsiest excuse, whether or not the celebration to which it is assigned is particularly celebratory. Neither the concept nor the record deserves to be so cheapened. 'Baggy Trousers' has survived better. Madness were staking a claim to longevity. Their second album, *Absolutely*, was as good as their first.

Now that I was sixteen, I was going to more gigs. We saw Orchestral

Manoeuvres in the Dark (can't remember where) who now had a big, fat Top 10 hit to their credit in 'Enola Gay', about the aircraft that dropped the bomb on Hiroshima. Some of us noticed that they had pinched the intro from 'Charade', a year-old single by the Skids, but it didn't seem to matter. They played 'Enola Gay' four times in the encores. The audience were increasingly energised with every repeat. If they'd played it a fifth time there may have been casualties.

We also saw the Jam, at the Hammersmith Odeon; just the three of them on a desolate stage, thrashing away before a packed house. We were up in the circle. There might have been a backdrop, perhaps a logo on a sheet or something; I can't remember. I do remember Paul Weller declaring the venue to be a "fucking shit-hole". I don't remember thinking *I must see them again* as we left.

I felt similarly about Madness, who we saw on December 23rd at the same venue. Lead singer Suggs opened the show by asking if we'd all done our Christmas shopping yet, for which he received an instant and synchronised "fuck off!" from right round the auditorium.

The crowd was predictably skinhead-heavy, but there were also large numbers of pop-heads and *Smash Hits*-heads. Somebody dared me to wear my Abba t-shirt, which I uncovered in time for a patrolling skinhead to notice. He stepped towards me, looked me in the eye, a gaze I calmly returned; then he sniggered and trotted off. Abba had been back at number one recently with the quietly likeable 'Super Trouper'. Perhaps he had quietly liked it, too.

Madness were rubbish. There was wonderful variation in their recorded tracks, but tonight they played everything in the same key and at the same speed; or at least that's what it sounded like to me. I didn't like their new single, either. 'Embarrassment' started, then finished, doing nothing whatsoever in between. It was almost as big a hit as 'Baggy Trousers'.

But the record that I loved above all others that autumn was a shock of delirium that came from nowhere. Built on rumbling, leathery war-drums, it raised ghosts of exterminated Red Indians beneath golden skies and crimson clouds with a power that reconquered the plains, turning every paleface into dust; spearing them with slogans, crushing them under guitar riffs, throttling them with righteous harmony; and to join these warriors, all we had to do was be innocent and proud.

I had seen the ridiculous name "Adam and the Ants" in various places. You might have seen it on xeroxed bills stuck haphazardly on brickwork around central London, or painted onto the backs of leather jackets worn by die-hard punks, or squashed into some dark corner of the music paper gig listings. There might have been a whip or high-heeled boot image alongside, some fetish thing that punks seemed to like. Occasionally there had been a review in *Melody Maker* but I barely bothered with the first sentence; it all seemed irrelevant.

This all changed in the space of a few minutes when I heard 'Dog Eat Dog'. It was like something I had always dreamed of but never thought I would be allowed to have. I trembled as I approached the record shop. In the following weeks, the thing that mattered most in the world was when I was going to get to listen to it again. Four, five times on the trot; it was never quite enough. Its chart peak of number four was definitely not enough.

One of my biggest regrets is having turned down a ticket to see them in those weeks. I think it was a cash issue; I had committed to seeing other gigs and doing other things and their Lyceum appearance was one date too many and I was being sensible. I heard stories about it afterwards, about the mad dancing near the front; twisting, twirling blokes whose flailing arms thumped each other with the force of a tomahawk blow.

We had seen the band on telly. There were two drum kits. That bit, I got. The rest needed getting used to. They wore a strange kind of fancy dress, with strips of fabric secured to waists and arms that dangled and flew, hair twisted into weaves and tied with short, thin ribbon, zigzags of make-up, black lipstick. The singer – Adam, presumably – had a Charge of the Light Brigade tunic, one of those covered in horizontal gold braids, which he wore open so that it shifted as he danced. A broad white stripe was painted across his face, traversing the bridge of his nose. He was a pop star; he could do what he wanted. And he was the one who had made 'Dog Eat Dog', so it was fine. This, clearly, was what an innocent and proud warrior should look like.

It was Malcolm McLaren who had taken this punk scruff and set him on the road to becoming *Top of the Pops* pretty-boy material, overseeing the assemblage of a new line-up and wardrobe overhaul, before buggering off with half of said line-up to form a dodgy new band called Bow Wow Wow. We'll come back to them.

Years later I would hear a story about how they got the mix through. Some executive at their new label CBS had heard 'Dog Eat Dog', turned his nose up at the sound, and asked them to go and re-mix it. They returned days later without having changed a thing and, having re-listened, he triumphantly declared: "That's much better. Told you, didn't I? Knew it needed something".

Actually, I've no idea what he said. I've no idea if he said anything. I've no idea if the story is true. The dialogue was invented in an excited huddle. But I don't care.

I bought the album *Kings of the Wild Frontier*, which extended the Red Indian thing but had pirate things and purely "ant" things, too. No, give it time. Some of it, like pirate thing 'Jolly Roger' was simply silly. Some of it, like 'Antmusic', a song about appreciating this new "ant music", was over-tidy and a bit dull. But there was also the tense, dark 'Ants Invasion', the fantastic riff-thrash of the narcissistic 'The Magnificent Five', plus, most importantly, the mighty title track, claiming identification in the modern world with redskins made to suffer for centuries.

It used the Burundian drum pattern from Africa as its foundation; condensed but not neatened, a fantastic sound that would be practised on countless thousands of school tables. It did what 'Dog Eat Dog' did, but at a different pace; grander, more enormous. Blary guitar riffs and masses of drums - I loved this album, warts and all.

If the kind of look they displayed on *Top of the Pops* needed some adjusting-to, we would soon get more practice. Our sixth form was in a consortium with two others, pooling students via minibus runs to make courses viable. This brought more new faces into our school, frightfully confident kids who called frightfully confident things across the common room in frightfully confident voices. Their heads seemed to be slightly tilted; their faces seemed to be *higher*.

They wore crisp vests, black cotton trousers and slender coats that came down way beneath the hip. They were doing 'A' Level History of Art. One of the bands they spoke about had the gratuitously stylish name Spandau Ballet. It made me think of people in their twenties and thirties, moving around grand old buildings in formal wear. My joke about calling them Potsdam Opera was ignored. I assumed that, like many other bands spoken about by the frightfully confident, they wouldn't be troubling the chart. But their single 'To Cut a Long Story Short' almost immediately started climbing it.

The main feature of its sound was the singer's shocking voice, a macho posture of sustained muscle-flex that showed us all where we had been going wrong. I got used to it because this was a good record; dry, lazered catchy bits and a driving beat.

They had a similar look to Adam and the Ants, but with more time spent in the hair salon. In addition to the dangly fabric, they wore blousey white shirts and picnic blankets, occasionally looking like half-opened parcels abandoned by children. Pirates appeared to have been jumbled up with ancient Greeks in a dressing-up box carried to castle dungeons for the video. It was all a million miles from mod.

It was coming from a gratuitously stylish scene which had just begun to emerge, with an approach to going out and looking good which was very different to that of Secret Affair. We heard it being called "New Romantic" I can't remember when I first heard the term. It may not have been quite that early. But I merely acknowledged it. Pop stars could look as ridiculous as they wanted as long as they made good records and, so far, this lot seemed to be two-nil up.

In this, I wasn't counting 'Ashes to Ashes' by David Bowie, which had been number one at the end of the summer. It had seemed important and I tried hard to like it. It took itself pretty seriously. There were lyrical references to the Major Tom character in 'Space Oddity'. In its video, he dressed as a Venetian clown, promenading down a radioactive beach pursued by a bulldozer. It was Art; how could I possibly understand? The look, attitude and atmosphere were representative of this New Romanticism thing. So I later discovered. I didn't link Spandau Ballet to it.

'To Cut a Long Story Short' added a new layer of texture to my record collection and there was then another, unexpected influx. My baby sister, now two, was going to a childminder whose husband had once run a mobile disco, playing at parties and weddings for years until he got a massive tax demand and had to sell his rig.

But the records remained, dust-gathering remnants of a former life, in piles behind the sofa and beside the bookcase. His sons had been using them as frisbees and it was time to get rid of them, perhaps in exchange for a bit of beer money. Once the childminder mentioned this to Mum, a meeting was swiftly arranged. It was not long after my seventeenth birthday and I took as much beer money as I could gather.

We sat on the floor in his lounge, between columns of singles, mostly without sleeves. As we sorted through them, memories returned. He enjoyed these with a low voice and a smile: *They used to love this one... Blimey, that always got 'em going... I used to put this on and then watch how many blokes moaned and went back to the bar...*

One was a reggae instrumental with its own cackling gargoyle, a terrific record by Dave & Ansil Collins called 'Double Barrel', which had been number one in 1971. He told me he used to play this as he was setting up, its frequency range being ideal for checking that the rig was working properly, "...because it used to set *all* the lights off". I loved that. I remember thinking that if anyone from now on asked me what kind of music I liked, I would tell them it was music that set all the lights off.

They were in good condition. Most were from the early 70s. They included two huge number ones from 1970, Freda Payne's soul-pop standard 'Band of Gold', plus 'Love Grows (Where My Rosemary Goes)' by Edison Lighthouse, beloved of the drum hippy and easily one of the best pop records ever made. From the same year's snowy Christmas there was 'Ride a White Swan' by T.Rex and 'When I'm Dead and Gone' by McGuinness-Flint, plus its number one, 'I Hear You Knocking' by Dave Edmunds' Rockpile.

There were two by the Jackson 5; 'I Want You Back' and 'I'll Be There'. There was another T.Rex one, the growling, woozy, stomping

'Metal Guru', which I subsequently played like crazy, likewise David Bowie's wonderful 'Starman'. There was another classic reggae instrumental, 'Liquidator' by Harry J. All Stars. There was 'Brown Sugar', one of the Rolling Stones' best. I also picked up 'My Generation' by the Who, on a strange Decca imprint, which I subsequently realised was its original US release. All the others were UK originals. My excitement could have boiled every kettle in Camberwell.

Having UK originals of singles which were (a) revered, and (b) really good, was too much of a dream. I had no idea that there were networks of collectors and traders; nobody had told me about dedicated second-hand record stores. I just assumed that desirable old originals were either fiercely guarded or in the bin, as scratched and mangled as any other former amusement.

This pile was amazing. We joked about how much they might be worth. I tentatively offered him twenty pounds for the seventeen I wanted. He suggested we simply make it a pound apiece. I felt guilty, but he was happy for me to have them. Seventeen incredible singles for seventeen pounds for my seventeenth birthday. It felt like destiny. I used sleeves from the summer fete haul to house them. They looked decidedly odd, with Tamla-Motown discs in Stiff sleeves and T.Rex in Gem ones.

I used a plain black sleeve to house 'Imagine', John Lennon's distinguished love and peace reverie, which was familiar even though I didn't remember it from 1975 when it had apparently been a hit. I chose it because it seemed important, and black seemed to be suitable for a serious record on the Apple label. I was perhaps influenced by an unconscious memory of 'Hey Jude' having arrived in a black company bag. I don't know. I was glad to own it, even though I didn't play it as much as 'Metal Guru' or some of the others.

Then, barely two weeks after it had been one of the seventeen, we awoke to the news that Lennon had been shot dead in New York. He was outside his apartment building and he got shot by some nutter. Just like that. Out of nothing. One of the Beatles. Finished.

There was nothing to say. You just had to absorb it. I had just started buying the music paper *Record Mirror* and I've still got the copy that carried the obituary, with a small picture of him in a mass of black on the cover. He had a new single out, a squarely unremarkable love song called 'Just Like Starting Over' which parodied rock 'n' roll era styles and had just edged into the Top 10 before dropping into the twenties. A week later, it was number one.

People played their old Beatles records. I had bought a few of their early albums a couple of years before and hadn't liked much on them, so I didn't join in. All the same, I was numbed. I didn't know what to think.

'Imagine' was played on the radio a lot. I got a message from the childminder, saying that she wanted their copy of it back, as if it had been a rental. Not knowing how to respond, I didn't respond at all. There were discussions about who would front the Beatles now, if they ever re-formed. At our sixth form fancy dress Christmas party, the knowledgeable friend with the strong views on 'Babooshka' went as John Lennon, wearing a t-shirt peppered with blood-stained bullet holes.

Life, of course, went on. Adam and the Ants disappointingly released 'Antmusic' as their next single and it went to number two. 'Runaway Boys' by the Stray Cats heralded another rock 'n' roll revival – rockabilly, to be exact – but was startlingly good. The picture cover of 'Same Old Scene' by Roxy Music made me realise how single I was. 'Celebration' by Kool and the Gang was played at parties all over the place. Life went on. But it was, nevertheless, a definite kind of ending for a Beatle baby.

Nine

When people let you down, when they bite hands that reach out to them, when they abandon you, your records don't. When people don't understand, when they don't see what's right before their eyes, when they don't care about injustices, your records do. The right record can tip you over the edge into tears, when a good cry is what you need most. The right record can drain anger from you like the lancing of a boil. When you want to be nowhere, the right record can give you somewhere to disappear to. Because of your records, you can be alright. Relying on them is safe.

By the time John Lennon died, I was familiar with an entire spectrum of roles that they were capable of fulfilling. Having records was like having your own well-stocked mansion to wander through: you could go into the planning room, you could go into the soppy room, you could go into the healing room, the groovy room or the laughing room. It was all in place and it was all staying. I was at cruise speed. My faith was solid. Experience and maturity would deepen it, not diminish it. Decades would pass before priorities would affect any change.

Yet change was soon all around. The next two years would see rather a lot of it. Technology usually drives change, but this time the gadgets and gizmos would be right up front and bound up with far-reaching transformations in culture. I'm warning you, this chapter is going to be nuts.

A few months into the new year, the LSM's mum threw a party. Adults mingled in the back rooms among drinks, ashtrays and bowls of food, while youngsters mingled everywhere else. In the dimmed lounge, music blasted fuzzily from the stack system, so-called because the radio deck, cassette deck, amplifier and turntable came in separate units which stacked up in a space-saving tower.

A specially-made-up cassette was providing the sounds – all house parties had to have at least one specially-made-up cassette. Adults occasionally threaded their way into the front for a dance to something not too recent; the hostess had made sure that the specially-made-up cassette had something for everyone.

One of the not too recent things was 'You've Got to Hide Your Love Away' by the Beatles; but this is not a dancer and, in any case, I didn't hear it on the stack system. A woman was moving around the party with a Walkman, a cassette player only slightly bigger than a cassette, its headphones like two spongy draughts pieces joined by a silver strip. All its buttons fit along one side. Its compactness was incredible. How was it possible? Because it worked on just two of those small AA batteries. Just two of the small ones. Wow.

She looked very pleased with herself and had every reason to be - the Walkman, made by Sony, was the newest and hottest thing; a music player that you could listen to while walking around; one that would fit into your coat pocket. We had heard about them and read about them. Now, here was one.

One of the adults steered her my way, saying that he bet I wanted a listen, and with a murmur of approval, she slipped off the headphones and handed them to me. I had worn headphones before, substantial cups of plastic trimmed with coated foam that covered the ears completely and sealed off the outside world. I wasn't expecting much by comparison. But the sound of this thing was wonderful; soft, warm and crystal clear, your own little private world right in the middle of a crowd. I can only imagine the look on my face. They cost £105. Who the fuck had £105?

That woman did. So did a mate at school, who produced one from his bag in the seclusion of the sixth form library. He let me listen to it, but nervously and only in a couple of sixty-second bursts, as if he had been letting me dance with his girlfriend then suddenly had second thoughts.

But people could be precious about cassettes in general. You could achieve status making up tapes for parties. You could influence the tastes of a crowd if you got it right. 1981 was when I entered this world. I could record direct from our Sanyo music centre, but the sound was murky. Kids with access to newer systems arrived at parties with productions that were bright, clear and loud. Mine were none of these things. Nobody wanted them. There was all sorts of fiddly technology involved with the various grades of cassette; but I concluded that it only made a difference if you were *refining* the quality of your sound. I was some way off all that.

Cassettes were routinely annoying, but they were in demand. With the right kit, you could at least produce impressive compilations. If you didn't get them played at parties you could play them in the car. Plus, importantly, taping other people's vinyl saved you a fortune if all you wanted was the music. Singles were now over a pound a pop. By the summer, you couldn't get a charting single in London for less than £1.10. Knowing that they would now be £6 if their price had risen in line with the general cost of living since the late 50s did not help.

Consequently, home taping was rife. People not only taped each other's records, but also radio programmes, most often the Top 40 countdown. The British Phonographic Industry, or BPI, the trade association for the UK recording industry, properly got their tassels in a tangle over the issue and launched the apocalyptic "Home Taping Is Killing Music" campaign, which had virtually no effect.

Happily fanning the flames of its anxiety was Malcolm McLaren, whose new product, Bow Wow Wow, had announced themselves the previous summer with 'C'30, C'60, C'90 Go', a song about the virtues of taping records instead of buying them. It was a terrific single, using a speeded-up Burundi beat, thrilling guitars and an energetically stroppy performance from teenage singer Annabella Lwin. But it stalled outside the Top 30. It was easy to surmise that people had taped it instead of buying it.

In fact, it had originally been released on cassette only – the first-ever "cassette single" - with the B-side blank, presumably to invite owners to tape somebody's vinyl thereon. Their label, EMI, refused to promote it. I got a copy when it came out on vinyl.

As far as I was concerned, having a track on cassette was not having it properly. Having a hit single as part of a compilation album was not having it properly either. My propensity for wanting the highlights of Best Ofs on 45 has already been noted.

But I was now beginning to attract peer criticism as a result of this preference for the seven-inch format. "Nobody buys seven-inch singles any more", was what I was starting to hear from the pastel cardigans, something that was true in the same way that nobody goes to certain well-frequented clubs or wears a certain brand of shoe that you see everywhere.

But those *somebodies* meant it – buying seven-inch singles was a mark of immaturity. Two of my sisters now had their own singles stacks, cared for in singles cases, bought with their pocket money. I was, in essence, being compared to them. It was okay for twelve-to-fifteen-year-olds; but they, presumably, were the nobodies, along with saddoes of our own age; those failing to atmospherically absorb the fact that we had to buy albums and twelve-inch singles instead, even if we didn't like them as much. So now, if I slipped out to buy one at lunchtime, I was careful who I showed it to. I was defiantly unrepentant, but there's no point making trouble for yourself.

In time, I would own a good stack of twelve-inches, but to begin with I thought of them as pointless. The main reason is this: any record, however good it is, has only so much to say and do. Having said and done it, it should end. When, in a well-documented moment, John Peel fell in love with 'Teenage Kicks' by the Undertones live on air in 1978, he simply put the needle straight back to the beginning and played it again. This is a reasonable and logical response to being enthused by a record you have just played. He did not flop back and wail in regret that it wasn't two minutes longer. By contrast, if 'Don't Stop 'Till You Get Enough' by Michael Jackson was a minute and a half shorter, you would be left wanting more – it would go from being a good record to being a great one. So making a record longer just to fill a bigger disc is stupid.

Sometimes the record companies didn't even bother doing that. Eighteen months previously, I had laughed myself stupid at a mate who had bought the twelve-inch of the novelty hit 'The Lone Ranger' by Quantum Jump for £1.50, only to discover that it was exactly the same length as the 90p seven-inch.

And that was only the first kind of rip-off. I would hear twelve-inch singles where songs had been artificially stretched out with longer intros, extra passages in the middle sections and interminable fade-outs, completely diluting the impact of the version that had sounded so good on the radio. I would even buy twelve-inch copies of records I had listened to on air for weeks, because I thought the rhythms and atmosphere were capable of holding their effect over a longer version, only to find that some of their most defining features had been edited out of the twelve-inch altogether. It drove me up the bloody wall.

It could be partially explained by the fact that, as the 80s wore on, different formats were allowed to count when compiling sales figures for the charts, meaning that if fans were happy to buy the seven-inch plus two different sets of re-mixes on twelve-inch, it would register as three individual sales, which of course the record companies were delighted with. Clearly the work of marketing people who were not music fans, except to the extent that music had paid for the Alfa Romeo. Bastards.

But I'm jumping way ahead. In the early weeks of 1981, peer pressure was taking its toll and there came a point where there was nothing to do but decide what my first twelve-inch single was going to be.

I opted for 'Bed's Too Big Without You' by Sheila Hylton, a cover of a well-known Police album track. It was reggae, it was on the Island label where lots of reggae lived, and it could be bought at Red Records on Brixton Road, so it was going to be okay. And so it proved, although I never played it much.

But there would be more in the summer. Abba released an unremarkable discoey hymnal from their *Super Trouper* album called 'Lay All Your Love on Me', as the first ever twelve-inch-only chart single. It went to number seven and of course I got it. Mum voiced her amazement at my continued loyalty to them. She sensed, correctly, that their credibility had long begun to wane. On the cover of 'Lay All Your Love on Me', they looked like tourists waiting for their coach to pull up.

It all coincided with my early visits to night clubs, where youngsters drifted and nested in sullen groups and few of them danced. The night club was the exclusive domain of the twelve-inch and I allowed this to affect my judgement. I suppose I wanted to fit in; buying twelve-inch records would help me on my way.

I bought the twelve-inch of 'Dancing on the Floor (Hooked on Love)' by Third World, a pulsating groove with a similar feel to their 'Now That We've Found Love' which was now a golden oldie. It had an incredibly *clean* sound. It got to number ten.

I also got 'Body Talk' by Imagination; a cavernous, gently swaying beat, adorned with meandering piano and falsetto vocal. A touch of class. You will become one, not with words, but with body talk alone. Ooh, yeah. My copy was crap. It started crackling as if it had been left in the cat tray for the weekend. Some pieces of vinyl do this, no matter how carefully you look after them. 'Body Talk' went to number four.

I finally came to realise that some records were indeed better on twelve-inch. It depended, simply, on whether or not the longer version was the more complete one. I reconciled myself to creating a third facility in my well-established vinyl storage system and just got on with looking after them.

One good thing was that the labels were all paper ones. Seven-inches were increasingly coming with silver rings, although some companies coloured theirs; so that Chrysalis, for example, had blue plastic rings, while Polydor still sometimes used the red rings they had been pressing throughout the 70s, alternating them with silver ones. But for now, at least, the majority were still paper. This was true for seventy-one of the ninety-seven seven-inch singles I bought in the first six months of 1981. Now say that sentence three times quickly.

But what you saw as you watched your records spin on the turntable was undergoing newer types of change. EMI, who had regularly allowed Queen to have their own designs, were embracing other novel ideas. The label on the A-side of 'C'30, C'60, C'90 Go' had been plain black, with all of the credits for both sides squashed into their long-established caramel-and-red on the reverse. This idea was also used by Stiff; all four of Madness' 1981 hits had an image covering the A-side label which echoed the picture cover, with all credits beside the B-side. Tenpole Tudor's good-time knockabout hits from that year did the same.

At the end of the previous year, EMI had changed their main design shockingly. The caramel-and-red was ditched in favour of plain cream, yes *cream*. They incorporated the logos of some acts, but they went further for others – these New Romantics, for instance. As well as being able to grab anything made of fabric and present it as an item of clothing, they were allowed to have bespoke label designs.

EMI's New Romantic hopes rested with recent signings Duran Duran from Birmingham who, in early spring, took 'Planet Earth' into the Top 10, a record whose electronic effects put a smart finish on its charm. Its themes were both contemporary and retro-futuristic. The lyric blatantly referenced New Romanticism. The band were named after a character in the 1968 space romp movie *Barbarella*. It all hung together and worked.

Their follow-up single 'Careless Memories' was similar and okay, but in late summer they raised the bar with the rollicking 'Girls on Film' which put them firmly in their stride, aided by the notoriety of the boobs-out version of its accompanying video. There were no boobs on their labels. Instead, a series of clean lines and rectangles in strong colours, creating an effect reminiscent of strip-lights on space ships. Nobody else on EMI had this.

The other major artist allowed to deviate from the ghastly cream was Kate Bush, whose four single designs the previous year had all been bespoke. That July, she released the madly percussive 'Sat in Your Lap', a song about somebody wringing their hands over their academic development. It reminded me of counting sequences on the educational kids' TV programme *Sesame Street* – perhaps the learning link was intentional. A bit too intense for many, it peaked only at number eleven, but it's bloody great. The label design was pale green with dark green text in a small, rounded font, all lower-case, and the image of a swan in the same colour to go with its B-side, 'Lord of the Reedy River', a song written by Donovan. *Donovan!* Oh, Kate – if you do Planxty next, I'll get a tattoo.

Like Duran Duran, Spandau Ballet had been allowed bespoke label designs by their hosts, Chrysalis. Theirs were all classical splendour; Athenian patterns and Spartan lettering at the statuesquely handsome end of the New Romantic spectrum. Label-mates Ultravox, by contrast, had the credits of their excellently grand synth number two 'Vienna' moulded into a plain blue plastic ring.

A&M gave bespoke designs to the Police, with colour images of the group gleaming through lettering spelling the band's name, but other A&M acts were on the same bulbous faun design that had been around since the mid-70s, although in a few months this would be replaced by an abrupt red with white and black trimmings.

Virgin, on the other hand, gave bespoke licence to everybody, ditching the idea of a brand design altogether. They had Genesis, whose lead singer and drummer Phil Collins had just released a solo album called *Face Value*, amidst hype that seemed justifiable once you had heard its first single, the colossal, spiritual 'In the Air Tonight', which got to number two.

Other labels had overhauled their look dramatically. At the start of the previous year, the ubiquitous Epic had switched from orange to sky blue, with a new logo made of yellow swirls. RCA chose the same year to ditch their longer-standing orange in favour of a businesslike black with silver type. On a smaller scale, Gem mercifully swapped their horrible shade of green for a nice, comfortable blue.

Others stuck to their guns. Polydor we have already mentioned. Motown were still on the blue spokes. Island retained the sunset design they had used since 1975 and CBS still had the orange and yellow meld, although they occasionally put out plastic rings in an unpleasant kind of terracotta. But the champions of dogged conservation were, without doubt, RAK.

Their yacht had now been a-sail for over ten years and it was now being given a fresh lick of varnish by the appearance of Kim Wilde. Her brightly powerful noise-pop would deliver hits throughout the decade, most of which would go Top 10 and a small number of which would be from the very top drawer. Early that spring, her first, a pulsating blur with its own mind entitled 'Kids in America', went to number two. It was disappointing that she was singing about living in America when she was from west London, but it's remembered enthusiastically, even by those who didn't think it was good.

So, a question: if 'Kids in America', 'In the Air Tonight' and 'Vienna' were all number twos, what the heck was getting to number one? Well, there was the novelty of 'Shaddap You Face' by Joe Dolce's Music Theatre; a skyward roll of the eyes at how cute those dumb foreigners can be. There was also – and get this – Shakin' Stevens; yes, he, of the other version of 'Jungle Rock'. He had shivered our good rockin' timbers the previous summer by getting 'Marie Marie' to just outside the Top 20, only to now cap it all, and then some, with 'This Ole House', whose gratuitous niceness annoyed the crap out of many, although good record it certainly was.

Aside from these, number one belonged to John Lennon. 'Imagine' arrived there in January, then a song of worship from his most recent album called 'Woman' did the same. Finally, another old one, 'Jealous Guy', was covered in tribute by Roxy Music, giving them what would be their only chart-topping single. They married their irresistible smoothness to the song's irresistible melancholy. It said "a tribute" on the cover. Britain solemnly held the doors open for it.

That Kim Wilde single brings us to another development – the increasing number of picture covers that were made from paper, rather than from anything that could reasonably be called card. Of the seventy-one singles that came in picture covers from the ninety-seven mentioned above, nineteen were made of paper, and I'm not even counting those with a glossy laminate.

The problem was their vulnerability. Singles slid up and down in their delivery boxes and, additionally, were often handled un-gently by store staff when taken out. The circular ridges bordering the run-out grooves rubbed together through the covers, with the result that an arc of whatever colour was on the back, was printed on the front of the next copy. If the back was a dark colour, your main cover image could be distinctly blemished.

The back of 'Kids in America' was black and the front was a mono picture of the singer's face beneath magenta lettering. The more I stared at the black arc beneath Kim's left eye, the more annoying it became, particularly given the level of feminine allure involved. I felt sure that a pencil rubber would do the trick, but I only succeeded in replacing a neat black arc with a straggly white one. I ended up buying another copy. I've resented paper picture covers ever since.

'Kids in America' was gratifyingly blary, yet it wasn't quite like anything from a year before. The soundtrack was becoming unrecognisable. The mod and 2-Tone scene had withered in the space of a few months and now seemed very old hat. New wave had calmed down. Clean sounds were moving in, growly guitars were being edged out. In the late autumn, I would bring a tape in to the sixth form common-room of a new guitar band I liked, and have it sneeringly dismissed as "stone age".

Production was now warm and close; reverb was contained, no longer echoing freely, but housed in huge acrylic towers where the air could be shut off. There are always exceptions, but this was the trend, one which would consolidate until, by mid-decade, there would be a quintessential, out-sized "80s sound". It was down to a revolution in the focus of technology. Specifically, it was down to the rise of the synthesizer.

The name "synthesizer" derives from the ability of a piece of technology to create a synthetic noise. Experimentation was happening as early as the 1920s, but constructing a synthetic sound and steadying it into something recognisably tonal, let alone musical, was a very specific challenge, one met only through lots of adjustment and twiddling. The 1963 theme for the TV series *Dr Who* – made exclusively from synthetic sounds – is history's finest example of this being done successfully.

Once the possibilities had become clear, the next thing was for all the knobs, buttons and dials controlling the sound to be standardised. A company called Moog stepped up to the mark. The same company also took the next step when, in 1970, they produced a synthesizer with a built-in keyboard – the Minimoog. Experimental musicians leapt at the chance to work with its sounds and they featured on a clutch of memorable hit records in the following few years.

In 1975, the Yamaha company introduced *digital* synthesis, condensing the various processes to provide tones that were more accurate, clean and versatile. The company's name would become synonymous with electronic keyboards as a result. Limitations remained; many keyboards were unable to play chords because they could only produce one note at a time. But it did mean that sounds could now be made and adjusted simply by pressing keys and buttons.

Such machines would be expensive until the mid-80s. In 1979, a simple keyboard synth could set you back £800 and the Fairlight CMI, a state-of-the-art studio synthesizer with an early sampling facility, cost upwards of £18,000, at a time when the average UK house price was £13,650.

Musicians and producers nevertheless adopted them in increasing numbers. Within a few years, atmospheres which only the very best orchestrators had been able to establish would be within reach of anyone prepared to fiddle around with the controls for long enough.

But the "80s sound" owed an equal debt to spread of electronic percussion; for, alongside the synthesizers, stood drum machines – boxes that could be programmed to play whatever drum parts were required and perform them at the press of a button. By mid-decade, having a drummer was often seen as an unnecessary extravagance. In many types of music, they simply disappeared.

The drum machine taking mainstream pop by storm in 1981 was the "Linn machine", the Linn LM-1, which was popular because it included a digital sampling facility. Its built-in sounds were rich and relatively convincing, comprising everything but a crash cymbal, although a subsequent, less expensive version, LinnDrum, would add this feature (I'll be testing you later).

The Roland company, meanwhile, launched their analogue TR-808.

This was less appealing to the industry because it didn't have digital sampling, but it was more affordable for DIY musicians and had its own range of sounds that would, as a result, become synonymous with street-level genres. You couldn't mistake these sounds for the real thing – they were metallic, cloned, machine-gun like – but they fit their own bill with panache. A completely new percussion sound had been born.

These technological developments were quietly welcomed by the BBC. The previous year, a decision to disband some BBC orchestras had led to a strike by the Musicians' Union. Part of the remit for these orchestras had been providing live backing for hit acts in the studio. A good, regular earner for them, but a frustration for young fans as these renditions were fuddy-duddy compared to the records.

During the dispute, of course, they stopped. Several editions of *Top of the Pops* were broadcast without any studio music at all – videos were shown instead and the lack of complaints from viewers changed the game. *Top of the Pops* had a long-standing habit of getting artists to mime to records; the percentage now went up. For years, the show had featured videos as a break from studio performances; their numbers now increased. And when bands played live, they didn't need an orchestra because they had synthesizers.

Not everybody did, however. The mod and 2-Tone acts did not quite disappear overnight. The Jam carried on undiminished. Bad Manners and the Beat would have hits for another couple of years. Madness would adapt and prosper. And there was one more serious biggie.

The Specials, who began the year with the gloomy, groovy and wonderfully loud 'Do Nothing', would top everything in the summer with 'Ghost Town', a song lamenting the condition of British youth – dismissed, disregarded, angrily wrecking their environment and each other. There had been riots in Brixton in the spring, sparked by confrontations between the police and black youngsters who felt harassed and invaded. Buildings and cars had burned for days. The song's lyric reflected the acrid pessimism giving rise to these events and the record's haunted-house effects were underpinned by a genuinely bleak atmosphere.

But, as it climbed to number one, new riots erupted in cities all over the country. It was like some kind of prophesy. The authorities briefly feared for general order. It was a big deal. 'Ghost Town' represented an important moment in our economic and social history and will forever be remembered as such. Having achieved this feat, the group immediately fell apart in acrimony and three of its key members, singer Terry Hall included, left to form the dismal, inappropriately-named Fun Boy Three. You could only shrug.

The event both accelerated and symbolised the rate of change. Alongside 'Ghost Town' in the summer charts were three records representing this new synth pop with distinction. The first was by the Human League, who had been around for a while as an all-male outfit. They had just swapped two blokes for two girls and got poppier. Their new single, 'The Sound of the Crowd', was mesmerising - all angular groove and buzzing riff, with male and female vocal hovering around it as if daring each other to get closer.

Second: 'New Life' by Depeche Mode; a brightly bleeping rush, whooshing along with the roof down, performed by clean-cut guys standing at their keyboards looking younger than us. The third I initially liked because it sounded Motowny and I later found out it was indeed a cover, a synthed-up version of a northern soul favourite. At the start of the school holiday I excitedly spread the word about it, along with another record called 'Japanese Boy' by Aneka (which I mention only in passing) and by the end of the summer both had been number one, which made me quite smug.

The record was 'Tainted Love' by Soft Cell; bleeps, catchy stomps, pained wailing; fantastic distortion. An old-style song done in a bang-up-to-date way. People of all persuasions lost their minds. At parties I went to it got played six, seven times. It was the best-selling single of the year. Three terrific records. And not a drummer in sight.

So it wasn't all gloom. Indeed, amidst the desolation of abandoned youth and burning cities, there were genuine causes for national celebration. In June, there was a royal wedding; HRH Prince of Wales married Lady Diana Spencer at St Paul's in a blizzard of splendour and we all got the day off.

But more importantly, the UK tasted Eurovision glory again. As before it was two blokes and two girls doing a dance, but Bucks Fizz in '81 were a different proposition to Brotherhood of Man in '76 and 'Making Your Mind Up' was a better song, an encouragement for us all to follow our own instincts in love unswayed by what others think. It was super-catchy. It bounced and twisted its hips.

The stage performance was slickly choreographed – a blur of blond hair, sparkling eyes and pale cottons. There was even a saucy bit. Near the end, when the lyric talks about wanting to "see some more", the boys, in perfect synchronisation, tore away the girls' short skirts to reveal still shorter versions beneath. First rate family-friendly pop with extra thigh – it was no contest. Victory was ours.

It was enormously popular and a big number one, but it wasn't played at the parties or night clubs I went to. The growing range of danceable pop meant it wasn't needed.

Let's think about "danceable" for a second. You could, of course, dance to anything you wanted, but some beats were more favourable than others for dancing in ways that didn't alarm those around you. Kids had looked cool dancing to glam in the early 70s, but only occasionally – the beats had rarely been right. More often, they had been left either with yoga-like workouts bequeathed by the hippies, or with bouncing. Soul, funk and disco had rarely had such problems – these were the tempos to emulate.

Synths and drum machines delivered fresh possibilities and rhythms with room to groove in began popping up all over the place. It might have been a brisk *dong, chang, dong-dong, chang;* it might have been a busy *digga-digga dang-digga, digga-digga dang-digga* or variations thereon. 'Planet Earth' had been danceable but not particularly bassy and, in the circles I moved in, bassy was a pre-requisite for danceable and danceable was the only thing that would do. When people turned their noses up at a record it was often because of "tinny bits", which meant treble, the opposite of bass and therefore a badge of shame. 'Planet Earth' had perhaps been a bit too tinny.

But 'Chant No.1 (I Don't Need this Pressure On)' by Spandau Ballet, which got to number four in the summer, was definitely not. This was explicitly danceable, going as far as to include funky horns alongside its bongos and its crunching beats. I played it to death. 'Tainted Love' was just as much of an all-out dancer, so was 'New Life' if you could keep up with it. The Human League planted their flag right in the middle of the dance floor, following up 'The Sound of the Crowd' with 'Love Action', which, along with its B-side 'Hard Times', was a fixture at parties right through the autumn. Dancing to this stuff wasn't quite like the smooth cool of moving to George Benson – there was more combustion involved, more elbows. But it was definitely dancing, not bouncing.

In any case, it was rendered glorious by comparison to what had happened to the disco beat. *Dom-tiss dat-tiss* had been reduced to *dom chack, dom chack* and the unscrupulous were now plonking anything on top of it that they thought could make money. Singles appeared by Starsound which were collages of clips, first by the Beatles ('Stars on 45') and then by Abba ('Stars on 45 volume 2'). These clips came one after another after another, never lasting more than a few bars, never sustaining or building anything – they were simply snipped out of the original recordings and dumped onto *dom chack, dom chack*.

Both got to number two. There were more to follow. A *Stars on 45* album was top of the charts for five weeks. People were paying money for this stuff. They danced to it at family parties. The horror was dizzying. When you objected, people complained: "But young kids might not get to know the Beatles otherwise". Really? That's like saying that they wouldn't find out about gravity unless someone pushed them out of a tree. It was depressing and it smelt of decay. Because it *was* decay. 'Stars on 45' was the home for the bewildered in which disco took its final breath.

Thankfully, better things were close by in these charts. Among them were the fresh wafts of warm maturity drifting in from American FM radio, the two best examples of which were 'Bette Davis Eyes' by Kim Carnes and 'Keep On Loving You' by REO Speedwagon, much derided but nevertheless splendid. I did mean splendid. I have thought long and hard about the best word for describing 'Keep On Loving You', but I keep coming back to splendid.

There was also great soul. The hand-over in recording styles was explicit in the best of its 1981 moments. At the start of the year, the swaying, synth-heavy 'Don't Stop the Music' by Yarborough and Peoples had been an enormous hit in our common-room. Later, the Whispers caused just as much excitement with the more traditionally-produced 'It's a Love Thing'. Summer dance floors heaved to the explicitly synthy 'I'm In Love' by Evelyn King, as well as the very un-synthy 'Going Back to My Roots' by Odyssey.

In a summer of riots and racial tension, 'Going Back to My Roots' was positive and upbeat; real ethnic resonance with its head held high. People loved it all the way to number five. But this summer was also the one when Bob Marley died, of a cancer that his Rasta beliefs forbade him to have treated. On the day the news broke, a woman at the bottom of our road had her front door and all her windows open, Marley blaring from inside, as she paced up and down the front garden, howling abuse at any white person who walked past. I only wish I could have understood my share.

Marley had used the traditional guitar-and-drum-kit format right to the end, and this continued in other enclaves. Heavy metal was one. I have already casually referred to this in the confidence that you, dear reader, have some background knowledge of it. Perhaps you agree with those who think of it as a rage-soothing facility for youngsters suffering growing pains at the opposite end of the scale from those of the pastel cardigans; a reality-free world of grisly themes and incalculable decibels where you can immerse yourself in hair, sew-on patches and questionable hygiene. There will always be a market for it. Where the distinction lies between heavy metal and "rock" is a discussion for others to have. Perhaps it's to do with the amount of denim.

The genre has produced some great stuff and the current market leaders were the brilliant AC/DC and the glossy but slightly dodgy-of-lyric Rainbow, with a band called Iron Maiden moving up through the ranks. If I've forgotten anyone it's tough. When you listen to the best AC/DC, you really do get the point. Their most recent album was *Back in Black* and their best previous one was *Highway to Hell*. Own both.

Other guitar-and-drum-kit loyalists stood among the huddle of survivors from punk. The Stranglers and the Jam have already been mentioned. The Boomtown Rats were petering out. Elvis Costello was making a country album. No, he really was. He was absolutely fine.

So too were Siouxsie and the Banshees. They had an amazing summer with the consecutive releases 'Spellbound' and 'Arabian Knights', two of the year's very best singles which, despite their quality, got no higher than twenty two and thirty two respectively. This was a screaming insult. On the other hand, it was proof that they were a specialist interest. As were John Lydon's Public Image Ltd. Their 1981 single 'The Flowers of Romance' was jarring and superb; massive drums, a violin and *that* voice. The strangest kind of comfort. God only knows what the pastel cardigans made of it.

Meanwhile, Lydon's former manager Malcolm McLaren was seeing his Bow Wow Wow project amount to not as much as had been hoped. The marketing strategy seemed, more than anything else, to centre on the fact that singer Annabella Lwin was "underage". This is now testing your dodgy-ometer. It's going off? Good. Keep it charged. The following year, they would make the Top 10 with 'Go Wild in the Country'. Its picture cover aped Manet's painting *Le Déjeuner sur l'herbe*, with Lwin posing naked. A few months on, they would release an old album track called 'Louis Quatorze', about a character whose name apparently derives from his taste for fourteen-year-old girls, one of whom is narrating. He has his way with her at gunpoint and she ends up adoring him. Best not dwell on this. Let's move on to Blondie.

We last met them when number one with 'The Tide Is High'. Their next single was 'Rapture', a classy, laid back groove with a blissed-out vocal over the top, the climax of which was Debbie Harry doing a rap. Yes, a rap. Like most other people, my sole experience of rap so far had been 'Rapper's Delight', which had since been enhanced by hearing a twelve-inch version where one of them boasts about what he's going to do with his "super sperm".

Debbie Harry is chronicled as being brave and ground-breaking to rap on a Blondie record and was arguably only reflecting the emerging sound back home. What I remember is people looking at each other and pulling faces. The rap bit starts with something about cool people that I couldn't make out, and then it's like My First Rhyme – going real far in your car, driving all night and seeing a light... There's then a story about a man from Mars who starts eating the cars, after which he eats the bars, then finishes by eating – wait for it – the guitars! I couldn't quite believe my ears. But others loved the gimmick, or loved Debbie Harry doing anything, and it gave *Smash Hits* a good reason to run features and print glossy shots. It got to number five.

Our final punk survivor had had to wait the longest to achieve proper success, but he was now the biggest pop star in the country. He was also one of the few remaining champions of growly guitar. Following 'Antmusic', Adam and the Ants had returned to number two with the title track from *Kings of the Wild Frontier*. Having played it all winter I was now hearing it on the radio going into the spring, but it was hard to get tired of.

His record labels prior to CBS quickly re-released old recordings, which were no better than curiosities; except for a B-side called 'Kick', which is an intoxicating explosion of noise as well as a tantalising sign of ant things to come. Adam was the man of the hour; pretty, brooding, a bit of a show-off, with that combination of man and boy that women struggle to resist. He took his image very seriously, but in service to his audience, not mockery.

Clearly, unless his next single was a complete duffer, it was going to be number one. His themes, in keeping with the New Romantic ethos, had largely been to do with looking good and dismissing the shabby, ugly and the old-hat. He kept this up. Having been a preening, precious redskin and then a preening, precious pirate, he now became a dandy highwayman. No, bear with it. In another galloping, thunderous arrangement, he stood by the roadside in his triangle hat, cape and mask, brandishing his pistol, making sure we knew that none of us looked as good as he did.

It was called 'Stand and Deliver'. Well of course it was. The sound was cleaned up. The vocals were right out front and you could hear every word of a lyric which was a jumbled summary of doctrine and playful anachronism. The only things nailing it to highwaymen was the costume and time-honoured highwayman turns-of-phrase in the chorus. It went straight in at number one – the only record that year to do so. It stayed there for five weeks.

At the end of the chorus he sings the phrase "Your conscience will be mine" and, in the video, as he repeats "all mine", he flicks his eyes skyward. I would watch it on *Top of the Pops* sitting with my girl-friend and, when he did this, she would blush and fidget. Then she would turn to me and apologise. Every time.

There was no point getting upset. You couldn't compete with Adam. In any case, I was a fan. Tracks from that album were on the brain regularly throughout the year, and 'Dog Eat Dog', 'Kings of the Wild Frontier' and 'Stand and Deliver' were clearly records of sub-stance.

'Stand and Deliver' was, without doubt, a *big* number one. I was get-ting good at identifying those. I felt that records of substance should command respect, whether or not I liked them. I was now buying records that I wasn't particularly enthusiastic about, if they seemed important and I thought my collection ought to include them. I didn't want to let any genuine classics go by. There were limits to this, but they were fairly arbitrary.

I was developing my perspective. Armed with the current edition of the *Guinness Book of Hit Singles* and tuning in regularly to oldies programmes including the *Golden Hour*, I was deepening my knowl-edge with determination. So, was I preoccupied with great oldies? Was their time-honoured quality overwhelming the current soundtrack?

Well I have some statistics, because 1981 was the only year when I kept a diary, all the way through, with a narrative on each day's events, or lack of them, that I didn't subsequently get rid of for being too cringeworthy.

It's an interesting source. At the top of each page I wrote the name of the record that I had on the brain that day, what we later came to call an "ear-worm". There always was one. On some days there were two. On one exceptional day there were three. There, those are your first stats.

The next is that 256 of the 372 titles were of current and recent records, i.e. from the last three months. Less recent ones, from back to circa 1978, totalled 47. There were 36 from the earlier 70s, mainly Abba or the Supremes with Jean Terrell on lead, and the other 33 were from the 60s, mainly the Supremes with Diana Ross on lead. None were from the 50s. So it was overwhelmingly new records that were doing the business.

Who, then, was serving up these irresistible new sounds? Well, the daytime line-up on Radio 1 was looking very different. I did occasionally listen to Capital, but not enough to remember names. The Radio 1 lot were also on *Top of the Pops*, so it was easier.

The roster now included the blond mop and calm enthusiasm of Kid Jensen, alongside the blond mop and loud enthusiasm of Peter Powell, both of whom had a taste for the relatively alternative. Tone was now on mid-afternoon duties and had also taken over *Junior Choice* from Ed "Stewpot" Stewart at the weekends, as well as presenting the Sunday Top 40 countdown.

His old late-morning slot now belonged to Simon Bates, whose formal baritone would make the show its own until well into the 90s. The *Golden Hour* was now unimaginable without his challenging growl: "But *what* was the year?"

Yet it was a new feature, *Our Tune*, that became his real trademark. Listeners would write in with true stories of emotional turmoil and tragedy, often involving the worst things that a person could ever deal with, and Bates would read them out solemnly, with marked, respectful pauses; pacing out syllables in the particularly difficult bits, until playing the special record. When *Our Tune* came on at 11am, huge swaths of the nation stopped what they were doing and grabbed a tissue. The unworldly sincerity of the show was a constant invitation to satire, but I've never known anyone who could do a decent Simon Bates impression.

In January, Dave Lee Travis left the *Breakfast Show* and was replaced by Mike Read, who I much preferred. He was enthusiastic, colourful and humorous; but reassuringly within boundaries, like your favourite teacher. He sat up straight and spoke clearly.

I wrote to him three times under different pseudonyms with comments which were supposed to be witty, all of which were read out. One of these was rumbled as phoney and, in retaliation, he immediately played the Shakin' Stevens record 'You Drive Me Crazy' that I had slagged off.

I also wrote in to volunteer for participation in a quiz called *1-2-3*, where you answered three graded questions on your favourite group or artist and won a £5 record token for each correct answer. In the last week of the summer holiday, his producer called our house to set it up and the next day I was on, joking pleasantly with the host and answering questions about the Supremes.

I got the answers right. I knew that the other groups they had had hits with were the Four Tops and the Temptations, I knew that Jean Terrell had replaced Diana Ross and I knew that their original name had been the Primettes. Relatives had been tipped off, but apart from family, one girl from school and one teacher heard it.

During that same holiday, there was an event on the other side of the Atlantic that we need to note. August 1st saw the launch of Music Television, or MTV, a cable and satellite channel with the sole purpose of playing music videos presented by "video jockeys".

Cable and satellite channels were a strange and exotic concept for we Brits. We still only had three channels – BBC1, BBC2 and ITV – and we seemed to get by okay. But the idea of a full-time music channel was intriguing, especially since there was an established tradition of British acts promoting singles on videos. We had seen them on *Top of the Pops*. We had sometimes seen them on *The Old Grey Whistle Test*, a late-night BBC2 show featuring "serious" music, consisting mainly of live studio performances. We had seen them elsewhere. But never in one place for hour after hour.

I've got a problem with music videos. The best of them enhance the record and show a real understanding of its purpose, but others do quite the opposite. Each is like a see-saw, with the importance of the record at one end and the importance of the video at the other. When the video is made the star of the relationship, it begs the question: *What is the point of the record?*

Too often, as I watched videos for records I liked, I found them contradicting their meaning and ruining their effect, making a mockery of the fulfilment they delivered coming out of the radio or from the speakers in the mansion. There are exceptions. But too few. Intrinsically, videos tell us - *the record alone is not enough.*

Yet most people take their entertainment broadly, as they find it; and there are laughs, great imagery and plenty of wow-moments in videos. For the devoted, unquestioning fan, it was all brilliant. They could drool over their favourites in new TV contexts, adoring their every movement, perhaps without scrutinising the quality of the record at all. *All his songs must be brilliant because he's got such lovely eyes.* This was nothing new, but with music video it was amplified. It's easy to see a smooth link between this and a time, two decades later, when making good records would be rock-bottom of the priority list for establishing and maintaining a chart act.

The launch of MTV had immediate impact in the States. One result was that young audiences could now see the people whose records had sounded so soft, warm and mature (not to mention splendid) on FM radio, discovering with alarm that they were old, going bald and a bit overweight.

But if this was deflating, they soon perked up at the sight of a group of girls cruising around Los Angeles with the roof down, dancing through fountains and generally mucking about in the sun, singing an excellent, sparkle-infused song about gossip called 'Our Lips Are Sealed'.

This was a surfy new-wave band called the Go-Go's. Guitarist Jane Weidlin had put its tune to lyrics written by Terry Hall following UK support slots with the Specials. The Go-Go's had the US hit with it. The Fun Boy Three reached the UK Top 10 with their rendition two years later, but anyone who seriously thinks theirs is the better version should lie down and be spoken to by someone with a soft voice and a certificate.

MTV made stars of the Go-Go's and their debut album, *Beauty and the Beat,* was an American phenomenon. I liked them a lot. I went silly over 'Our Lips Are Sealed'. I bought the album early. I went to see them at The Venue in Victoria. I evangelised about them. But nobody cared. An all-girl group was seen as a gimmick, particularly by girls. More than that however, they were, as someone noisily declared in our sixth-form common room one morning, "stone age".

There were few black acts on MTV to start with. Not even Michael was on yet. MTV's management claimed that this was because record companies were failing to fund videos for black artists; therefore there was nothing to play. Michael's ambitious, well-funded 1983 videos would change all that.

But the first black faces on MTV were in the line-up of the Specials, whose 'Rat Race' was played on the opening day. British acts featured heavily. The UK's established video tradition meant we had the vital content. The result would be a few years of huge stateside success for UK acts.

In truth, I don't remember that many videos from that period. To the credit of my peer group, our music conversations were mainly about the records, ranging from "It's good"/"It's crap" to "That music all sounds the same to me – I like soul", to the animated swappings of notes that often enabled you to sort out your own feelings about things as you went along.

These exchanges did, occasionally, prove that there was real thought going on. One girl was delighted to discover a piece of lyrical wordplay in a Squeeze single called 'Tempted', where the narrator says he fumbles for his clock – *alarmed.* She told everyone she had noticed this. I, meanwhile, was trying to get that horrible single out of my head. It was from an album called *East Side Story,* a gathering of dramas and portraits from the council estate which I spent a lot of time with that summer.

Squeeze were probably my favourite band at this point. Though sadly unable to maintain the giddy heights of 'Cool for Cats' and 'Up the Junction', they had continued to put out fine stuff; the anticipation and delusion of real young people set in flats, curry houses and trips to the seaside, painted in loving detail. It was properly stone age; with tinny bits, twangy guitar and driving beats behind the contrasting sounds of the two main vocalists, Chris Difford's deep geezer and

Glenn Tilbrook's clear alto, the latter a voice I absolutely loved.

I just didn't get on with 'Tempted'; it was a bit too impressed with itself. It didn't bother the Top 40. The big *East Side Story* hit was the countrified ballad 'Labelled with Love', which would go all the way to number four in the autumn, putting its cave paintings on the walls of the Top 10 for a whole month.

Nobody danced to 'Labelled with Love'. But I danced to their oldie 'Take Me I'm Yours' at a couple of parties that autumn. A friend put it on and we danced to it as a kind of dare, as others shuffled out of the way. 'Don't Stop the Music' by Yarborough and Peoples had referred to "dancing and prancing", a piece of gratuitous rhyming I sneered at; if you had started "prancing" at some of the parties we went to, you wouldn't have lasted five minutes. But our movements to 'Take Me I'm Yours' went dangerously close. We did it again at my 18th a few weeks later, temporarily turning up the lights in the dark room, tolerated because it was my birthday.

This was quite an event, because the dark room was sacred at teenage parties. A pecking order of DJs held sway, playing smooth soul sounds; the right records for serving the scene and maintaining the intimate atmosphere. People could get close in the dark room. If you were able to project unbroken cool, you could hack it. Even our happy soul weekender friends had to tone it down a bit.

At some parties we ended up at – cellar parties that never seemed to have a host – it could all be like this. But most house parties had contrasts, with different crowds doing different things in different rooms. The atmosphere was good. There was rarely any trouble.

Night clubs were a contrast. You danced just because you were there, with no idea if it looked okay or if anyone could tell how uncomfortable you were. Almost always, they were intimidating, dull, alienating places where smiling seemed to be outlawed. Occasionally, someone might try and lighten the mood by grinning and doing a funny dance or something, but the general atmosphere would soon put a stop to such nonsense. Then of course there were the groups of lads happy to find a bit of conflict with other groups of lads. Spotting an innocent attempt at mood-lightening was often the excuse they were waiting for. It all added up to an assault on your confidence and sense of ease. Girls picked up on this and steered clear. Plus, each drink was at least the price of a single. These things can't help but cross your mind.

But once in a while, a record appears that sweeps all mutual suspicion and anxiety away at a stroke. That autumn, it was 'Let's Groove' by Earth, Wind and Fire. When I think of it, I see crowds of dancing youngsters – contented and relaxed if not downright cheerful – in living rooms, school halls and clubs; its bassy, robot-voice riff and bright call to action doing the business for all. At its climax, the vocal commands us to "boogie on down"; and that's what people started doing, bending the knees and sinking lower, shimmying the shoulders, lines and circles of them. I'm not sure anybody ever took the lead on this – it just felt like the thing to do.

Gatherings through Christmas and into the new year bristled in anticipation of the unifying force that was 'Let's Groove'. Its only rival was Kool and the Gang's 'Get Down on It', coming from a similar, ultra-cool place but a bit too serious to get anyone shimmying.

It was a good end to this year of change. The football team I played for was top of its league. My love life was in decent shape. For my 18th birthday, I had got a gleaming stack system made by JVC, enabling me to make party tapes that were more readily accepted. And, as if to underline what a crossroads of a year it had been, the number one single at Christmas was by the Human League.

Yes, the Human League. Even now, I marvel at that fact. Just over a year ago, Queen had gone disco. Now, the Human League were the Christmas number one thanks to 'Don't You Want Me', a tale of painful moving-on with a sky-punching belter of a chorus. After an autumn of number ones as awful as 'It's My Party' by Dave Stewart and Barbara Gaskin, 'Under Pressure' by Queen and David Bowie (yes, together) and 'Begin the Beguine' by Julio Iglesias – all a triumph of style over substance – the good guys were winning again.

And there was more good stuff surrounding it. A Scottish group called Altered Images had provided something genuinely alternative earlier in the autumn with 'Happy Birthday', a feisty, zesty chang of xylophone and guitar with a breathy, super-girly vocal, made for bouncing, not dancing. It had gone all the way to number two. Now they were back in the Top 10 with the more reflective but no less shimmery 'I Could Be Happy'.

With it, was 'Mirror Mirror' by Dollar and a new one by Bucks Fizz called 'The Land of Make Believe', both of which seemed to be attempting the world record for sparkles in a confined space. There was 'One of Us', a quality moper from Abba; there was the nuttily cute 'It Must Be Love' by Madness.

And then there was 'Ant Rap'. No, there really was. Adam Ant had got very excited about his success. He had been at number one again in early autumn with 'Prince Charming', a manifesto for narcissism based on an old variety show rowing song. It was the title track of the Ants' new album. But whereas *Kings of the Wild Frontier* had had dirt under its fingernails, those on *Prince Charming* were all immaculately polished. There was silk, there was satin, there was pearly lip gloss. On the cover, they looked less like a pop group and more like a gift-set of novelty bubble bath.

The music was likewise silk, satin and gloss; mainly mediocre. The rap track was a lot of stitched-together nonsense. A chanted chorus name-checked the band and ended with Adam praising himself. This was doing nothing for the status of rap. Neither was the fact that the small number of rap records by black artists I had heard since 'Rapper's Delight' had been so uninspiring. Rap was an amusement, something to be prodded and smirked at, like game show contestants having a go on a potter's wheel. Bit of space left on the album? Do a rap.

But perhaps the novelty would give them another hit, for the sake of having another hit. It was decided to release 'Ant Rap' as a single. They re-recorded it, adding layers of rafter-rattling drums and a whole lot of other gratuitous noise until, through sheer will, it had become an extremely loud chunk of ridiculous fun.

It appeared just before Christmas, in a sleeve that was a half-arsed attempt at an advent calendar. If you used the perforations to push the windows open, you could see the band members on the inside as you listened to the single. I had no desire to do so. But I did listen to the single a lot. It got to number three.

North from A1 Stores along the Walworth Road stood Sundown Records, a Superdisc-like cube with a policy of selling albums at a rock-bottom £1.99. There was another shop like it at Camberwell Green called One Price, its name an echo of Our Price, the chain that had taken over all of Harlequin's properties in central London and flooded the music press with ads. I was a frequent visitor to both, topping up the collection here and there with stuff I felt I ought to have.

Months after 'Ant Rap', a couple of football mates began working at Sundown, joining a throng of young guys crammed behind the counter, comfortably outnumbering the browsing customers. I found a copy of *Prince Charming* and took it up. They looked at me quizzically. I said: "Well it's got to be worth £1.99, hasn't it?" They both said: "No".

But however silly Adam and the Ants may have looked on their cover, they were only reflecting the times by being shiny. Everything was shinier. Affordable fashions were shiny. Local youngsters wore smooth, glossy shirts with a subtle glint, and throat-chains of bronze called "belchers". Farah slacks were the only trousers, some designs betraying a slight sheen. Technology was making music shiny. Even live strings sounded shinier. The next two years would be brightly shiny for the 45. The number ones were mostly rotten, but sod those. If we jump into the middle of 1982, we can see how things were developing. The chart at the end of May is a particularly good snapshot.

So what was in it? A Madness number one, that's what. One of the few decent chart-toppers of the year, 'House of Fun' was about being old enough to buy condoms, and the video was three minutes of nutty elation.

Roaring up behind it was – well looky here – Adam Ant. Or at least according to the plastic terracotta ring it was Adam Ant. The cover insisted it was Adam *and the Ants*. Somebody at CBS needed to take command. 'Goody Two Shoes' was another leg-shaking drum rumble, this one bemoaning judgements suffered as a result of being sober in a world of boozing and drug-taking. Mischievously, its last four beats were the first four from Elvis Presley's 'Jailhouse Rock'. It took over from 'House of Fun' at the top. Behind both and destined to stick at number two, was a synth lovely; the aching 'Only You' by Yazoo, a duo comprising a departed Depeche Mode member and a girl called Alf with a distinctive voice of rich hazel.

Spandau Ballet and Duran Duran were heading for the Top 10 again with good, pacey records in the new sound-mould, respectively 'Instinction' and 'Hungry Like the Wolf'. Close by were a bunch of New Romantic new arrivals called Simple Minds, with the restlessly groovy 'Promised You a Miracle'. Soft Cell, meanwhile, though back in the Top 10, had gone a bit funny. 'Torch' was a difficult listen: jazzy, sleazy and alienating.

The antidote was 'The Look of Love' by ABC, a slamming, crescendo-building rollercoaster ride in a jewelled hat, with soaring strings and echoes of yester-classics: by the end of it you were knackered. It was produced by former Buggle front-man Trevor Horn, also responsible for the exceptional sound of the current Dollar album. Meaningful new reputations were being forged.

This slick, new, shiny pop had its naff moments. Thankfully slipping out of the charts was 'My Camera Never Lies', a third number one from Bucks Fizz, although what possessed people to buy it I've no idea. Flimsy, fluttery wafers of fleeting noise that wouldn't settle on anything for longer than it took to dash off again. Made you want to punch a hole in the partition. It was hard to swallow so soon after 'The Land of Make Believe' and only a year after 'Making Your Mind Up'. This year's Eurovision entry, 'One Step Closer' by Bardo, was cut from the same cloth. But it didn't win and now it too was dropping out of the charts. Good.

You might have thought that Tight Fit would be peddling the same stuff. They were choreographed pretties with a male lead in sweatbands, which was so frightfully *now*. Sweatbands were bloody everywhere. A fashion accessory to convince audiences that they were taking their health seriously. As if they had invented exercise. As if they were the first generation to get hot on stage. Utter bollocks.

Tight Fit had induced bucketloads of vomit in the spring when granny-pleaser 'The Lion Sleeps Tonight' had been number one. Now they were back, with something called 'Fantasy Island'. Well, you had to give it a listen. So you did. And before long, you were in the grip of a quite extraordinary chorus, which spiralled and hurtled, defying every effort to keep it under control. You couldn't imagine that they'd actually set out to please you, let alone thrill you like that. They'd made a good record by mistake.

Soul was a bit thin on the ground but there was contrast in what was there. 'Forget Me Nots' by Patrice Rushen was hushed and contained, whereas 'Mama Used to Say' by Junior was in-yer-face and stompy, with swipes of synth noise that pointed the way to a future norm.

Below these and now dropping, was 'I Can Make You Feel Good' by Shalamar, who had been around for a few years. This was the kind of bright, warm, optimistic sound that our happy soul weekender friends liked best and the two guys and girl looked bright, warm and optimistic on the cover of the single. These images would be replicated on that of the album, called - brightly, warmly and optimistically - *Friends*. Its next single, 'A Night to Remember', would be even better. Soon this album would be in just about every house I visited.

Peaking lower down this late May chart was a stodgy Siouxsie and the Banshees single called 'Fireworks'. It got to number twenty two. I thought it incredible that it had done ten places better than 'Arabian Knights', which I was still playing, but there you have it. The sound was unmistakable.

So too was that of Altered Images, whose two singles this year had both been good although progressively less well-placed. The new one, 'Pinky Blue' was wonderful, but in a world of its own. Not shiny in the current sense. The flatly un-shiny Go-Go's had another go-go with 'Our Lips Are Sealed', released as a double A-side with their huge American hit 'We Got the Beat'. It did a bit better this time, missing the Top 40 by a mere seven places.

However, if you're talking about sounds, the record with the most distinctive one was, without question, 'Ever So Lonely' by Monsoon. Black kids, as in Afro-Caribbean kids, although still experiencing prejudice and resentment, were gradually being accepted by urban society for being cool and good at stuff. How nice of Whitey. The cultures had interfaced. Rednecks, in certain moods, might look at a black kid and think of them as something approaching a "proper" Londoner.

Not so Asian kids, those whose parents were from the Indian subcontinent. They were caricatured viciously and horribly as ugly, smelly and penny-pinching. Asian kids at our school were quiet, which, given the above, was hardly surprising. They weren't known for fighting and they weren't in the football team. But everybody knew sounds from that culture, gleaned from the hippy era and from trips to the curry-house. It was kind of inevitable that one day someone would pull them together into a contemporary pop record.

People rolled their eyes about 'Ever So Lonely'. Many saw no more than a gathering of clichés; the sitar and the tabla drum sounds, the singer Sheila Chandra appearing on the cover in ceremonial pose – *doing one of them dances with one of them red spots on her forehead.* On the back was a picture of the Taj Mahal. The B-side was called 'Sunset Over the Ganges'. Perhaps it didn't do itself every favour it might have done.

But the point was, it existed. It got to number twelve. I bought it partly because of the novelty, but listening to it loud on headphones removed all inhibition. It's a hypnotic sound spectacular. The rhythms and arrangement may be authentic for all I know; you'll have to ask an expert on Indian music. But if they use the discussion as a stick with which to beat 'Ever So Lonely', send them to me.

However, the single I loved the most and played the most that spring got nowhere near the charts. Those of us in the boroughs of Lambeth, Southwark and Lewisham were used to the sight of flyers pasted to walls, bollards and junction boxes for an act called True Life Confessions. They featured grainy images of women in stockings and suspenders, items of clothing associated with sex even though, aside from some practical advantages, they were utterly ridiculous. It made you wonder what might be on show at one of their performances. I never seriously planned to investigate.

But then one morning they were on the Radio 1 *Breakfast Show.* Mike Read played a single called 'Banana Split'. It had lots of drums, growly guitar with the treble turned up, sprightly keyboard and a strong riff. There were percussive female voices that seemed to veer in and out of French. It was bouncy and frivolous. It was neatly edited. Its chorus went: *Bah-nana-nah, bah-nana-nah – banana spleet, wooh!*

I fell in love on the spot. In a world where you had to be cool all the time and were not allowed to smile in night clubs in case strangers punched you and your friends turned away, it felt like a rescue. I thought that if I didn't own a copy within twenty four hours, I might actually die. It took a whole afternoon of scouring London until the Leicester Square Our Price yielded a copy. Mike Read played it once more. I don't think anybody else ever did.

Except me. I'm still playing it now. I play it when I need a change of atmosphere. I play it when I need to be rescued. I play it for fun. When I played it at the time, people were embarrassed. It wasn't shiny, it wasn't smooth, it wasn't cool. Pacy records with lots of toms were dismissed as having "that jungle beat". Pastel cardigans love little classifications like this; you can put things in their place with those. Nobody I knew thought it was any good and nobody else – perhaps in the whole country – bought it. So on that basis, you might conclude that the frequent and firm judgements of "shit" were correct.

But I refute that on two counts. The first is this: it's a good record that was simply released four years too late. In 1982, it was stone age with knobs on; but back in the days of 'Ca Plane pour Moi', 'Jilted John' and 'King Rocker', with all those growly guitars, thundering toms and bounciness, not to mention French, it would have fit right in. Its cartoonishness would have appealed to younger kids, too. With more than a couple of radio plays, it would certainly have made the Top 30 and might have done much better. Those two girls at the back of the classroom would have driven everyone nuts with it.

The second count is this: whenever I hear 'Banana Split' by True Life Confessions, I am flooded with joy. If I was listening to shit, that wouldn't happen.

Thirty-three years after its release, completely out of the blue, I would make a shocking discovery. It's a cover version. 'Le Banana Split' was first performed by Belgian singer Lio. It came out in 1979 and was a big number one in France. Her record is a softly-blipping piece of synth bubblegum, notorious for its sexual suggestiveness (I had always had my suspicions about the lyrics). The line-up of True Life Confessions included two French-speaking north African girls, so there's the link.

'Le Banana Split' is dreadful; almost entirely devoid of life by comparison to the version I love. The discovery was a lot to take in. I had no idea it existed. It blew my mind. Like finding out I had a brother.

This then, was the balance of the soundtrack in May 1982. The following year would be pretty much more of the same. So I'm going to race through it, headlines only.

First headline: a good rap record. In fact, one of the best records of that or any kind, in that or any year. For mainstream radio listeners, it was nothing short of astonishing. Immediately, this was different. Immediately, you knew this was a record of substance. This was 'The Message' by Grandmaster Flash and the Furious Five.

Over a downbeat bass pattern, with echoing keyboard flourishes and alien sound effects, a man describes the urban world to which his circumstances have consigned him. It's one of dirt, vandalism and casual, life-threatening violence. It's non-stop stink, non-stop noise, non-stop menace. The only people doing well are the thugs. Pimps, drug dealers and loan sharks have the money, the cars and the girls. Kids see this and can't wait to drop out of school to start emulating them. One about to do so is the narrator's son. He doesn't see the point in studying. What he sees looks to him like evidence. Another layer of stress for a father who is trying to impose values despite it all.

He gets no break. He warns us not to push him, he's on the verge of losing it; one more thing and he might tip over into God knows what. His manic, nervous laughter – *huh-huh-huh, huh, huh* – is a major feature of the record. The final verse adheres most closely to the title; it's a parable – the tale of a boy who does exactly what the son is threatening to do, but who is overtaken by reality; he gets arrested and put in jail where he's at the bottom of the pecking order, left with nothing but the status of victim. Life is now an endless torment. His only escape is to hang himself in his cell. And so that is what he does. This, the narrator tells us, is what happens. It is happening somewhere out there right now, somewhere in his neighbourhood – so don't push him. This is fucking heavy. Even at the fade-out it doesn't stop; now there's police harassment. A group of youths are hanging out on the street when a squad car screeches up; the cops pick a fight, then bundle at least one of them into the wagon to cart them off, the fading siren blending into the general din.

Now contrast these gangster scenes with those painted in the same weeks by Kid Creole and the Coconuts. I had first encountered them via something called 'Latin Music'; a single full of Hispanic reference and cha-cha, purveying images of Caribbean islands where señoritas wiggled up and down for the delectation of men with dollars. In 1982 they had three fat hits – 'I'm a Wonderful Thing, Baby', 'Stool Pigeon' and 'Annie, I'm Not Your Daddy' – which moved closer to straight pop while keeping many of the trappings. There were horns, there were stylish clothes, there was dancing.

Kid Creole cut a sharp dash out front, with his sharp suits, his sharp moustache and his sharp moves. It was as shiny as you like. The album they came from was called *Tropical Gangsters*, but these gangsters were cabaret and, steamy though it was, it lay closer to custard pies than dirty needles.

Yet the tropical bit mattered. The young decade was embracing all things tropical. Tropical settings, once an occasional foray, would preoccupy movie studios. Night clubs would be decked out in plastic tropical vegetation as standard. The tropics meant distance and glamour, jet-setting available only to those with the means to experience it. It was aspirational. It therefore fit the contemporary bill to an increasing extent, since, as everybody knows, the 1980s invented aspiration. Plus, all that moisture made the tropics naturally shiny.

Out of all this crawled a taste for Bossa Nova rhythms, the light, cool shakes of Latin sound associated with evenings in sophisticated settings and a better class of company. The basic Bossa Nova went *chickada chickada chicka-dada chickada chickada*, but the one we began hearing most went *dit, d'diddit, dit-dit d'dit* and it was soon infecting large parts of the soundtrack.

I may have heard it first at what is officially my All-Time-Best Gig.

In the early part of that autumn, the Beat were getting a lot of air-play with a cutely catchy single called 'Jeanette' and I went with the LSM to see them at the Hammersmith Palais. Despite the changes to the soundtrack in the previous two years, the place was packed with Harrington jackets, 2-Tone badges and pork-pie hats. The sense of excitement was high.

We got there early enough to see both support acts. The first was the Alarm, who played stodgy, sky-punchy rock in denim trousers and lumberjack shirts, while a group of perhaps twenty of their fans stood in a uniform of ankle-length leather coats with hair stiffened into an extremely high, forward-leaning wedge. The contrast with their surroundings could not have been greater. It was like the aliens had landed. They were bunched right at the front, aggressively belting out the words. The Beat fans left them to it. When their boys finished playing, they simply disappeared.

Next were Aztec Camera. I instantly disliked them because of the name. They appeared on stage like mummy had just rung the bell for supper, then started tamely tapping and strumming, with the singer doing something like *hing or hudda, hing oh har*, the kind of vocal affectation that needed a very different audience to this one. In fact, all of it needed a very different audience to this one.

Once the first bottle landed, their fate was sealed. The whole crowd seemed to be chucking something. One by one, the group walked off, until finally there was just the singer, strumming defiantly, dodging the missiles, or trying to, until he too took his guitar off and left, to ironic cheers from the crowd.

The softie in me felt sorry for them, but, really, they shouldn't have been there. Being bottled off may only have stiffened their resolve, however. They had perhaps abandoned the stage before playing 'Oblivious', a horrible song that would breach the Top 20 a year later. It's a *dit, d'diddit, dit-dit d'dit* classic. Members of the Bible Society would perform it in Student Union bars to gain attention before a good news announcement. A simple "Excuse me, everyone" would have been much less painful. This was the kind of thing that was lying in wait.

Time had left 2-Tone and mod behind, yet tonight, here, the Beat were massive and relevant – they made themselves so before a passionate, physical crowd and we were right in the middle of it. The sound was incredible, the energy pulsating, the set-list perfect. Apart from a few tracks from the new album, we knew all the words and every detail of every arrangement, almost all of which was exactly like the records – an issue I had always had with live performances and one which simply did not apply tonight. They did everything we loved and other things that they made us love right then and there.

We were deep in the mosh at the front, completely swept along, minds unnecessary. During the instrumental section of 'Mirror in the Bathroom', the band danced and skipped around, each in a groove of their own; but as it ended they had somehow lined up; and as the riff kicked back in, they began advancing towards us in formation. The two of us threw our heads back and screamed like a pair of girls. What a moment. What a night. When we emerged into the West London air, our ears were ringing and our clothes dragging with sweat.

But out with the old, in with the new. In November, we began hearing a record which encapsulated the new sounds but with extra flash attitude caked on top with a trowel. This was 'Young Guns (Go for It)' by Wham! - a stupid, gimmicky name for an act. Lyrically, it was an update on 'Too Much Too Young'; a guy was berating his mate for leaving the single life behind to settle down and be under the thumb of some girl. It sounds a bit twinkle-toed when it begins, with its tinny keyboard and perfunctory dance beat, but it builds and builds into something good enough to make you ignore the ridiculous Americanisms. By the end, it's taken your breath away.

Wham! were two English guys in the best high street fashions; like the coolest among us, but with more money. There were two things about them I instinctively *didn't* like. First, they were clearly neither a vocal act nor a band, even though they had trappings of both (i.e. one of them was seen with a guitar sometimes and they performed the song by dancing and singing). They were something different: the image and look were being promoted above all else. It was glaring, and it ruffled the feathers.

But the second reason was more critical, and perhaps amplified the first. They were the first non-novelty chart act that I knew for sure were almost the same age as me – they would have been in the school year above and therefore in the same circles. I had already experienced the trauma of having a first footballing hero who was as young as I was. The musical equivalent was somehow even harder to deal with.

In with the new, out with the old. There were three break-ups we need to mention. The first was sudden and shocking. The Jam had spent the whole year at the top; 'Town Called Malice' had gone straight in at number one, built on a fast, energetic beat inspired by 60s soul records; closest to 'You Can't Hurry Love' by the Supremes and 'I'm Ready for Love' by Martha and the Vandellas (people would call this "that Motown beat", as if there was just one). There followed the sweeping, string-laden 'The Bitterest Pill (I Ever Had to Swallow)', which went to number two. The sound was changing, you could hear it across their new album, *The Gift*. Horns were creeping in and clarity was being swamped by too many words. At the end of the year they went straight in at number one again with 'Beat Surrender', a double single-pack with extra goodies that wasn't very good. Then Paul Weller suddenly announced that they were splitting up. He was off to do something different. Out of nowhere. Serious.

Then Squeeze split. After an album called *Sweets from a Stranger*, which seemed to follow the blueprint of 'Tempted' and was therefore drab, they put out the half-baked 'Annie, Get Your Gun', followed by a Best Of, called *Singles – 45s and Under*, which did well. And that, we were told, was going to be that. They had lost the big hit formula and so there seemed little point carrying on.

A group in a similar situation, succumbing to a creeping inevitability, was Abba. Since 'One of Us', they had released three singles, one of which was good, one sort-of good and one unlistenable dross. None of these had done better than number twenty-five. The world had changed around them. They were looking decidedly middle aged. There was only one option. Suddenly, they were gone.

But newly arrived, was a fourth TV channel, Channel 4, which I'll mention because its flagship show was *The Tube*, a music magazine programme specialising in live studio performances, which put me off a bit, but I tuned in. It was giggly and chaotic, like *Top of the Pops* without the behavioural guidelines. The most interesting thing in its first few weeks was a video of an all-girl guitar band from America called the Bangles, performing a riffy, urgent song called 'How Is the Air Up There?' while rolling around on the grass. I found it months later, on an import EP on IRS, the same label as the Go-Go's.

So now I've mentioned imports, which were another important new feature in our landscape. Imported twelve-inch singles were desirable. They were exclusive; they were not in the charts; they had thicker sleeves and unfamiliar designs. They had hand-written cards stuck on by store staff, giving you bits of information. Some of them played at 33rpm. They were pricey; a fiver, sometimes more. People around me were casually mentioning them.

In the end, I got one. I can't remember where I first heard about 'E.T. Boogie' by the Extra T's. It was on the Sunnyview label, whose sky-blue and yellow design evoked neat suburban lawns. Well it did for me; you may well wonder about sky-blue and yellow lawns. A few people I knew liked it. It was made from warm bubbles of synth and TR-808, mixed with brightly reverberating pips; robotic voices went "E.T." and" funky" every so often. It was inspired by the year's big cinematic hit, *E.T., the Extra-Terrestrial*, about a cute kid making friends with a cute alien who can make bikes fly over trees. The alien is home-sick and picks up enough English to say "E.T. phone home" in cute moments. The record pauses to replicate them. I liked its oddness. I wished there were a whole scene full of records like this.

What I *didn't* want, was a whole scene full of current chart acts doing cover versions. The reason is simple: cover versions default to being annoying. We have a duty to be suspicious of them. Unless you are going to do something radical to a known song, completely re-working it so that it is either vastly different and therefore interesting (like 'Banana Split' by True Life Confessions), or vastly improved and therefore good (like 'Banana Split' by True Life Confessions), there's no point. Keep your tributes to yourself, or chuck them at fans during an encore.

But if anybody was sharing such wisdom that winter, Phil Collins wasn't listening. He released a cover of 'You Can't Hurry Love'. Yes, *that* 'You Can't Hurry Love'.

They had a good go at the sound – there's an attack of treble, there's choppy guitar, there's a lick of strings and something high up in the background playing the main melody. It sounds a lot more like the Supremes than Duran Duran. But it's a tribute, an attempt to reproduce the original. This automatically lowers its value.

Yet alas, on an immeasurably depressing day in January 1983, it became Britain's number one. Part of the explanation is that it was climbing the chart during the Christmas festivities, proving itself fun for all the non-discerning family, even perhaps for more discerning ones affected by alcohol.

Phil Collins slotted into this picture. He was your favourite uncle; at his jovial, have-another-one best when party time has de-activated the quality controls. As the decorations came down, leaving nothing to anticipate but cold trudge, its zingy, upbeat tone kept people buying it. It was an antidote. For some.

Here's a question. If there had been no Supremes version, if it had been Uncle Phil that introduced us to 'You Can't Hurry Love', would it have been a hit? Here's an answer: probably. The tune is good, the feel is galvanising, the lyric has universal relevance - *when oh when am I going to find that special someone?* It would have filled the airwaves and done solid business. But there *is* an original which we *do* know well. So here's another question: is the meaning of the song as clear in the cover? This is a question that needs to be asked because the original lyric was modified. Yes, *modified.* A Holland-Dozier-Holland lyric *modified.*

Here are the facts. On the Supremes record, the first verse opens with "I need love, love, to ease my mind; I need to find, find, someone to call mine". Love, love; find, find. A balanced piece of Holland-Dozier-Holland word-play with concentrated meaning. The modified version went: "I need love, love, to ease my mind; I need to find time, someone to call mine". What? Find *time?* We're talking about finding love. Do you need to find time to find love? It's entirely possible that you might. So then say so. In another verse. Or, preferably, another song.

But did the public roll its eyes and turn away? Did they heck. It was, after all, "just a bit of fun". They sang along and bought more copies. For me, seething away beneath my tin hat, it was like a kick, kick in the teeth, teeth.

There was more in the chorus. The original: "You've got to trust; give it time, no matter how long it takes". The modified version: "Just trust in the good times, no matter how long it takes". Good times? What good times? You're longing for someone to give your love to, don't undermine our empathy by saying there are good times to trust in. And if, by chance, you mean the good times that will come when you have found someone, then bloody well say so. English is our first language; we'll get it.

Is it a waste of energy caring about this? Clearly, any artist has the right to make modifications. But I hated this record. I hated its success in doing better than the original, which had peaked at number three. I hated the fact that nobody seemed to care about the modified lyrics. I hated the feeling that it was tarnishing the memory of 'In the Air Tonight' as well as 'You Can't Hurry Love'. I hated the video, which approximated the performance of a male vocal group, presumably the Four Tops or the Temptations. I hated it, in immaculate seclusion, while its success further enhanced Uncle Phil's status and wealth, and the British public finger-clicked away those January blues.

To be fair, it wasn't the only offender. Soft Cell's 'Tainted Love' had a cover of 'Where Did Our Love Go' on its B-side. The original song uses the same idea as 'Baby Love' – she is crying and desperate as he ceases to care and withdraws. Its phrases include "don't leave me all by myself" and "don't you want me no more?" But on the Soft Cell record, the lyric is modified to "don't you leave me *no more*". What? That's a completely different meaning. He's leaving her now, for the first time, which is why she's so devastated; it's not like "don't leave the toilet un-flushed no more", which suggests a habit. And if he is repeatedly leaving her, then she must be repeatedly taking him back and we would have less sympathy for her.

I could go on. Believe me, I could. But I don't think anybody cares. Nobody seemed to at the time. Even though I took the trouble to explain it. I used words like "negligence" and "abuse". They used words like "shut" and "up".

There were shinier singles at number one in the months following Uncle Phil's success. Michael Jackson got there for a week with 'Billie Jean', the opening single from the album that would follow *Off the Wall*. It was about some fan claiming that he was the father of her son. Michael shimmered as he shimmied, across an expensive set built especially for the video. Where he trod, the paving lit up. He sprinkled magic dust on a tramp who promptly became the wearer of a tuxedo. Touch Michael and you are healed. Or else you just light up. The record was a mid-paced plod with a non-event of a chorus. But Michael's people wouldn't hear a word against it. It had no trouble getting on MTV.

The decade was setting out its stall in earnest, ushering in all shades of exclusive and upmarket, whether you were off for cocktails or off to the tropics. Duran Duran had last been seen in the tropics, shearing through exclusive and upmarket waters on a yacht in the video for 'Rio'. It wasn't one of their best, but their stock was high. It seemed about time that they had a number one, and 'Is There Something I Should Know?' duly became one, going straight in. This wasn't one of their best either, but it was better than 'Rio'.

It was knocked off the top spot by David Bowie, who was once again on the crest of a trend with 'Let's Dance'. The record was more new noise; big beats and shuddering shards of synth, but somehow carrying the scent of mid-century jazz, evoking exclusive and upmarket nights on Manhattan rooftops.

Not to be out-shone, Spandau Ballet promptly conjured up their own chart-topper, but theirs required a makeover and a sideways move into blue-eyed soul. They were suddenly kings of shiny; fit to stand beside any plastic tropical vegetation in any nightclub anywhere. The suits were crisp, the top buttons were done up and the hair was neat. You could almost smell the aftershave.

The song was 'True'. It was a cloakroom record, so-called because it signalled the start of the slow dancing – time to get your coat. Indeed, it was not just a slow record that happened to be good for smooching; it was engineered specifically for the purpose. The plan worked. 'True' was massive. It was all a long way from 'To Cut a Long Story Short'.

The Sun & Doves pub on Coldharbour Lane had a DJ blaring away in the public bar at weekends. It was a sea of belchers, pastel cardigans and amber pints. 'Billie Jean' and 'True' were among the records to occasion hushed reverence when they came on. People would stop talking and start gently nodding their heads, gazing out into the crowd rather than at each other.

Many records from 1982-3 make me think of perching somewhere in there, being lectured by the wise, having first experiences of this and that, or just fannying about. I can't mention them all. But to show the range of what was available in the months following 'Billie Jean', I've picked four particularly remarkable ones.

I went to the Camden Palace on Tuesdays for a while, to a night called *Slumming in Style*. I still didn't really "get" night clubs, but this was un-threatening, mainly because there never seemed to be many people in its cavernous, multi-storeyed space. Dress was eclectic and the music was better. 'Let's Dance' was top dog on its playlist - everyone there seemed to light up when it came on.

The only other thing played as often was 'Blue Monday' by New Order, a padded cell of synth in which a manly voice ruminated above machine-gun drum patterns, deep bass and deep guitar twangs. It was a hard, assertive sound; an alternative record made exclusively for dancing. Nothing else sounded like it and nothing else felt like it to dance to. It came as a twelve-inch only, in a minimalist yet intricate cover, black with coloured flecks, and bits that stuck out at the lip of the outer sleeve. You had to put it back in very carefully to avoid damaging it. I failed at the first attempt. A small, galling rip remains its one scar.

Then, 'Temptation' by Heaven 17, who featured former members of the Human League. This spent a week at number two while 'True' was on the throne. It was fully contemporary, but twisted; something that might frighten a child in the same way that 'River Deep – Mountain High' had once spooked me. It began like a warning cloaked in stompy northern soul; it ended like a final judgement drenched in fire and brimstone. There were cowled male voices; there was a female vocal of celestial power; there were rising chords slamming like fists from a thunder-god, tormented by apocalyptic strings and four-to-the-bar snare. It climbed and intensified until dials veered into the red, walls shook and your head spun. There was as much energy in this record as all those shiny number ones combined. Best single of the year.

Now: how do you fancy a piece of folk-rock, with one of the loveliest melodies you've ever heard, sung by the clearest, purest female vocal you can imagine, augmented by thrashes of acoustic guitar to set the pulse racing, all at just the right pace so you don't miss a thing? Well I bloody do. But if you just turned your nose up at the mere mention of "folk-rock", you may be helping to explain why 'Moonlight Shadow' by Mike Oldfield only got to number four, albeit staying there for three weeks. Two of the five records above it in that time were good, but not *as* good.

All sorts of people succumbed to its vast charm. On an afternoon's sunbathing at Brockwell Park lido, we found ourselves lying beside an old mate from cubs days, now a bit of a Jack-the-Lad with - he would have us believe - football hooligan credentials. There were radios on all around us and, when 'Moonlight Shadow' came on, he became restless; fidgeting on his towel, turning over, then turning over again, every thought of looking cool so close to all these girls forgotten. He sat up. He was grinning. "I like this. It's good this, 'nit? It is good, 'nit? I really like this". We were happy to reassure him, as he began playing to the gallery, conducting with an invisible baton, giving nursery tick-tocks of the head. He had risen further in our estimation.

Mike Oldfield had been around for ages. So too, now, had Malcolm McLaren. He had popped up as a solo artist the previous winter by taking 'Buffalo Gals' into the charts, a record I will go into detail on some other time. His new one that summer was 'Double Dutch'. It was about teams of girls competing with ropes and hoops to be the best at formation skipping; the "Double Dutch" being one of their routines.

It opens with the sound of a rope cutting the air, then the band comes in; African rhythms, African strings; upbeat and bright, met with handclaps, and settling into a rhythm which quickly becomes a new best friend. Malcolm starts talking over the top of it, introducing us to these contests which, apparently, happen all over the world. He speaks each verse and the girl choir responds with choruses of resounding crispness, saluting the Double Dutch and their team, the Ebonettes.

The pace whips you along. All its sounds are great. "What a strange record", a friend's Mum exclaimed, as it came on during the drive to a football match. I was working in West London and went to the ice rink at Queensway a couple of times; they played records over the tannoy and when 'Double Dutch' came on, everybody suddenly sped up so that the unconfident had to scramble for safety at the sides. Such was its euphoric power. It was a three-and-a-half-minute carnival.

Records like these provided the highs that kept the soundtrack vital, balancing out the dullness and horror elsewhere. With records like these, things were okay. Music was performing its full range of services and all areas of the mansion were well-trodden. For me, each reaction had the sweet smell of familiarity – there had been something like it at some significant point before.

Yet the new order of things, this shiny, exclusive and upmarket trend, was not for everybody. Not everyone aspired to aspiration. Wham! had put out decent stuff, but they were well-turned out and confident, which could be alienating. They crowned their upward trajectory in the summer, with a single about a luxurious destination for people who were well turned-out and confident, a destination which was shiny, exclusive and upmarket. The single was called 'Club Tropicana'.

There had always been people we could turn to at moments like this. But the new zeitgeist was filtering through some surprising gaps. Many of those who once stood and railed now reclined, smoothing their spotless fabrics, tolerating the plastic tropical vegetation, sipping their espresso, dreaming of status and tapping their fingers to something going *dit, d'diddit, dit-dit d'dit.* It was, perhaps, time that the mansion was re-furbished.

Acknowledgements

The author wishes to recognise the writers of the lyrics used in this book and the relevant copyright holders.

The songs, in order of appearance, are: 'The Song of Reproduction', 'A Transport of Delight', 'The Hippopotamus' and 'The Gnu Song', all written by Michael Flanders and Donald Swann, © Warner/Chappell; 'When It Comes to the Crunch (It's Smiths It Is)' written by Howard Barnes and Cliff Adams, © Thames Music Ltd.; 'The Ballad of Bonnie and Clyde' written by Mitch Murray and Peter Callander, © Peermusic Publishing, Universal Music Publishing Group.; 'Last Night in Soho' written by Ken Howard and Alan Blaikley, © Carlin America Inc.; 'Hey Jude' written by John Lennon and Paul McCartney, © Sony/ATV Music Publishing LLC; 'Blackberry Way' written by Roy Wood, © T.R.O. Inc; 'Bridget the Midget (the Queen of the Blues)' written by Ray Stevens, © Kobalt Music Publishing Ltd; 'Co-Co' written by Nicky Chinn and Mike Chapman, © Universal Music Publishing Group; 'I'm Still Waiting' written by Deke Richards, © Sony/ATV Music Publishing LLC, Universal Music Publishing Group; 'Poppa Joe' written by Nicky Chinn and Mike Chapman, © Universal Music Publishing Group; 'Goody Two Shoes' written by Adam Ant and Marco Pirroni, © Sony/ATV Music Publishing LLC, Universal Music Publishing Group; 'Golden Brown' written by Hugh Cornwell, Jean-Jacques Burnel, Dave Greenfield and Jet Black, © EMI Music Publishing, Sony/ATV Music Publishing LLC, Universal Music Publishing Group; 'Good Grief Christina' written by Giorgio Moroder and Pete Bellotti, © Warner/Chappell Music, Inc; '48 Crash' written by Nicky Chinn and Mike Chapman, © Universal Music Publishing Group; 'Yesterday Once More' written by Richard Carpenter and John Bettis, © Warner/Chappell Music, Inc, Universal Music Publishing Group; 'Little Boxes' written by Malvina Reynolds, © Schroeder Music Company; 'Maids When You're Young Never Wed an Old Man' written by Luke Kelly, John Sheehan, Barney McKenna, Ciaron Bourke and Ronnie Drew, © Carlin Music; 'When I Needed a Neighbour' written by Sydney Carter, © Stainer & Bell Ltd.; 'Tiger Feet' written by Nicky Chinn and Mike Chapman, © Universal Music Publishing Group; 'This Town Ain't Big Enough for Both of Us' written by Ron Mael, © Imagem Music Ltd; 'Window Shopping' written by R. Dean Taylor, © EMI Music/Jobete Music; 'Achoo' and 'How Are You Getting Home?', both written by Ron Mael, © Imagem Music Ltd; 'Space Oddity', written by David Bowie, © Peermusic Publishing; 'Bohemian Rhapsody' written by Freddie Mercury, © Sony/ATV Music Publishing; 'Love Machine' written by James Griffin and Michael Zane Gordon, © Warner/Chappell Music, Inc; 'DAT' written by Leighton Shevrington, © Calderwood, Inc; 'Daddy Cool' written by Frank Farian and George Reyam, © Sony/ATV Music Publishing LLC; 'Pool Hall Richard' written by Rod Stewart and Ron Wood, © Sony/ATV Music Publishing LLC, Warner/Chappell Music, Inc; 'Jamming', written by Bob Marley, © EMI Music Publishing; 'Jilted John' written by Graham Fellows, © Graham Fellows; 'Ever Fallen in Love With Someone You Shouldn't've' written by Pete Shelley, © Universal Music Publishing Group; 'Pop Muzik' written by Robin Scott, © Universal Music Publishing Group; 'Don't Stop 'Til You Get Enough' written by Michael Jackson, © Sony/ATV Music Publishing LLC; 'Breathing' written by Kate Bush, © Sony/ATV Music Publishing LLC; 'And the Beat Goes On' Written by Leon Sylvers, Stephen Shockley and William Shelby, © Sony/ATV Music Publishing LLC; 'Trans Siberian Express' written by Tony Wood, © BMG Dinsong Ltd; 'Making Your Mind Up' written by Andy Gerard Hill and John Danter, © Sony/ATV Music Publishing LLC, Universal Music Publishing Group; 'Rapper's Delight' written by Nile Rodgers and Bernard Edwards, © EMI Music Publishing, Sony/

Thanks

In making this book a reality, I am indebted to Kerstin Muggeridge for her help and support; to the Oxygen Company of Tiverton and Ashford's in Exeter for their expertise; and, in particular, to my partner Sarah for her skill and advice. I am hugely grateful.